Proxmire

PROXMIRE

Bulldog of the Senate

JONATHAN KASPAREK

WISCONSIN HISTORICAL SOCIETY PRESS

Published by the Wisconsin Historical Society Press
Publishers since 1855

The Wisconsin Historical Society helps people connect to the past by collecting,
preserving, and sharing stories. Founded in 1846, the Society is one of the nation's
finest historical institutions.
Join the Wisconsin Historical Society: wisconsinhistory.org/membership

Publication of this book was made possible in part by a grant from the Amy Louise Hunter
fellowship fund.

Front cover image: WHI 58403, William Proxmire Walking Across US Capitol Lawn

Printed in Canada
Dustjacket design and typesetting by Wendy Holdman Design Ltd.

23 22 21 20 19   1 2 3 4 5

Library of Congress Cataloging-in-Publication Data
Names: Kasparek, Jon, author.
Title: Proxmire : bulldog of the Senate / Jonathan Kasparek.
Description: Madison, WI : Wisconsin Historical Society Press, 2019. |
    Includes bibliographical references and index. |
Identifiers: LCCN 2018035648 (print) | LCCN 2018044146 (ebook) |
    ISBN 9780870209093 (ebook) | ISBN 9780870209086 (pbk. : alk. paper)
Subjects: LCSH: Proxmire, William. | Legislators—United States—Biography. |
    Legislators—Wisconsin—Biography. | United States. Congress. Senate—Biography. |
    United States—Politics and government—1945–1989. | Waste in government
    spending—United States. | Wisconsin—Biography.
Classification: LCC E840.8.P7 (ebook) | LCC E840.8.P7 K37 2019 (print) |
    DDC 328.73092 [B]—dc23
LC record available at https://lccn.loc.gov/2018035648

♾ The paper used in this publication meets the minimum requirements of the American
National Standard for Information Sciences—Permanence of Paper for Printed Library
Materials, ANSI Z39.48-1992.

For my family, Jody, James, William, and Alden
And for Ellen Proxmire (1924–2015), whose determination to ensure
her husband's legacy made this project possible.

CONTENTS

INTRODUCTION

Every Marathon Comes to an End

A t ten o'clock in the morning on August 27, 1987—thirty years to the day since he was first elected to the United States Senate—William Proxmire stunned the people of Wisconsin by announcing that he would not be a candidate for reelection in 1988. Packed into a parlor adjacent to the Assembly chamber in the State Capitol, where he had begun his public career in 1951, the crowd of reporters and onlookers gasped when it heard the news. Proxmire called it a "very, very difficult decision" and cited his age as the key factor, noting he would be seventy-three at the beginning of his seventh term. Later that afternoon he told *Milwaukee Journal* reporter Dennis McCann, "The reason I'm not running is because I'm just too old. In your seventies, that's long in the tooth. You never know when something's going to hit you." Having served in the Senate for thirty years, Proxmire had seen too many senators unwilling to retire despite fighting senility or physical ailments. He wanted to retire before his health deteriorated. Ironically, Proxmire was in excellent health. "I ran five miles this morning, did a few hundred pushups," he boasted. Nonetheless, Proxmire had made up his mind that it was time to step down.[1]

A political maverick and something of a loner in the Senate, Proxmire had made the decision by himself. Most assumed he would serve one final term in the Senate and retire in 1995. The day before his announcement, former senator Gaylord Nelson confidently predicted Proxmire would seek reelection. "I'm startled to tell the truth," Nelson said after hearing of Proxmire's announcement. "I don't think there was any doubt that he could get reelected without any serious challenge in either party." Proxmire had even surprised his family, telling his wife, Ellen, and their son, Douglas, only two days earlier. "You're not going to like this," he told them at dinner, "but I'm announcing on Thursday morning in Madison that I'm not running." Other members of his family found out by hearing news reports after his announcement.[2]

1

Proxmire's absence from Wisconsin politics was almost unthinkable. He had first been elected to the US Senate in 1957 to finish out the term of Joseph McCarthy, who had died that May. He was reelected in 1958, 1964, 1970, 1976, and 1982 and would serve a total of thirty-one years and four months. Proxmire was currently third in seniority in the Senate, behind John Stennis of Mississippi and Strom Thurmond of South Carolina; had he run again, he would have chaired the Senate Appropriations Committee and served as president pro tempore. No one from Wisconsin had ever served in Congress that long, and few state elected officials could match his years of service.[3] He was also, he noted at his press conference, the first senator to retire voluntarily since Isaac Stephenson in 1915, wryly suggesting, perhaps, that few elected officials recognized when it was time to bow out. Even before his election to the Senate, Proxmire was a major figure in Wisconsin politics, serving one term in the Assembly and running for governor three times in a row in the 1950s. His retirement thus capped nearly forty years of almost nonstop political activity.

Moreover, Proxmire was one of the last of those Democrats who had reinvented and revitalized the party in the late 1940s and early 1950s, changing it from a conservative party that rarely won more than two dozen seats in the legislature to a liberal party that regularly controlled one or both houses of the legislature and won six out of eleven gubernatorial elections between 1958 and 1988. Proxmire's election to the Senate in 1957 heralded the Democratic landslide of 1958, and his tireless campaigning helped make the Democratic Party a force in Wisconsin politics. Most of the others responsible for the party's success had long ago left the scene. James Doyle, Thomas Fairchild, John Reynolds, and Horace Wilkie retired from partisan politics for federal and state judgeships. Some had lost re-election bids, including Philleo Nash, defeated for lieutenant governor in 1964, and Gaylord Nelson, who lost his Senate race in 1980. Patrick Lucey had resigned as governor in 1977 to become ambassador to Mexico. Others, like Carl Thompson, had simply retired after a long career in electoral politics. Proxmire began his career as a youngster from Illinois, and he ended it as an elder statesman of the party, a figure from another era who had witnessed a new generation of politicians emerge.[4]

Beyond simple longevity and his historic role in the midcentury Democratic renaissance, Proxmire had left a deep impression on the people of the state. His campaigning was legendary. In the 1950s, he pioneered the combination of radio and television advertising with street-corner appearances, shaking hands with thousands of voters every day. Factory workers arriving at the plant gate at six thirty in the morning found Proxmire waiting to say hello to each one. Visitors to the Wisconsin State Fair found him greeting voters at the flower show. He was a fixture at Lambeau Field in Green Bay and Camp Randall Stadium in Madison. Even while the Senate was in session, Proxmire returned home on weekends, often spending 120 days a year or more in the state. Critics mocked his desire for publicity, but at football games, parades, or fairs, Proxmire wanted to make sure that the people of Wisconsin knew he was *their* senator.

Proxmire was memorable not just for his ubiquity but also for his eccentricities. He was a health zealot, and got up early every morning to jog the five miles from his home to his office following a hundred or more pushups. He never smoked, didn't drink coffee or alcohol, and went to bed early. He ate all manner of other health food that baffled his friends and staff and even published two books on healthy living, *You Can Do It* in 1973 and *Your Joyride to Health* in 1993. Proxmire was also notoriously frugal, carrying his own lunch while traveling, peanut butter sandwiches early on and later the more health-conscious option of cottage cheese or sardines, and running his later campaigns and his office on a shoestring. By one estimate he returned over $1 million from his office payroll and expenses (although his staff admitted that he paid them well) and spent less than $200 out of his own pocket on his last two Senate campaigns, the state filing fee and postage to return unsolicited and unwanted contributions. He extended this frugality to the US government as well, and in 1975 began the "Golden Fleece" program, which probably brought him more publicity than any other activity. The program publicized wasteful government expenditures, including an $84,000 study on why people fall in love, a seventeen-page instruction manual for purchasing Worcestershire sauce that cost the army $6,000, and a $200,000 grant to build a replica of the Great Wall of China in Indiana. Taxpayers howled in mirth as well as indignation at Proxmire's amusing and pun-filled press releases designed to show how easy it was to waste taxpayers' money.[5]

Proxmire's antics—from his factory gate appearances to his Golden Fleece Awards to his infamous facelift and hair plugs—would in themselves make him a memorable figure in the history of the US Senate, an institution whose history was already filled with memorable characters. Americans do like to poke fun at the old-fashioned pomposity that tends to surface among those whose job it is to guard the republic from both the powerful president and from the excesses of popular democracy. That the US Senate is the greatest deliberative body in the world is a cliché, but the truth of that statement depends to a great extent on the quality of its members. The greatest senators—Henry Clay, Daniel Webster, John C. Calhoun, Robert La Follette, Robert Taft, Arthur Vandenburg, Robert Wagner, Oliver Ellsworth, and Roger Sherman are the Senate's own choices—rose above personal quirks and political inclinations to make major contributions to the institution.[6] Proxmire took his role as a US Senator seriously, deeply honored to be entrusted in a position to shape the direction of the country. In an extraordinary testament to this dedication, Proxmire almost never missed a roll call vote—nearly ten thousand between 1966 and his retirement—but he spent most weekends in Wisconsin.

Beyond his popularity and his own eccentricities, Proxmire was in many ways the model senator, an incorruptible, dedicated public servant thoughtfully guiding the republic and protecting it from executive tyranny and popular passions, as envisioned by the framers of the Constitution.[7] Although he consulted his own staff and kept close tabs on what the people of Wisconsin thought, he reached his own decisions about important issues without bowing to pressure from lobbyists or his caucus. His colleagues called him a maverick. "He's recognized as a loner," Nelson remarked. "People didn't dislike him or hold personal grudges against him. I never had a quarrel with him in eighteen years. But he never played ball. . . . What he thought was right, what he wanted to do, he always ran his own show."[8] From the beginning, senators were expected to exercise their own judgment, a responsibility Proxmire took very seriously, rarely deferring to party leadership. In fact, shortly after he joined the Senate he publicly criticized Senate majority leader Lyndon Johnson, charging that he dictatorially controlled the Democratic caucus and as a result essentially ruled the Senate. Most thought his actions were political suicide, but Proxmire refused to back down and survived Johnson's displeasure. Although a Democrat, he sometimes refused to toe the party line on issues such as abortion or federal spending, instead relying on his own judgment.[9]

Indeed, reducing federal spending—except for dairy price supports—was Proxmire's greatest consistency. Even though he supported the Vietnam War in the early 1960s, he later turned into a critic of military spending. He forced a Pentagon engineer to testify before Congress about cost overruns in Lockheed Martin's C-5A transport plane in 1968, and later opposed the development of the MX missile and sank funding for the supersonic transport. Nor was it solely military spending that caught his ire. In 1985, he cast the lone "no" vote on an emergency farm credit bill, arguing that it would raise the federal deficit at a time when the biggest obstacle to farm prosperity was the deficit itself. Wisconsin Republicans and Democrats alike complained that Proxmire's high-minded efforts to control government spending did little to end the pork-barrel legislation that most members of congress viewed as essential to their states and thereby to their own careers. Instead, they charged, Proxmire's opposition to federal spending in other senators' states diminished his own ability to gain support for federal spending in Wisconsin, a particular sore point for Milwaukee mayor Henry Maier.[10]

Proxmire rejected that argument, insisting that his unwavering support for dairy price subsidies showed that he represented the state's major economic interest. Moreover, he believed a senator had to do more than simply look after the interests of his own state and consider the nation as a whole. The biggest threat to individuals and small businesses, he believed, came not from the government but from corporate interests using their influence to shape legislation for their own benefit. Through his experience as a political reporter for Madison's *Capital Times* and later as a member of the Wisconsin legislature, he learned about the influence wielded by corporate lobbyists. He remained hostile to lobbyists throughout his career and showed particular interest in curtailing the power of financial institutions. After the use of credit cards became widespread in the 1960s, Proxmire introduced the Truth in Lending Act, which required lenders to disclose the full cost and terms of loans to borrowers to counter the glitzy ads that could mislead unsuspecting consumers. In 1971, he wrote the Fair Credit Reporting Act, which allowed consumers to obtain information about their credit rating from credit bureaus and to fix information that was incorrect. As ranking member or chair of the Senate Banking Committee, Proxmire oversaw some of the most important financial legislation in the late twentieth century and shaped federal policy in the 1970s. In 1977, he was the prime mover behind the Community Reinvestment Act to prevent banks from "redlining" or denying mortgages for property in undesirable neighborhoods and encourage investment in poorer neighborhoods. The ability of most Americans to manage their credit and to obtain a mortgage directly results from Proxmire's passionate concern about these issues.

Although he eventually opposed the Vietnam War and criticized most military spending, Proxmire believed the United States had a critical role to play in world affairs. He often spoke of his fear of nuclear war and supported arms reduction treaties with the Soviet Union. It was imperative that the United States behave morally. Between 1967 and 1986, Proxmire spoke every day the Senate was in session urging ratification of the United Nations Genocide Convention, declaring genocide a crime that required military intervention. Conservatives feared the treaty would give the United Nations undue control over American foreign policy, but after more than three thousand speeches, by Proxmire's count, he finally convinced the Senate to approve the treaty. As he left the Senate in 1989, he took the greatest pride in his record of roll-call votes and his triumph in committing the United States to the convention.

The issues that Proxmire tackled remain relevant more than twenty years after his retirement. Decades before the Jack Abramoff lobbying scandal, Proxmire warned of the obvious danger of allowing corporations to use lobbyists to influence legislation. The explosion of lobbying into a billion-dollar business and the regular employment of former members of Congress as lobbyists (the so-called revolving door) would have shocked him, and his efforts in the Wisconsin Assembly to expose lobbying to public scrutiny are worth revisiting. The vast amount of money required to mount a senatorial campaign, and the unceasing fundraising and expenditures required by PACs, would trouble him as well. Before there was a "Troubled Asset Relief Program" in 2008 to aid banks that had overextended credit during the housing bubble, there was a federal bailout of Chrysler and the city of New York. Proxmire shaped both of those—what might he have said about requiring substantive reforms for banking institutions that profited from regulations loosened in the 1990s? He regretted that the federal budget grew every year. What his colleagues

derided as naïve or sanctimonious concern over federal spending has become the major national debate over abuse of federal earmarks, such as
the oft-derided Gravina Island Bridge "to nowhere" in Alaska. Certainly
the emergence of military contractors in wars in Iraq and Afghanistan
would cause Proxmire to rise in indignation as hundreds of millions of
dollars disappeared into private coffers with no public accountability. Tax
policies that emerged in the 1980s to shift the tax burden away from corporations and wealthy individuals and toward middle- and low-income
Americans would no doubt infuriate him. He began his career advocating a fairer tax system that recognized the importance of rewarding hard
work while at the same time requiring those who benefited from a secure
infrastructure and an educated and healthy workforce to pay more into
the commonwealth to help preserve them. These issues remain vital, and
Proxmire's perspective is badly needed in the public debate. Without it,
the Senate—and the nation—is a much poorer place.

Beyond specific issues of lobbying, taxation, banking, and federal
spending, Proxmire also possessed a lack of cynicism that few elected officials can match today. He devoted his life to serving the nation, and he
never forgot what a privilege that was. In one of his later speeches, he
mused on the rare opportunity he had in the Senate: "Where else can you
not only dream of the direction the country is going in, but play a significant part in getting it there? Now, let's not kid ourselves. Senators may ac-
complish little or nothing. But we have a chance, a remarkable chance."[11]
All the handshaking comes back to that—a chance to guide the nation and
make a difference. William Proxmire saw the challenges and opportunities
presented by the economic and political upheavals of the late twentieth
century and never abandoned the basic principles of fairness and equality.
And he made a difference.

1

POLITICAL AWAKENING

Lake Forest, Illinois, was an unlikely place for a liberal Wisconsin Democrat to grow up. Nonetheless, it did have a profound effect on the future senator, named Edward William Proxmire at his birth on November 11, 1915. A close-knit and well-off family and a wealthy community provided the young boy with a privileged upbringing. Although many politicians try to downplay such a childhood, preferring the populist narrative of rising from poverty and overcoming adversity, Proxmire made no secret of the advantages he had. Writing to journalist Jay Sykes in 1971, he described his family life as ideal: "If I could choose, I would want to be the second child in a family of three with an older brother and a younger sister and that is exactly what I got."[1] His father, Theodore Proxmire, a physician and one of the most respected men in the community, had moved to Lake Forest to establish a practice in 1906, after graduating from Rush Medical College in Chicago in 1904. Theodore himself had been born in Lancaster, Ohio, in 1881 and graduated from Ohio State University prior to enrolling in medical school. In 1912, after six years spent establishing a practice, he married Adele Flanigan, a gregarious, affectionate woman born in St. Louis in 1881 to Irish immigrants. Although they had by all accounts a very happy marriage, one that produced three children—Theodore was born in 1913, and Adele was born in 1917—their personalities were quite different. Pleasant and well-liked, Theodore was also serious and hard-working. His routine rarely varied; he made house calls Monday through Saturday mornings and saw patients in his office Monday through Friday afternoons. He tried to not work on Saturday afternoons and Sundays, but was often called out on emergencies, the very model of a dedicated physician. Adele, in contrast, enjoyed socializing. She smoked heavily and drank, and enjoyed going to parties and entertaining guests long after her husband had gone to bed. Theodore sought to instill the importance of hard work and often took his children along with him on house calls. Adele was exuberantly affectionate, showering them with kisses as she tucked them in at night. Both parents were devoted to their children, and because his medical office was in their home, both parents were actively engaged in raising them.[2]

Theodore Proxmire was not just a successful physician but also a widely respected leader in the community. World War I furthered his reputation after he was assigned to be a reserve medical officer with the rank of captain at nearby Fort Sheridan. He earned a promotion to lieutenant colonel and assumed command of the base's Lovell General Hospital, taking decisive action when the 1918 influenza pandemic reached the United States by removing all men from the crowded barracks, housing them in pup tents, and inoculating them. There was not a single casualty at the fort during the outbreak, and he was decorated by former post commander Colonel Robert McCormick. His practice thrived after the war, providing a comfortable income for the family that allowed for live-in help provided by an African American couple. Later, Theodore founded Lake Country Tuberculosis Sanatorium in Waukegan and served as chief of staff of Lake Forest Hospital. In 1956, the fiftieth anniversary of his arrival in Lake Forest, the annual Lake Forest Day—an event he helped found in 1908 with the Women's Club—was dedicated to him, and a parade of "Proxmire Babies" walked past him, ranging in age from almost fifty years to twelve days. Throughout his life in Lake Forest, he delivered speeches to civic organizations such as the Woman's Club and was instrumental in the success of the Young Men's Club, a group that organized athletics and social events. Theodore's hard work and dedicated community service made him a role model for his son.[3]

Growing up with respected parents in an affluent community brought great privileges, and from an early age, Edward Proxmire recognized how fortunate he was. The community provided excellent public schools, and young Edward attended the Halsey School (originally built in 1895 and rebuilt and enlarged in 1912) for kindergarten and Gordon School for grades one through six. For one year, Proxmire attended Alcott School, a private school run by Allen Chartis Bell (it was renamed Bell School in 1934). His father continually emphasized the importance of education and willingly paid to send all three of his children to preparatory schools and private universities and even financed his son's graduate work at Harvard. As a boy, Proxmire supplemented his formal education through extensive reading while waiting in the car as he accompanied his father on house calls. In addition to Onwentsia Country Club, of which the Proxmires were members, Lake Forest provided the Winter Club, organized in 1901 by Lake Forest residents who wanted year-round recreational opportunities for their families. Edward played football in the fall as well as basketball, hockey, and bowling in the winter. Spring brought baseball and track, and during the summer, members had access to the club swimming pool. The Proxmire children spent nearly every afternoon after school and much of the weekends at the Winter Club. Education, disciplined hard work, and physical activity remained core values for the rest of Edward's life.[4]

Young Edward particularly embraced the gospel of exercise and dreamed of athletic glory. He idolized sports heroes like Red Grange and Jack Dempsey and covered the walls of his bedroom with pictures of Big Ten football teams and the Chicago Cubs. His father shared his love of athletics and took the children to football games at Soldier Field and to baseball games at Wrigley Field, as well as to amateur and professional boxing tournaments. As a boy, Edward Proxmire dreamed of scoring the winning touchdown in a big game or knocking out the reigning heavy-weight champ, what he later referred to as "Walter Mitty daydreams."[5] One other figure held a significant place in his imagination: William S. Hart, the glowering leading man of silent films. In 1921, inspired by one of Hart's films, Edward insisted on being called "William." His parents indulged him, perhaps realizing his irritation of being "Ed" while his older brother was called "Ted." For a time, he went by "E. William," but he eventually dropped his first name altogether and was almost universally known simply as Bill.[6]

Proxmire may have remembered his position as middle child as ideal, but he often chafed under the shadow of his older brother, Theodore. Theodore was intelligent, athletic, popular, and good-looking—exactly the characteristics to generate both admiration and irritation in a younger brother. The two competed against each other for their parents' attention

and fought often. Once, Theodore held Bill under water for nearly a minute. Another time, Bill hurled a steel piggy bank at his brother; he missed,
but Theodore retaliated by giving Bill a black eye with a vicious punch. By
the time he was in eighth grade, Bill had begun to focus on boxing as his
particular sport, in part to be able to defend himself or to clobber his older
brother in revenge. The competitive streak endured, and Proxmire later
found himself competing with his own children. The youngest Proxmire
sibling, Adele, named for their mother, got along with both brothers. She
was a quiet, hardworking, and exceptionally intelligent girl ("a real sweet-
heart," Proxmire called her) who was consistently at the top of her class.
Proxmire admired her studiousness and quiet hard work, and the two
remained close until her death in 1967.[7]

In 1929, Theodore and Adele Proxmire purchased a summer house
in Desbarats, Ontario, on Lake Huron about thirty-five miles southeast
of Sault Ste. Marie, and their vacation home had as great an impact on
the teenage Bill as Lake Forest did. Accommodations were a far cry from
comfortable suburban Chicago: the house had neither indoor plumbing
nor electricity. But Proxmire loved it because it offered unlimited hik-
ing, canoeing, and swimming, and he spent every summer there for the
next ten years. While at Desbarats, Proxmire developed a peculiarly regimented life, much to the amusement of his family. He set up a punching
bag and weight-lifting equipment in a cabin his father built on the property
and exercised rigorously every day. While the rest of his family slept late
and danced into the night, Proxmire rose every morning at six thirty and
swam before breakfast. In the morning he pumped water for the house
before canoeing and swimming again. After lunch, he read for an hour
before going on long hikes and working out in his makeshift gym. His
family thought he was crazy, but Proxmire was developing the disciplined
routine that would continue for the rest of his life. His family would "enjoy
life up there with beer, square dances at night, sleeping late in the morning, and generally having a ball," he later recalled. "I couldn't understand
that kind of wasted time, even in a place like [Desbarats]. I had a certain
amount of reading I wanted to do, a certain amount of physical condition-
ing I wanted to achieve, so I set out to do it and I did."[8]

In the fall of 1929, after spending his first summer in Desbarats, Proxmire joined his brother at the Hill School in Pottstown, Pennsylvania.

Founded in 1851 by the Rev. Matthew Meigs as a "family boarding school for boys and young men," the college preparatory school offered the fourteen-year-old Proxmire his ideal educational setting. Since its founding, the school had emphasized character building through a rigorous and traditional academic program combined with strictly enforced routine and discipline. Under James I. Wendell, headmaster from 1928 to 1952, The Hill increased its enrollment and expanded and modernized its curriculum in response to John Dewey's ideas of progressive education. Tradition remained, from mandatory chapel services to dress codes to petty rules regulating all aspects of student behavior, but the school gained a reorganized and modernized library, science building, and gymnasium. For a young man who craved physical activity and routine, it was perfect, and it fostered in Proxmire a lifelong fixation with ethical behavior. He was determined to demonstrate his academic ability and to show up his older brother. As a "second-former" (equivalent to eighth grade) Proxmire made the "A lists" by earning straight As on biweekly reports in six courses fourteen straight times, a school record. Proxmire minimized his accomplishment as the result of hard work and determination rather than innate intellectual brilliance, and he later eased up and focused more on athletics than academics, finishing five years with good though not extraordinary grades. At The Hill, he pursued boxing—becoming the 145-pound intramural champion in 1934—as well as track and football. Less socially active than some of his classmates, Proxmire nonetheless was secretary of the English Club and the YMCA Executive Committee. In recognition for his diligent study habits, his sixth-form classmates voted him "biggest grind" just before graduation, though he also received votes for "biggest sponger" and "most energetic," two labels that would no doubt amuse those who knew him later in life.[9]

After completing five years at The Hill, Proxmire—again following his brother—enrolled in Yale University in 1934. He majored in English literature, but athletics continued to be a major part of his life. He joined the freshman boxing team and later, through diligent practice, fought on the varsity team for three years in the 145-, 155-, and 165-pound weight classes. Although illness prevented him from fighting in the Eastern Intercollegiate championship his senior year, he did fight to a draw the captain of the Army team, who went on to win the championship. Proxmire was equally determined to do well in football, but his slight frame brought him much less success. Despite participating in practice every fall and spring, he was simply too slender to be an effective player. He scored exactly one touchdown, in a practice game against Colgate University. Yet his hard work earned the respect of the head coach, who sent Proxmire in as right end for a single play in the first half of a game against Princeton. It was the only varsity play Proxmire ever experienced, and he was nowhere near the ball, but it earned him a letter in football. As at The Hill, Proxmire spent more of his time in the library than most of his fellow students. Combined with boxing and football, his studies left him little time for an active social life, though he did join Chi Psi fraternity and "had [his] share of dates with Smith, Vassar, and Sarah Lawrence girls in New York City."[10]

College also began to reshape Proxmire's political views. His father was a staunch Republican, and Lake Forest was a solidly Republican community, but moving into the wider world, Proxmire began to see the very real poverty of the Great Depression and the effects of President Franklin Roosevelt's New Deal programs. Home for Christmas in 1934, he went to a movie with his father and stood to applaud Roosevelt as he appeared in a newsreel. Theodore yanked his nineteen-year-old son back into his seat, warning him that his action would be bad for business. Despite his father's opposition, Bill thought that increased federal spending was exactly what the economic crisis called for.[11]

Proxmire's real devotion to education began in 1938, when he graduated Yale and enrolled in Harvard Business School, specializing in financial management. No longer distracted by athletics, Proxmire focused on his courses and graduated in the top ten percent of his class with an MBA in 1940. As a result of his academic record at Harvard, J. P. Morgan and Company hired him as an executive trainee. During the summer of 1940, the three months between earning his master's degree and beginning his career on Wall Street, he returned to Lake Forest for a final athletic binge, playing thirty-six holes of golf every day at Onwentsia Golf Club. One day he played ninety holes just to prove he could. He got his handicap down to nine and averaged a score in the low eighties. After that summer, Proxmire rarely had time for golf.[12]

The golfing binge was also a form of therapy. While Proxmire was a student at Harvard, tragedy struck his family. After graduating from Yale in 1936 Ted went to work as a clerk for American Airlines. The older Proxmire boy had always been obsessed with speed, and his parents indulged his daredevil nature. At fifteen, he owned a motorcycle that he would ride down the highway at speeds in excess of seventy miles per hour, weaving in between vehicles and terrifying his more cautious younger brother, who once walked home several miles rather than ride with him. At Yale, Ted tinkered with the Buick convertible his father had given him but quickly developed an interest in flying, participating in stunt flying meets. Needing more experience in order to become a pilot for American Airlines, he enlisted in the army air corps. Early in 1939, he flew into an airport near Lake Forest to meet his parents and his brother. After a picnic lunch, Ted took off in his airplane and terrified his family: "After he had gotten half a mile from us," his brother recalled years later, "he turned around, gunned it, and did a series of barrel rolls only fifty feet off the ground, then he turned around and came back and flew upside down, wide open. My mother literally screamed with fright." In retrospect, it was eerie foreshadowing. A short time later, in February 1939, Ted died when the fighter plane he was flying crashed in Florida. He was only twenty-five.[13]

Ted's death devastated his parents. Theodore sank into a depression while he struggled with his son's death. It was the saddest Proxmire ever saw his father. "We never in our wildest dreams think our children are going to predecease us," Proxmire later said, "and when that happens, it's very devastating." Adele coped better because of her religious belief, attending Mass every day. The tragedy—Bill referred to it as the saddest day of his life—haunted him for years as he struggled with the shock.[14] The family continued to experience personal hardship. Proxmire was very close to his sister, Adele, who earned a degree from Sarah Lawrence University in 1937. Shortly thereafter, she married a Lake Forest lawyer, John E. Baker Jr. The two were a devoted couple and had two children. After the second daughter was born, however, doctors diagnosed Adele with multiple sclerosis, which over the next twenty years crippled her and robbed her of her eyesight and voice before her death. Proxmire's mother, who mourned Ted for the rest of her life, died in 1951. The tight-knit family had been wrenched apart, and the middle child experienced both the sudden death of one sibling and the slow deterioration of the other.[15]

With degrees from Yale and Harvard and a job at J. P. Morgan, Proxmire was poised to become a successful Wall Street financier in the fall of 1940. His flirtation with the Democratic Party also seemed to have died out, since he actively supported Republican nominee Wendell Willkie for president, largely based on his opposition to a third term for Roosevelt. He gave two dozen speeches for Willkie around New York City, though he was careful to label himself an independent rather than a Republican. To his chagrin he found that Roosevelt's brilliant use of radio easily undid his efforts. He was, however, eager to improve his public speaking skills and enrolled in a speech course at Columbia while working at J. P. Morgan. His career in high finance proved short-lived. After six months, Proxmire began to realize that a career on Wall Street was not satisfying. It was too easy, perhaps, to make money for others without having to work hard— that was not the way he was brought up and it was not the way he wanted to live. Foreign affairs also made Proxmire's departure easier. Roosevelt signed the first peacetime draft on September 16, 1940, and Proxmire drew a low draft number. Perhaps competing with his brother's service in the army air corps, Proxmire chose to enlist in the army rather than wait to be drafted. For whatever reasons, the Ivy League Wall Street hotshot found himself in basic training at Camp Roberts, California, in March 1941.[16]

Unlike most recruits, Proxmire delighted in basic training, later calling it "really a happy period of my life." His devotion to physical activity and disciplined work habits fit perfectly with life in the army, and he loved the exercise and competition. He even enjoyed KP duty. Given his education and background, the army transferred him to the Finance Department of the army, and then to Fort Sheridan, his father's old post near Lake Forest. After the Japanese attack on Pearl Harbor, he transferred to the Counter-Intelligence Corps. His training in Chicago fascinated him. He took copious notes on principles of espionage and technical information on codes, surveillance, gathering evidence, and undercover work. Practical assignments—especially transforming raw information into a properly organized and formatted report—appealed to his sense of order. Lectures on German espionage and propaganda and on recent revolutions also caught his attention, and he carefully preserved those notes.

After completing training, Proxmire spent three and a half years in Chicago working in the Military Intelligence Service at the Sixth Service Command headquarters. His principal task was conducting background checks on military personnel as "Investigator 201." His hard work was noticed, and he moved up the ranks from private to master sergeant by March 1943. Proxmire was commissioned a second lieutenant on December 6, 1944, and transferred to Fort Meyer, Virginia, and later to the War Department working to decipher Japanese codes. It was an eye-opening experience as he suddenly found himself surrounded by graduates from the best colleges around the country and felt for a time like a bumbling fool. Many of his fellow officers in the CIC—jokingly referred to as "Christ, I'm Confused"—had backgrounds in mathematics or engineering, and Proxmire developed a tremendous respect for them and their abilities. Because of the confidential nature of their work, employees were forbidden to discuss it. Instead, lunch conversation revolved around sports, so Proxmire and others would read the sports page religiously every morning in order to be able to participate in discussions. The camaraderie made it almost like being at school again.[17]

When the war ended, Proxmire found himself at a crossroads. Promoted to first lieutenant at the end of the war, he nonetheless had no interest in continuing in the service. While in Washington, he regularly visited the Capitol and watched Senate debates from the visitors' gallery. His time in the army and his visits to the Senate Chamber made him realize that financiers had far less influence in public life than they'd had in the past—the big decisions were made in Washington, not on Wall Street. The challenge of working for the CIC also made him reluctant to return to the financial world, which offered no real intellectual challenge. He knew he could be successful at it, but he would stagnate intellectually. He considered enrolling in the Columbia School of Journalism, but when he was discharged in January 1946 he instead returned to Harvard and entered the Graduate School of Public Administration.[18]

Proxmire threw himself into his coursework with characteristic fervor. He took meticulous notes on the lectures and readings for courses on economic theory and on public opinion and politics, which became the foundation for his later interest in economics and fiscal policy. The economics course began with John Stuart Mill's *Principles of Political Economy* and continued through Edward Hastings Chamberlain's *Theory of Monopolistic Competition*. One of the major ideas Proxmire described in his notes was the relationship between the law of cost and the law of supply and demand, particularly in an era of rapid technological advance. What was the consequence for a society, for example, when technology lowered consumer costs but drove down wages or increased unemployment? In his government course he also learned concepts that would later guide his political campaigns, especially strategic use of media and how to tailor political messages to fit radio, magazines, or newspapers.

The ideas of John Dewey particularly intrigued him as he took careful notes on *The Public and Its Problems*. Dewey described how special interests obfuscate real social needs and prevent the public from perceiving the need for change, and how the distractions of modern life and popular culture diminish civic engagement. Modern life had become so complicated that citizens simply did not know what to think and increasingly depended on experts to guide them, posing a potential threat to democratic government. The solution to this problem of disengagement was for journalists to freely investigate issues and distribute their conclusions widely, as Proxmire underlined in his notes: "Communication of the results of social inquiry is the same thing as the formation of public opinion." In other words, the real power of a journalist or a politician was the ability to tell the people what they needed to know. The class brought personal satisfaction as well. On March 28, Proxmire noted in his notes, "Exams were handed back—for some mysterious reason [I] received an A– although it was a very badly written, badly organized exam, but the result should add confidence that in the future there's no reason for the fine frenzy."[19] Proxmire had finally found his calling.

The influence of the press over political behavior continued to fascinate him. In August, he submitted a term paper titled "The Role of the Press in American Politics," a 110-page inquiry into "how can the newspaper achieve the crucial objective of disseminating the relevant political facts to the sovereign electorate with the greatest degree of completeness, accuracy and objectivity technically possible" while remaining profitable for its owners. Since newspapers depended on advertising revenue, could they be truly neutral, or would they unintentionally mirror their advertisers' views? Should the government subsidize newspapers because they performed a valuable public service? Proxmire argued that major newspapers in the United States tended to disseminate the point of view of a single economic interest group at the expense of other interest groups, thus failing in objectivity. His solution was a new model of newspaper that eliminated the editorial page with a "battle page" in which opposite sides of a controversial issue would present their arguments for the readers to judge. Reporters would need to follow strict rules on objectivity and avoid any language that might insert opinion. Such an endeavor, he argued, would be attractive to readers and therefore profitable for the newspaper itself.[20]

While at Harvard, Proxmire met Elsie Rockefeller at a wedding in New York City in January 1946. Elsie was the great-granddaughter of William Avery Rockefeller Jr., brother and business partner to John D. Rockefeller and the second-largest shareholder of Standard Oil Company. In the 1880s, William relocated to New York to head the company's international operations and then diversified into mining, railroads, and utilities and increased his wealth. He bought a summer home in Greenwich, Connecticut, where Elsie was born on April 4, 1924, to William Avery Rockefeller III and Florence Lincoln. Elsie grew up in Greenwich, living a sheltered, privileged life and attending Miss Porter's School in Farmington, Connecticut, an elite boarding school for the children of prominent families, including those of the Bush family and Jacqueline Bouvier herself. Despite her sheltered life, Elsie developed a strong social conscience that belied her family's privileged background. After graduating from Miss Porter's, she volunteered for medical service in the impoverished communities of eastern Kentucky, assisting with childbirth and living under her mother's maiden name rather than being identified as a Rockefeller. Seeing firsthand the daily struggles that the people of Appalachia endured profoundly affected her. Although her family and friends had always been steadfast Republicans, she began to realize the positive impact of New Deal programs and how government intervention could benefit those who most needed assistance. After working as a nurse's aide during World War II, she worked at Scribner's bookstore in New York just prior to meeting her future husband.

On the surface, William and Elsie made a good match. Elsie's two brothers and father had graduated from Yale, which immediately gained Proxmire acceptance into her family. Although they both came from conservative families, they had both recently become interested in Democratic politics, and Elsie assumed he would pursue a respectable career in public service or finance. They were married on September 14, 1946, in a ceremony at Christ Episcopal Church in Greenwich, with Proxmire's father as his best man. After a reception at the home of Elsie's mother, Florence, and stepfather, George Sloan, and a honeymoon in Bermuda, the couple returned to Cambridge for Proxmire to continue his graduate work at Harvard. Their first child, Theodore Stanley, was born on October 6, 1947.[21]

Continuing his graduate studies kept Proxmire busy, but he found the problems presented in his courses intellectually stimulating. In the winter of 1946–1947, he tackled the problem of increased government subsidies of higher education, submitting his conclusions in the form of a 104-page dialogue among four characters staying at the Statler Hotel in Washington prior to their testimony before the Senate Committee on Labor and Public Welfare: Platon, president of Harvard University; Aristo, professor of public administration at Tricago University; Thomas Jeffers, United States senator; and Andrew Jacks, New York state senator. Proxmire concluded that the cost of expanding college education to more citizens should be borne by the federal government as well as the students themselves through a plan whereby the government would pay tuition and living costs of those who gained admission to colleges and recover those costs from graduates' future earnings. His professor called it a "very successful tour de force" and awarded Proxmire an A minus.[22]

Another major project addressed the question of whether cabinet officers should clear their public statements with the president. On the one hand, the president needed to ensure that his administration spoke consistently; on the other hand, cabinet officers also needed to be able to express themselves freely. Proxmire's research strategy was straightforward: he wrote to government officials requesting their opinions. Among those responding to his inquiries were former president Herbert Hoover, ten cabinet officers, other federal officials, and eight journalists. The responses proved to be a fascinating glimpse into the psychology of government. Hoover insisted that as the president's appointees, cabinet officers owed him loyalty; if they opposed the president's views they had no choice but to resign. Walter Lippmann, Henry Wallace, Harold Ickes, J. W. Fulbright, and Joseph P. Kennedy voiced similar views, although those with experience in the executive branch admitted that there were no firm rules in place governing such statements, which sometimes resulted in conflict among departments rather than with the White House. Proxmire argued that the need for a coherent public message from the executive branch required some standardized procedures to ensure that the president's cabinet spoke uniformly in support of administration policies.[23]

Not every academic endeavor was a happy one, however. Enrolled in a political theory course that covered the development of western political thought from Machiavelli through Marx, Proxmire discovered that professors could sometimes be dismissive of their students' ideas. The professor in this case was Louis Hartz, who had recently arrived at Harvard and would later publish one of the most influential works in American political science, *The Liberal Tradition in American Politics*. On March 21, Proxmire wrote in his notes:

> Hartz started out the lecture by answering my letter criticizing his notion of separation of powers with a wholly unfair blast which made no effort to consider the problem I raised but placed me in the position of a low grade idiot, charging that he had meant separation of governmental powers—classes—<u>not</u> separation or division of labor. It taught me to be awfully careful in writing letters to tailor them to the degree of maturity, self-confidence, emotional balance of the recipient as well as to his intelligence; and when in doubt to couch the letter in utterly adulatory terms in order to be sure not to injure the recipient's vanity in such a way that the letter has a reaction entirely different from that desired.[24]

Academics could have thin skins, but so could Bill Proxmire.

Economics provided more room for Proxmire to develop his own ideas. Foreshadowing his interest in tax policy that would distinguish him in Wisconsin politics, Proxmire tackled the question of corporate income tax in one of his final projects at Harvard. He described corporate income tax as "a unique fiscal policy weapon. Because it affects private investment directly (that is by modifying profits) instead of indirectly (through demand or cost) it is a more incisive tool of fiscal control of private investment than other fiscal measures." Free market advocates insisted that corporate taxation was purely punitive and, by reducing profit, would slow economic growth. On one side stood those who argued for corporate taxation to prevent the kind of maldistribution of wealth that made the Great Depression last so long. Proxmire cautiously came down in the middle and recommended the elimination of corporate taxation but with increased personal income tax rates on large incomes and increased capital gains tax to maintain revenue while encouraging investment. Government certainly had a role to play, but proper fiscal policy depended above all on a fair tax policy.[25]

The year 1948 was a busy one. There was a new baby at home, and not only had Proxmire earned a master's degree and continued with coursework leading to a PhD, he also began teaching political theory and comparative government. Teaching undergraduate courses was a major challenge: "I had to learn the course first," Proxmire later wrote. "I really worked my tail off." He also earned money by delivering speeches ($25 each) on the issues of the 1948 election throughout New England for a lecture bureau. He strove to appear objective and often made his audiences wonder if he was a Republican or a Democrat. His time at Harvard, however, had convinced him to support Democratic nominee Harry Truman. Writing about this later, Proxmire noted that "on all the political problems, the Republicans had reasons not to act, while the Democrats worked at solving the problems. It made a tremendous impression on me . . . Democrats came up with the answers, while the Republicans always seemed to give explanations that nothing ought to be done."[26] For the intellectual, active Proxmire, that was a profoundly unsatisfying position. For his dissertation, Proxmire proposed a study of how newspapers affected political behavior. His plan called for a historical overview of the role played by newspapers followed by criteria for evaluating the service of newspapers based on accuracy, comprehensiveness, comprehensibility, attention winning, readership, and discussion. Proxmire prepared a long list of sources and proposed studying six major newspapers and several smaller ones and interviewing reporters and editors, as well as state and national representatives. His ambitious timeline called for him to begin gathering research material on May 15 and complete a content analysis of newspapers in the summer and fall, with November and December saved for writing and revisions. His committee—or perhaps Proxmire himself—might have questioned his devotion to the project and his increasing commitments to family, public speaking engagement, and interest in developing a career in journalism or politics. On the last page of his proposal he added a note: "During the period May 15, 1948 to January 1, 194[9] the dissertation will be my exclusive concern—seven days per week!"[27] No doubt Elsie was less than pleased by this single-minded dedication combined with his other commitments, which left almost no time at all to spend with his family.

In truth, Proxmire had little interest in finishing his dissertation. He had already decided on a career and started looking for a suitable place to work on a newspaper and then move into politics. Accordingly he, Elsie, and Teddy moved in with his parents in Lake Forest while he conducted his job search. Proxmire ruled out any of the large city newspapers—the same he had chosen for his dissertation—reasoning that he would not have the opportunity to stand out in a large staff. He was also too impatient to become involved in an urban political machine and wait his turn while bosses dictated candidates—he had talent and wanted to make his mark immediately. He focused on Oregon, Washington, Indiana, and Wisconsin and sent letters to about fifty medium-sized newspapers (with a circulation between 15,000 and 75,000) offering his services as an editorial writer or investigative reporter. He got interviews at several newspapers, including the *Indianapolis Star*, the *Yakima Herald-Republic*, and the *Daily Olympian*. Job offers came from newspapers in Washington, Indiana, Illinois, and Michigan, and from the Madison *Capital Times*, where he had been interviewed by chief editorial writer Miles McMillin. Proxmire received a strong recommendation from one of his Harvard professors, John Gaus. Gaus had been a political science professor at the University of Wisconsin from 1927 to 1947 before moving to Harvard, where he met Proxmire as a graduate student. More importantly, Gaus had been a close friend and political advisor to former governor Philip F. La Follette in the 1930s and had supported his progressive policies that included increased relief spending, government reorganization, and the nation's first unemployment compensation program. Based on Gaus's enthusiastic recommendation, McMillin hired Proxmire to be a reporter on political and labor issues for forty dollars a week. There was at least one dissenting voice. When Proxmire encountered *Capital Times* reporter Aldric Revell on a fellowship to Harvard, he asked his opinion of moving to Wisconsin, working on the newspaper, and then running for office. "It's one of the most foolish things I've ever heard of," snapped Revell.[28]

Proxmire, however, thought Wisconsin offered more prospects than anywhere else. Washington State already had a well-established Democratic Party, with too many well-known figures that would hinder his ability to break into electoral politics. Illinois offered a similar situation: Paul Douglas and Adlai Stevenson led a Democratic party with a strong presence in state and local politics, and Proxmire did not want to wait in line for a chance for higher office. Wisconsin offered a much greater opportunity.[29]

In Wisconsin, the political landscape was very different. While most states had a competitive two-party system, Wisconsin featured a Republican Party that had dominated Wisconsin politics between the Civil War and the 1930s. Of twenty-one governors elected between 1861 and 1932, only three were Democrats (William Taylor in 1873, George Peck in 1890 and 1892, and Albert Schmedeman in 1932). With a few brief exceptions, Republicans controlled both houses of the state legislature and the congressional delegation. The Democratic Party remained marginal, made up of old Jacksonians who were often even more conservative than the Republicans. Wisconsin politics, however, was not uncontested. As the leadership of the Republican Party became more closely aligned with the state's manufacturing and commercial interests, and more dictatorial about choosing candidates, young, reform-minded men began to organize a faction within the party in the 1890s. First called "half-breeds" by their conservative opponents, the group became known as "Progressives" and secured the nomination of Robert M. La Follette in 1900.

La Follette and his supporters sought to change fundamentally the political and economic landscape of the state by establishing primary elections, reforming corporate tax structures, regulating railroads, and instituting a civil service law. When La Follette went to the United States Senate in 1906, Progressives continued to grab national attention through reforms: new labor laws, workers' compensation, conservation laws, corporate regulation, and the nation's first constitutional income tax law. La Follette ran unsuccessfully for president on the Progressive ticket in 1924 and died shortly thereafter; his son, Robert Jr., served in the Senate from 1925 to 1946, and his younger son Philip was elected governor in 1930. Philip's administration pushed through increased expenditures for relief for the unemployed and created the nation's first unemployment compensation program. When Democrats swept into power on Franklin

Roosevelt's coattails, the progressive faction abandoned the Republican Party and formed a third party, the Wisconsin Progressive Party, led by the La Follette brothers. The Progressive Party was much more closely aligned with the New Deal than the Wisconsin Democratic Party, but it went into decline after 1939 and disbanded in 1946.[30]

In 1946, then, Wisconsin Progressives faced a choice. Some, especially those who had supported the senior La Follette, returned to the Republican Party. Robert La Follette Jr. led this return and ran for the Republican senatorial nomination but lost to a political newcomer: Appleton judge Joseph McCarthy. Now dominated by conservative businessmen and openly hostile to the New Deal, the Republican Party offered little attraction to younger people who had come of age under Roosevelt and Philip La Follette. Instead, these younger liberals began remaking the moribund Democratic Party. The first move in this direction was actually the former Socialist mayor of Milwaukee, Daniel Hoan, who ran for governor as a Democrat in 1944 and 1946. The so-called "Young Turks" included Gaylord Nelson, Lester Johnson, Carl Thompson, John Reynolds, James Doyle, Ruth Doyle, and Horace Wilkie. Many were part of the Wisconsin Young Progressive Club at the University of Wisconsin and had earned degrees from the UW Law School. Meeting at a hotel in Fond du Lac in 1948, these young leaders established the Democratic Organizing Committee, an organization to sidestep the older, more conservative party leadership and to raise funds through membership. Gradually, the DOC organized units in county after county and held its first convention in Green Bay in November 1949, where the featured speaker was the liberal Democratic senator from Illinois Paul Douglas. They claimed to be the inheritors of the La Follette tradition and provided a perfect opportunity for someone as energetic and ambitious as Bill Proxmire.[31]

In January 1949, Bill, Teddy, and Elsie—five months pregnant—arrived in Madison. Proxmire had tried to find a house to rent but found nothing to his satisfaction. Instead he borrowed money from his father to purchase a run-down, twenty-five-year-old farmhouse on ten acres on Buckeye Road on the eastern edge of Madison, and then borrowed more money from his father to repair and modernize it. He began working for the *Capital Times* in February. Publisher William T. Evjue had founded the newspaper in 1917 as a pro–La Follette alternative to the *Wisconsin*

State Journal. He remained a devout La Follette supporter until 1938, when he broke with Philip La Follette over the governor's effort to reorganize state government and the La Follettes' isolationist foreign policy—both Phil and Young Bob opposed Roosevelt's efforts to aid Great Britain in 1940 and '41, while Evjue supported Roosevelt in foreign policy as well as domestic policy. Evjue made the *Capital Times* into a crusading newspaper that became the mouthpiece for Wisconsin liberal thought, by 1950 firmly aligned with the reborn Democratic Party. By that time, Evjue remained a strident and cranky critic of political corruption and corporate power. His weekly radio program, "Hello Wisconsin," carried his views into every corner of the state, though he had largely turned over the editorial page to Miles McMillin, who had joined the paper in 1945.

It seemed like a good fit, since Proxmire, too, had a deep desire to fix problems. Shortly after moving into the house on Buckeye Road, he wrote:

On this twenty third day of January I resolve to do all in my power to make the morally right decisions.
Right in that they are the most just to all concerned.
Right in that they are usually the hardest.
Right in that they so often only involve me, but require doing that which is wearying or boring or dull.

Based on Evjue's hostility to corporate lobbying, Proxmire began to investigate lobbying, and McMillin had him focus on the Wisconsin Manufacturing Association, the Wisconsin Chamber of Commerce, and lobbyists representing insurance firms and construction companies. Proxmire immediately began building a file on key members of the legislature interested in efforts to curb lobbying and those eager to quash reforms. His efforts to understand its inner workings quickly made him an expert on the state legislature. He also made himself a nuisance to public figures by taking advantage of public disclosure of income tax returns. As long as Proxmire confined his investigations to those whom Evjue already targeted, he got along fine with the publisher, though some criticized his writing style as clichéd and overtly partisan. Trouble began when he turned his attention too close to home. When Proxmire began trying to unionize those departments of the newspaper that were not already organized, he became a source of irritation to management. According to Miles McMillin, Evjue finally fired Proxmire not over his labor organizing but when Proxmire critiqued a story Evjue had written about a murder trial. The cantankerous editor had finally had enough insubordination, although publicly the separation was by mutual consent in order to allow Proxmire to run for office. Evjue himself had served a single term in the Assembly before deciding that one could be either a good journalist or a good politician, but not both.[32]

Proxmire's union activities led him to the Madison *Union Labor News*, published by the Wisconsin Federation of Labor. His primary role was business manager, which mostly involved securing revenue through advertising. As he put it, his new job involved "selling advertising for Madison Union Labor News, on commission-only basis; earnings negligible." While he worked for *Union Labor News*, the Proxmires received significant financial support from both families, although, as Proxmire noted, "None of us is happy about it."[33] And while it paid little, his connection to the *Union Labor News* gave Proxmire a public voice through a weekly radio program called "Labor Sounds Off," broadcast Thursdays at six thirty p.m. on WKOW. Proxmire used his program to criticize Madison businesses, including Oscar Mayer, Ray-O-Vac, and A&P grocery store, that, in his opinion, were hostile toward organized labor or treated employees unfairly. Elsie usually appeared on these broadcasts as well, playing the role of the "average housewife," asking questions about unions and bargaining rights in order to allow Proxmire to correct common misinformation and antilabor viewpoints. Their often humorous repartee reflected a style popular on radio comedies, although it sometimes bordered on the farcical, as when they staged a mock argument that culminated in physical violence complete with sound effects to make a point about press coverage of labor conflicts. Proxmire began naming a weekly "Friend of Labor" and a "No Friend of Labor" and urged listeners to patronize businesses based on their record of good labor relations. Proxmire also took great pains to point out those businesses where management had a good working relationship with employees. This was unapologetic opinionated journalism, and WKOW soon started each broadcast with a disclaimer to avoid losing advertising revenue.[34]

Proxmire also used his radio broadcasts as a way of singling out those whom he decided deserved particular scorn. He frequently targeted Senator Alexander Wiley, the Republican incumbent who had represented Wisconsin since 1939, as well as Don Anderson, the publisher of the conservative *Wisconsin State Journal*. In December 1949, Proxmire made one incident with Anderson into a short-lived cause célèbre after Anderson ran over a union picket and the judge dismissed assault charges against him.[35] Other targets included Republican Party leader Thomas Coleman and Governor Oscar Rennebohm for reporting $80,000 and $90,000 respectively in tax-free dividends and then opposing efforts to change the tax code to make income from dividends taxable. He complained about lobbyists and contrasted record corporate profits and tax-free dividends with stagnant wages for working people. Still interested in being an investigative journalist, Proxmire also uncovered fraud in the Department of Agriculture and the theft of confidential files from the Dane County attorney general's office.[36] Sensitive to red-baiting, Proxmire also channeled the staunch anticommunism of most national Democratic politicians, including Harry Truman, whom he admired. When Senator Joseph McCarthy called the *Capital Times* communist-influenced, Proxmire made it his "laugh of the week." After reminding listeners that McCarthy had failed to pay taxes on over $42,000 of income until that newspaper uncovered the story, he quoted McCarthy as calling the *Capital Times* "the red mouthpiece for the Communist party in Wisconsin." Instead, Proxmire praised the newspaper for fighting communism, "the evil thing that means the utter destruction of institutions like *The Capital Times*." Again and again, Proxmire warned listeners not to be misled by such reckless accusations and false comparisons.[37]

"Labor Sounds Off" provided a platform for Proxmire to boost the new Democratic Organizing Committee as well. He regularly praised former attorney general Thomas Fairchild ("a man of absolute integrity"), who was running against Wiley in 1950. He also celebrated Dane County delegates to the Green Bay meeting in December 1949, including Carl Thompson, Jim Doyle, Gaylord Nelson, Horace Wilkie, and Virginia Hart, throwing his entire weight behind this newly energized and liberal political faction. Although not part of this inner circle of Democratic leaders, Proxmire was quickly becoming a significant part of the Dane County party. In the fall, the Dane County Democratic Club made Proxmire the head of its speakers' bureau, giving him the task to recruit Democrats—including himself—to speak to civic clubs, women's groups, labor unions, and other interested parties. At first Proxmire hoped it would be a paid position, as he dourly noted: "Democrats (DOC) had thought couple of months ago of giving [me a] salary for heading speaker's bureau, but that fell through."[38] Paid or not, Proxmire was making important friends, like Warren and Ellen Sawall, who worked for the Democratic Party in Madison, as did many volunteers. Ellen later recalled:

> There was a group of us in Madison that included Pat Lucey and Gaylord Nelson and Carl Thompson and Horace Wilkie. We began very slowly, very quietly and all volunteer. . . . We all loved it. We socialized together. We all knew our children. None of us had any money. Pat Lucey hadn't even begun his real estate business then. And Gaylord and Carrie Lee [Nelson], we were contemporaries and their children were contemporaries with my children and it was an interweaving of this volunteer interest with the practical aspect of making a living and raising your family.[39]

At the end of 1949 and the beginning of 1950, then, Proxmire had already made a name for himself as a liberal journalist, mastered the art of radio broadcasting, and become a part of the new Democratic Party. And he began to think about running for office: "Definitely interested in politics," he mused, "but for present if [I] ran for anything wouldn't be above assembly level." Although running for the assembly was a small start, it was the beginning of an almost forty-year career in politics.[40]

2

THE PEOPLE'S BUSINESS

As the "Young Turks" slowly reinvented the Wisconsin Democratic Party, William Proxmire, already familiar to Madison residents as a reporter and radio commentator, reinvented himself as a candidate for political office. On February 16, 1950, a reporter for the *Capital Times* wrote that Proxmire was "strongly considering" a primary election challenge to first-term incumbent John M. Blaska in the Dane County Second Assembly District. At first glance, Proxmire had little chance of winning. Blaska was a sixty-five-year-old farmer from Sun Prairie with a long record of public service: he had served for twenty years as town chairman and had represented his community on the Dane County Board before winning election to the legislature in 1948. Prior to Blaska's election in 1948, the seat had been held for three terms by Earl Mullen, elected as a Republican in 1946 and as a member of the Progressive Party in 1942 and 1944. Lars Lein, another Progressive elected in 1940, served a single term. Between 1917 and 1939, the seat was held by James C. Hansen, a loyal supporter of Robert La Follette, who joined the Progressive bolt from the Republican Party in 1934. For over thirty years, then, Dane County's second district was a safe seat for liberals regardless of party labels. This boded well for Proxmire. Blaska, Mullen, and Hansen, however, were lifelong residents of the district with long records of local public service.[1] How would voters respond to a young outsider who had lived in the district for only a year?

Proxmire made the early announcement in that *Capital Times* article to test public reaction to his potential candidacy. He had made himself a reasonably well-known figure in Blooming Grove (population 5,428) and Burke (2,569) since he was active in building a Democratic organization in

these small communities of eastern Dane County.[2] Nonetheless, his background posed some potential difficulties. First, he was a newcomer, having
lived in Wisconsin only since January 1949. Wisconsin voters—especially
in rural areas—preferred candidates who had local roots and who based
their candidacies on personal connections developed over many years.
Blaska, Mullen, and Hansen fit this pattern, but Proxmire certainly did
not. In fact, his election would make him one of the youngest legislators in
the state. Second, in the short time Proxmire had lived in the rural district,
he was mostly closely identified with organized labor. He worked for the
Union Labor News and chaired the organizing committee of the Madison
Newspaper Guild, the labor union for newspaper workers. Radio station
WKOW broadcast his weekly program "Labor Sounds Off" on Thursday
evenings.[3] Efforts to forge an alliance between industrial workers and
farmers were notoriously difficult in Wisconsin. Earlier attempts in the
1930s, based on the Farmer Labor Progressive Federation, were only mod-
estly successful for a few years, and the Cold War had only deepened suspicion of alleged labor radicalism among rural voters. The new Democratic
Party struggled to unite these two constituencies.[4]

Proxmire recognized these potential liabilities and met them head-on.
Sitting down for an interview with reporter Sterling Sorensen, he insisted
that a candidate "should be judged on his merits, on his integrity, on his
intelligence and on his ability, rather than on the length of time he has
lived in a community." Electing candidates based on residency, he continued, would result in government by self-selected aristocracy. His refusal
to defer to others with longer records conjured up the same image that
had riled voters since the appearance of Robert La Follette in the 1890s.
This tugged powerfully at the memories of Dane County voters, but it was
unclear if they would see such a threat from their neighbors, or whether
they would resent someone making that comparison. Moreover, Proxmire
made clear that he was not the "labor" candidate: "I welcome the support
of all economic groups, farmers, workers, business and professional people
and housewives."[5]

The biggest obstacle to his election, however, was Elsie's family, the
Rockefellers. Her father, William A. Rockefeller, was, as Sorensen noted,
"extremely wealthy." Moreover, Elsie's mother had later married George
A. Sloan, who sat on the boards of directors of US Steel and Goodyear.

Would these connections to industrial wealth taint Proxmire in the militant heartland of La Follette progressivism? Again, Proxmire preemptively distanced himself from that image by declaring himself a "New Deal/Fair Deal Democrat" and promising that none of his rich relatives would provide financial support. Besides, he added, Wisconsin election laws limited primary campaign expenditures to $225, meaning the Rockefeller fortune would be irrelevant. The editor of the *Capital Times* later said that the extensive coverage of the almost-announcement and the inflammatory headline linking Proxmire to the Rockefellers and Sloans was a deliberate attempt to scuttle his candidacy. William Evjue, himself an old La Follette ally, still had an axe to grind with his former employee. Instead of ducking the issue, Proxmire welcomed the challenge and used the publicity to his own advantage.[6]

Proxmire did not officially enter the Democratic primary until May 10, but in the interim he continued to circulate among Democratic Party activists in his district to make himself known. In late February, at a meeting of the Stoughton local of the Democratic Organizing Committee (DOC), he and State Senator Gaylord Nelson discussed the state budget and the possibility of a sales tax, already emerging as a divisive issue in the state.[7] Nelson was a major figure in Wisconsin politics, and immensely popular in Dane County, so Proxmire benefited from the connection. Although often linked to the Madison-based Democratic leadership—the *Wisconsin State Journal* linked Proxmire with *Capital Times* editor Miles McMillin, Roland Day, and others as a cadre that sought to dominate city and county government—Proxmire remained outside the inner circle. The Dane County DOC named Nelson, Horace Wilkie, James Doyle, Ruth Doyle, and Thomas Fairchild as delegates to the 1950 State Convention, but Proxmire was sent only as an alternate.[8] Rather than working up through the ranks of the Democratic Organizing Committee, then, Proxmire essentially planned to bypass the party leadership and talk directly to the people, again following a pattern established by Fighting Bob.

And talk he did. Proxmire used his weekly radio program to discuss both labor and farm issues, although he never mentioned his own candidacy. More importantly, he began a door-to-door campaign to introduce himself personally to the voters, easily outpacing the much-older farmer who did not have the time to spare. Proxmire's relatives may not have contributed to his campaign, but his independently wealthy status certainly made his marathon campaigning possible and gave him a decided advantage in old-fashioned politicking. His background as a reporter helped prepare him, too. Proxmire carefully planned his race to reach those constituents most likely to vote in the primary in the most efficient way possible. He filled a reporter's notebook with the election results from 1944, 1946, and 1948 for every precinct in the district, adding where he could the names of personal contacts who could help organize those areas. After identifying the twenty most Democratic precincts, Proxmire then went door-to-door, visiting every farm and every house and following up each of these visits with a letter. In the last two weeks of the primary, every family in the district received a handwritten postcard, and in the final two days, nearly three thousand of them received a telephone call from the candidate or his wife. In a few months, Proxmire had made himself as well-known as the lifelong resident incumbent and demonstrated his energy and willingness to completely devote himself to politics.[9]

Despite the stark differences in their backgrounds, the two candidates embraced very similar positions on the key issues of interest to Dane County voters. Responding to written questions from the League of Women Voters, both Proxmire and Blaska favored reforming the utility tax and both favored increased state aid to public schools. Proxmire demonstrated his grasp of state issues by citing recent legislative committee reports on both questions and calling for taxation of corporate dividends to fund educational improvements.[10] In fact, the candidates' positions were so similar, Proxmire spent more time criticizing the "pro-business and anti-organized labor" state Republican platform and candidates than challenging his Democratic opponent.[11] Proxmire's strenuous efforts and connections to labor unions paid off when voters went to the polls on September 19. Blaska led in early returns, but a strong turnout among workers in Stoughton, where Proxmire had a two-to-one advantage, put the younger man over the top. The total vote was 1,885 to 1,674.[12] The cost of the campaign—mainly postcards, stationery, and postage—amounted to $203.12.[13]

Proxmire's opponent in the general election, Edgerton attorney Claude Stout, attempted to rile rural voters by charging that Proxmire's candidacy was an attempt by organized labor to buy control of the seat, held for decades by farmers. Stout's chances for election were slim, and he knew that Proxmire's positions on issues—and the Democrats' generally—were popular in the district. His best chance was to drive a wedge between farm and labor interests and force Proxmire to either downplay his connections to organized labor and thereby risk alienating those supporters, or else make rural voters see him as a tool of the labor unions. Proxmire didn't take the bait and instead calmly reiterated the Democratic Party's position favoring a corrupt practices law limiting campaign expenditures by outside groups, including labor unions.[14] The district's voting history made Proxmire's election in November likely, so for most of October, Proxmire campaigned with other Dane County Democrats and emphasized state and national issues. Appearing at a League of Women Voters meeting on October 16, Proxmire joined Ruth Doyle in calling for income tax changes, including higher inheritance taxes and the elimination of the exemption on dividends, in order to reduce property taxes and increase funds for local schools.[15]

Tax reform, especially property tax reform, was a bread-and-butter issue for liberal voters, but Proxmire also addressed issues of national importance that most of the voters in his district had little interest in. Anticipating how important the civil rights movement would become in the state, Proxmire embraced the state party's support for civil rights at a meeting of the NAACP on the University of Wisconsin campus. In the 1949 session of the legislature, seven civil rights bills—all introduced by Democrats—were debated. Three passed, outlawing discrimination in the National Guard, in public housing projects, and in public schools. Republicans defeated the other four, which would have raised fines for resort owners who discriminated and increased funding for state programs studying discrimination. Proxmire summarized the party's position as "probably the best record on civil rights of any state political party in the country."[16] Although civil rights was not yet a major issue in his district, Proxmire nonetheless staked out an unequivocal position based on his principles.

The other looming issue in both state and national politics was Wisconsin's own Senator Joseph McCarthy, who was alleging communist infiltration in the federal government, universities, and other spheres of American life. Proxmire joined other Democrats in attacking the senator's record as he ramped up these allegations. When McCarthy addressed the

La Crosse Kiwanis Club at the Stoddard Hotel in October, Proxmire and other Democrats set up a loudspeaker across the street to confront the senator on charges of unethical conduct. Warren Sawall, editor of the *Wisconsin Democrat*, and University of Wisconsin student Norman Anderson distributed copies of a *Capital Times* editorial questioning McCarthy's conduct as a circuit court judge and demanding to know why he had paid no state income taxes the previous four years. At the conclusion of McCarthy's speech, State Senator Gaylord Nelson spoke to the crowd as it left the hotel. Challenged by state Republicans who objected to this attempted disruption, Proxmire defended the action as an exercise in free speech. It was the people's right, he said, to know about any elected official's alleged ethical lapses.[17]

Buoyed by their attacks on McCarthy, Democrats were optimistic about their chances on Election Day, but they badly misjudged the mood of the electorate. Dissatisfaction with President Truman, anxiety about Communism, and the Korean War all contributed to a national swing toward the Republican Party. Republicans gained five seats in the US Senate and twenty-eight seats in the House of Representatives, a major setback for President Truman, who had struggled to get his proposals through Congress despite Democratic majorities. Republicans made noteworthy gains, particularly in the Midwest, where McCarthy's charges reached the most responsive audience, leaving the national Democratic Party torn between liberals and conservative southerners.[18] In Wisconsin, even though Democrats improved from their 1948 showing, the entire Republican ticket swept into office. Walter J. Kohler Jr. defeated Carl Thompson in the race for governor by better than eighty thousand votes (nearly 54% of the total). State attorney general Thomas Fairchild lost to incumbent US senator Alexander Wiley by a similar margin. Voters, worried about inflation and higher taxes brought on by the Korean War, blamed the Truman administration but had little reason to be dissatisfied with the state Republican Party. Dane County, however, proved once again to be a major source of Democratic strength as Democrats Ruth Doyle, Proxmire, and Herman Eisner were elected to the county's three Assembly seats.

Proxmire won his race 8,094 to 4,132 and carried all but three precincts. Led by Gaylord Nelson, the Dane County delegation would be in the minority: Republicans retained solid control over the Assembly and the Senate.[19] Although Proxmire was the least experienced of the group, it was clear that he intended to make his mark. Despite his earlier hostility, William Evjue now praised the newcomer and editorialized that "Bill Proxmire is a new figure in Wisconsin politics who will be heard from. . . . He is already planning to introduce a bill that will close the present loophole in the tax law under which top income boys in this state are escaping taxes on dividends from Wisconsin corporations."[20] It was clear that Proxmire had no intention of being a quiet back-bencher.

Even before he took office, he began challenging governor-elect Kohler over tax issues. After Kohler testified at the state budget hearing that Wisconsin was adequately enforcing its tax laws, the head of the tax commission, Arthur Wegner, reported that he had asked for thirty auditors for the 1949–1950 biennium to review tax returns and received only fifteen, and still needed more. "So there it is," Proxmire wrote in a letter to the *Capital Times*. "The 1949 legislature and the governor of Wisconsin have failed to live up to their trust by refusing to permit the state to enforce its income tax laws. And no one can deny it."[21] He was the junior member of a small minority, but Bill Proxmire would indeed be heard. A few weeks after the election, Proxmire announced that he would be the new general manager of the three-year-old Midwest Company, a construction company based in Sun Prairie that manufactured homes and buildings. He made clear, however, that his work as a legislator would be his first priority.[22]

As Elsie watched from the Assembly chamber gallery on January 9, Chief Justice Oscar Fritz swore in Proxmire and the other representatives. Also in the gallery were James E. Doyle, one of the leaders of the new Democratic Party, and his wife, Ruth, who was beginning her second term as the representative from Dane County's first district, encompassing the city of Madison. Together with Gaylord Nelson, the three would make their mark as the progressive vanguard of the party, much to the irritation of some Democrats from Milwaukee, who disliked the "Madison Ring."[23] Given his low seniority and the Democrats' minority status, Proxmire received only one committee assignment: the committee on taxation. Despite this, he quickly emerged as the principal Democratic voice on all matters of tax policy. Other members deferred to his rapidly growing expertise in large part because he was one of the few legislators who—despite his job—had the financial means to devote himself full-time to politics.[24]

Proxmire's first major proposal in the Assembly built on a theme he had raised during his campaign: the influence of big business on public policy. On January 17, he and five other Democrats introduced a bill that would create a full-time counsel to represent the interests of the people on the Public Service Commission, the state agency that regulated utilities.[25] In a public hearing before the Assembly judiciary committee, Proxmire explained that lawyers for utility companies "are extremely well-paid and backed by a battery of accountants and engineers. The city attorneys who generally have to oppose them just aren't any match. They don't have the training or the background." Unless the people of the state had this kind of ombudsman representing their interest, he argued, the Public Service Commission would be too easily swayed by the corporations it was charged to regulate. The proposal quickly gained support from other Democrats and from the state CIO, but in mid-May the committee recommended against passage.[26] A final vote in the Assembly came a week later, and the measure failed 54–33. Clearly most Republicans in the Assembly did not share Democrats' suspicion of utility corporations, and many were skeptical of *any* increase in state authority over private business. One Republican declared the "people's counsel" unnecessary and claimed it would be a step toward creating "people's courts" like those in European communist states.[27] It was a revealing moment to the man from Blooming Grove: using the state government to protect the interests of Wisconsin consumers was not an obvious decision in Cold War America.

Despite his devotion to liberal policies that weren't likely to get a hearing in the Republican legislature, Proxmire cosponsored some legislation that was less controversial and garnered bipartisan support. In February, he cosponsored a bill with three Republicans to create a state-run grading system for tobacco farmers to eliminate their dependence on tobacco buyers to assess the quality and value of their crop. A related measure exempted tobacco crops from personal property tax if the crop was held as collateral for federal loans through the Department of Agriculture. Although not a major Wisconsin crop, eastern Dane County was the center of production, so Proxmire and other legislators were acting in the interests of their constituents while at the same time siding with small-scale producers at the mercy of large, well-funded purchasers who naturally opposed the bill. Moreover, meeting with tobacco growers to discuss the bill gave him an important public relations opportunity, especially after tobacco dealers opposed the bill and the attorney general's office revealed that it had recently investigated tobacco buyers for price-fixing. Despite its 65–21 passage in the Assembly, the Senate killed the bill.[28]

Proxmire introduced some measures to reform state government and introduce greater efficiency. With Ruth Doyle, he proposed a constitutional amendment requiring the legislature to meet annually instead of biennially. He reasoned that this would lead to more efficient government, since actual tax revenues often differed markedly from estimates, and inflation worries encouraged department heads to submit deliberately oversized budget requests, badly skewing the real needs of the state. This made it virtually impossible to accurately budget two years in advance. Although the idea generated support among some administration officials, including the state auditor, the assembly rejected the resolution 68–31.[29]

Some of Proxmire's bills in the Assembly were aimed at traditional Democratic voting blocs. The most important of these dealt with organized labor. On March 1, Proxmire and three other Democrats in the Assembly introduced a bill to prohibit employers from requiring employees to attend lectures for "political or economic indoctrination" unless equal time was provided for speakers of the employees' own choosing. The impetus for the bill, strongly supported by the Wisconsin CIO, was a series of mandatory "Freedom Forums" held during working hours in factories in Milwaukee, Oshkosh, Racine, and other cities that linked organized labor with "un-American" activities. The measure lost 57–35.[30] Proxmire vigorously supported other labor-related bills, including measures to allow employees six years instead of two to sue employers for back wages, establish sick pay for Wisconsin workers, allow public employees to organize unions, raise the minimum wage, and establish rent controls.[31] Although none of these passed the Republican-dominated legislature, Proxmire's support cemented his reputation as reliably pro-labor. "The membership," wrote G. T. Owens, president of the University of Wisconsin employees union, "is keenly aware of your fine record in introducing and supporting legislation beneficial to state employees." Yet it was more than just appealing to the base: Proxmire consistently argued that the well-being of American workers was necessary for American prosperity in general.[32]

In addition to protecting the interests of Wisconsin workers, Proxmire also supported the elderly and called for increasing state old-age pensions to $75 per month. "Old people are in bad shape," Proxmire told the Assembly Public Welfare Committee. "Their buying power has been cut in half in recent years by inflation. We are remiss in caring for our aged. All neighboring states do better. Some 32,000 folks would benefit if we passed this bill." A lobbyist for the Wisconsin State Chamber of Commerce complained that "the poor little taxpayer already is taxed to the limit," a comment that particularly drew Proxmire's anger. He pointed out that the new tax would cost an individual earning $3,500 a year only another $2 in income tax. This was a small sacrifice for those who needed aid and could no longer work. To Proxmire, refusal violated the unwritten social contract that a society took care of its members and complaints could only be motivated by selfishness.[33] Although the increase in itself was not controversial (Governor Kohler supported it, and the bill passed unanimously in the Assembly), the method of financing the increase was. The original bill called for the state to pay 60 percent of the increased cost; the remaining 40 percent would be paid by counties and financed by property taxes. Proxmire proposed increasing the state share to 80 percent as a fairer way of raising revenue. Property taxes, Proxmire argued, were not based on ability to pay. If funding was needed, then, the fairest way would be to raise income taxes, rather than let county governments take the heat from taxpayers for raising property taxes. The Assembly rejected Proxmire's amendment before passing the pension bill unanimously.[34]

Although a relatively minor skirmish in the 1951 legislative session, the old-age pension fight highlighted several critical issues for Proxmire. First was the presence of lobbyists in the capitol. This was certainly nothing new, but for Proxmire, lobbyists were one of the major flaws in representative government, and he and Doyle introduced a major bill to curtail their influence. Their bill required registered lobbyists to list their employers and file weekly reports in which they itemized their expenditures and listed the public officials they visited. Violations of these provisions would result in the suspension of the licenses of both the lobbyist and his employer. Proxmire saw this as a moral issue, writing that lobbyists influenced legislation for "their own selfish ends," and "short-circuited" democracy.[35] Once again, Proxmire did his research. He consulted with former Dane County district attorney Robert Arthur, who had experience in prosecut-

ing lobby law violations, and he discovered that registered lobbyists had
spent $33,000 entertaining legislators in 1949. Proxmire cast the bill as
part of a populist crusade, calling it a measure on behalf of "the millions of
unorganized persons in the state who have no representatives to lobby for
them before the legislature." He claimed to have spoken to seven thousand
residents of his district in his 1950 campaign, most of whom disapproved
of lobbying.[36] Miles McMillin, chief editorial writer for the *Capital Times*,
poured fuel on the fire by publishing articles listing lobbyists and their expenditures, amounting to over $18,000 in the first four months of 1951.[37]
As with other Democratic measures, the lobbying bill failed. The Assembly
referred the bill to the judiciary committee, but the committee failed to
report it back. Proxmire did succeed in forcing a roll-call vote to withdraw
the bill from committee; his motion failed 51–39, but it did encourage
representatives to take a stand for or against tougher rules on lobbying,
which provided an issue Democrats could use in the next election.[38]

The second lesson Proxmire learned from the old-age pension issue
was the complexity of taxation. Over the course of the legislative session,
Proxmire quickly emerged as the Democratic expert on tax policy, a position enhanced by his position as the sole Democrat on the Assembly Tax
Committee and by his careful research. Proxmire sponsored or cosponsored several pieces of tax legislation during his term. The first, cosponsored by Herman Eisner of Cross Plains, required railroad corporations
to pay state income taxes. Railroads had been exempt from income taxes,
paying only property tax. Proxmire and Eisner estimated that repealing
the exemption would raise $1 million in new revenue.[39] During committee
hearings on the bill, Proxmire defended the tax hike by pointing out that
Wisconsin was the only state not to tax corporate income of railroads.
When representatives of the Wisconsin Railroad argued that the tax would
raise freight and passenger rates, Proxmire quickly countered that the
railroads could deduct their state income tax from their federal income
tax, making it unnecessary to pass the cost on to customers. Republicans
uniformly opposed the measure, and the Assembly rejected it by a vote
of 62–29.[40] The battle for public opinion, however, continued, and Proxmire's research fueled the editorial pages of the *Capital Times*. On May 12,
Miles McMillin published a scathing column accusing the railroad lobby
of manipulating Republican lawmakers. A few days later, the newspaper

again denounced the "million-dollar subsidy" to railroads and listed the names of those representatives who voted against Proxmire's bill. Arguments about this issue continued for months. On his weekly radio address, carried by fifteen stations around the state, William Evjue continued to decry the railroad lobby and cite research showing that the railroads were taxed less than other state corporations.[41]

A second fight over taxes erupted in February, when Proxmire and other Democrats introduced a bill to reenact a 3 percent tax on corporate dividends and allow individuals to exempt only that 3 percent of dividends from their individual income tax, rather than the entire amount. The increased revenue this move would generate was earmarked for state aid to local schools. When Republicans criticized the bill because it would raise taxes on small and out-of-state stockholders, Proxmire retorted that two-thirds of the out-of-state stockholders had incomes of over $12,000 and could afford the tax, an argument similar to the one he had made defending his support of increasing old-age pensions. Once again, the issue was not simply taxes, but *fair* taxes.[42]

The battle continued to simmer during the spring months, and Proxmire once again demonstrated his skill in using detailed evidence to support his position while making it clear to the public. The key difference between his plan and an alternative, introduced by Melvin Laird of Marshfield, was that Proxmire's bill would force out-of-state shareholders to pay as well. Retaining the 3 percent dividend rate on corporations while allowing Wisconsin residents an equivalent deduction not available to residents of other states, he argued, would be as fair as other states collecting sales tax on Wisconsin residents making out-of-state purchases, and it would raise $1.8 million in state revenue, of which $620,000 would be distributed to local governments. To the surprise of many, the Assembly passed the bill on June 6, but the Senate rejected it the next day and instead passed a bill that eliminated the 3 percent corporation tax and taxed dividends as normal income for individuals. Governor Kohler signed the bill after the Assembly concurred. Once again, corporations won a major victory and Wisconsin taxpayers footed the bill.[43]

Shortly after the corporate tax bills were introduced, Proxmire and two others Democrats introduced a third bill to close loopholes in the state's gift and inheritance taxes. First, the bill would aggregate gifts from one person to another over a period of years, rather than calculating the tax rate based on the calendar year. Second, it would tax income from life insurance policies when the policy belonged to a person other than the deceased.[44] In March, Proxmire and Ruth Doyle introduced another measure to increase penalties on those filing late or fraudulent income tax returns. The issue, once again, was fairness. "The state government," Proxmire told the Assembly judiciary committee in April, "owes it to the honest taxpayer to provide adequate penalties for the dishonest one." He then named several prominent figures ("moral leaders in their communities") who had avoided paying state income taxes, including Joseph McCarthy and several members of the legislature.[45] In June, forcing a vote to withdraw the bill from committee, Proxmire launched into a vigorous argument in favor of increasing the penalties, noting that tax fraud cost the state $20 million in revenue every year, basing his charge on discrepancies between Department of Revenue estimates of gross state income and the total of what residents reported on tax forms. The *Capital Times* once again turned Proxmire's proposal into a crusade, publishing editorials condemning tax evasion. Proxmire's efforts succeeded, and the Assembly approved the measure 78–5. The Senate, however, adjourned without considering the bill, effectively killing it.[46]

A final major battle over taxation involved banks that invested in tax-exempt federal securities. For years, banks in Wisconsin had profited by investing in federal securities while paying no state income taxes on these profits. In fact, two-thirds of Wisconsin banks paid no income taxes whatsoever, including some of the largest and most profitable, like First Wisconsin National Bank in Milwaukee. In March, Proxmire introduced a bill to assess a franchise tax on banks in order to tax their entire income, including income derived from US securities that were exempt under the current corporate tax law. Other states had begun doing this as well, after a federal law permitted states to tax these securities. Basing his bill on a similar law passed in Oklahoma, Proxmire proposed to plug this loophole and tax banks on all their profits. He noted that in 1920, state corporation taxes on banks brought in $2 million; by 1950, this had dropped to $90,000. Republicans in the Assembly challenged the bill as unconstitutional and requested an opinion from the attorney general. In June, Attorney General Vernon Thomson reported that the measure was invalid because it would discriminate against banks; nonbank corporations owning federal securities would *not* be taxed. The Assembly promptly rejected the bill 60–20.[47] Thomson's ruling, when paired with the legislature's refusal to tax railroads' corporate profits, aided Democrats' arguments that the Republican Party served only the interests of the wealthy and of corporations, not those of ordinary Wisconsin taxpayers. When Republicans gathered at Wisconsin Rapids for their convention in July, Democrats continued to heckle them about their tax policies that favored the rich, citing as evidence how little income taxes banks paid. As late as December, the *Capital Times* continued to publish figures showing how plugging the loophole would increase revenue, claiming that the ten largest banks paid only $73 in state income taxes in 1951. Proxmire's bill would have increased that figure to nearly $1.9 million. The Democrats had found a potential campaign issue for 1952.[48]

Proxmire's dogged work researching and defending the Democrats' tax bills reflected his conviction that state tax policy needed to be reformed. The increasing costs of education, infrastructure, and social services required increased state expenditures, which in turn called for increased state revenue. This money, however, had to be raised fairly. Plugging loopholes used by corporations to avoid state taxes was a far better option than increasing property or income taxes or—most dreaded of all—imposing a sales tax. Proxmire had also found an issue he could engage the public in, and he spoke frequently on the radio and to groups around Wisconsin about state finances. He also spoke on the floor of the Assembly in earnest efforts to convince his fellow legislators, sometimes sparking the ire of Republican members who were coming to resent Proxmire's populist inclinations.[49] It could also, however, be politically dangerous at a time when increasing taxes worried voters. One anonymous correspondent demanded, "Are you an assemblyman from Moscow, or Wisconsin?" and predicted that raising taxes on wealthy individuals and corporations would encourage people to quit their jobs and stand in bread lines.[50]

The overall state budget passed in April was a record $211,844,769. Democrats, the majority of whom voted for the final budget, issued a statement expressing dismay at the increased cost of government. Indeed, the biennial budget passed in 1945 was only $95 million. This put Democrats in an awkward position, since they had consistently favored increasing expenditures in education and public employee salaries. Defending the spending priorities of his party, Proxmire argued that the legislature needed to curb wasteful spending rather than enact across-the-board cuts or tax increases. He pointed to, for example, the nearly $10,000 in new equipment that sat unused at the Department of Motor Vehicles, as well as the $59,000 spent to print the biennial *Blue Book*, which legislators distributed to constituents for free. The list of expenditures went on: free fountain pens for legislators, highway maps, and other small expenditures that added up to—in Proxmire's estimation—$20 million.[51]

Proxmire's most significant contributions to the legislative session of 1951 included arguing the Democratic position on tax reform and state revenue. Wisconsin would continue to struggle with inflation and increased expenses for the rest of the decade. The other great political issue facing Wisconsin was US Senator Joseph McCarthy, who had begun making his reckless charges of Communist infiltration of the federal government in 1950. Proxmire took the lead in the legislature, not against McCarthy himself but against his tactics, already known as "McCarthyism." In March, a resolution introduced by Republican Arthur Peterson would have allowed citizens who believed they had been slandered on the floor of the legislature to sue the legislator who had made the allegedly slanderous remarks. This was a significant change to the traditional privilege of immunity that representative bodies enjoyed, but at the height of the Cold War, a careless accusation could destroy a person's life. Speaking in support of the resolution, Proxmire referred to an ugly incident in which children were beaten on their way home from school because McCarthy had wrongly accused their father of being a Communist. Similar tactics should not be used in the legislature, he said: "I could stand here and say there are thirty embezzlers in the state Department of Agriculture . . . I could say the governor was a sex pervert, and that McCarthy is a homo-sexual. . . . If I did . . . those charges would be spread in newspapers all over the state."[52] The resolution was defeated, 66–28, with only one Democrat voting against it: Hermann Eisner, who represented Dane County's third district and subsequently earned condemnation from the editorial page of the *Capital Times*. Eisner took the unusual step in defending himself publicly through letters to both Madison newspapers, arguing that his vote was to protect legislative immunity, which he saw as a rarely abused and necessary part of free government, not a vote to endorse McCarthy or his tactics. Proxmire, he wrote, was simply tilting at windmills.[53]

The Democrats' attacks quickly shifted to McCarthy himself. In March, Proxmire hinted at the strategy his party was going to employ in an address to the Dane County Organizing Committee. He charged that McCarthy "dominated" the Wisconsin Republican Party and linked the senator's antics with the record of the 1951 legislature: "Although [McCarthy] has used the most brutal and ruthless methods, he has failed and failed completely." Likewise, the legislature had failed to provide increased old-age pensions, increase salaries for teachers, or plug loopholes in tax laws used by corporations. Proxmire and other Democrats intended to make McCarthy the reason for these failures, or at the very least, use McCarthy as an issue in local and state elections.[54]

The crusade against McCarthy began in earnest in June, when Democrats began "Operation Truth," a statewide effort to promote party policies and to attack McCarthy at every opportunity. Launching the campaign in Janesville on June 2, Henry Reuss, James Doyle, Gaylord Nelson, and Proxmire outlined the need to defeat McCarthy, up for reelection in 1952. Proxmire's own remarks again linked the actions of the Republican legislators with McCarthy, arguing that Republicans cooked up the red scare in order to distract voters from the influence lobbyists had over state government. McCarthy, was, he asserted, "a smart, brutal, and distinguished liar" steeped in corruption. "His circuit court was a little Reno for lawyer friends seeking divorces," he said, referring to allegations that McCarthy had used his position as judge to arrange quick divorces. "He was only paid up on his income tax when he was caught."[55] The Democrats repeated the charges in Madison on June 11 and argued that their party had a far better record of combating Communism in Europe and in Asia. Proxmire pointed to the Marshall Plan and the Korean War as evidence of the Truman administration's successes. Moreover, Proxmire called the Democratic platform a "great liberal program" helping farmers and businessmen alike, and stopping domestic subversion and espionage.[56] Not every Democrat approved of the tactic. William B. Rubin, a longtime party leader from Milwaukee, thought the effort would benefit McCarthy and encourage his supporters and suggested that the four young Democrats responsible for the street-corner gatherings should have deferred to the "older heads" of the party. Proxmire defended "Operation Truth" by noting that conservative newspaper publishers in most cities also tended to own local radio stations, and that people simply never heard the facts.[57]

The four moved on to Fond du Lac on June 14 before Proxmire took to the airwaves to refute McCarthy's criticisms of Secretary of Defense George Marshall and Secretary of State Dean Acheson. Speaking on WIBA on June 22, Proxmire outlined the Democrats' charges concerning McCarthy's record. Proxmire began by challenging McCarthy's honesty, recounting how the State Board of Bar Commissioners had recommended disbarment, how McCarthy had filed fraudulent income tax returns, and how the State Supreme Court itself had refused to believe McCarthy's testimony. He then dismantled McCarthy's criticism of Marshall by noting that McCarthy had himself voted for the Marshall Plan in 1947. Moreover, McCarthy had played no role in the conviction of any person for subversive activities. "Let us remember," Proxmire solemnly told listeners, "the best weapon against Communism is the truth."[58] Despite the energetic efforts of Proxmire and the other Democrats, "Operation Truth" met with limited success. It bolstered those who were already opposed to McCarthy, but it did nothing to change the minds of his admirers. Despite the charges leveled against the senator, one columnist noted that an appearance by McCarthy himself would easily draw a crowd of supporters three times as large as one for Democrats. Proxmire and the other Democrats simply underestimated McCarthy's popularity as well as the futility of trying to challenge his conduct with facts and numbers.[59]

These determined attacks on McCarthy fueled speculation about the senator's prospects for reelection in 1952, and Proxmire's sudden emergence as a major political figure made him a possible opponent. Many Democrats seemed willing to take on McCarthy. Party activists favored James Doyle, Edward Fairchild, Henry Reuss, or Gaylord Nelson, all of whom had devoted time to rebuilding the state Democratic Party. Daniel Hoan, former Socialist mayor of Milwaukee, retained a strong following in that city. Proxmire assured party leaders that he would not run for the Senate seat, but his continued public appearances suggested otherwise. This put Kohler in a difficult position. Personally disgusted with McCarthy, he nonetheless depended on the senator's supporters for votes. Repudiating McCarthy might jeopardize his own chances for reelection, or, at the very least, badly divide the Republican Party. If, however, he affirmed his support of McCarthy, he risked alienating moderate Republicans and independents. At the very least, Kohler would look weak and vacillating.[60] The operation against McCarthy received even greater coverage when the Democrats attempted to force delegates to the Republican state convention to take sides. On July 6, Reuss, Doyle, Nelson, and Proxmire sent Governor Kohler a telegram at the convention challenging him to repudiate McCarthy's tactics, especially his charges against Secretary of Defense George Marshall, as a threat to national security.[61] For a moment, it appeared that Kohler would indeed respond to the goading of the Democrats and take a stand against McCarthy. When two anti-McCarthy Republicans were booed at the convention and denied the floor, Kohler criticized the action as "disgraceful" and announced that he would meet personally with the four Democrats to discuss his views.[62] The governor, however, proved too wily to risk widening the division among Wisconsin Republicans. He called off a planned meeting and instead demanded that the four Democrats join him in rejecting "Trumanism," which he defined as "government by crony and government by mediocrity."[63] Indeed, even some in the Democratic Party thought the four were engaging in a transparent attempt to gain publicity, as Democratic State Senator William Schmidt of Milwaukee accused them in late July. Others chided them for wasting the governor's time. What had begun as an attempt to divide the Republican Party now threatened to exacerbate Democratic divisions between the young liberals of Dane County and the older, more conservative members from Milwaukee.[64]

In the midst of this political intrigue, however, Proxmire was forced to leave for Lake Forest with Elsie when his mother fell ill. Adele Proxmire died on July 16, the second devastating loss for the family. Proxmire adored his extroverted mother, who for nearly forty years had been the ideal doctor's wife: social and friendly, entertaining visitors late into the evening. She had been an extremely affectionate mother, supportive of her children but more indulgent than their father. Proxmire remained close to his father until his death in 1959, and Theodore continued to support his son's business and political ambitions. Yet his father's support—both generally as well as financially—masked a great loss. Now as Proxmire was beginning his public career, he had lost that vital connection to his childhood that might remind him to temper his long hours of work with spending time with his own children.[65]

Returning from Lake Forest, Proxmire's influence in the Democratic Party continued to grow in the late summer and fall of 1951, as did his public appearances and speculation over his political future. In August, Ruth Doyle and Elizabeth Runge announced the formation of the Midwest Lecture Bureau and listed Proxmire as a speaker on taxation. The "nonpolitical" nature of the bureau raised eyebrows, but it confirmed Proxmire's reputation not only as an effective public speaker but also as an expert on tax issues.[66] Reapportionment based on the 1950 census increased Dane County's representation in the state senate and assembly, and Proxmire seemed a likely candidate to run for the new Senate seat. Proxmire was also frequently mentioned as a potential challenger to Congressman Glenn Davis of Waukesha in the first district, or even McCarthy himself.[67]

In October, Proxmire attended the Democratic convention in Wausau as speculation continued to swirl around the 1952 elections. Proxmire had already made a mark on the convention, working on a committee chaired by Henry Reuss to draft a statement of principles for the party, but he had unequivocally taken himself out of the running for the US Senate prior to a straw poll a week prior to the convention. He later announced that he would not run for the second congressional seat then held by Davis.[68]

In public, his political future remained an open question. Proxmire had built up his reputation in the Democratic Party and demonstrated his willingness to work tirelessly. He was a gifted public speaker. He would have more time to devote to politics, too, because that summer he became part owner of the Brooks Farm Implement Company of Sun Prairie, serving as its vice president in charge of advertising and publicity but leaving the day-to-day management to others. Privately, he was already thinking about his next undertaking, a campaign for governor to unseat the popular Walter Kohler.

3

THE SHADOW GOVERNOR

After completing a remarkable first term in the Wisconsin State As-sembly, William Proxmire seemed to have a clear political future. Political commentators in the state newspapers assumed that the young Democrat from eastern Dane County would easily be reelected to a second term in 1952, perhaps moving up to the State Senate if Gaylord Nelson, the incumbent senator from Dane County, chose to run against Republican US Senator Joseph McCarthy, also up for reelection that year. Proxmire had demonstrated his ability to research complex issues, especially those involving tax policy, and explain them clearly to his fellow legislators and the public. He had tirelessly argued the Democratic Party's position on the issues, and his collaboration with Nelson, James Doyle, and Thomas Fair-child indicated his growing importance in the party. Under these circum-stances, a patient politician would hold a seat in the legislature, continue to work hard for the party, and wait his turn to try for higher office. But Proxmire was not patient. He had the energy and believed he had the abil-ity to rally the voters of Wisconsin behind the Democratic Party's banner, and so launched three unsuccessful campaigns for governor, making him the best-known political loser in state history. He remained a maverick and an important figure in the state Democratic Party, even though he refused to defer to the party leaders and remained the incumbent governor's chief critic. Despite the fact that he held no elective office, he acted, essentially, like a shadow governor, a public foil for the policies of Governor Kohler and the Republican legislature.

Proxmire officially announced his candidacy on Saturday, March 8, 1952, vowing to campaign in every precinct in the state. His announcement continued a theme he had begun during the previous summer's street-corner attacks on McCarthy: that the state Republican Party had identified itself with "the evil thing that is mccarthyism [sic]." Only the Democrats, he claimed, could offer the farmers, laborers, and small-business owners a constructive alternative to the Republicans in state government, distracted and divided by McCarthy's charges and dominated by corporate lobbyists. Running for governor was, of course, a daunting task. Governor Walter Kohler Jr. was generally popular and had already announced his reelection bid in January. Proxmire himself acknowledged the "stiff, uphill fight" but was optimistic about his chances, noting that the Democratic vote for governor had increased from only 10 percent in 1938 to 47 percent in 1950. He was just the candidate to continue that momentum.[1]

Not everyone was convinced. Claude Stout, his Republican opponent in the 1950 assembly race, published a letter in the *Wisconsin State Journal* deriding Proxmire's chances of persuading Wisconsin voters to abandon the Republican Party. "After such a short residence here he knows all the answers," Stout huffed. "Are we old-timers in Wisconsin so dumb that we will fall for that stuff?" Here Stout raised a potentially damaging issue. Proxmire had lived in Wisconsin for only three years, whereas Kohler was the son of a prominent business family from the state. During the campaign, Kohler did indeed occasionally dig at "the visitor to Wisconsin."[2]

Even Democrats had been skeptical of Proxmire's chances, and some tried to dissuade him from running for governor. In December 1951, federal judge Robert Tehan summoned Proxmire to his home and tried to talk him out of running. He predicted that the Democratic nominee for US Senate would be Thomas Fairchild from Madison. Voters, Tehan argued, would not support a Democratic ticket headed by two Madison-area liberals. Furthermore, charges of "carpetbagging" would guarantee Proxmire's defeat, Tehan predicted, and he would thereby drag the other Democrats down with him and guarantee McCarthy's reelection to the Senate. McCarthy was the Democrats' principal target, not Governor Kohler. Refusing to defer to party leaders, Proxmire decided to run anyway.[3]

Tehan's arguments may have been sound, and yet no other Democrats were willing to run against Kohler. Herman Jessen of Phelps in Vilas County—a banker, mink rancher, and chair of the Tenth Congressional District Democratic Organizing Committee—announced his candidacy in October 1951 but withdrew in February 1952, sensing a lack of support from his fellow Democrats.[4] Carl Thompson had mounted two campaigns for governor, in 1948 and 1950, the second with great reluctance. He had no interest in running against Kohler again. The other major party figures all had their eyes on McCarthy's Senate seat, which produced significant conflict among them. Gaylord Nelson, Henry Reuss, James Doyle, and Thomas Fairchild all sought the nomination but feared a primary contest would weaken the party and drain critical resources that were better used against McCarthy. Informal negotiations produced only bitterness. Doyle withdrew from consideration to become party chair, and Nelson withdrew after Reuss abruptly announced his candidacy. Fairchild announced his candidacy in June, forcing a Democratic primary. The result of the focus on McCarthy meant that Proxmire was the sole claimant to the Democratic gubernatorial nomination, and since other Democratic leaders saw the incumbent Kohler as virtually unbeatable, they were delighted to let Proxmire run as a "sacrificial lamb," a role that no one else was willing to perform. Proxmire, in turn, embraced the opportunity to build a statewide reputation, even if it meant losing.[5]

Once Proxmire made his announcement, Democrats around the state lined up behind him and offered him advice. Gaylord Nelson chaired the Proxmire for Governor Committee, while Madison party activist Ellen Sawall served as treasurer. James Dillman of Sheboygan agreed with Proxmire's insistence that failing to wage a vigorous campaign for governor would certainly result in the reelection of McCarthy. "I know," he assured Proxmire, "that you will carry on an energetic and hard-hitting campaign and get our story to the people." Lester Johnson urged him to focus on building up local organizations and making a list of the "old Progressive groups" in every county to pull those voters into the Democratic Party. Leonard Zubrensky, who would become Proxmire's Milwaukee campaign manager, wrote Proxmire that he was so impressed by the candidate's announcement "that I have decided to run against Kohler myself."[6] Carl Thompson peppered him with suggestions: recruit candidates to run for local office, use photographs of himself with Elsie and their children for campaign literature, meet with newspaper editors, and so on.[7]

Proxmire launched his campaign on Friday, March 21, in Mauston, where he told the Juneau County Democratic Organizing Committee that the centerpiece of his administration would be tax reform. The central goal of his tax program was to lower property taxes. He claimed that "the farmer, the home-owner, the small businessman in Wisconsin pays one of the stiffest property taxes in the nation." In order to decrease them, Proxmire promised to increase state aid to local governments; the increase in state expenditures would be funded by closing loopholes that allowed railroads, banks, and other corporations to avoid paying income taxes. This is essentially the same argument he had made in Assembly: the problem was not that taxes were *too high*, but that they were *unfair* because those with the greatest wealth could avoid paying their share. Proxmire thus revived the same economic policies Progressives had argued for in the 1900s and 1930s.[8]

On this issue, his experience in the Assembly proved invaluable, and his campaign literature described six bills he had introduced that would have lowered property taxes.[9] Indeed, Proxmire made the issue very simple. Property taxes in Wisconsin were higher than in neighboring states because local governments carried a much larger share of the costs of schools, highways, and social services. The solution was to increase state aid to local governments and to increase state revenue by raising taxes on corporations and wealthy individuals. No politician could base a campaign around *raising* taxes, but Proxmire described this as an issue of tax fairness, claiming Republican policies "discriminat[ed]" against wage earners, small-business owners, and farmers: "Rather than levy fair taxes upon their railroad friends or upon their banker buddies . . . the Republican administration prefers to force the burden of educational, highway and relief costs upon the property owner." He also called for stronger laws to stop income tax evasion, which he claimed cost honest taxpayers millions of dollars a year. For most of the campaign, Proxmire continued to hammer away at what he saw as the principal issue facing the state.[10]

Yet Proxmire knew he was in for a difficult fight and would almost certainly lose. "I am writing you because I want your support," his form letter to supporters began. "Believe me, I do need it." Why would people donate money, volunteer their time, or otherwise support a candidate when they were satisfied with the incumbent? The answer was McCarthy. Running an aggressive race for governor, Proxmire wrote, would discourage citizens from voting a straight Republican ticket and thereby increase the possibility of defeating McCarthy. Lackluster state races would only discourage Democrats, who might then simply stay home on Election Day. National Democrats also hoped for a McCarthy loss and thought about supporting Proxmire on those terms. In response to an appeal from Elsie, Eleanor Roosevelt sent $25 and expressed hope that "Senator McCarthy's defeat would help the future of freedom of the United States."[11]

In late March and April, Proxmire continued to travel around the state. On March 28, he spoke to the Dunn County Democratic Organizing Committee in Menomonie on the importance of enforcing the state's antitrust laws and charged that the Republican administration encouraged "monopolistic collusion" that hurt Wisconsin taxpayers.[12] He told University of Wisconsin students on April 8 that the railroad lobby would cost the state $1 million in lost tax revenue in 1952, which could have been used for aid to education or property tax relief.[13] On April 16, he spoke to the Milwaukee Junior Chamber of Commerce at noon and to Democrats in the city's fifth ward in the evening. He again emphasized the dangers of lobbying, telling the JCC that the $35,000 spent by lobbyists to buy liquor and food for legislators in the 1951 session was either "an incredible waste of time or legalized bribery" and suggested a four-point program to end such influence in the legislature. That evening, he emphasized economy. Under fourteen years of Republican administration, expenditures tripled, and the number of state employees increased by 50 percent. Only the Democrats, he said, were serious about reining in the state budget for the benefit of Wisconsin taxpayers.[14] On April 24, Proxmire traveled again to Milwaukee to speak to the Milwaukee CIO Political Action Committee. There he called for an end to executive sessions—"secrecy" in state government—which he said "breeds misunderstanding, concealed inefficiency and all too often outright corruption."[15]

It wasn't all after-dinner speeches to loyal supporters, however. His campaign chronically short on funds, Proxmire usually packed peanut butter sandwiches and carrot sticks to eat and often stayed at the local YMCA, sometimes for as little as one dollar a night. At dawn, he was at factory gates to shake hands with employees as they arrived. In between these more formal speeches, Proxmire developed his method for "meeting the folks." In cities and small towns, he spoke on street corners through a megaphone as volunteers passed out buttons and campaign pamphlets. He dropped by the offices of local newspapers to introduce himself and offer an immediate interview. Failing those, he simply drove up and down Main Street looking for people to talk to. After Mississippi River flooding badly damaged homes in Prairie du Chien, Proxmire sloshed through the mud to talk to the victims. By one estimate, he drove thirty-five thousand miles and shook hands with two hundred fifty thousand people. Not since Philip La Follette's barnstorming tours of the early 1930s had so many in Wisconsin seen so much of one politician.[16]

Proxmire's central theme was taxation, but he tailored his message to fit his audiences. One of the earliest interest groups Proxmire courted was farmers. His campaign brochures identified him as "an executive of a successful farm implement dealership" who "has learned the problems of the farmers of Wisconsin." One photograph shows Proxmire, dressed in a suit, talking to a man on a tractor. His campaign stops in small towns were usually centered around farm issues. In Black River Falls, Proxmire derided the "myth" that the Republican Party represented the interests of farmers. For fourteen years, he argued, Republican legislatures had raised property taxes on farms by depressing local government aid.[17] When challenged on his assertion that farmers in Wisconsin paid the highest per capita property tax, Proxmire cited a 1942 US Census Bureau study and a 1951 Michigan study that surveyed property taxes in agricultural states.[18] He reiterated his arguments throughout the summer, eliciting a snide comment from the editorial board of the *Wisconsin State Journal* that his agricultural knowledge came from "having Pappy buy him a piece of a farm implement business," and that farm property taxes were 30 percent higher in Illinois. Proxmire responded with an advertisement in the same paper pointing out that the statistics used by the *Wisconsin State Journal* included low-value cutover acreage in northern Wisconsin that bore insignificant property tax. Productive farmland was taxed at a much higher rate.[19] Getting farmers to support a Democratic candidate was a tough sell, since many were dissatisfied with Truman's agriculture policies and the generally declining farm prices since 1946. Nonetheless, Democrats began to see the need to pull in rural voters. Dan Hoan, for instance, singled out Proxmire's analysis of farm taxes in his speech to the Democratic

Organizing Committee Convention dinner. Proxmire's courtship of farmers laid the groundwork for their future support of Democrats.[20]

Proxmire combined his call for tax reform with a demand for greater
economy in state expenditures. He had raised the issue in the legislature,
but it received new interest in late September when it became clear that
Wisconsin would experience a budget shortfall. The projected $40 million
deficit would almost wipe out the state surplus fund, requiring the next
administration to either sharply raise taxes, cut spending, or both. The
Republicans, he charged, refused to talk about the issue. Proxmire blamed
not only unfair tax policies but also frivolous and wasteful spending, pointing to recent newspaper reports of construction costs for the state mental
hospital. He also derided other state expenditures, like the $30,000 spent
on printing state *Blue Books* for legislators to distribute to constituents, and
cited the fact that Republican administrations had increased state spending from $35 million in 1938 to $125 million in 1951. Proxmire promised a
thorough reorganization of state government to make it more efficient and
cut waste, noting that other states had saved millions of dollars through
similar efforts.[21]

At the same time that he was arguing for changes in taxation and frugality in state government, Proxmire also called for increased spending
in several areas. Several times during the campaign, he complained about
the "gross mismanagement" of the state highway system. How, he asked,
could Wisconsin drivers pay so much in gasoline tax and get so little in
roads? He compared Wisconsin's highways ("always seem to be detoured,
torn up or just falling apart") with those of other states, which were built
faster and well maintained. This was a particularly important issue in
northern Wisconsin, whose economy depended upon tourism.[22] In addition to appealing to frustrated drivers, Proxmire also appealed to parents
by deriding the Republicans' record on education. Wisconsin spent less
proportionally than many southern states, he charged, and many school
buildings were no longer adequate. The solution was to increase taxes on
railroads and banks to relieve local property taxpayers.[23]

At the Democratic National Convention that July, Proxmire plunged
into national politics and generated renewed publicity for his own campaign. The issue was the party's position on civil rights and the conflict
over two delegations from Texas. Proxmire was Wisconsin's representative

on the Credentials Committee and favored the liberal Democratic delegation led by former Texas congressman Maury Maverick. Proxmire urged
the committee to seat this delegation, but it instead voted 36–13 to seat
an anti–civil rights delegation led by Governor Allan Shrivers. Unwilling
to back down in the interests of party harmony, Proxmire attempted to
rally support among other liberals and took his case to the floor of the
convention. In a passionate fifteen-minute speech, he cited Texas law and
denounced the Shrivers delegation as disloyal: it "has never supported
President Truman, never supported the New Deal or Fair Deal, never supported Civil Rights, and has never supported labor." Moreover, he criticized those same party leaders who had urged him not to risk dividing the
convention. "I say to you," he told the convention, "the Democratic Party
has never followed any leader." Proxmire cut a fine figure at the rostrum
and reminded many of Robert La Follette's often inflammatory minority
reports decades earlier. Nonetheless, the convention rejected Proxmire's
arguments and seated the Shrivers delegation, which left Proxmire "discouraged and disappointed." Despite the outcome, Proxmire impressed
many with his efforts. Hubert Humphrey wrote, "I have heard many fine
comments about your own presentation at the convention and the fine
way it was received over the television network."[24]

Proxmire soon found himself on the losing side once again. He and
other Wisconsin delegates went to the convention pledged to support Senator Estes Kefauver of Tennessee. After leading on the first ballot, Kefauver
lost to Illinois governor Adlai Stevenson. There were no hard feelings. In
response to a letter outlining his prospects in Wisconsin, Stevenson wrote
Proxmire that he was "much impressed with the vigor of your campaign
for governor and I only regret that we have had no opportunity to talk." In
October, when Stevenson campaigned in Madison, Proxmire introduced
him to a crowd of about nine thousand and later accompanied the presidential candidate to Milwaukee.[25]

For much of the campaign, Proxmire emphasized Democratic policies, but he grew increasingly critical of Kohler and sought to link him to
McCarthy. Speaking in Dodge County, Proxmire challenged Kohler "to
tell the people of Wisconsin frankly and openly why he is supporting . . .
McCarthy" and promised to repeat the challenge every day until Kohler
responded. Proxmire listed several instances when Kohler had publicly

defended McCarthy and pointed out that the governor had never publicly criticized the senator.[26] The following day, Proxmire broadened his attack by declaring that the Republican Party as a whole "was now the party of mccarthyism." He charged that, like McCarthy's use of "the big lie," the Republican Party had falsified its record on taxation, expenditures, government secrecy, and other vital issues.[27] In August, when Kohler took over campaign appearances while McCarthy recuperated from surgery, Proxmire renewed his attacks, and continued raising the issue throughout the fall. Kohler's support of McCarthy was "the mistake of Kohler's life," he charged, and insisted that the Truman administration had waged an effective campaign against communism at home and abroad.[28]

These attacks angered Kohler, who personally detested McCarthy but recognized the senator's popularity. He did not want to alienate conservative voters and recognized the potential dangers of Republican division. He frequently called for party unity and hesitated to take a firm stand on some controversial issues, which the Democrats used to depict him as vacillating.[29] Although intended to generate publicity and support, these comments were not just campaign rhetoric. Proxmire was beginning to position himself as the Democrats' shadow governor, commenting on decisions made by Kohler and offering alternatives.[30] Kohler had no interest in responding to Proxmire's criticism, unwilling to give him more publicity. Since neither candidate was opposed in the primary election, Proxmire proposed that the two debate each other in what would become the state's longest gubernatorial campaign between two candidates who differed on almost every issue. Kohler refused. "While I appreciate your offer," he wrote sarcastically, "I believe it would be unfair for me to take advantage of your prominence in Wisconsin politics by sharing your audiences for my campaign appearances."[31]

Proxmire nonetheless continued to hammer away at Kohler in the days leading up to the September primary and came up with new ways to get publicity when most of the state newspapers afforded him very little coverage. On August 15, from twelve a.m. to six a.m., Proxmire conducted a marathon broadcast session on a Superior radio station, discussing his positions and answering questions from callers. He even conducted the station breaks by himself. He followed his radio talk with street-corner speeches in small towns in northern Wisconsin, and then held an even longer radio broadcast in Wausau, beginning at ten forty-five p.m. on August 20 and ending at six thirty the next morning. Proxmire held a third overnight broadcast in Green Bay on August 28–29. In between his second and third broadcasts, he and Elsie recorded a series of five-minute programs where they talked about some of the key issues in a conversational tone, as if they were sitting down to lunch. Proxmire was certainly not the first to use radio for political purposes, but he was the first to recognize how effective such "stunts" could be in gaining publicity, as well as making his views known to voters.[32]

The results of the primary election on September 9 brought mixed results for the Democrats. Proxmire's candidacy was unopposed, but the contested primary for the US Senate seat between Thomas Fairchild and Henry Reuss increased Democratic turnout. The two Democratic candidates for governor in 1950 received a total of 167,522 votes; Proxmire received 178,133, making him the top vote getter among all Democratic candidates that year. Republicans, however, did even better. Two Republican candidates for governor in 1950 split 422,454 votes. In 1954, Kohler alone won 699,082. Democratic efforts to unseat McCarthy backfired and increased Republican turnout, with its own contested senatorial primary, more than it increased Democratic turnout. Proxmire responded to the results by urging Democrats to come out fighting: "It will be a tough, uphill race against a demagoguery with a sledge hammer kick. But if anyone thinks we will duck, or evade, or pussyfoot around the issue of mccarthyism [sic] let him think again." Liberalism was dead in the Republican Party, Proxmire warned, and urged anti-McCarthy Republicans and former Progressives to join the Democrats.[33]

Heading into the general election campaign, Proxmire knew he faced long odds in defeating Kohler. In a speech in Wisconsin Rapids the week after the primary, he described the effective and well-funded Republican machine as ready to spend five times what the Democrats could and eager to take advantage of thousands of precinct workers. More importantly, he accused state newspapers of failing to cover his campaign at all. In contrast, he told radio listeners in Eau Claire, "I do not have one single paid or part time paid worker: no campaign manager, no publicity man, no speech writer, no advance man, no secretary. My wife and I are running this campaign together and we're enjoying every minute of this battle."

Instead, he continued to rely on street-corner appearances, speaking from a car equipped with a loudspeaker.[34] In these speeches, he accused Kohler and the Republicans in the legislature of selling out the interests of the people of the state in order to give tax breaks to those who donated to the party, and he continued to hammer away at the lobbying issue, calling it "legalized bribery."[35] Proxmire frequently expressed his frustration that Kohler refused to talk about these issues, acting as if the electorate "owed" him a second term, a "jellyfish" who spent most of his time campaigning for Dwight Eisenhower and Joseph McCarthy and neglected to make the case for his own reelection.[36] Not until the very end of the campaign did the two candidates actually meet face-to-face, the first time by accident. Proxmire and Kohler attended separate events in Racine on October 31 and met when both stopped for breakfast at the Racine Hotel. Proxmire invited Kohler to join him, and the two chatted for a while. Kohler cheerfully paid Proxmire's eighty-cent bill. Two days later, they both appeared on television in Milwaukee to close out their campaigns in a polite but firm disagreement over state aid to local governments, McCarthy, and other issues.[37] Still frustrated with the lack of press coverage, Proxmire took to the airwaves a final time to end his campaign, hosting a thirty-hour radio broadcast carried by stations around the state on November 2 and 3. Proxmire kept his suit coat on the entire time as he fielded a thousand calls from voters, taking only an occasional thirty-second break and sitting next to a vacant chair "reserved for Gov. Kohler." Signing off at midnight, he slept in the back seat of his car all the way back to Blooming Grove.[38]

Wisconsin voters went to the polls on November 4 and delivered a Republican landslide. Eisenhower defeated Stevenson in the state 979,744 to 622,175, and McCarthy won reelection by a margin of over 139,000 votes. Clearly the strategy of linking state Republicans with McCarthy had failed. Despite his vigorous campaigning, Proxmire lost decisively, gaining just under 602,000 votes compared to Kohler's more than a million. On election night at the Ambassador Hotel in Milwaukee, when it became clear that he had lost, Proxmire confided to Leonard Zubrensky his plan for the future: "I'm going to run in two years and lose. I'm going to run in 1956 and win." His strategy was simple, he told Zubrensky: "I'm going to a plant gate this morning and I'm going to a plant gate every morning I'm in the state of Wisconsin. I'm going to issue a press release every afternoon." The next morning, he was at a factory gate shaking hands with workers.[39]

In a letter to a friend after his loss, Proxmire waxed philosophical. "I had predicted two weeks before the election that I would lose," he wrote. "We will now make the Republicans assume the responsibility in the Nation as well as in the State and we can now hold them completely and strictly responsible for whatever happens." Nonetheless, he was chagrined, confiding to Carl Thompson that he felt his loss was a disappointment to the party after Thompson's much closer race in 1950.[40] Having sacrificed his safe seat to run, Proxmire now held no elective office and therefore lacked a platform, but he worked quickly to solidify his status in the party. Within a few weeks of the election, he wrote letters of congratulation to those few Democrats who had won (Clement Zablocki in the fourth congressional district and Carl Thompson in his old Assembly seat), promising to help them in the future. He also wrote letters to Ruth Doyle, Horace Wilkie, Thomas Fairchild, and Adlai Stevenson, commiserating with them over their losses and reassuring them that the Democrats' day would come. To Patrick Lucey and James Doyle, Proxmire wrote effusive thank-you letters for their "generosity" toward his campaign and praised their effective leadership. Proxmire's candidacy had made him a statewide name, and he intended to keep that status by maintaining connections with party leaders.[41]

He also intended to make himself the public face of the party. The 1953 legislature began its session in January, and from the beginning, Proxmire became the chief opposition spokesman, a shadow governor who critiqued the administration's every move and suggested a Democratic alternative. Stanford Goltz of the *Wisconsin State Journal* noted that Proxmire "is leaving no press release unturned to keep his name before Wisconsin voters. Bill has kept a steady stream of statements fluttering down on state newspapers."[42] Recognizing the looming budget problems that would plague Wisconsin later in the decade, Proxmire focused on the state budget. In Green Bay in late February, he called the budget "irresponsible" and predicted that the state would spend far more than it would collect in revenue. This threatened dire consequences for taxpayers: reduction in state spending would likely lead to increases in local spending funded by property taxes, hitting small earners proportionately harder, or, as Proxmire put it bluntly, "The less you make, the more taxes you will pay." Three weeks later in Wausau, he called on Kohler to admit that the amended budget approved by the legislature's joint finance committee would require increasing taxes or else force a $1.5 million deficit.[43] He continued to sound the alarm as he traveled the state to talk to local Democratic organizations; issuing press releases kept him in the spotlight. In 1953, he gave about two hundred speeches to Democratic groups around the state, sending follow-up letters to each member who attended. Proxmire had become a permanent fixture in state politics.[44]

Critics joked about Proxmire's apparent appetite for publicity, but given the media's generally conservative bent in the state, he thought his efforts critical to future Democratic success. In February, he requested two half-hour segments from Milwaukee television station WTMJ to discuss legislative issues and the governor's budget address. The station refused, stating its policy of not selling time for politically oriented programming outside of election season. This struck him as a violation of the FCC requirement that television stations provide equal time to political parties, and he filed a complaint. The chairman of the commission, however, refused to intervene, pointing to the obvious fact that Proxmire was not running for any elective office and so the FCC had no authority to require a broadcaster to carry any programming. The "equal time" requirement was irrelevant.[45] When a Beloit radio station carried a broadcast by Governor Kohler, Proxmire again complained about partisanship and demanded equal time; the station refused to grant a "private citizen" a partisan broadcast.[46] He even investigated the possibility of become a media owner himself. In late 1952, he had organized "Fort Broadcasting Industry, Inc.," financed by a $5,000 stock purchase from his father. In March 1953 Proxmire began negotiations to purchase radio station WTKM in Washington County and then transfer the license to Madison. These negotiations fell through, and he instead purchased time on WIBA in Madison, speaking at four thirty p.m. on Sunday afternoons, when he could rebut the governor's one forty-five p.m. remarks. Proxmire continued trying to purchase a radio station but eventually bought a half-interest in a Waterloo printing company, Artcraft Press, which would eventually print much of his campaign material.[47]

Proxmire claimed the right to speak in opposition to the Republican administration as the "titular head of the Democratic Party in Wisconsin," even though he held no elective office and had no leadership position within the party itself. In his broadcasts, he criticized Kohler's budget (April 12) and his highway proposals (April 19) and mocked Kohler's suggestion of toll roads as a way of raising highway funds (April 26). His fiercest comments involved tax issues as it became clearer that the state did indeed face a potentially large budget deficit. His solution was simple: he called for stricter enforcement of existing tax laws to raise $20 million in revenue, claiming—with little evidence—that one out of every three or four citizens cheated on their tax returns. Failure to increase enforcement and close loopholes would force the Republicans to enact a sales tax to make up the shortfall. When the legislature finally passed the budget, he criticized state spending and inefficiency in state agencies. His weekly attacks on Kohler and the Republican administration continued through the spring and early summer.[48]

In fact, having a Republican president as well as a Republican governor to criticize was a great boon to Democrats. Economic problems were national, and Proxmire no longer had to defend the policies of an unpopular Democratic president. In Medford, he accused President Eisenhower of "establishing a welfare state for big bankers," stating that a few thousand banks received four times the subsidies given to millions of farmers. Instead, Proxmire praised the results of federal farm subsidies enacted under Democrats Roosevelt and Truman, noting that after twenty years, mechanization had increased efficiency and average farm wages had risen from 3 to 75 cents per hour.[49] Proxmire's continued focus on rural interests became even more important when Democrats scored a major upset in the ninth congressional district. Longtime incumbent Merlin Hull, a former Progressive who had returned to the Republican Party in 1946, died that May. In a special election held on October 13, Democrat Lester Johnson defeated his Republican opponent, Arthur Padrutt, by a 57 percent margin. Padrutt, misreading the popularity of Eisenhower in the district in the 1952 election as an endorsement of the administration's policies, campaigned as the pro-administration candidate. Johnson criticized the policies of Eisenhower and Secretary of Agriculture Ezra Benson. Kohler and the state Republican Party devoted much time and money to the race but were unable to persuade disgruntled farmers to support a Republican. The message was clear: Democratic success depended on abandoning the single-minded focus on McCarthy and broadening the party's economic appeal to farmers.[50]

In fact, Benson played a critical role in helping Wisconsin Democrats gain favor with farmers. In January 1954, he announced a reduction in dairy price supports, giving Proxmire even more ammunition against the Republican administration, especially after Governor Kohler refused to protest against the Eisenhower administration's farm policies. Benson was a deeply conservative Republican who believed that farmers would do best without any interference from the federal government. Large producers were receptive to this measure, but small-scale farmers saw a return to pre–New Deal poverty. Rural discontent would be a critical factor in 1954.[51]

Proxmire's solo efforts during the spring and summer of 1953 started to irritate other Democrats who were unwilling to let the still relatively new and ambitious politician claim the 1954 gubernatorial nomination uncontested. Proxmire may have thought he deserved a second attempt for devoting so much of his energy to the lost-cause campaign of 1952, but his unwillingness to defer to party leaders or to work within the DOC framework worried those who had devoted more of their careers to rebuilding the party. In October 1953, James Doyle, stepping down from his position as state chairman, began seriously considering running for governor. Fearful that a contested primary would drain resources and split the party, some Democrats began arguing for a convention endorsement of candidates. Only those candidates endorsed at the state convention would receive support from the party. Proxmire saw this as a way for party leaders to undermine primary elections and vigorously argued against it. He charged that "an influential group" in the party was behind the move and saw it as a return to the age of "boss rule." Although it was cloaked in the traditional language of La Follette insurgency, Proxmire had a very real worry. In a convention vote, Doyle would likely beat Proxmire to get the party's endorsement and thus the full support of party machinery, but in an open primary, Proxmire's energy would likely prevail. When Doyle introduced endorsement at the party convention, Proxmire led the successful effort to reject the plan. The two remained cordial, but it was clear that Proxmire had an unpredictable independent streak.[52]

To nobody's surprise, Proxmire announced his second candidacy for governor on March 25, 1954. He was the first candidate in the field, but now other Democrats wanted to run, too.[53] Much had changed since 1952 that put Kohler in a more vulnerable position. He was running for a third term; no governor had been elected to a third consecutive term since John Blaine in 1924, and voters had decisively rejected third-term attempts by Philip La Follette in 1938 and Julius Heil in 1942. The state budget surplus had dwindled from $49 million to $15 million, and the Joint Finance Committee predicted a $7 million deficit by July 1955. Even though Kohler's party controlled the 1953 legislature, conservatives had rejected the governor's plan for a merger of the University of Wisconsin with the state college system, an increase in the size of the state patrol, greater authority to cut spending, and other measures. The discord among Republicans over state finances became obvious when Kohler vetoed a record thirty-four bills passed by the two houses of the legislature with large Republican majorities. Kohler's own appeal among voters appeared to be fading as well. He had campaigned hard for Republican Arthur Padrutt in the October special election against Lester Johnson but was unable to convince traditionally Republican voters that the decrease in farm prices was the Truman administration's fault. For the first time in years, the incumbent looked truly vulnerable, and James Doyle announced his candidacy on May 4, two days before Kohler formally announced his reelection bid.[54]

From the outset, the Proxmire campaign was far better organized than it had been two years earlier. His radio "talkathons" in 1952 had basically been publicity stunts, but they had taught Proxmire the importance of radio and television advertising, and so he hired Milwaukee advertising firm Dayton, Johnson & Hacker to produce print, radio, and television ads to run in Green Bay, Eau Claire, La Crosse, Milwaukee, Madison, and even smaller markets. He was a very hands-on—and probably quite difficult—client, rewriting copy and suggesting images, once urging the firm to find "any kind of a fresh, new gimmick which will dramatize my background and experience." Elsie and the children put up with being filmed in their home by a Madison crew to appear for a few seconds in one television ad. Essentially, Proxmire used a "media blitz" to coincide with his personal appearances, combining radio and print ads to promote fifteen-minute television speeches. Combined with his mailings and street-corner appearances, Proxmire seemed to be everywhere at once. "You are the fastest moving candidate I've ever worked with," wrote his advertising agent, Robert Vail.[55]

Most of his primary campaign was directed against the Republicans rather than against Doyle, out of fear of alienating some Democrats and also out of a genuine respect for his opponent. Proxmire did, however, take great care to emphasize his qualifications. In July, he prepared a detailed memorandum for use by his advertising firm distinguishing his record from Doyle's. He stressed his own record as a campaigner and legislator, noting that Doyle "never ran for political office," had "no record as a campaigner," and had "no experience in state government." When letter writers to the *Capital Times* challenged him on his chances of beating Kohler—Proxmire was convinced that Evjue was trying to aid Doyle by deliberately running pro-Doyle letters—his campaign manager shot back that Proxmire had been the only Democratic candidate to win Milwaukee County and led all other Democratic candidates for state office in number of votes. Moreover, he reminded Evjue that after the 1952 election, Democrats were "fulsome in their praise" of Proxmire's efforts. Only when he challenged the older, more established party leader did Democrats suddenly begin to question his suitability as a candidate. Nonetheless, at joint appearances, the two Democratic candidates professed their admiration for each other and promised to support whoever won the nomination.[56]

Proxmire opened his campaigns with attacks on McCarthy, but in July and August, Proxmire increasingly emphasized economic issues, particularly the looming state budget deficit and agricultural prices. The "Joe Must Go" recall campaign launched by Sauk City newspaper editor Leroy Gore in March collected insufficient signatures to trigger a recall election, but it had demonstrated how much McCarthy's popularity had declined among farmers, especially since the senator had done nothing to challenge Secretary Benson's reductions in dairy price supports. In Stevens Point, Proxmire predicted Democratic victory now that the Republican administrations in Madison and Washington had begun to "sputter and stall on the bumpy road of McCarthy and falling farm prices."[57] Radio spots promoting his appearances emphasized his knowledge of taxes and the need to maintain price supports for dairy farmers. Proxmire's radio spots ran in Beaver Dam, Janesville, Wisconsin Rapids, Fond du Lac, Oshkosh, and Wausau, and he appeared fifteen times on five different television stations between August 11 and September 9.[58] As he had two years earlier, Proxmire complained about the lack of press coverage. Milwaukee newspapers sent reporters to cover the candidates only in late August, prolonging his reliance on purchasing radio and television time. Even normally friendly papers like the *Capital Times* did not print his press releases as frequently as he wanted.[59]

Proxmire's combination of personal appearances on street corners and at factory gates with radio and television appearances worked brilliantly. Patrick Lucey later recalled that while he "thought Doyle would come through as a very warm person and very articulate . . . on TV, he was no match for Proxmire at all." Although Doyle was more popular with the "Madison intelligentsia" (as one observer dubbed them), Proxmire was more popular with working-class voters. He defeated Doyle 141,548 to 85,187, winning all but fourteen counties. He ran best in those areas where he invested the most in media coverage, besting Doyle by almost 19,000 votes in Milwaukee. In smaller media markets, like the southwestern and far western counties, the vote was much closer. Voter turnout, however, was only slightly larger than it had been in 1952 (when Proxmire received 178,133 votes unopposed) and Governor Kohler, running unopposed in the Republican primary, received more votes than the two Democrats combined (331,006). Only in Dane, Milwaukee, and Kenosha counties, and three sparsely populated rural counties (Iron, Jackson, and Langlade), did the combined Democratic vote exceed Kohler's. Proxmire had won the primary, but the general election would be much harder.[60]

Publicly, Proxmire remained optimistic, asserting that "Wisconsin Democrats have the best chance in 25 years in the coming fall election" and promising a "vigorous, all-out campaign." He planned to continue the same campaign strategy into the general election, citing the lesson he learned in the primary about the potency of television advertising, which he "expected to use quite a bit." Citing the increase in Democratic voters in Brown County, he wrote John Reynolds Jr. that he planned to use television to the maximum extent in the campaign against Kohler, continuing his pattern of coordinating media use with personal appearances. Local party leaders, however, warned him not to neglect personal contacts, especially those who had supported Doyle in the primary and now needed encouragement to continue working for Proxmire. Others

warned him of trying to do too much himself. It was fine, one supporter
told him, "to put on a one man show before the primary, but this thing now
means [a] lot of organization and ACTIVE participation by a lot of people."
This was really Proxmire's great weakness as a candidate. Determined to
do everything himself, he sometimes failed to make use of the resources
of the Democratic Party.[61]

As he had in the 1952 campaign, Proxmire invited Kohler to debate
the big issues, clearly staking out the Democratic platform of improving
education and welfare, eliminating "special interest domination" from
state government, and fighting for 90 percent price supports for dairy
farmers and more jobs for the unemployed. Kohler refused and instead
grew increasingly sarcastic about Proxmire and accused him of lying about
state finances. Other Republicans were more aggressive. Warren Knowles,
running for lieutenant governor, accused Proxmire of trying to buy the
election with out-of-state money. Proxmire responded that he received
only two out-of-state contributions: $6,000 from his father and $4,900
from his sister.[62]

Yet by October, Republicans were sweating. McCarthy was becoming a liability, and Proxmire continued to hammer away at the senator
and suggest that Kohler and other state Republicans gave him "the rever-
ence of a feudal lord." It was an off-year election, so the party lacked the
power of President Eisenhower's coattails. In September, Maine elected
a Democratic governor, Edmund Muskie, for the first time since 1932,
perhaps signaling the beginning of a trend that would sweep Wisconsin
Republicans out of office.[63] Republican worries helped produce the major
controversy of the campaign when Proxmire used Stoughton dairy farmer
Oscar Holte in a television commercial to dramatize what had happened
to farm incomes. In the commercial, Holte showed Proxmire photocopies
of two checks from the same dairy company for the same quantity of milk.
The check from 1952 was for $1,022; the one from 1954, for only $574. It
was an effective ad and forced Kohler to respond. The Kohler campaign
purchased time on twenty-eight radio stations to rebuke Proxmire. Speaking at six forty-five a.m., when farmers would most likely be listening,
Kohler reminded rural voters that Proxmire had until just five years ago
"lived in the fancy suburb of Lake Forest, Illinois" and had tried "to put
over on Wisconsin farmers the most scandalous hoax I have ever seen."

Proxmire, he argued, compared wartime prices with peacetime prices, and he accused Democrats of never giving dairy farmers prosperity without war. Proxmire was furious and demanded Kohler meet him face-to-face in a live radio broadcast in Madison. Kohler did not attend, but Oscar Holte did and told listeners that Proxmire had been right and was a "100 per cent honest man."[64]

On Election Night, Democratic optimism proved to be well-founded. Nationally, Democrats gained control of both houses of Congress; in Wisconsin, they picked up eleven seats in the Assembly, two seats in the Senate, and one congressional seat (Henry Reuss in the fifth). Months of courting the farm vote paid off as well, as Democrats made strong gains in rural areas. Yet it was not enough to put Proxmire in the governor's mansion: Kohler won, 596,158 (51.5%) to 560,747 (48.4%). Proxmire won large margins in Milwaukee, Kenosha, Racine, and Dane counties, as well as the rural northwest in the best showing of a Democratic candidate since 1934.[65] "It was close, but no cigar," Proxmire quipped to one correspondent. He professed not to be disappointed, but the close loss was hard to take after such a hard campaign, and Proxmire briefly considered a recount. Repeatedly, Proxmire told friends that Democratic prospects for 1956 looked even more promising, especially if Republicans continued their policy of reducing farm subsidies. The morning after the election, he was at a Milwaukee factory shaking hands, and within weeks he was working with Carl Thompson to build up stronger precinct organizations in preparation for 1956.[66]

All of this political activism, however, took a tremendous toll on his personal life. A few days after the election, one of his friends wrote to congratulate him on his campaign. "You are young," William Benton wrote. "You have the right attitude and the right Party—indeed, I even seem to remember that you have the right wife."[67] Elsie, despite her support of Proxmire's early political ambition, had grown to resent his time away from the family. She was nine years younger than her husband, and lonely. Hosting teas for supporters and making telephone calls to raise contributions was not what she wanted. Her husband's frequent absences deprived her of the comfortable home life she had hoped for, and she was unhappy about the late nights and campaign workers who practically moved in. Upset by her husband's neglect, she had fallen in love with Miles McMillin, the chief editorial writer for the *Capital Times*. Shortly after the election, she took Theodore and Cici to the Washoe Pines Ranch in Reno, Nevada, for six weeks to establish residency and take advantage of that state's liberal divorce laws. Alone in Blooming Grove, Proxmire put their house up for sale but refused to discuss the situation. In February 1955, he flew to Nevada for the court appearance, and on February 9, a judge awarded Elsie an uncontested divorce and custody of the children. Proxmire retained visitation rights and final say over Theodore's education. After conferring with Adlai Stevenson, himself a divorcee, Proxmire issued a statement to the press: He "did not want the divorce and deeply deplored it" and claimed that he would have given up all political activity to save his marriage. There was more to it, however, and he noted cryptically that giving up politics would not have prevented the divorce.[68]

Elsie and the children moved into a new house about a mile away while Proxmire remained in the old house, no longer for sale, where the children often stayed on weekends and for most of the summer. Personally devastated by this turn of events, Proxmire remained bitter about the divorce and worried about how it might affect his political future. The two stayed cool toward one another, despite their proximity. Elsie warned him not to let "your resentment towards me and your feeling of wanting revenge" affect the children. Six months later, Elsie married McMillin, who had divorced his own wife a year earlier. Over time, Proxmire and his former wife grew more civil for the sake of the children. They never spoke badly about each other in front of others and tried to ensure that the children spent equal amounts of time with both parents.[69]

In 1955, Proxmire held no elected office or any leadership position in the Democratic Party, but he nonetheless provided analysis and advice—usually unsolicited—with an eye to the 1956 election. He was particularly interested in farm policy. An analysis of 1954 election returns by the Farmers Union shortly confirmed what Proxmire had already figured out as he campaigned around the state: farmers were angry about Agriculture Secretary Benson's farm policies and voted Democratic in protest. Proxmire wrote to Democratic members of Congress explaining the political implications of the farm vote and urged them to offer a specific farm proposal prior to the 1956 presidential election.[70] When Minnesota governor Orville Freeman announced legal action to open markets outside of Minnesota for its milk and milk products, Proxmire wrote Governor Kohler and urged him to cooperate with the effort in order to open up more national markets for Wisconsin dairy producers. Although Kohler responded positively, Proxmire remained skeptical of Kohler's interest, and warned Freeman that "the only real chance of effective Wisconsin co-operation in this fight is a hotly partisan political fire built under him."[71]

That summer, Proxmire waged another fight at the Democratic convention against the endorsement system. James Doyle was the leading voice supporting convention endorsement of candidates, and he had some reasonable concerns. The Fairchild/Reuss primary in 1952 and Doyle's own race against Proxmire had caused hard feelings among party workers, and many wanted to avoid the expense of a primary. Labor leaders particularly favored convention endorsement since it gave them more influence over the nomination. Others simply wanted to announce early and preempt Proxmire before he had a chance to get started. In August, Madison mayor George Forster announced that he was considering a run for the Democratic nomination in 1956, and Proxmire encouraged him to do so but warned that he might contest the nomination. If they did face each other in a primary election, "It would be good for Wisconsin, good for the Wisconsin Democratic party and good for the eventual winner." He wrote to local Democratic Party leaders urging them to oppose endorsing candidates at the party convention and received generally favorable responses. Joseph Schantz, the Monroe County chairman, wrote back, "We old timers setup the primary system a long time ago under old Bob, and it would be fulish [sic] to destroy it now." At the Green Bay convention, the executive committee rejected endorsement. Once again, Proxmire took his case to the people rather than defer to the wishes of the party leaders.[72]

Proxmire clearly planned to run for governor again in 1956 and spoke in glowing terms about the party's chances to oust the Republicans. At a birthday celebration for former president Truman in Kenosha, Proxmire predicted that the prolonged decline in dairy prices combined with McCarthy's growing unpopularity and concerns about state finances meant an "excellent" chance of Wisconsin Democrats electing a governor. Months later, he predicted a potential seventeen-vote swing in the Assembly because of voter discontent with Republican farm policies.[73] Despite Proxmire's continued devotion to politics, some Democrats hoped that two losses in two years would end the tireless senator's aspirations. Yet Proxmire forced party leaders to acknowledge him. Although he was not well-liked among party regulars, voters found him an appealing candidate, and his willingness to campaign hard could not be ignored. John Reynolds urged Proxmire to run again, stating bluntly that "no other Democrat in this state is so well known to the man on the street as you are."[74]

Proxmire announced his candidacy in early February 1956 and immediately began rallying Democratic leaders around him. Supporters created a "Proxmire for Governor Committee," chaired by William Foster with John Reynolds as secretary. Co-chairs included Daniel Hoan and James Doyle. Foster rehired the advertising firm that had handled the 1954 campaign. Proxmire began his campaign with a series of sixteen farm rallies in the southwestern counties of Crawford, Grant, Iowa, and Monroe, a part of the state in which he ran poorly in 1954. Having come within a few thousand votes of winning in 1954, Proxmire was confident that reusing the most effective aspects of his earlier campaigns while shoring up where he had been weak would lead to victory. The election of 1956 would be his most optimistic campaign, and no other Democrat challenged him for the nomination, leaving Proxmire free to campaign against the Republican Party for nine months.[75]

Things looked even brighter in March when Governor Kohler announced he would not seek a fourth term. It was widely assumed that he would run against Senator McCarthy in 1958, but Kohler had also grown weary of trying to hold together a fractious party split between moderates and pro-McCarthy conservatives. Despite his often bitter criticism in the past, Proxmire praised Kohler's moderate leadership. The only Republican candidate to seek the nomination was attorney general Vernon Thomson, more conservative than Kohler and a consummate political insider, having served in the assembly from 1935 to 1951 and as attorney general since 1951. He was not as popular as Kohler, and in a campaign in which Proxmire would focus on Republican fiscal mismanagement, he was the weaker candidate. In fact, Proxmire's impressive performance in 1954 may have frightened other Republicans away from pursuing the open seat.[76]

Proxmire did indeed intend to make the economy the focus of his campaign. For the first six weeks, he prioritized farm prices. He told one audience that the drop in farm income disguised a sharp rise in inflation. The

Eisenhower administration, he argued, had caused this inflation by ballooning the national debt by more than $13 billion in three years. Declining
food prices, however, kept the cost of living relatively flat, meaning that six
out of seven Americans were "riding on the back of the American farmer."
The solution to declining farm prices was farmers limiting production
until they received 90 percent parity. Proxmire challenged Thomson to
meet him in a televised debate over farm problems, but Thomson refused.
All through May, Proxmire continued to emphasize the problems facing
dairy farmers and the Republicans' failure to adequately address them.[77]

As with his earlier campaigns, fund-raising and publicity were problems. Proxmire accused Republicans of planning to spend $1 million on the
campaign and bemoaned his own limited resources. He urged supporters
to contribute to his campaign in order to pay for television and radio ads
that the Republicans could easily afford. Mass mailings to party members
went out in April asking for donations of $5 or $10. One campaign worker
discovered that calling supporters and asking for only a dollar raised more
money than asking for five or ten. By the fall, all those soliciting campaign funds concentrated on the $1 amount, and by September, the cam-
paign had raised nearly $4,000, exclusive of county campaign efforts.
Fund-raising efforts continued through September and October, but the
advertising firm continued to be a drain on campaign funds. Proxmire,
though, believed that his continued presence on television was critical.[78]

In July, Proxmire turned his attention to cities in the Fox Valley and
Milwaukee in what was fast becoming his most grueling campaign. He
worked eighteen-hour days and longer, greeting factory workers at the
plant gates at five thirty a.m., shaking hands with voters at shopping centers and on street corners, and talking to local Democrats long into the
evening. By one estimate, he was in a car over thirty hours a week, sitting
in the back seat typing press releases on a wooden board fastened to the
back of the front seat. Late July found him once again in the southwest,
and by early August, he was campaigning in central Wisconsin.[79]

As he had in 1952, Proxmire took time out from his campaign to attend
the National Democratic Convention as an alternate delegate. Tennessee senator Estes Kefauver won the Wisconsin presidential primary, but
after he withdrew in favor of Adlai Stevenson, Proxmire led the effort to
convince Stevenson to choose Kefauver as his running mate. New York

governor Averell Harriman, however, persuaded some Wisconsin delegates to defect to him and deny Stevenson the nomination. Proxmire used
the incident to argue in favor of the open primary. Referring to the large
number of letters, telegrams, and telephone calls received by Wisconsin
delegates, Proxmire asked, "Can anyone question that this campaign by a
delegate is bypassing the public and taking any kind of determining voice
out of the hands of the people?" Although he admired Harriman's liberal
record, Proxmire disliked his tactics and worked with Kefauver to convince
most of the Wisconsin delegation to support Stevenson. Stevenson won
the nomination and left the choice of a vice presidential nominee up to
the convention. Proxmire then worked through the night to convince the
Wisconsin delegation to support Kefauver, whom Proxmire asserted had
the enthusiastic support of Wisconsin farmers. Wisconsin's twenty-eight
votes for Kefauver on the first ballot helped secure him the nomination.
Despite his success at the convention, his stance against "boss rule" would
come back to haunt Proxmire before Election Day.[80]

Returning to Wisconsin, Proxmire continued his campaign and predicted a smashing victory in November, increasingly focusing on the national race, and hoping that a Wisconsin swing away from Eisenhower
toward Stevenson would sweep Democrats into state offices as well. He
reasoned that a strong farm plank in the national Democratic platform
and Kefauver's nomination would attract votes from farmers, and state
financial problems would build on a Democratic surge that began with
Lester Johnson's election to Congress in 1953. On television and in radio
appearances, he sought to link inflation and unemployment to the Republicans. Economic problems facing ordinary Wisconsin voters, he said, were
made worse by big business's domination of the Republican Party, which
thereby exerted influence over state regulatory agencies at the expense
of farmers, small business owners, and consumers. "Eighteen years of
conservative Republican appointments of these 'referees' have given the
big boys a real whip-hand in Wisconsin," Proxmire stated on a Sheboygan
broadcast. In Oshkosh, he slammed the Eisenhower administration's increase in interest rates and described how rising interest rates would hurt
dairy farmers and school districts struggling with construction costs that
would ultimately be borne by the property-tax payer.[81]

The results of the primary election were encouraging. Both Proxmire and Thomson were uncontested, but other primary races increased voter turnout among Republicans. Proxmire received 265,475 votes, emerging once again as the leading vote getter among Democrats. Thomson polled only 400,442 votes, far fewer than Kohler had during his last three races. If Democrats could continue to emphasize basic economic issues and build on their momentum, Proxmire looked likely to be the next governor of Wisconsin.[82]

Proxmire, however, retained his maverick streak and took a stand on principle that shook up the Democratic Party and jeopardized his chances to defeat Thomson. In the primary, voters had nominated Robert La Follette Sucher, grandson of Fighting Bob, to be the Democratic candidate for attorney general. His name was certainly an asset, but he was also "not professionally or temperamentally qualified to be attorney general," as Proxmire wrote in a mass mailing sent out to seven thousand party members, urging them to support the defeated Frank Nikolay as an independent candidate. Proxmire had acted alone, without consulting party leaders and infuriating state chairman Philleo Nash, who called Proxmire's action a "bombshell." Sucher gleefully pointed out the contrast of Proxmire's move against him to his past stands against endorsement and in favor of primary elections. If Proxmire had really thought him unqualified, why had he not said so during the campaign? Did he not trust voters to decide qualifications for themselves? Was he now trying to dictate candidates? In reality, it was a matter of principle. Proxmire was essentially correct about Sucher's credentials. He had graduated from the UW Law School in 1955, and his only legal experience was as a legal representative for the Madison Building Services Employees Union. Proxmire regretted not doing more to draw attention to these issues during the primary. It also reflected his conviction that Democrats would win in November, and he had grave reservations about saddling the state with an unqualified officer, stating that it would be a "real catastrophe for Wisconsin." Proxmire used his radio and personal appearances to collect signatures for Nikolay's nominating papers. Some Democrats, like James Doyle and John Reynolds, supported Proxmire's efforts, but others in the party resented his attempts to be a "kingmaker." He proved his success as a campaigner when he managed to collect enough signatures to place Nikolay on the ballot within a week. Nonetheless, the impression that Proxmire might be trying to overrule Democratic voters generated suspicion in the minds of many.[83]

In the final month of the campaign, Proxmire remained confident of victory. He told the state Democratic convention that the Republican campaign was "crumbling" because candidates refused to acknowledge the state's fiscal problems. Thomson emphasized his long experience in state government, but he lagged behind Proxmire's seemingly superhuman ability to talk to voters, averaging between five and six live television appearances in different cities every week. Ads for Thomson in the closing days of the campaign listed his accomplishments in state government compared to the thin record of "the man from Illinois." Proxmire criticized Republican tax policies that burdened small earners in favor of the rich and corporations and predicted that Republicans would be forced to enact a sales tax in the state. Thomson countered that Democrats would raise income tax rates on those earning less than $5,000 a year. Exchanges between the two candidates grew more and more heated throughout October as each accused the other of trying to mislead voters about state finances and distort the opposing party's position on taxes. It was not particularly illuminating to voters, but Proxmire sensed Republicans' anxiety and kept up his attacks. In late October, state tax commissioner Harry Harder released an analysis of Proxmire's tax plan that showed it would raise only $4.4 million per year, not the $75–$80 million Proxmire claimed. Proxmire, caught off guard for once, replied that Harder failed to take into account changes to the revenue distribution formula. Few voters understood such technicalities, and in trying to simplify his message, Proxmire instead looked deceptive. It was a rare stumble from someone who knew taxes better than anyone else in the state.[84]

It remained a close race down to the end, but once again Proxmire came up short. Thomson won 808,273 (51.9%) to 749,421 (48.1%). Proxmire carried industrial lakeshore counties (Kenosha, Racine, Milwaukee, and Manitowoc) and farm counties in the west and northwest. He ran far ahead of the other Democratic candidates, including Stevenson, demonstrating his popularity with voters. Yet it was not enough to overcome the power of Eisenhower's coattails. The nation—and Wisconsin voters—had rallied behind the president during a time of international crisis: Israeli troops invaded the Sinai peninsula, British and French forces launched air strikes against Egypt, and the Soviet Union invaded Hungary to suppress a reform movement led by Imre Nagy. Proxmire blamed these events for his loss and called the defeat "especially painful" because of the years of organizing and high hopes that had built in the last few years in the lead-up to this election. Supporters were shocked. "The mentality of a public that failed to elect a Proxmire and a Stevenson seems hopelessly subnormal to me," wrote one correspondent. "People seem not to want anyone with brains, ability, and ethics in public office." Dejected supporters left campaign headquarters early, leaving behind piles of uneaten food ordered in anticipation of long celebration. It looked like the end of his career, as the *Wisconsin State Journal* editorialized: "After six years of employing himself at little more . . . than constant campaigning and spending thousands upon thousands of dollars on it, the three-time loser ought to be convinced that he's all done."[85] Yet it was not the end to his career in politics; the three-time loser suddenly saw his political fortune reversed with the death of Joseph McCarthy. The siren song of another statewide campaign lured him away from home once again, eventually leading him to the United States Senate.

4

To the Senate

D espite his frustrating third loss in six years, William Proxmire had good reason to be happy in the winter of 1956. While in Chicago for the Democratic National Convention that July, Proxmire had taken a break from the swirling activity for a quiet stroll in Grant Park with Ellen Sawall, the executive secretary of the Wisconsin Democratic Party. Sawall had worked on Proxmire's campaigns and been active in the party since 1950, serving as precinct committee chair, fund-raiser, and event organizer. Like Proxmire, she was a relative newcomer to Wisconsin, born in Pittsburgh and raised in Washington, where her father worked in the US Patent Office and her mother was a teacher. She was attractive (voted "most beautiful girl" of the Woodrow Wilson High School class of 1942) and intelligent (Phi Beta Kappa from the University of Richmond in her junior year) with degrees in French and psychology. While at the University of Richmond, she had met Warren Sawall, an airman from Wisconsin stationed in Richmond. After he returned from overseas in 1945, the two were married and moved to Wisconsin, where they both finished their education at the University of Wisconsin, living in "Badger Village," a collection of Quonset huts quickly set up to house returning veterans. After graduating, they moved to Wisconsin Rapids, where Sawall worked for the local newspaper. While in school, their first child, Mary Ellen, was born in 1946, and Jan Cathy was born in 1949. The family soon returned to Madison to work for the Democratic Organizing Committee and became part of the group that included most of the major party figures, including the Doyles, Nelsons, and Proxmires. The Sawall marriage, however, was not a happy one, and Warren and Ellen eventually divorced.

Single once more in 1955, Ellen and Proxmire gradually began seeing more of each other. As they talked about their lives—both were divorced with two children—they decided to get married. It was not particularly romantic, Ellen later recalled, but, "It seemed so natural and proper," she wrote a few years later, "in the light of our feelings for each other and our mutual interest in politics and in children." Politics postponed any public announcement of their engagement since they worried that an announcement would remind voters that Proxmire was divorced—still a stigma in socially conservative Wisconsin—and they saw very little of each other until after the election. The two were married on December 1, 1956, at Lake Edge Congregational Church in a small ceremony with their families present. Friends were delighted. "Ellen is one of the finest girls that we have ever met," John Reynolds wrote him after their engagement was announced. "Likewise, you are one of the finest men we have ever met, so it is well the two of you are getting together."[1]

After the couple's short honeymoon in Chicago, Ellen Proxmire moved into the farmhouse in Blooming Grove to preside over the household of six. She brought her two daughters, Mary Ellen, age ten, and Jan Cathy, age seven, to the family; Proxmire's two children, Teddy, age nine, and Cici, age eight, lived in the house on weekends. The children, Ellen later recalled, got along beautifully, especially since they all attended the same school and the households were close to each other on Buckeye Road. The Roney family owned a farm next door and often took care of Teddy and Cici, and soon also helped look after the other girls as well. The new family often visited Proxmire's father in Lake Forest, and the elderly doctor quickly became "Grand Popsey" to Ellen's children. Ellen continued to work for the state party part-time as financial secretary, while Proxmire returned to running the business side of Artcraft Press, badly neglected during his campaign, and assumed a much more conventional role as husband and father, home at six p.m. every evening and all weekend instead of racing from one town to the next.[2]

Although he adopted the schedule and habits of a conventional businessman, Proxmire kept his hand in politics as well, forming the "Wisconsin Committee to Beat the Sales Tax" in late November 1956. He recruited an executive committee that included longtime supporters from around the state, including Roland Day, Betty Graichen, Frank Nikolay, and John

Reynolds. Proxmire himself was listed as president and Ellen served as secretary. By January 1957, Proxmire had researched state finances thoroughly and projected that the state would need $100 million in the coming biennium and $375 million by 1965–1967. This increase in spending would clearly require new sources of revenue, but Proxmire's numbers also showed how regressive the tax system was in terms of percentage of income—that is, wealthier individuals and corporations could use a variety of loopholes to pay a smaller proportion of their income than middle-class and working-class taxpayers did. A sales tax—even with exemptions for food or other necessities—would only increase this disparity. He prepared a detailed analysis of tax rates and projected state spending for the committee and recommended increases in marginal income tax rates and elimination of exemptions for corporate income, all of which would increase state revenue while reducing taxes for those with lower incomes. This kind of thinking was consistent with the tax reforms advocated by earlier progressive governors, especially in the 1900s, 1910s, and 1930s, and he had advocated similar changes while a member of the Assembly. His detailed research and uncanny ability to explain complicated matters to a general audience, however, contributed to a growing debate over state taxation.[3]

Many Republicans, including former governor Kohler, favored a sales tax to bring in new revenue. Business leaders claimed that Wisconsin's income tax system already discouraged business expansion, and a citizen's committee in late 1956 recommended a 2 percent sales tax, the proceeds of which would be earmarked for education. In March 1957, first-term state senator Kirby Hendee, a Republican representing the northern suburbs of Milwaukee (the fourth Senate district), introduced a 2 percent sales tax with an exemption for food. Proxmire testified before the Senate taxation committee against the measure, arguing that it would fall heaviest on those least able to afford it. A taxpayer with an income of less than $2,500 a year would see a 30 percent increase in the total amount of taxes paid to all levels of government, Proxmire calculated, whereas those with an income of over $50,000 a year would see a net tax cut by taking advantage of new deductions. Proxmire made similar arguments before the Assembly taxation committee in May.[4]

Proxmire's public fight against the sales tax irritated those in the Democratic Party who thought that the former nominee should let party officials lead the opposition to the Republican administration. In March, Governor Thomson recorded a twenty-eight-minute film explaining the workings of state government, which was distributed to fourteen television stations around the state. Proxmire charged that these recordings were more than just educational and were in fact "to advance his political viewpoint and personal political fortunes," and promptly wrote to each station demanding that they provide him equal time to challenge the governor's statements, as he had done in 1956 with Kohler's radio broadcasts. Most stations refused, noting that since neither he nor Thomson was running for political office, the equal time doctrine did not apply. His presumption irritated party leaders. Acting chair of the administrative council Herman Jessen declared flatly that Proxmire had no right to speak for the Democratic Party, while Daniel Hoan said simply, "I move we inform Proxmire he is not the Democratic Party." In the future, the council decided, the state chair would be the one to request equal time if the party deemed the governor's media appearances overtly partisan. By the time the council had made its decision, however, two stations had offered Proxmire equal time, and Proxmire turned the whole issue over to state party chair Philleo Nash, noting sardonically that "this is now your baby" and urging him to pursue the opportunity to counter Thomson's message.[5]

The sales tax would remain a hot topic in Wisconsin in the coming years, but events in Washington were pointing Proxmire in a new direction. He had been considering a challenge to Senator Joseph McCarthy in 1958 for some time, and it was widely assumed that Kohler would challenge McCarthy in the Republican primary election. McCarthy was indeed vulnerable, as he had been censured by the Senate and as rumors of his alcoholism circulated around the state. Plans for 1958, however, were suddenly obsolete when the forty-eight-year-old senator died in May 1957 at Bethesda Naval Hospital of liver failure. Shortly before six o'clock on May 2, a friend telephoned Ellen Proxmire with the explosive news; when Proxmire returned home a few minutes later, she could tell by his expression that he had heard as well. Patrick Lucey called and urged Proxmire to run, over Ellen's objections, arguing that the short campaign required someone who already had statewide name recognition and donating $500 for the cause. Proxmire had decided to begin his fourth statewide campaign.[6]

Despite nearly a decade of organizing and campaigning, the Democrats had won only one statewide race since 1946, and their efforts to fight McCarthy publicly had done little to diminish his popularity. This election, however, was different. It was the first open Senate seat since 1925, and the Republicans seemed determined to tear their party apart. Rumors swirled about who would enter the race, or even if there would be a race at all. Some Republican Party leaders wanted the legislature to pass a law allowing the governor to appoint a successor to fill out the remainder of McCarthy's term. Thomson seriously considered asking the legislature for such a law and was potentially interested in cutting a deal with Lieutenant Governor Warren Knowles to resign and be appointed himself. From Washington, senior senator Alexander Wiley, who had fought his own battles against party leaders and won reelection over their opposition in 1956, grumbled that there must be no appointment or party endorsement and insisted he be consulted in all developments. Muddying the waters still further was former governor Oscar Rennebohm, who announced that he would be willing to serve if Governor Thomson offered him the appointment. The Republican State Executive Committee met to advise Thomson but adjourned without coming to any recommendation on appointment.[7]

The Democrats were only slightly better organized. The 1956 nominee, Henry Maier, bowed out. Proxmire made no secret that he was considering the race, but Milwaukee labor organizations began actively promoting congressman Henry Reuss. James Doyle publicly supported Reuss as well, along with most of the Democratic leadership. It soon appeared that Reuss would be the Democrats' anointed champion. Proxmire refused to let Reuss preemptively walk away with the nomination and sent a telegram urging him to run but warned that he would also likely be a candidate. "A primary contest," Proxmire promised, "would stimulate an interest and enthusiasm that will greatly enhance the chances of our party." Not everyone shared Proxmire's relish for a primary fight. State Senator Gaylord Nelson, also rumored to be interested in McCarthy's seat, announced that he would not run but urged party officials to agree on a candidate quickly to avoid a costly primary campaign. Nelson also tried to discourage Proxmire from running, assuring him that he could defeat Thomson and be elected governor in 1958. The University of Wisconsin's Young Democrats urged Proxmire to step aside in favor of another candidate because voters had "rejected" his name three times. Despite efforts to throw cold water on his nascent campaign, Proxmire continued to promote himself and his chances. He made the special election a referendum on national issues, criticizing Secretary of State John Foster Dulles's "inept" foreign policy and Eisenhower's "enormous" federal budget despite drops in farm income and increases in the cost of living. He particularly focused on the policies of Secretary of Agriculture Ezra Taft Benson, who had cut farm subsidies for Wisconsin farmers.[8]

Republicans remained divided. Thomson delayed calling a special election, and candidates abounded. On May 14, former governor Walter Kohler announced that he would be a candidate if there were a special election. The next day, Knowles and former congressman Glenn Davis, who had run a close second to Senator Wiley in the 1956 Republican primary, announced their candidacies, and on June 4, a fourth Republican, Alvin O'Konski, entered the race, even though Thomson still had not called for a special election. The Democratic contest changed when congressman Clement Zablocki told reporters he would run, effectively scuttling Reuss's candidacy. Reuss had hoped for Zablocki's endorsement and was shocked when Zablocki himself entered the race; this put Reuss in an awkward position, having publicly stated he would not run against the party's most senior congressman.[9] Finally on June 6, Thomson announced that a special election would be held on August 27, with a primary—by this point clearly necessary—to be held on July 30; candidates could begin circulating nomination papers on June 18 and had to file them with the secretary of state by July 12. The next day, Proxmire announced his candidacy.[10] His declaration contained some familiar themes but focused on national rather than state issues. "Since the last election," he said,

> Wisconsin people have become increasingly more concerned with an Eisenhower-Dulles foreign policy that has repeatedly brought us to the brink of war without advancing the strength and stability of the free world. In every month since the last election tens of thousands of Wisconsin citizens whose incomes are fixed, have helplessly watched the cost of living rise to one new high after another. Meanwhile the

> Republican administration has followed a monopoly-coddling policy
> that permits big business to shove up the price of almost everything
> we buy in spite of record profits and near-record supplies.

This was La Follettism revised for the Cold War: a populist demand for economic justice combined with a strong foreign policy. Americans could not be free from foreign threats if they endured growing economic inequality at home.[11]

Philleo Nash and other Democratic leaders feared a contested primary would drain party resources and weaken the eventual nominee; Nash in particular was eager to see Proxmire's campaign quashed, worried that having rejected him three times in six years, voters would hand an easy victory to the Republican nominee. In order to resolve the nomination without a primary, the party's administrative council sponsored a series of three public meetings, dubbed "Operation Sounding Board," in Green Bay, Eau Claire, and Sheboygan. These meetings would give potential candidates the opportunity to offer their qualifications and platforms, and the audience could participate in a straw poll to gauge candidates' support among likely voters. The operation was clearly aimed at Proxmire to prevent him from obtaining the nomination over Zablocki or another potential Democratic candidate by default as the best-known Democrat in the state, only to lose to the same candidate who had defeated him twice before. Proxmire angrily wrote Nash and demanded his assurance that the meetings would not lead to endorsement or the elimination of any candidate. The plan badly backfired. Rather than discouraging Proxmire, the meetings demonstrated his popularity among voters. In Green Bay on June 8, eleven of the twenty-one attendees who shared their views on candidates supported Proxmire. Those who supported Reuss said they preferred Proxmire to Zablocki as their second choice. By the Sheboygan meeting on June 11, Proxmire had emerged as the overwhelming favorite. The attempt to discourage his candidacy irritated Proxmire, but he took gleeful delight in seeing how quickly voters showed their support. Despite vociferous support from labor groups, Reuss kept his word and withdrew from consideration in favor of Zablocki, narrowing the Democratic contest down to Proxmire and the Milwaukee congressman.[12]

The Republican primary turned out to be even more complicated and divisive. Kohler was the likely nominee, but he was distrusted by the more conservative elements of the party. He was the only candidate to solidly support the policies of the Eisenhower administration, and his coolness toward McCarthy had become well-known. It was unclear whether he could survive the primary if conservatives voted in large numbers. Attendees at the Republican convention in La Crosse booed him when he outlined his moderate policies shortly after they had cheered the more conservative Davis and Knowles. Altogether, seven Republicans sought their party's nomination: Kohler, Knowles, Davis, O'Konski, state senator Gerald Lorge, former state Supreme Court justice Henry P. Hughes, and former congressman John C. Schafer.[13]

Proxmire threw himself into the campaign with characteristic fervor. The morning of June 17 found him outside factory gates in Watertown at six thirty a.m., the beginning of a typical week that included visits to factories, shopping centers, and public buildings in Milwaukee, smaller cities, suburbs, and rural areas around the state. His campaign rhetoric was familiar. He charged that the Republican candidates were enslaved to big business and favored "tax relief for the big corporation and the big earner and little or no tax cuts for the rest of the taxpayers." Since he was running for the Senate rather than the governor's office, he added a great deal of campaign material to his usual criticism of state tax policy. In Kenosha on June 19, he claimed Dulles's foreign policy resulted in record budgets for the Departments of State and Defense, using two-thirds of federal revenue. During a television appearance in Madison on June 20, he claimed that the oil lobby burdened American taxpayers, who had to pay higher taxes to offset corporate tax breaks and higher gasoline prices. On a radio broadcast from Marinette on June 28, he blamed Republican policies for rising consumer prices during a time of record corporate profits. Proxmire called for nuclear disarmament with "air-tight" inspection on July 9 in Wauwatosa. In a Milwaukee radio address, he criticized the treasury for borrowing from social security funds at 2.5 percent rather than the more typical 3.5 percent, thereby costing "hundreds of millions of dollars in benefits" to the elderly. He also came out in favor of civil rights and called for changes to the Senate filibuster rule that allowed southern senators to kill legislation. In Milwaukee on July 24, he greeted workers at factory gates before moving on to West Wisconsin Avenue to meet shoppers. "Say, you're persistent," quipped one diner at a West Allis restaurant when Proxmire introduced himself.[14]

Proxmire and Zablocki rarely referred to each other during the primary, usually focusing on the Eisenhower administration or the Republican candidates. In Green Bay on June 13, Proxmire charged that Kohler, Knowles, and Davis all favored tax relief for corporations but nothing for average taxpayers. He also attacked both Kohler and Knowles for supporting a sales tax. After Kohler criticized Davis for being "beholden" to Milwaukee industrialist Walter Harnischfeger, who had made several large donations to Davis's campaign, Proxmire listed twenty-five donations from corporate executives to Kohler totaling $6,636 and charged the former governor with blatant hypocrisy. All of this bolstered his argument that the number one issue in the campaign was the domination of government by "big business."[15] Zablocki, too, criticized the president's agricultural and foreign policies and chided Kohler for being such a staunch supporter of the president. Both candidates promised to support the winner of the primary, so Proxmire "took it easy" on Zablocki so that he would not alienate him or his supporters during the campaign.[16]

Republicans, however, targeted Proxmire, the heavy favorite. "Let me warn you right now," growled O'Konski, "that our real enemy in this campaign is 'Foxy, Proxy Proxmire.'" Davis was eager to take on Proxmire in the general campaign, vowing to make the Democrat "eat his words." When not attacking Proxmire, Republican candidates attacked Kohler, depicting him as too liberal and soft on communism. Kohler was an easy target. Overconfident about his own nomination, he did not begin campaigning until June 29, but even then his campaign was not well organized or well-funded. Kohler tried to steer a moderate course and thus attract Democratic voters, but his positions ended up drawing fire from both Democrats and more conservative Republicans, especially Davis, who outspent Kohler by over $30,000 in the primary.[17]

On the day of the primary election, July 30, voter turnout was light— under five hundred thousand votes. The results of the Democratic and Republican primaries were starkly different. Proxmire, a far better campaigner than his opponent, easily defeated Zablocki 86,341–56,817. Proxmire carried every county but Milwaukee, Zablocki's home, and Portage, with its large Polish American population. Zablocki and the Democratic

Party immediately lined up behind him and looked forward to a unified campaign to win the Senate seat. Democrats would certainly need to be united behind a single candidate: the total Republican vote in the primary was twice that of Democrats. Republicans, however, remained badly divided. Kohler emerged the victor—as expected—but by only 9,000 votes. Davis and O'Konski together bested Kohler by 50,000 votes and together carried fifty-one counties to Kohler's seventeen. Of those seventeen counties, moreover, Proxmire had carried seven in 1956, leaving Kohler's base of support in the Fox Valley. It was not clear if the other candidates' supporters would swing toward Kohler as much bitterness remained after the ballots were counted. Out of all the Republican candidates, only Knowles immediately pledged to support Kohler. Belatedly and reluctantly, the others offered lukewarm support. Kohler had beaten Proxmire twice, but now it appeared he was a far weaker candidate than he had been in 1954, the last time he had faced Proxmire. Nonetheless, Democrats were still facing an uphill battle to win only their second statewide race since 1946. If Republicans could pull together, as conventional wisdom said they would, it looked likely that Kohler would defeat Proxmire a third time.[18]

The first major handicap facing Proxmire in the general election was a lack of funds. Although Lucey was chairman of the campaign committee, Ellen served as her husband's campaign manager, and she saw firsthand that her most important task would be to keep the money flowing from many small donations to major expenses, like television airtime. When he announced her role in his campaign, Proxmire said she "knows Wisconsin and its politics from solid experience as a poll worker, precinct committeewoman, work group organizer, fundraiser, and editor of the state Democratic newspaper." Ellen's brilliant coordination made the campaign work. She turned their farmhouse kitchen into a campaign headquarters and put the children to work answering the telephone, stuffing envelopes, and delivering campaign literature door-to-door. Proxmire's use of media belied the campaign's precarious finances. Donations were in such small amounts and so sporadic that Ellen made daily trips to the Greyhound depot in Madison to put checks on the bus. In Milwaukee, the campaign's advertising agent would take the check and see what airtime, when and where, could be purchased with the funds available. The party tried to bolster Proxmire's campaign by soliciting small donations from many people, the "100 for 100" campaign, which tried to get one hundred people to pledge to collect $100 from their friends. Most donors gave between $5 and $25, though some organizations donated larger amounts. The United Auto Workers donated $2,000, and the United Steelworkers gave $5,000; the Democratic Senatorial Campaign Committee and the Pennsylvania Democratic Party made several contributions, totaling over $8,000. As with earlier campaigns, Dayton, Johnson & Hacker provided radio and television advertising, by far the largest expense. Despite a few large contributors, the Proxmire campaign continually struggled to pay its bills.[19]

In contrast, Kohler and the Republican Party seemed to have no shortage of campaign funds and spent freely on print advertising. The numerous billboards promoting Kohler irritated Proxmire, and he accused the former governor of trying to win the election through a "billboard buildup" rather than through a frank discussion of the issues. According to Proxmire, the $15,000 spent by the Republican Voluntary Committee on three hundred billboards around the state was based on the principle that "if you pour enough money into selling a name you can forget the issues." Campaign expenditure reports filed with the secretary of state showed that Kohler outspent Proxmire five to one, and the Republican Party outspent the Democratic Party ten to one.[20]

A second obstacle that Proxmire needed to overcome was the stigma of being a "three-time loser." Normally, three consecutive losses would end any political career, but other Democrats tried to turn Proxmire's losses into a virtue. Reuss noted that both Lincoln and La Follette had lost elections before winning. Speaking on WFOX in Milwaukee, Proxmire embraced the label: "Let my opponent have the support of the man who has never proposed to a girl and lost. I'll take the losers. . . . If all those who have ever lost in business, love, sports or politics will vote for me as one who knows what it is to lose and fight back, I will be glad to give my opponent the support of those lucky voters who have never lost anything."[21] Despite the public optimism, Proxmire remained gloomy about his chances. Republican candidates had vastly outpolled the two Democrats in the primary, and despite the fractious nature of that contest, all but O'Konski now backed Kohler. Every major newspaper in the state, with the exception of the *Capital Times*, endorsed Kohler, as did President Eisenhower.[22] Expecting a somber election night, the campaign arranged for a small room at the Wisconsin Hotel in Milwaukee but did not order food or drink—the oversupply of refreshments ordered in 1956 in anticipation of a victory party still stung.[23]

Proxmire faced these obstacles by campaigning even harder than he had before, driving from one end of the state to the other and buying as much radio and television time as he could. In the closing weeks of the campaign, he attacked Kohler's support for Agriculture Secretary Benson's farm policies, which cut price supports to dairy farmers. Small-scale farmers in the west and north were particularly receptive to this criticism. He pushed for increased tax exemptions of an average of $200 per family while criticizing Kohler for supporting a 3.5 percent sales tax. Proxmire also assailed Secretary of State Dulles for wasting billions of dollars of foreign aid in an ineffective war on communism. He called for extending and increasing Social Security benefits and blamed economic monopolies for inflation. Every day he was in a different city, greeting workers at factory gates in the early morning, visiting with voters in shopping centers and main streets, and writing press releases on important issues in the back seat of his car as he rode to the next location.[24] On a typical campaign day in late August, Proxmire spent the morning in Beloit at the Fairbanks, Morse & Company factory before fielding questions at the Hilton Hotel on taxes, foreign policy, social security, and the federal budget. After lunch, he drove to Janesville but found few people to talk to downtown and so wandered over to an auction that was in progress. He drew attention to himself by buying a tennis racket for $1.50, to the delight of the crowd when the auctioneer recognized him. After a Democratic dinner at the Parker Pen Company cafeteria, he drove to Milwaukee to start the same daily routine over again.[25]

Even on Election Day, August 27, Proxmire continued to campaign. After voting with Ellen in Blooming Grove, they dropped the children off with friends and drove through Racine, Kenosha, and Milwaukee to visit party volunteers working the phone banks to get out the vote in those crucial industrial cities. As Ellen inspected the election-night headquarters, the first results from rural areas began to trickle in. To her astonishment, Proxmire was ahead, and the lead remained constant throughout the evening. As more returns were reported, the growing crowd at the Hotel Wisconsin became more jubilant. The election was decisive: Proxmire defeated Kohler 435,985 to 312,931. After three attempts, Proxmire had finally won a statewide election and was now a United States Senator.[26]

Why had Proxmire won? The farm vote is the first part of the answer, as he did extraordinarily well in rural areas of the northern and western parts of the state, the same areas where La Follette progressives had always come out ahead. Townships with farm populations that topped 50 percent voted for Proxmire an average of 64 percent, up from 49 percent in 1954. Support for Proxmire among rural communities stemmed from unhappiness with the Agriculture Department's cutting subsidies to dairy farmers. Proxmire promised to fight these policies. Kohler tried to avoid the issue, but when asked directly, he admitted that he favored Secretary Benson's policy of reducing subsidies. Proxmire's assiduous courting of the farm vote and his continual haranguing of Ezra Benson had at last paid off.[27]

Labor unions had also effectively backed Proxmire by manning phone banks in Milwaukee, Madison, Racine, Kenosha, La Crosse, Eau Claire, and Sheboygan to get out the vote on Election Day. Hundreds of union members had made forty-five thousand telephone calls, even though labor leaders had initially favored Henry Reuss. Once the Wisconsin CIO and Wisconsin State Federation of Labor both endorsed Proxmire in early August, union support was critical. Proxmire's factory gate appearances undoubtedly helped his image as a candidate concerned for the welfare of working-class families. In Milwaukee, he did better in 1957 than he had in his earlier races, largely because of the positive light in which workers viewed him. Moreover, Kohler had the misfortune to be associated by name to the strike at the Kohler plant, even though he no longer had any connection to that company. It was not a tough sell to get factory workers to vote for the man who was willing to be at the factories at six thirty in the morning and against the stuffy industrialist whose family was part of the longest strike in state history. Proxmire had accomplished a daunting task that the La Follettes themselves had never quite managed: building a solid electoral coalition of farmers and laborers.[28]

Winning every large city in the state as well as the farm vote in all but one county west of the Wisconsin River was a potent electoral triumph, but part of Proxmire's landslide was due to lingering bitterness on the part of Republican voters who had not supported Kohler in the primary election. Although Democratic turnout in the general election more than tripled from the primary, Republican turnout actually decreased by more than four thousand votes, and Kohler struggled to overcome the apathy he encountered. Since Davis refused to campaign for Kohler, it seems likely that many of his supporters in the primary simply refused to vote for someone they found only marginally more palatable than the Democratic candidate. Robert Boyle ran as an independent "pro-McCarthy" candidate and gained 3 percent of the vote, not enough to throw the election to Proxmire, but enough to indicate a sizable dissatisfaction with the moderate Kohler among more conservative Republicans. Kohler himself might have been overconfident, running a bland campaign that stressed his record as governor and his support for Eisenhower, rather than engaging in serious debate with his opponent. Vice President Nixon observed that "it was the old story of a unified, vigorous minority party, with a hard-fighting, resourceful candidate, defeating a divided, bickering, over-confident majority."[29]

Whatever the reason for the victory, Proxmire's supporters were jubilant on Election Night; it was a "mob scene," Ellen later recalled. The small room was suddenly filled with revelers, and campaign workers danced outside in the rain. Telephone calls came in from Lyndon Johnson, Adlai Stevenson, Estes Kefauver, and others. The Proxmires tried to leave the pandemonium to return to their hotel room, only to find reporters waiting for them in the hallway. Telegrams continued to arrive all night until there were hundreds piled up on the coffee table. In the early hours of August 28, Proxmire did two things that guaranteed his future success at the polls. First, before leaving the celebration, he announced that he would run for a full term in 1958, just fourteen months away. Second, he and Ellen left the hotel at five thirty to stand outside factories in Milwaukee—the Wisconsin Motor Corporation, the Heil Company, and the Nordberg Company—shaking hands with workers as they arrived and thanking them for their support. After three painful losses, he was determined never to lose another election and would do whatever he could to stay connected to voters. As astonished workers shook hands with a politician *after* his election, Proxmire remarked to a reporter that he did not want voters to think that he would forget all about them after getting their votes. He had been a different kind of politician, and now, he assured them, he would be a different kind of senator.[30]

The Proxmires had little time to celebrate their victory. After finishing breakfast at their hotel, they learned that they had reservations on a late-afternoon flight from Milwaukee to Washington because Senate majority leader Lyndon Johnson was eager to have Proxmire sworn in as soon as possible. The Democrats held 49 of 96 seats, but Matthew Neely of West Virginia was gravely ill (he would die four months later), and the governor of West Virginia was expected to appoint a Republican successor. Combined with the potential election of Walter Kohler, Neely's death meant that there would be 48 Democrats and 48 Republicans, with Vice President Richard Nixon breaking all ties in favor of the Republicans, who were eager for the opportunity to take back control of the Senate. Proxmire's election guaranteed that Johnson would remain majority leader. Shortly after his victory, Proxmire gleefully told Johnson, "I've got the biggest birthday present of them all for you—me!"[31]

Ellen burst into tears at the news of their quick departure because it meant there was no time to return to Madison to say goodbye to the children. Still wearing the same clothes from the previous day, the Proxmires boarded the plane with State Democratic Chairman Philleo Nash and reporters from *Life*, who snapped pictures of Proxmire sipping a glass of milk while he looked through papers. Proxmire had worked tirelessly to make himself a state figure, and now he was, overnight, a national figure. Johnson and four others senators (Ralph Yarborough of Texas, Hubert Humphrey of Minnesota, Estes Kefauver of Tennessee, and Mike Mansfield of Montana), as well as the Democrats in Wisconsin's congressional delegation, met Proxmire when he stepped off his plane at National Airport and escorted him to the Capitol. The Proxmires arrived in time to witness a historic moment in the Senate: South Carolina Senator Strom Thurmond was in the midst of his filibuster against the Civil Rights Act of 1957, the longest in Senate history. Thurmond had agreed to temporarily yield the floor so that Proxmire could be sworn in immediately. Republicans, still smarting that the upset had deprived them of the chance to reorganize the Senate, were in no mood to be so gracious. When Johnson asked for unanimous consent to swear in Proxmire, Senate minority leader William Knowland of California objected because Governor Thomson had not yet sent a telegram confirming Proxmire's election. A twenty-five-minute argument ensued, Johnson becoming furious that the governor was allegedly unable to contact the Senate because he was on his way to the annual Midwest

Shrine Bowl to watch the Green Bay Packers play the Philadelphia Eagles. "I assume Western Union was operating," snarled Johnson, before giving up on Knowland. Instead of joining his fellow senators on the floor, Proxmire waited in the office of the Secretary of the Senate to meet individual senators before leaving for Ellen's parents' home in Bethesda. The next day, after the telegram arrived from Madison, Vice President Nixon swore in Proxmire, who wore a tie borrowed from his father-in-law. The new senator had not had enough time to pack.[32]

Johnson's enthusiasm for Proxmire remained unabated. He hosted a lunch with the new senator as guest of honor in the Old Supreme Court Chamber. The Senate majority leader also assigned Proxmire to a seat on three committees, all voluntarily relinquished by fellow Democrats to make room for the newcomer: Banking and Currency, Post Office and Civil Service, and Small Business. Overwhelmed with his reception, Proxmire broke the Senate protocol that required new members to remain silent; he gained recognition from the chair to thank Johnson on the floor. Johnson then announced that he would name Proxmire one of four senators to travel to West Germany to attend the opening of the Bundestag, an unusual privilege for a junior senator. That evening, Thurmond ended his filibuster and the Senate passed the Civil Rights Act by a vote of 60–15. Proxmire voted yea. The Senate also passed bills appropriating funds for foreign aid and easing immigration restrictions, and a measure establishing rules allowing defense attorneys to access FBI files. After conferring with Senators Humphrey and Joseph Clark, Proxmire voted in the affirmative on all measures. The Senate adjourned for the rest of the year, but Proxmire's work was just beginning. On Friday, he and Ellen found his space in the Senate Office Building, just down the hall from Senator Wiley's. They despaired at the ringing phone, the four thousand unopened letters, and a line of prospective employees waiting in the hallway. Over the next two days, they quickly organized a staff, ordered supplies, and answered the most pressing messages. Proxmire hired Andrew Rice, then working for Henry Reuss, to run his office in Washington, and Robert Lewis, editor of the National Farmers Union newspaper, as his administrative assistant. Proxmire also hired University of Wisconsin political science professor Ralph Huitt as an advisor, adding further to an already talented staff. Just before returning to Madison on Sunday, Proxmire appeared on a live ABC television program, *Open Hearing*, discussing farm problems, foreign policy, and other subjects. Realizing they would not make it from the studio to the airport in time to catch their flight, the Proxmires gratefully took advantage of their senatorial privileges and received a police escort. The plane was already loaded, however, so the two newest celebrities in Washington good-naturedly climbed in through the baggage compartment. When the Proxmires' plane landed in Madison, they found more than one thousand supporters waiting for them. After finding their children, they began making their way back to their Blooming Grove house to find that friends had prepared a reception to welcome them back. Someone had tacked a sign on the back door that perfectly summed up Proxmire's career to this point: "The glory is not in never failing, but in rising every time you fall."[33]

Although he had voted on only four bills during his first few days in the Senate, Proxmire demonstrated his willingness to take politically dangerous stands. On an *Open Hearing* program broadcast just before he left Washington, he called for the resignation of Secretary of Agriculture Benson, noting that his own election was a sign that farmers had repudiated Benson's policies. Benson denied this, probably correctly, but his office was clearly alarmed by the new senator. Farm discontent had been a factor in the election, but it was not a specific repudiation of Benson himself. When Proxmire sent the vacationing Eisenhower a telegram urging him to replace Benson, the president refused. "The president asked me to continue and I have consented to do so indefinitely," Benson told reporters after meeting Eisenhower in Newport, Rhode Island. The feud became more heated when Proxmire reported that a special assistant to Benson, Bert Tollefson, had telephoned Proxmire's office and warned Robert Lewis to "take it easy" on Benson, or else Wisconsin Republicans would launch a smear campaign against Proxmire in 1958, reminding Catholic and Lutheran voters that Proxmire was divorced. Tollefson denied the threat, calling the report "a gross distortion"; Benson, too, quickly tried to assure Proxmire that no one in his department would make such a threat, but Proxmire remained convinced that it was a deliberate plan to silence an administration critic.[34]

Proxmire refused to back down on his criticism of Benson's farm policy. When the *New York Times* published an editorial asserting that most economists agreed with Benson's policies, Proxmire fired back that his policies had reduced farm prices by 14 percent and lowered farm income by nearly 25 percent. Although beneficial to large-scale producers, Proxmire argued, Benson's policies were destroying family farms.[35] In December, Benson announced further cuts to dairy price supports, and Proxmire immediately responded with plans to introduce legislation to maintain them at then-current levels. Throughout the rest of Eisenhower's administration, Proxmire remained one of Benson's most trenchant critics, especially after being assigned a seat on the Senate Agriculture Committee, as the Agriculture Secretary's popularity among Midwestern Republicans dwindled.[36]

Proxmire's criticism of Benson could be dismissed as simple partisanship rather than political independence, but the senator also took pains to distance himself from organized labor and from the leadership of the Democratic Party itself. On September 26, Proxmire addressed the Wisconsin CIO convention in La Crosse. Rather than praising the importance of organized labor, he promised that he would not be beholden to any special interest group. "I was not the candidate of top leaders or [of] organized labor before the primary or after the primary and I am not their candidate now," he told the delegates. "I will take no dictation, no instructions, no discipline on the part of labor leaders." He made it clear that his role was to represent all the people of Wisconsin, not just those necessary for his reelection. For labor leaders who had vigorously—if somewhat reluctantly—supported his candidacy, this was a slap in the face.[37] He also continued to cause problems for the Democratic Party. At the party convention in October, he supported Patrick J. Lucey, a Madison real estate broker and key figure in his senatorial campaign, against Philleo Nash as state chairman. Proxmire's independence, as evidenced by the Robert Sucher incident, irritated Nash, who had hoped to scuttle Proxmire's candidacy and only half-heartedly supported him when it became clear that Reuss would not run. Many Democrats were opposed to Nash's reelection, but Proxmire's active support of Lucey resulted in charges of bossism and claims that the new senator was trying to seize control of the party and form his own personal machine. It was not true, of course, and Lucey's subsequent successes in building party strength and winning elections as party chair from 1957 to 1963 proved Proxmire's judgment correct.[38]

Proxmire was not afraid of the Eisenhower administration, organized labor, or even his own party, but he did worry about public opinion. He had promised economy and independence, and to show his commitment, he announced that he would not accept gifts or favors of any kind from anyone who might have an interest in legislation before Congress. Reporters quickly pounced on his trip to West Germany. When questioned about his "junket," he replied testily that it was "filled with legislative purpose" and was being paid for by the West German government anyway. Nonetheless, Proxmire smarted at the insinuation that he was personally profiting from his position. He decided that he would travel alone to save money, and just before he departed, he announced that he would pay for the trip himself rather than accept money from a foreign government. He traveled tourist class with a small suitcase, briefcase, and dictating machine, and managed to cut the cost of his trip nearly in half. It was certainly an education. He marveled at West Germany's rapid recovery from the war and was especially impressed by the massive factories in Dusseldorf and Cologne, as well as the Autobahn. He inspected schools and interviewed educators about vocational training, and even went to a movie "to get the feel of the populace." He toured a printing factory at Bad Gotesburg—after arriving at six a.m. to shake hands with the workers—and questioned people about their opinions on American foreign policy. On a side trip to Poland, he was struck by the "dismal failure" of communism. Banners on the walls of the factory that he toured denounced "American imperialist plotters," but Proxmire found that Polish workers admired and respected Americans, despite the Polish government's alliance with the Soviet Union.[39]

Proxmire returned to the United States in late November. Ellen had made preparations to relocate the family to Washington, and so the two of them packed as much as they could into their 1956 Chevrolet and drove to their rented house in Bethesda to settle in for a few days before the four children flew in to join them just before Christmas. In January, the girls started a new school and Proxmire began a new session in the Senate.[40]

The 1958 congressional session began in January and lasted until August, and it was quickly evident to the Proxmire family that a senator's life was not all victory celebrations and European trips. Since he had to run for reelection, Proxmire soon began regular weekend trips to Wisconsin, by Ellen's count spending 156 days away from Washington. Yet he never missed a roll-call vote. This diligence came at a cost. To maintain his presence in Wisconsin and attend to duties in Washington, Proxmire usually took a midnight flight from Milwaukee on Sunday nights and arrived in Washington several hours before dawn. Rather than drive the ten miles to their home in Bethesda for a few hours of sleep, Proxmire slept on his office couch in order to be at work early Monday morning. The government reimbursed only three trips, leaving the Proxmires to pay for the rest. The return to almost constant activity disconcerted Ellen, who was disappointed that there were few opportunities for the whole family to be together.[41] The stressful home life took a tragic turn in early July. Proxmire announced Ellen's pregnancy in early January, and the baby was due at the end of June. While he was working in his office or on the floor of the Senate, and when he was in Wisconsin for the weekend, Ellen managed the household and took care of the children while she was pregnant. William Wayne Proxmire was born on July 3, weighing only four pounds, twelve ounces, and died the next day. The death deeply saddened his parents and the siblings, who had been looking forward to having a new member of the family.[42]

Proxmire's first few months in the Senate were disappointing and downright dull for a reform-minded, energetic man. He came to Washington armed with a legislative agenda that included, among other liberal issues, increasing social security payments and tax reform. Senatorial tradition at first scuttled his ambition: a freshman senator had little chance of pushing any kind of program when he was expected to sit quietly. At first, Proxmire played by the rules and was seen rather than heard. He sat in the presiding officer's chair—a tedious job doled out to less senior members—longer than any other senator and sixteen times as long as the nominal president, Richard Nixon. He slowly began to draw attention to himself in the "morning hour" when senators introduced bills or inserted material into the *Congressional Record*, and he waited patiently to be invited to participate in debate by other senators. He worked diligently in committee, challenging Postmaster General Arthur Summerfield on a proposed increase in postage rates to five cents that would increase small business costs. He later introduced an amendment limiting the rate discounts offered to large-circulation publications. Proxmire cosponsored civil rights legislation and a public works program with fellow Democrats

but remained a minor figure in the Senate. He did not give his first formal speech until the Easter recess, and then only two senators heard him:
Frank Church, who was presiding; and Paul Douglas, who arranged to
be present so Proxmire would not have to address an empty chamber.
Frustrated with the expectations that new senators should remain silent
and defer to their party leaders, Proxmire began to speak more and more
in debate. His staff soon began to receive gentle warnings that their boss
was becoming too presumptuous. Older senators presiding over the debate
tried to discipline the young upstart by refusing to recognize him as he
stood by his desk waiting to speak. What was the point of being a senator
if he couldn't participate in floor debate, which he regarded as the heart
of representative government?[43]

Proxmire finally abandoned all pretense of passivity in late May, when
he announced that he would challenge a major cornerstone of American
foreign policy. In 1951, Congress passed the Mutual Security Act, which
created the Mutual Security Administration to distribute foreign aid for-
merly handled by the Mutual Defense Assistance Act (MSA) of 1949 (military aid) and the Economic Cooperation Act of 1948 (nonmilitary aid). The
MSA was to provide assistance to those nations threatened by communism
as part of the larger foreign policy of containment. In May 1958, the House
of Representatives passed a $3 billion bill to fund the MSA, and Proxmire
used the Senate bill to make a statement about US foreign policy as well
as challenge the deferential role he was expected to take by offering four
amendments from the floor. Proxmire's proposed amendments reduced
the funding by $339 million from the total amount approved by the Senate
Foreign Relations Committee. He also offered amendments to ban foreign
aid to dictatorial governments, specifically Saudi Arabia, Yugoslavia, and
the Dominican Republic. In offering amendments from the floor, he was
questioning the judgment of his most senior colleagues, but he was also
challenging the basic thrust of US foreign policy in place since the beginning of the Cold War. "It is time for the Senate," he lectured his colleagues,
"to act on the basis of principle rather than expediency." American money
should be used to promote democracy, he argued, not just prop up dic-
tators who chose to ally themselves with the United States. He criticized
General Rafael Trujillo's government in the Dominican Republic and said
that Saudi Arabia was "the most ruthless and vicious dictatorship probably

on the face of the earth." Instead, the Senate should ask four questions before approving any foreign aid funds: "Does it really bulwark the free world substantially; does it encourage individual freedom; will it in the long run promote peace; are we assured it will not entrench tyranny?" The Senate rejected all amendments, with even some of the most liberal senators unwilling to question the pragmatic need to support foreign allies.[44]

For the rest of the summer, Proxmire continued to, in the words of advisor Ralph Huitt, "talk when he pleased on whatever subject he chose." He criticized Milton Eisenhower, younger brother of the president and president of Johns Hopkins University, for using a military plane to fly him from his vacation in northern Wisconsin to Washington, "mooching" at taxpayers' expense.[45] In early June, Proxmire proposed a bill to cut tax depletion allowances for producers of oil and natural gas—a tax break (from 27.5% to 15%) to help pay for new oil exploration, which he argued would raise $500 million in revenue. Lyndon Johnson tried to prevent Proxmire from introducing the bill and ordered the Senate floor cleared to prevent a quorum. Proxmire demanded a roll call, and his amendment received thirty-one votes. His effrontery infuriated Johnson. On July 18, Proxmire announced on the floor that he intended "to rise every day, from now until social security improvement is adopted" to plead for increased payments, and did so for twenty-seven consecutive days.[46] In August, he lectured the Senate on tax issues and proposed a plan that would reduce taxes on individuals and small businesses while increasing expenditures on social security and education, all paid for by closing tax loopholes on capital gains, gambling expenses, and corporate dividends.[47] He even threatened filibuster at the very end of the session over a bill to allow Chicago to increase its diversion of Lake Michigan water for its sewage system. The chief backer of the bill was the liberal Democratic senator from Illinois Paul Douglas, and it had the support of the Senate leadership. In a rush of last-minute legislation, Proxmire refused unanimous consent to consider the bill immediately, delaying it for a day. On the final day of the session, August 23, Proxmire held the floor from nine p.m. (his desk stacked with material for him to read in a filibuster) until midnight, when the bill was tabled. Defying Senate custom, the first-termer had won.[48]

The Senate session ended at four a.m. on August 24, and the Proxmires immediately drove back to Wisconsin to start campaigning seriously.

Proxmire was favored to win reelection, but he took nothing for granted—
no statewide Democratic candidate had won reelection in Wisconsin since
Governor George W. Peck in 1892, and it was unclear if his triumph in 1957
was the beginning of a Democratic resurgence or just a fluke. This time,
Republicans viewed Proxmire with more respect. Only one Republican
entered the race against him: former state Supreme Court justice Roland J.
Steinle, who was endorsed by the party convention in May. A conservative
Republican, Steinle based his campaign on characterizing Proxmire as "the
most dangerous man in the US Senate." Two Democrats challenged Proxmire in the Democratic primary, both former supporters who had axes to
grind. Harry Halloway, Proxmire's Milwaukee campaign manager in 1956,
had made the lavish arrangements for a victory celebration that deeply embarrassed the candidate when he lost to Thomson. Proxmire subsequently
refused to pay for the unauthorized expenses. Halloway claimed that he
was running in order to challenge Proxmire's attempted bossism of the
party, angry over Proxmire's support of Patrick Lucey as state chairman
and Vel Philips as national committeewoman. Proxmire warned his staff
to ignore Halloway when possible or to refuse to answer any charges he
might make in the campaign. The second opponent was Arthur McGurn of
Kenosha, whom Proxmire had refused to hire for his 1957 campaign. Proxmire easily defeated the two candidates in the primary, winning 220,146
votes; Halloway won 20,880, and McGurn won 16,104.[49]

The campaign against Republican nominee Roland Steinle differed
significantly from Proxmire's earlier gubernatorial and senatorial campaigns. In his early races, he had been the challenger and eagerly attacked
his opponents' records at every opportunity. Now he was the incumbent
and focused on appearing senatorial. He blandly remarked that Steinle
was a hard worker and would make a good senator, even though Steinle
ridiculed Proxmire as a hypocrite who sanctimoniously refused token
gifts (like two rolls of aluminum foil from a West Virginia senator) but
accepted large donations from labor unions. The Proxmire campaign was
also significantly more organized and better staffed than his 1957 race
had been. Proxmire's secretary, Nancy Barkla, moved into the Blooming
Grove house to manage Senate correspondence and type press releases,
and Proxmire's status as an incumbent and likely victor made recruiting
volunteers far easier. Ellen managed the campaign and hosted the report-

ers who came to observe, including Marquis Childs, who arrived before dawn and woke Ellen by rummaging around in the kitchen to make coffee. One thing remained the same: Proxmire was always on the move, racing from one end of the state to the other. Days typically began at factory gates and included live radio broadcasts, visits to shopping centers, evening meetings, and interviews with reporters. Seldom home before ten, Proxmire rose every morning by six to start again.[50]

Although he was the heavy favorite to win, Proxmire was vulnerable to one charge: the accusation that he was a big spender. In May, Congressman John Byrnes of Green Bay charged that Proxmire was "the greatest spender in the history of the US Senate." He claimed that the bills Proxmire introduced would have cost $23 billion and driven the national debt over $300 billion. Proxmire quickly defended his record, noting that Byrnes included tax reduction proposals when he talked about increased spending. He also argued that by cutting waste and closing tax loopholes, his proposals would actually save the federal government $9 billion. Nonetheless, President Eisenhower gleefully called Proxmire "billion dollar Bill." When Proxmire proposed to increase spending on Social Security, Byrnes again argued that such spending was essentially a tax hike on working people. The two antagonists met in a debate broadcast on Green Bay television station WBAY on 28 October, each armed with charts and graphs. Even Vice President Nixon, campaigning for Republican candidates, challenged Proxmire's record on spending, stating that if more Democrats like Proxmire were elected to the Senate, "You will be in for a wild spending binge by radical Democrats drunk with visions of votes." Proxmire did not respond to the attack.[51]

Steinle continued to call Proxmire a "spendthrift" in his campaign appearances. In Green Bay on 13 October he charged that Proxmire's proposals would increase taxes and inflation: "Proxmire not only wants to stick the young people of America with the bill for his politically inspired spending program, he also wants to bury them under a mountain of socialistic controls aimed at squelching their freedom of opportunity." In Stevens Point later that month, he charged that Proxmire's proposals would have added $400 a year to individuals' federal income taxes.[52] Until the very end of the campaign, the basic issue was over taxes and spending. In late October, however, anti-Catholic campaign literature endorsing Proxmire began circulating in the state. Proxmire quickly denounced the pamphlets as an "appeal to religious bigotry." Proxmire's repudiation did not satisfy Steinle, who remained bitter about the incident.[53]

The results of the election were spectacular, not just for Proxmire, but for Wisconsin Democrats generally. Proxmire defeated Steinle 682,440 (57%) to 510,398 (43%), an increase in both absolute numbers and in percentage of the total vote from 1957, confirming his popularity among Wisconsin voters. Moreover, in four of the ten congressional districts (the 6th, 7th, 8th, and 10th) Proxmire did better than the Democratic congressional candidate, and in three districts (the 1st, 2nd, and 3rd) he garnered more votes than *both* candidates put together. Voters in rural areas had voted for a Republican representative and a Democratic senator. Only incumbents Lester Johnson, Henry Reuss, and Clement Zablocki outpolled Proxmire in their districts, and then by only a few thousand votes. The election of 1958 was also a major turning point for the Wisconsin Democratic Party, in large part due to Proxmire's energetic campaign. For the first time since 1932, voters elected a Democratic governor, Gaylord Nelson. Democrats also took three other state offices: Philleo Nash, John Reynolds, and Eugene Lamb were elected lieutenant governor, attorney general, and treasurer, respectively. Only the immensely popular Robert Zimmerman survived the Democratic sweep. Democrats also gained twenty-two seats in the Assembly, giving them a majority for the first time since 1933, and three seats in the State Senate. Within six years, the Wisconsin Democratic Party had grown from a small and ineffectual minority to a fully mature governing party. Proxmire had gone from a one-term assemblyman quixotically challenging entrenched political authority to one of the most popular politicians the state had ever produced.

5

A WHITE KNIGHT IN CAMELOT

In January 1959, William and Ellen Proxmire returned to Washington. While Proxmire went to his office to prepare for the next Senate session, Ellen drove to their new house in the Cleveland Park neighborhood in northwestern DC near Rock Creek Park. They had purchased the house on a "flying trip of five days" the month before, now certain of at least six years' residency, four and a half miles from the Capitol. Ellen found the house initially listed for $45,000 and called a friend in a panic because her husband told her they could not afford more than $35,000. On his advice, she successfully offered $37,500, and when she reported her triumph, Proxmire's first concern was whether it had a good shower. The location, close to parks and good schools, was perfect for the children. Ellen registered them in nearby schools and spent the next month unpacking and setting up their new home.[1]

While Ellen worked on getting their home in order, Proxmire began his first full term as a United States senator by challenging two powerful Washington figures: secretary of agriculture Ezra Taft Benson and Senate majority leader Lyndon Johnson. First came Benson, whom Proxmire had frequently criticized in the past. In January, Proxmire pounced on a speech Benson made to the National Council of Farmer Cooperatives, in which Benson had stated that the administration's proposals "were the product of the best thinking of the nation's farmers and farm experts," but that Congress had failed to act on most of those proposals. Benson thereby blamed Congress for the continued decline in farm income, and Proxmire, now a member of the Senate Agriculture Committee, refused to let him get away with it. Would the secretary, Proxmire inquired politely, send him a list of all these proposals and a statement outlining which ones had not passed Congress? Benson complied with Proxmire's request, but not before Proxmire went public with his criticism of the administration's most recent proposals. The Eisenhower administration proposed to abandon the old parity method of maintaining farm prices in favor of a price support system based on market prices, which would result in lower federal price supports. Citing studies by the department's own Agricultural Marketing Service, Proxmire asserted that the changes to farm subsidies recommended by the administration would result in a 10 to 25 percent drop in prices and overproduction of dairy, livestock, and poultry products.[2] After Benson testified before the House and Senate Agriculture committees, claiming that farmers were more prosperous than at any time in history and calling for the elimination of unsustainable levels of federal price supports and the adoption of a policy that emphasized increased consumption of agricultural production, Proxmire zeroed in on dairy price supports. He challenged Benson to approve plans developed by the National Milk Producers' Federation (NMPF) to maintain milk prices even without the long-standing federal guarantee of 90 percent parity. Assistant Secretary Marvin McLain defended the department's record of promoting efficiency in production and marketing dairy products and the success in the distribution of federally purchased dairy products for school lunch, emergency, and foreign aid programs. The long-term solution, he insisted, was expanded consumption, not continued price supports. Refusing to back down, Proxmire issued a press release accusing Benson of deliberately leading dairy farmers on a wild goose chase by encouraging them to develop "self-help" plans to maintain price supports, like the one proposed by the NMPF, while actually opposing those plans in favor of a market-based approach to farm prices.[3]

On one level, Proxmire's attack on Benson and the administration's farm policy was the legitimate concern of a senator from an agricultural state protecting the interests of his constituents. It was an article of Midwestern Democratic faith that it was in the best interests of the nation to maintain agricultural prosperity, and the changes proposed by the administration would indeed have lowered price supports and reduced farm income. Yet there was also a political element. Proxmire had been instrumental in drawing farmers into the Democratic Party and he knew better than to neglect their concerns. If farmers drifted back to the Republicans, it would hurt Democrats' chances in Wisconsin and around the country. Essentially, he was still in campaign mode, publicly fighting with Benson to draw attention to an issue important to Wisconsin farmers. His attack on the administration's farm policy was a direct continuation of his gubernatorial and senatorial campaigns, in which he acted as the champion of small farmers.[4]

That he began his second term challenging Benson surprised no one. His next target, Lyndon Johnson, surprised just about everyone. Over the past several years, Johnson had assumed unprecedented influence over the Democratic caucus and thus the entire Senate. As majority leader, chair of the Democratic conference, chair of the Democratic Policy Committee, and chair of the Democratic Steering Committee, Johnson could dole out committee assignments, office spaces, campaign funds, and special assignments to his supporters. He had an uncanny knack for gathering intelligence about the opinions of his fellow senators, and through friendly persuasion and bullying kept the Democrats in line and maintained the unwieldy coalition of liberal northerners and conservative southerners. Nothing occurred in the Senate without his knowledge and consent; aside from the president himself, he was the most powerful figure in Washington.[5] Proxmire himself had benefited from Johnson's beneficence when the majority leader rewarded the new senator with a trip to West Germany as a representative of the Senate in 1957 and a seat on the agriculture committee in 1958. In fact, when Gaylord Nelson criticized Johnson as too soft on key issues like civil rights to merit the unquestioning support of northern liberals, Proxmire leaped to his defense: "I think Lyndon Johnson has been an excellent party leader. He has been fair to everybody." Other liberals, including Wayne Morse, Paul Douglas, and Hubert Humphrey, likewise fell into line rather than risk their political futures by challenging Johnson's mastery of the Senate.[6]

As long as the Senate remained closely divided and a Republican remained vice president, Democrats acquiesced to Johnson's control for the sake of party unity. As a result of the 1958 elections, however, the Senate was now controlled by Democrats 64 to 34, and some northern liberals began to privately question Johnson's dictatorial control and the dominance of conservative southerners. The first whiff of Proxmire's rebellion occurred on February 2, when he announced that he would oppose the appointments of J. W. Fulbright as chair of the Foreign Relations Committee and A. Willis Robertson as chair of the Banking and Currency Committee because he feared a "high concentration of committee power in Southern members." At a time when "southern" was virtually equivalent to "conservative," Proxmire's actions suggested that a northern revolt was brewing. Joseph Clark of Pennsylvania wanted more liberals to sit on the Democratic policy and steering committees, and Patrick McNamara of Michigan wanted more frequent caucuses. Liberal frustration climaxed at the party caucus in January. Expecting to discuss issues, senators instead listened to a lengthy Johnson speech—already released to the press—that was full of clichés and largely for public consumption. Then Hubert Humphrey discussed his recent trip to the Soviet Union and his conversation with Nikita Khrushchev; Johnson gave no opportunity for senators to discuss their legislative program. What was the point of being a senator, Proxmire wondered, if they were simply supposed to do as Johnson said?[7]

Proxmire began his public criticism of Johnson after receiving private encouragement from Wayne Morse and Joseph Clark, and he fired the first shot from a Madison television station on February 15, following Paul Douglas's advice to take a potentially controversial stand at home rather than in Washington. On television, Proxmire asserted that Johnson's power over committee assignments and the legislative schedule led to "obsequious bowing and scraping senators" who followed orders so as not to risk losing their positions. "Initiative and responsibility appear to begin and end with the majority leader," he continued. "There is no place for senators outside his inner circle. We get no real report from the leadership and we don't even have an elementary knowledge of when his power is to be used and why." Such influence, he argued, made it impossible to pass the kind of legislation desired by northern liberals. Many senators shared these views, Proxmire asserted, but were unwilling to say so publicly, fearing reprisals from party leadership. Johnson refused to comment, but a Johnson supporter tried to dismiss the accusation as mere grousing, noting that Proxmire himself had benefited from Johnson's control of committee assignments and that the Democratic committee on committees had never overruled his decisions. Moreover, Johnson had indeed used his powers in the service of liberal goals, pushing through a civil rights bill in 1957 and proposing limiting senators' ability to filibuster. Johnson supporters dismissed this sudden protest as nothing more than sour grapes caused by Proxmire's disappointment at not getting a seat on the finance committee.[8]

After this opening salvo, Proxmire took his fight to the floor of the Senate. Monday, February 23, began with the annual reading of Washington's Farewell Address in honor of his birthday, a tradition that dated back to the nineteenth century. Few senators were actually present on the floor when the morning hour ended and Proxmire rose to speak—Johnson himself was at home in Texas recovering from a bad cold—"to protest the disintegration of the rights for all Senators in my party regardless of seniority or official position to take part in determining the most important decisions made in the US Senate."[9] Proxmire complained that the party caucuses of 1958 and 1959 had not been real caucuses but merely opportunities for Johnson to read a speech with no discussion of legislative strategy. He demanded that Senate Democratic leadership consult more with rank-and-file senators. "There has never been a time," he insisted, "when power has been so sharply concentrated as it is today in the Senate. The typical Democratic senator has literally nothing to do with determining the legislative program and policies of the party." Recalling Robert La Follette's criticism of the 1909 Republican caucus and citing Woodrow Wilson's *Constitutional Government* on the importance of party caucuses, Proxmire announced his intention to demand changes in how the Senate was run.[10]

He had distributed copies of his speech an hour before he read it on the floor but was disappointed by the lack of support he received. No one else was willing to join him on the barricades. Richard Neuberger, senator from Oregon and a loyal Johnson supporter, immediately demanded to know when Proxmire had reached this conclusion: "Unless my memory fails me the Senator from Wisconsin . . . before he was elected to a six-year term, probably buttered up the majority leader more than any other senator," Neuberger remarked. Proxmire suddenly found himself on the defensive and in the unusual position of being cross-examined by a fellow senator, who, warned by Proxmire's own release, had at hand nearly every public statement Proxmire had made about Johnson in the past two years. Proxmire bristled at the phrase "buttered up" and insisted that he had praised Johnson when he thought he was right, which was most of the time. Mike Mansfield then pounced on Proxmire. Had he ever asked for a party conference? Had Proxmire spoken up at the last caucus meeting when Johnson asked for questions? Proxmire had to admit that he had not. Neuberger's and Mansfield's questioning made Proxmire appear to have turned on Johnson either from petulance over being denied a choice committee seat or simple grandstanding. Undeterred, Proxmire vowed to continue to speak on the issue until Johnson gave rank-and-file Democrats more say in party matters.[11]

Proxmire did succeed in gaining national recognition on this important issue, but the support he expected from his Senate colleagues was slow in coming. Over the next few days, a few senators cautiously came to Proxmire's defense. Wayne Morse and Joseph Clark agreed that the party caucus should play a greater role in determining which bills should be introduced but stopped short of actually criticizing Johnson's leadership. Paul Douglas likewise refused to openly criticize Johnson but noted that Proxmire's suggestions might be worth some consideration, provided he avoided personal attacks. Other senators denounced Proxmire, including J. William Fulbright, who said Proxmire's performance came "with very poor grace and very little justification."[12] Most believed Proxmire's revolt would result in nothing except the end of his own career as he suddenly found himself on the outs with Senate leaders. *New York Times* columnist Arthur Krok compared Proxmire to the young Giocante Casabianca, standing "on the burning deck whence all but he had fled." Even though some senators might nod quietly in approval, they would not join Proxmire in open "unclubby" revolt against a majority leader who had been so good to so many of them. As one senator joked, "There were two farewell addresses yesterday—Washington's and Proxmire's."[13]

Yet Proxmire would not give up. Appearing on *Meet the Press* on March 1, he complained that Johnson had failed to pursue the party policies on federal aid to education, increased income tax exemptions, and unemployment compensation. His "one man" rule in the Senate thus prevented the majority party from carrying out the platform on which it had been elected. Johnson had no comment, but assistant majority leader Mike Mansfield testily asserted that any Democratic senator could ask Johnson for a caucus at any time. Senator Robert Kerr of Oklahoma was even more blunt: Proxmire's charges were "intemperate, unjustified and uncalled for."[14] Proxmire renewed his criticism of Johnson on the floor of the Senate on March 9, this time with Johnson present. Proxmire began by praising Johnson's political leadership ("a brilliantly instinctive performance by a man who has been called an authentic political genius") but demanded regular party meetings to make the majority leader more responsive to party members. Mansfield demanded to know why Proxmire had not attended meetings of the policy committee, open to all Democratic senators, if he did not know his party's position on pending legislation. Only Paul Douglas tepidly supported Proxmire's demands, predicting that the party's domination by senators from southern states, who often opposed civil rights or labor legislation, was endangering Democratic chances of capturing the White House in 1960. Johnson sat silently throughout the three-hour debate, but other senators defended Johnson's leadership and success in explaining Democratic positions to the general public and denied any "steamrolling" from his office. Once again Proxmire found himself on the defensive as Mansfield interrogated him.[15]

The public response to Proxmire's stance buoyed his courage. His office staff quickly found itself overwhelmed answering telephone calls, responding to mail from all over the country as well as from Wisconsin, and mimeographing lengthy press releases. Proxmire claimed that the flood of correspondence ran thirty to one in his favor. "Please accept my most sincere and hearty congratulations," wrote Leslie Bechtel from Port Wing in Bayfield County. "I cannot understand a liberal democratic majority meekly accepting such absolutism." Most correspondents critical of his position accused him of political grandstanding. "You are just a publicity seeking cheap lying politician—in other words a damned liar," ran one letter from Greensboro, North Carolina. Proxmire's staff sent a thank-you letter to each person who wrote in support of his position. Those who criticized his position received a polite response assuring them that the senator respected their views but could not agree.[16]

The attack on Johnson's "one-man rule" took a farcical turn a few days later on March 12, when senators gathered in the Senate Reception Room for an unveiling of portraits of the five greatest senators, which included Robert M. La Follette Sr. Proxmire and Alexander Wiley joined the La Follette family to hear remarks by John F. Kennedy, who chaired the committee that selected the five, and Vice President Richard Nixon.

Afterward Johnson circulated among the guests and managed to pose for photographers with each of the states' delegations. Yet when Proxmire later used the photograph of himself and Wiley standing in front of the portrait of La Follette with La Follette's daughter Fola in his monthly newsletter to constituents, he cut Johnson out of the picture. All that remained of the majority leader was an ear. Editorial cartoonists embraced the event. Jim Berryman of the *Washington Star* depicted Proxmire wielding a pair of scissors while Johnson lurked behind him, warning, "I'm afraid it's not that easy to get rid of me!" Proxmire defended his actions by insisting that the Texan did not belong in the Wisconsin gathering, but Johnson was furious and called the alteration "petty, cruel, and unfair."[17]

Slowly, additional senators began to join Proxmire in questioning Johnson's actions as majority leader. On March 19, Richard Neuberger called for a revision to the Senate seniority system, although he was careful to note his disagreement with Proxmire's criticism of Johnson's rule. The problem, he suggested, lay not in how the majority leader managed the Senate but in the practice of awarding committees by seniority; instead, committees should reflect geographic diversity and chairs should be elected by a secret ballot. Not until early April did another senator fully embrace Proxmire's demands to limit Johnson's authority. Agreeing with his colleague, Pat McNamara blamed a "serious breakdown in the majority's responsibility to the Senate" for a failure to increase unemployment benefits backed by northern liberals. A few days, later Joseph Clark stated that he also had written to Johnson, blaming him for the defeat of increased unemployment benefits. Faced with this growing revolt—famed editorial cartoonist Herbert Block depicted Johnson bemoaning to House Speaker Sam Rayburn that "Some of those Non-Texans are Getting Downright Unfriendly"—Johnson finally entered the debate on April 6. In a speech to the Texas Legislature, he deviated from his prepared speech to assert that "no one man speaks for the Democratic party in this nation."[18]

Johnson's full response to Proxmire's charges came on May 28. During debate on an appropriation bill for the District of Columbia, Albert Gore of Tennessee proposed an amendment and Johnson tried to convince him to offer the amendment in committee rather than on the floor, where it could be more efficiently discussed. Johnson lost his temper over Gore's disobedience and lashed out at Proxmire and other critics:

It is obvious that there is wide divergence of opinion in the Senate. The senator from Illinois is not in agreement with the senator from Tennessee. What power have I to bring those two strong men into agreement by waving a wand? The senator from Wisconsin thinks I might be able to do it; but I have been here long enough to know that no senator can be told what to do.

When Proxmire suggested that this disagreement was exactly why they needed more frequent party caucuses, Johnson exploded. "This one-man-rule stuff is a myth," he ranted. "This theory that one man is able to tell sixty-four other senators how they shall vote does not exist." Looking straight at Proxmire, Johnson suggested that Proxmire's charges stemmed from his own failure as a senator—what he really wanted was "a fairy godmother" to deliver majorities for his projects and when he couldn't get his way "he put the blame on leadership." Proxmire insisted that Johnson's testy remarks indicated that he knew most Democrats really wanted more frequent party conferences, but recognized the futility of trying to get Johnson to change his methods by a public assault. Senator Richard Russell later told Proxmire that his efforts against Johnson had reminded him of a bull that had charged a locomotive: "That was the bravest bull I ever saw, but I can't say much for his judgment."[19]

After halting his attacks on Johnson for the rest of the summer, Proxmire renewed his call for changes to the Senate Democratic leadership in November. The impetus for his renewed challenge to Johnson's leadership was the growing dissatisfaction of northern liberals frustrated by the limited results of the current session. In October, Americans for Democratic Action (ADA), the liberal advocacy group founded in 1947, had released evaluations of senators based on thirteen key issues that had come up that session. According to the report, Johnson voted the liberal position only 53 percent of the time. Proxmire, along with fourteen other senators (John A. Carroll, Joseph Clark, Paul Douglas, Philip Hart, Thomas Hennings, Hubert Humphrey, John F. Kennedy, Eugene McCarthy, Pat McNamara, Warren Magnuson, Wayne Morse, Edmund Muskie, Richard Neuberger, and Stuart Symington) received a 100 percent rating. The report validated not only Proxmire's place among the most liberal members of the Senate, but also his criticisms, since ADA called the session itself a failure and blamed

Johnson's leadership. A few weeks later, speaking at a Madison labor banquet, Proxmire acknowledged that Johnson had "overcome his regional limitations to a remarkable degree" but still conferred mainly with committee chairs who were overwhelmingly southern and conservative. "He is still a southerner," Proxmire said, and northern liberals were "on the outside looking in."[20]

By waving the bloody shirt, Proxmire did indeed voice the growing worry among northern liberals that a southern Democratic presidential candidate could not represent the true leanings of the party. Yet he remained unwilling to risk a split in the party that would guarantee the election of a Republican, vowing that he "would willingly and strenuously support Lyndon Johnson for the Presidency if he is nominated," but, Proxmire added, "He is not my first choice."[21] Three other senators looking for the Democratic presidential nomination—John F. Kennedy, Hubert Humphrey, and Stuart Symington—had much stronger claims on Proxmire's support. The interparty rift continued for the rest of the year and came to include the two dominant national party figures: Harry Truman and Eleanor Roosevelt. At a fund-raising dinner in New York on December 7, the two clashed over the criticisms raised by northern liberals such as Proxmire. When Truman chastised "self-appointed guardians of liberal thinking," the audience knew he was referring to Proxmire, Morse, and other liberal senators. Roosevelt leaped to their defense: "I know we want unity but, above everything else, I want a party that will fight for the things that we know to be right at home and abroad."[22] Not until January 1960 did Johnson move to placate his liberal critics by offering to hold party conferences when any senator requested, though retaining for himself the power to appoint members to the party's policy committee. Heartened by encouragement from other northern liberals, Proxmire promised to work for curbs on the majority leader's power even if it took ten years.[23]

Although his public criticism of Johnson and Agriculture Secretary Benson brought him recognition and some stature among liberals, the young senator was still in campaign mode, and his actions left him vulnerable to criticism and charges of hypocrisy. On March 15, the *Milwaukee Journal* published an editorial titled "Abuse of the Base," criticizing Proxmire's large staff and charging that the senator used the payroll system to provide "a small income to worthy supporters without exacting from them any real work of value to the Congress or the nation." Newspapers around the state reported that in 1958, Proxmire had one of the largest staffs of any member of Congress: eighty-three in the second half of 1958 with a payroll of $30,638. Angry constituents wrote letters demanding an explanation—how could the senator who made such a public show of economy require such a large staff? After consulting with the financial clerk of the Senate to verify the precise size of his payroll, Proxmire defended his staff. Most of it consisted of part-time employees, some hired for only a few weeks to work on specific projects. Many others were college students or interns. But by May, the total number of staffers working in the Washington office was down to seventeen, one of the smallest in the Senate. Proxmire had done nothing wrong but was angry that he had been caught off guard.[24] The controversy was especially troublesome because Proxmire had voluntarily disclosed his payroll, one of only a few senators who did not keep their staff and payroll information confidential. Expecting praise for openness, he instead met with unexpected criticism and was especially stung by the fact that *Milwaukee Journal* reporters were invited to see the Milwaukee office in action but never actually saw the kind of work that was done for constituents in that city. In fact, Proxmire's office was desperately understaffed, especially since he was determined to keep in touch with his constituents. On one afternoon as his staff mimeographed and collated one of his press releases, Proxmire gamely trotted out to bring back coffee.[25] The Johnson affair overwhelmed his staff since, as Ellen recalled, "Controversy not only breeds conversation, it means a lot of extra work. Office mail became astoundingly heavy, phonecalls were incessant, interviews with newsmen from all over the country piled on top of each other, and much midnight oil was burned tying up loose ends." Ellen herself became vital to the Proxmire office, spending several days a week there, answering letters (usually the most difficult ones, "real dogs" as she called them) and working on the newsletter. When visitors from Wisconsin appeared in the office, Ellen graciously chatted with them for a few minutes if her husband was unavailable.[26]

Despite her years of political experience, Ellen was particularly struck by some of the contradictory expectations of senators:

If you turn out as much mail as your office staff can possibly produce, constituents and newspapers sometimes complain about the use of the franking privilege; if you are late in answering a letter, you unquestionably hear about your inefficiency. If you entertained all the people who came to see you from your home state you could do nothing else; but if you don't happen to be around when a certain group comes by, you're not being hospitable, and obviously have ceased to care about the folks back home.[27]

In response to these pressures, the Proxmires developed a system to accommodate visitors while allowing Proxmire to diligently attend to his duties as senator. Visitors to the office signed a guestbook; if the senator was able to meet with them personally—even just a brief greeting—a staff member placed a check mark next to their name. Those he had not seen personally received a note from him expressing his regrets for having missed them while on the floor or in a meeting. Once, this system backfired when two reporters met Proxmire briefly in his office before Ellen escorted them to the Senate gallery and a tour of the Capitol. For some reason, their names were not checked, and they received a letter from Proxmire apologizing for having missed them. The confusion fueled a stinging editorial complaining about Proxmire's superficial and incompetent office.[28]

On the floor of the Senate in 1959, Proxmire was a fairly conventional and reliably liberal voice on national issues. In May, he joined with Joseph Clark, Paul Douglas, and Eugene McCarthy to introduce several tax bills that would end deductions used by corporations and introduce a withholding system for interest and dividend income, which they estimated would raise an additional $2.5 billion in revenue. These proposals made little headway in the Senate, in part because they lacked the support of the Senate leadership. Proxmire also cosponsored "fair trade" legislation to benefit small businesses by allowing manufacturers to set minimum prices and fine those stores that sold for less. This was a growing concern for Proxmire, who saw small, locally owned businesses outcompeted by large retail chains that could undercut prices. In a letter to the *New York Times* in July, he expressed concern over changes in retail grocery stores: "There are fewer retail food firms in business today than there were in 1939, although population has greatly increased. The trend of concentration in the retail food business indicates that in the foreseeable future the distribution of food at retail in this country may be controlled by a half-dozen giant chain organizations."[29] He also defended regional interests. In August, Proxmire and Alexander Wiley led the opposition to a bill that would allow the city of Chicago to divert more water from Lake Michigan to aid sewage disposal. On September 1, he launched a seven-hour speech against the bill, not as a filibuster but as an educational effort to convince senators that it would lower levels in the Great Lakes and threaten the lake shipping of other states. His effort succeeded: the Senate voted to refer the bill to the Foreign Relations Committee, effectively killing it.[30]

Proxmire worried that such efforts to protect his state's interests might make him seem provincial and narrow, so he took every opportunity to demonstrate his interest in national issues before a wider audience. In addition to his frequent trips to Wisconsin, Proxmire also traveled extensively to address various organizations on political and economic topics, up to thirty times a year. For instance, in June he traveled to New York to deliver the commencement address at Yeshiva University, while in August he spoke at a convention in Oberlin, Ohio, on "Change and Crisis in Rural America." He would accept just about any invitation to speak to any organization, provided the engagement did not conflict with a roll-call vote. This often resulted in last-minute dashes to the airport to catch the last flight to get him to his destination at the last possible moment. The moment he finished speaking, he had to rush to catch a flight to return to Washington. Occasionally these plans went awry. One last-minute trip to Providence in the spring of 1960 was foiled when weather diverted his plane to Hartford. Unable to make his engagement, Proxmire was forced to take a train back to Washington. He "arrived home at 5:00 a.m., heavy-bearded and cross, undelivered speech still in his breast pocket." During another mad rush to the airport, a desperate Proxmire pulled up to a policeman on Constitution Avenue. "I'm Senator Bill Proxmire of Wisconsin," he announced to the officer, hoping for an escort. "I'm in a hurry to catch a plane. Could you help me get to the airport." Unimpressed, the officer gave directions, and Ellen drove off with her chastened husband.[31]

Proxmire collected modest fees for his speeches, but the constant travel took a heavy toll on his office and household budgets. His Senate salary was $22,500, and he received reimbursement for three trips to Wisconsin (one

at the rate of twenty cents per mile and two at the actual cost). Proxmire
returned to Wisconsin nearly every weekend and paid for the trips out of
his own pocket. In addition, his office regularly overran allocations for
long-distance telephone calls, telegrams, postage, stationery, and other office supplies. Determined to keep in touch with his constituents, Proxmire
paid the overruns himself, despite the drain on the family's finances.[32]

Proxmire's enhanced status as an outspoken member of the party's
liberal wing proved important during the 1960 presidential primary, in
which Wisconsin played a key role. By early 1959, it was clear that the
Wisconsin presidential primary—the second in the nation—would be a
showdown between Kennedy and Humphrey, both of whom needed to
win the state to further their campaigns. Kennedy needed to show that he
could win outside the northeast, and Humphrey could not afford to lose a
neighboring Midwestern state. Sensing the opportunity to gain stature by
backing a winning candidate early, Wisconsin Democrats began to choose
sides, much to Gaylord Nelson's despair: "The candidates may not mind
making Wisconsin a bloody battle ground," he growled in June, "but that
doesn't mean we have to submit to it." Instead, Nelson remained neutral—
privately favoring Humphrey or Adlai Stevenson and fearing that a dead-
locked convention might pave the way for a Johnson nomination—and
vowed to "referee" the primary to keep it fair.[33] Like Nelson, Proxmire
remained officially neutral, but his popularity among voters meant that
both Kennedy and Humphrey sought his support, or at the very least tried
to emulate his positions. In April 1959, Kennedy appeared in Milwaukee
as part of a three-day tour of the state testing the waters for a presidential
bid. When asked about Proxmire's criticism of Johnson, he was cautiously
supportive, asserting that Proxmire had not made a *personal* attack on
Johnson but merely stressed the need for maximum possible discussion,
a point with which Kennedy, he assured reporters, agreed. A few months
later, when Humphrey spoke in the state in June, he began by attacking
Secretary of Agriculture Ezra Taft Benson, using some of the same language that Proxmire had been using for years. Both Kennedy and Humphrey had learned from Proxmire what worked with Wisconsin voters.[34]

It was unclear what role Proxmire would play in the campaign. Desperate to avoid a divisive primary in Wisconsin, Nelson even suggested that
Proxmire seek the nomination himself as a "favorite son" candidate, dis-

couraging Kennedy and Humphrey from running in the state and allowing Wisconsin's delegation to the Democratic National Convention to remain uncommitted. Proxmire confirmed that he was seriously considering the option, but privately he favored Kennedy. In August, Proxmire furthered Kennedy's campaign by releasing a poll he had conducted of Wisconsin voters as to whom they supported for the Democratic nomination; two thousand voters responded to Proxmire's questionnaire and favored Kennedy over Humphrey 42.5 percent to 17.3 percent. Humphrey refused to believe Proxmire's poll and refused to be scared off by a potential Proxmire candidacy, a possibility that lingered at the November state convention.[35]

In the early months of 1960, all eyes were on Wisconsin after Kennedy formally announced his candidacy in January. By then, Humphrey had announced plans to enter the Wisconsin primary, but Kennedy did not commit to it until January 21. Both Nelson and Proxmire reiterated their neutrality, Proxmire telling reporters that he had "great regard for both men," but indicating that he himself would run if Humphrey were the only candidate. He denied that he was secretly a stalking horse for Kennedy: "I would run with the idea of taking to the convention a delegation that would size up the situation and push from the beginning in a unified way for a candidate who best reflects the views of Wisconsin and who could be nominated." Once Kennedy announced his intention to be on the April 5 ballot, Proxmire finally laid to rest his own candidacy.[36] The press continued to associate him with Kennedy, however, and Proxmire continued to insist he was neutral. When former Proxmire staffer Jerry Bruno issued a letter calling on Proxmire supporters to vote for Kennedy, Proxmire angrily repudiated any attempt to associate his name with the senator's.[37] The contest grew bitter closer to Election Day. When polls showed Kennedy ahead, Humphrey attacked Kennedy's voting record on farm issues, arguing that Kennedy's position was almost the same as Nixon's. This drew a sharp rebuke from Proxmire, who called Humphrey's comments "deplorable." Proxmire later qualified his criticism of Humphrey by acknowledging his right to comment on his opponent's voting record, but argued that it was too simple a comparison.[38]

The divisiveness and negativity disturbed Proxmire. He had long argued that contested primaries benefited the party, but the lack of uniformity across the nation concerned him because a few early victories by a well-financed candidate could undermine the will of a majority of voters. That is, a candidate who won a few early victories might force other candidates to drop out, even if most voters in states with later primaries might have preferred someone else. Moreover, the disruptive nature of the Wisconsin primary brought calls to do away with primaries altogether and substitute new ways of choosing delegates to the convention. Proxmire took the opportunity presented by the Wisconsin primary battle—one of only fourteen in 1960—to argue for electoral reforms. He defended a presidential primary over other ways of selecting delegates, but rather than leaving a party's nomination to a patchwork of different requirements over fifty states, he proposed a national primary in August with limits on campaign expenditures and full disclosure of all contributions and expenditures, all based on his own experiences in Wisconsin.[39] On April 5, in a record turnout, Kennedy defeated Humphrey by a decisive margin, 476,024–366,753. Humphrey won four congressional districts in the more agricultural western and southern part of the state, three of which bordered Minnesota. Kennedy did overwhelmingly better in the eastern congressional districts, far more urban and industrial, and with a large population of Catholics. The tumultuous primary delivered 20½ delegate votes to Kennedy and 10½ to Humphrey.[40]

In the midst of the contention surrounding the Wisconsin presidential primary, the Proxmire family suffered a major blow with the death of Theodore Proxmire, the beloved "Grand Popsey," on December 16, 1959. Ellen received the telephone call early in the morning and immediately burst into tears. She adored her father-in-law, and the seventy-eight-year-old physician had been a major source of support for his family. Very successful in his practice and in his investments, the elder Proxmire had paid for his son's education and had funded his early political campaigns as well as his farm implement and printing ventures. Even after Proxmire was elected senator, his father was a source of financial support, paying for his trip to Germany when Proxmire received criticism for traveling abroad at public expense. Dealing with the estate kept Proxmire and his sister, Adele, busy for much of the winter. The Proxmires selected some personal items from the house, including an oil portrait of himself and his brother and the family Bible, and other household goods that would be of practical use, including an air-conditioner for the humid Washington summers. Adele received the property in Desbarats, their summer home in Canada, and Proxmire received the house in Lake Forest. Between property, life insurance policies, and investments, Proxmire inherited some $300,000. His prime objectives, he wrote George Maurer, the estate's executor, was to provide for the education of his children and have a source of economic security for his family. With careful investment in stocks and treasury bills, Proxmire's estate did just that, paying for a combined total of sixty-four years of education for his and Ellen's children. Unwilling to see anyone else living in the house he grew up in, Proxmire sold the building to the neighboring Presbyterian Church, for less than its assessed value of $41,000. The congregation razed the building to expand its parking lot. Later, worrying about an apparent conflict of interest, Proxmire sold almost all of his stocks and converted the inheritance into US securities.[41]

In his years in the Senate, Proxmire prided himself on such scrupulous honesty and tried to avoid anything that might be considered remotely unethical. He insisted that other officials should operate on a similar level and challenged those who did not live up to that standard. In January 1960, Proxmire launched another crusade by opposing Eisenhower's nomination of Oshkosh native James Durfee to the US Court of Claims. Durfee had a long record of public service that included acting as Langlade County district attorney and chairing the Wisconsin Public Service Commission before Eisenhower appointed him to the Civil Aeronautics Board (CAB) in 1956. Yet when Eisenhower nominated him in 1959, Proxmire blocked the nomination just before Congress adjourned, claiming the need for a more thorough investigation of a home-state nominee. Eisenhower resubmitted Durfee's name in January 1960, and this time Proxmire did not object to Judiciary Committee hearings, but announced that he would testify against the nomination. At the heart of the matter were three trips paid for by airline corporations that Durfee had made while head of the CAB: Flying Tiger Airlines and Overseas National Airlines paid for a three-day golfing trip to North Carolina in October 1956, Eastern Airlines paid for a four-day trip to Mexico City in September 1957, and Trans-World Airlines paid for a four-day trip to Rome in September 1957. Proxmire saw this as a clear violation of the CAB ethics code, since Durfee had accepted services of substantial value from those businesses he was supposed to be regulating. "On every one of these occasions," Proxmire told the subcommittee after submitting details of these trips, "it is clear that he accepted unusual hospitality and that the hospitality was provided by persons who had a pecuniary interest in the CAB, his agency."[42] Durfee denied any impropriety, noting that two of the trips were celebratory inaugural trips cleared by a House Legislative Oversight Committee and considered part of his official duties. It was a common practice, encouraged by the State Department, for CAB officials to travel on such flights inaugurating new service to foreign destinations. The third was hosted by two competing airlines, which made it impossible for one to later request special consideration. Despite his objections, which Proxmire renewed in March as the nomination moved toward a vote, and a four-hour floor speech opposing him, the Senate approved Durfee, 69–15.[43] In response to the Durfee appointment, Proxmire called for a more rigid ethics law modeled on Wisconsin statutes, forbidding federal employees from accepting anything of value from those under their regulatory responsibility.[44]

Although Proxmire never let up on Durfee, he did acknowledge when his accusations of ethical lapses turned out to be unfounded. In June, he issued a press release charging that an $89,400 government contract for furniture for the US embassy in Venezuela had been improperly awarded to a Michigan firm headed by the son of Commerce Secretary Frederick H. Mueller. He further alleged that Mueller Metal Corporations had received nine contracts from the State Department, none based on competitive bidding. Mueller denied any wrongdoing and sent Proxmire a report documenting the transaction, which he characterized as "proper" and "in the public interest." Faced with the documented transaction, Proxmire had to admit that there had been nothing improper in the sale.[45]

Yet the close connections between business owners and elected officials still irritated him. Any suggestion that officials might use their influence for personal gain struck him as immoral, and he elaborated on this idea when he began criticizing the Federal Communications Commission in the summer of 1960. At issue was the award of a television license to a station in Albany, New York, partly owned by five New York and New Jersey representatives. On June 19, the *Washington Post* reported that FCC policy gave advantages to firms whose stockholders included members of Congress. The next day, Proxmire called this policy "political payola" on the floor of the Senate:

This is morally as wrong as it can be. It sets up a firm pattern for predictable corruption. This means the congressmen who pass on all appropriations including the salaries and expenses of members of the FCC, and who determine every aspect of the basic law under which they are given the charter to operate, can enjoy a special compensation when it comes to handing out these enormously valuable television franchises, worth in some cases millions of dollars.[46]

As it had with the Mueller and Durfee controversies, the *Capital Times* gave Proxmire a great deal of publicity and published editorials supporting his accusations and demanding change. The congressmen in question insisted that they had never put any pressure on the FCC and in fact owned only a small percentage of stock. Proxmire later cited an anonymous source in the FCC who said it was long-settled policy to consider congressional ownership as a positive factor in awarding licenses. Encouraged by the *Capital Times*, Proxmire attempted to turn these alleged ethics violations into a major push for more efficient and honest government. In August, Proxmire introduced a measure to end such favoritism, even though he had no evidence of any kind of influence.[47]

In addition to publicizing cases of graft, Proxmire continued to be a reliable liberal voice in the Senate and a supporter of Wisconsin's interests. In January he cosponsored an election bill that would have ended poll taxes in southern states, and he later voted in favor of a constitutional amendment banning them. During a filibuster against the Civil Rights Act of 1960, Proxmire was one of the few Democrats who appeared at every late-night quorum call and cheerfully bedded down on a cot in the Old Supreme Court Chamber.[48] He steadfastly defended Wisconsin's dairy interests by protesting Eisenhower's move to raise quotas on imported cheese, grumbling that Wisconsin-made Edam and Gouda were superior. He blocked a bill that would have allowed the navy to serve margarine on ships, foiling an effort by southern senators to benefit the cottonseed and soybean oil industries of their own states. In May, he introduced a bill to raise price supports for milk from $3.06 to $3.22 per hundredweight, a measure that eventually passed and was reluctantly signed by President Eisenhower. While these efforts did not grab the headlines like his attacks on Durfee did, they did reinforce his popularity among farmers.[49]

In the weeks leading up to the Democratic National Convention of 1960, Proxmire made it clear that he supported Kennedy and confidently predicted his nomination on the first ballot. He was less confident about Kennedy's election, as he noted in a letter to his aunt: "I don't under-estimate Nixon—he has immense advantages in the press, the power, wealth, and the organization of the Republican Party." Kennedy's chances, he decided, were "a little better than even." At the convention, he met with Wisconsin delegates and urged them to back Kennedy. His support of Kennedy led some Wisconsin Democrats to launch a movement to nominate Proxmire for vice president. The state Democratic convention unanimously endorsed him and some at the national convention paraded with signs that read "Get Off the Rocks with Prox." Proxmire was flattered but insisted he was not a serious contender for the vice presidency.[50] He did not expect Kennedy to select him as his running mate, but he was mo-mentarily stunned when Kennedy tapped Lyndon Johnson, his nemesis from the Senate. Johnson's selection put Proxmire in an awkward position, since he had been so publicly critical of the Texas senator. The Wisconsin delegation, Gaylord Nelson especially, was deeply skeptical of Johnson, fearing that the powerful majority leader would easily dominate Kennedy and push him to more conservative positions. Many northern liberals shared Nelson's views. Surprisingly, Proxmire quickly came to Johnson's support and urged the Wisconsin delegation to back him. He told William Evjue that Johnson might actually be less of an obstacle as vice president than in his current position, and predicted that Hubert Humphrey would replace Johnson as majority leader, enabling the president to get a liberal program through Congress.[51]

Once Congress adjourned in August, Proxmire returned to Wis-consin, leaving Ellen in Washington with the children as he launched a three-month campaign tour through the state. Ellen herself headed up the Women Speakers' Bureau for the Kennedy campaign, wrangling con-gressional wives to speak to audiences when the highly sought after Ken-nedy sisters were unavailable. Although not up for reelection himself, Proxmire traveled to every corner of the state on behalf of Kennedy and the state ticket, headed by Nelson. He also crossed into Michigan, Illinois, and Minnesota to campaign for Senators McNamara, Douglas, and Hum-phrey. He spoke in glowing terms about how a Kennedy administration would raise farm prices and help small businesses, and he linked Nixon to Agriculture Secretary Benson in an effort to get farmers to vote Democrat. When Kennedy himself came to Wisconsin, Proxmire traveled with him from Madison to Milwaukee, Green Bay, and La Crosse.[52] Despite Proxmire's strenuous efforts on behalf of the Kennedy campaign, Nixon carried Wisconsin narrowly: 895,175 to 830,805. Most disappointingly, the farm vote that had been so crucial to Proxmire's past victories almost completely abandoned the Democrats. Kennedy carried only seven primarily rural counties in the western part of the state by small margins. Reliably Democratic Dane County gave him a 3,800-vote margin out of a total of more than 90,000 votes cast. Only Milwaukee went for Kennedy in a big way, giving him a 70,000-vote lead over Nixon. Proxmire had become a popular figure around the state, but he did not have the coattails to ensure a Kennedy victory.[53]

Given Proxmire's strenuous campaigning on behalf of Kennedy in 1960 and their personal friendship from the Senate, the new president might have seen Proxmire as a key supporter of administration policies. Proxmire, however, continued to be stubbornly independent and proved to be one of the administration's early critics, much to the annoyance of other Democrats. The first conflict occurred over Kennedy's nomination of Lyndon Johnson's protégé John B. Connally as Secretary of the Navy. Connally was also coexecutor of legendary Texas oilman Sid Richardson's estate. Proxmire, along with Oregon senator Wayne Morse, announced his opposition to the nomination because Connally's oil industry connections were a conflict of interest, since the Secretary of the Navy had control over the nation's naval oil reserves. When Connally's nomination came to the floor, however, Morse and other liberal Democrats acquiesced to the president's choice, leaving Proxmire the lone dissenting voice, despite vigorous lobbying by Robert Kennedy just before Proxmire delivered his speech against the nomination.[54] At the heart of Proxmire's concern over these nominees was the influence of the oil industry in Kennedy's administration and the conflict of interest that presented. In late March, he was the sole dissenter in the Senate's confirmation of John M. Kelly, an oil producer from New Mexico, as assistant secretary of the interior because he planned to retain his holdings while dealing with other energy companies as a government official. In his newsletter Proxmire cited both Connally and Kelly as evidence that the "oil interests" had achieved "enormous power" over the government's oil policies. He later called oil the administration's "Achilles heel," noting that Kennedy's tax program contained no reduction in the oil depletion allowance, what he called "the most notorious loophole in the federal tax system."[55]

Proxmire's biggest fight, however, was against the nomination of Houston oil executive Lawrence J. O'Connor to the Federal Power Commission (FPC). Testifying before the Senate Commerce Committee, Proxmire grew melodramatic in his opposition. Appointing O'Connor to the FPC, Proxmire told the committee, would be like appointing Mickey Mantle to umpire Yankee games. "It is about as fair as a fourth strike . . . about as ethical as brass knuckles." When O'Connor easily won committee approval, Proxmire vowed to fight the nomination on the floor and launched a marathon speech against it. He began his speech just before eleven on the morning of August 7, quietly speaking to an almost empty chamber from notes on his desk next to a chart that showed rising natural gas prices and listed O'Connor as a stockholder in twenty-nine energy companies. He spoke for nine hours before the Senate adjourned, and he resumed speaking the next morning, giving examples of how energy companies used their influence to vastly reduce their tax liabilities by using lax regulation by the FPC to extort high rate hikes for consumers. He insisted that this was not at attempt to filibuster the nomination but rather a sincere effort to change senators' minds. Proxmire stuck to his topic, a veritable dissertation on industry regulation, and avoided the usual tactic of reading from unrelated sources, but he finally gave up on the third day after holding the floor for nearly thirty-three hours with only brief respites as the Senate conducted other business. The Senate promptly approved the nomination 83–12.[56] Proxmire's criticism of the appointment of officials connected to the oil industry resumed in September when Kennedy nominated another Texas oil executive, Jerome J. O'Brien, as the director of the Interior Department's Office of Oil and Gas. An otherwise fine administration, he complained, had been "blackened by oil influence." Kennedy, he said, "owes the country an explanation for this latest in a string of appointments which wholly ignore the consumer and give the petroleum industry a stranglehold on US government policy affecting oil and gas."[57]

Despite his opposition to some of Kennedy's appointments, Proxmire supported much of Kennedy's domestic program. The most pressing issue was the recession that had begun in the spring of 1960. Encouraged by Walter Heller, chair of the Council of Economic Advisors, Kennedy favored using government fiscal policy to encourage economic growth, especially since he had called for a minimum annual 5 percent economic growth to provide for the rapidly growing population. In a special message to Congress, Kennedy asked for an extension of unemployment benefits, area redevelopment, increased minimum wage, housing and community development programs, and tax incentives for investment. Congress considered most of this legislation in the early spring. In March, Proxmire voted in favor of a nearly $400 million aid program to chronically depressed areas (a program first proposed by Paul Douglas in 1955) and for a bill extending unemployment benefits. Proxmire later supported a bill providing $2.55 billion in aid to public schools and another $8 billion housing bill.[58]

Kennedy, however, faced much greater criticism over his tax program. Prior to his inauguration, a task force headed by MIT economist Paul Samuelson had recommended to the new president increased government spending and temporary tax cuts as a way of stimulating the economy. Kennedy himself viewed Keynesian economics with some skepticism, but Proxmire responded to the administration's increasing emphasis on deficit spending with horror. When Walter Heller testified before the Joint Economic Committee, to which Proxmire had just been appointed, Proxmire argued that Congress would not accept planned deficit spending, and when the committee issued its report in April, Proxmire authored a critical dissenting report that opposed the administration's plans to cut taxes while increasing spending. If the federal government were to run deficits of 4 percent of GDP, as it did in the 1930s, the result would be a $20 billion deficit per year with only minimal improvement in unemployment. Such a plan had no chance in Congress, especially since Kennedy also called for increased defense spending that he deemed vital for national security.[59] Economists thought Proxmire's rejection of Keynesian principles outdated. University of Wisconsin economics professor Robert Ozanne compared Proxmire's economic views to those of Herbert Hoover, much to the senator's irritation. In the *New York Times*, famed Harvard economist Alvin Hansen criticized Proxmire's assessment of deficit spending in the 1930s and pointing out that the economic situation in 1961 was nowhere near as dire and required proportionately smaller deficits. Proxmire responded that reliance on fiscal policy to provide economic solutions was overly simplistic and ignored political and social realities of peak industrial production.[60]

Proxmire's criticism of deficit spending was part of a broader critique of government spending, and he found many proposals to criticize. In July, after Congress passed a $46 billion defense bill, Proxmire criticized unnecessary defense spending in a newsletter to constituents: "It is understandable that some congressmen, with aircraft plants in their districts and unemployment running higher, might seek to raise appropriations for bombers. . . . But the result is that taxpayers across the nation pay for this bit of localism as the bombers quickly become obsolete."[61] On the floor, he attempted to cut $525 million from a defense bill to pay for bombers deemed unnecessary by Secretary of Defense McNamara. He also criticized the appropriation for three new aircraft carriers costing $245 million each in an age when missiles were the most advanced military technology available. When the House and Senate Appropriations Committees routinely added money to requests made by the administration, Proxmire attempted in vain to remove them, including $60 million from an appropriations bill to fund NASA and other federal agencies and $297 million from a bill to fund the National Institutes of Health. The times were too perilous, he said, "to heap more spending on top of that thought necessary by the administration."[62] Alarmed by growing budget deficits potentially as high as $6 billion, Proxmire began targeting projects he derided as "trivial"—an aquarium for Washington, DC, an addition to the Library of Congress, and a pavilion at the 1964 World's Fair—and urged constituents to write to their representatives to vote against them as part of a "loud national taxpayer protest."[63] It was not just spending that worried him. When Kennedy backed away from his pledge to balance the budget, citing the risks of raising taxes before unemployment levels dropped further and the need for increased military spending, Proxmire was the first figure from either party to pounce on the president. He speculated that Kennedy might need to make the unpopular decision of increasing revenues by curtailing deductions for manufacturers. "If we cannot match spending and revenues when the economy has sharply improved . . ." he wondered, "when can we ever expect to?"[64]

Throughout 1962, Proxmire continued to buck the Kennedy administration and his own party over spending, tax policy, and agriculture policy but often found his efforts stymied. When the president asked for increases in defense spending, Proxmire's was one of the few voices in Congress to challenge the need for increased spending, blaming powerful Pentagon lobbyists and Cold War fears of appearing soft on communism as the real cause of escalating expenditures. In June, the Senate twice defeated his efforts to cut $400 from a bill for new bombers and carriers. Proxmire's criticism of Pentagon spending received unexpected support from Dwight Eisenhower, when the former president suggested a cut in defense spending, which he thought reflected "unjustified fears, plus a reluctance in some quarters to relinquish outmoded concepts."[65] Space exploration also struck Proxmire as unnecessarily expensive. Alarmed at the $20 billion plan to reach the moon by 1970, Proxmire challenged the need to spend so much in so short a time. "I do not object to our effort to land men on the moon," he told a House committee. "The significant question is . . . at what rate such a program is carried on and what specific goals are set for it." He recommended NASA present alternative proposals with smaller budgets for Congress's consideration. Yet when he proposed to cut $105 million from a $3.7 billion appropriation for NASA, the Senate rejected his amendment 66–4.[66]

Proxmire grew increasingly critical of the administration's spending when the Senate considered a public works bill that authorized the president to spend up to $1.5 billion on works programs if economic indicators suggested a recession.[67] He also challenged the Kennedy administration on the need for tax cuts to stimulate the economy. Economic conditions were good, and cutting taxes would only add to the budget deficit, he insisted. Lower interest rates would be far more effective in encouraging business investment. This put him at odds with the president, Senate Democrats, and the growing liberal economic orthodoxy. Of particular concern in the administration's 1962 Revenue Act was a 9 percent tax credit for investment, a "billion-dollar windfall" that businessmen did not actually want. He criticized the entire bill as "a special interest bill, a bill for the gas interests, a bill for expense account tax dodgers, a bill loaded with provisions for single companies." He voted against it, as did fellow liberals Paul Douglas, Albert Gore, and Wayne Morse.[68]

Nowhere was Proxmire's independence more visible—and more irritating to the White House—than in relation to the administration's agriculture policies. In January 1962, the president submitted a new proposal that would force farmers to accept much stricter production limits on surplus products or lose price supports, and for the first time, dairy farmers faced marketing quotas. The president also called on Congress to authorize Agriculture Secretary Orville Freeman to maintain milk price supports at their current level of $3.44/hundredweight until the end of the year; without such authorization, surpluses would force the secretary to reduce milk supports to $3.11/hundredweight by April 1, a stop-gap measure to maintain farm income before his own plan went into effect. At first Proxmire enthusiastically supported Kennedy's call for supporting milk prices at their current level and promised to "make an all-out fight for passage of the resolution." Proxmire did indeed go to bat for the president, appearing before the House Agriculture Committee to argue in favor of maintaining supports and pushing for them in the Senate Agriculture Committee. Despite his efforts, both committees rejected price supports, and Secretary Freeman dropped the maximum price. Proxmire estimated the cost to Wisconsin farmers at $35 million, a major blow to the state's economy.[69]

The Kennedy administration, however, made the mistake of equating Proxmire's support for maintaining milk prices with support for the president's farm bill. After touring Wisconsin communities in February, Proxmire returned to Washington and raised questions about Kennedy's farm plan at a news conference. He reported that farmers objected to the production limits, and the plan did nothing to increase consumption of dairy products or government purchases of surplus milk, though he insisted that he had not yet made up his mind and would wait to hear testimony from Freeman about the implementation of the new plan. When the Senate Agriculture Committee took up the measure in May, Proxmire's opposition to mandatory controls became clear. Freeman expected Proxmire to follow the party and support the president's bill, but without consulting the White House, Proxmire introduced a substitute measure in committee to extend voluntary production quotas and got the measure passed 9–8. One administration official expressed the widespread frustration with Proxmire: "This guy cut us without warning. He's a SOB to pull a trick like that."[70] Despite anger from his own party, Proxmire defended his stand.

Farm experts predicted farmers would reject mandatory controls and thereby lose all price supports. The resulting drop in farm income would produce "a first-class farm depression" and would leave Wisconsin dairy farmers stuck with permanently low milk prices. Despite his criticisms, the Senate passed the administration's bill 42–38, with Proxmire voting against it.[71]

Proxmire also broke with the administration on foreign aid. In a surprise move in June, Proxmire moved to amend a $4.7 billion foreign aid bill to preclude any aid from going to Yugoslavia, as he had done in 1959. Frank Lausche quickly moved to broaden Proxmire's amendment to bar aid to *any* communist nation, and the amendment easily passed. In an attempt to persuade the Senate to reject the amendment, National Security Advisor McGeorge Bundy wrote to Senate majority leader Mike Mansfield that aid to Yugoslavia was necessary to allow the Yugoslav government some ability to resist total control by the Soviet Union. Proxmire's actions sent the White House into a panic. Returning from delivering the commencement address at West Point, Kennedy phoned Senate leaders to discuss ways to undo the damage. An amendment allowing the sale of surplus food to Yugoslavia and other communist nations was quickly written and passed, saving the administration from a major defeat. Proxmire voted against the administration's change but voted for final passage of the bill.[72] Proxmire's move did, however, damage his reputation and brought him criticism from several sources. George F. Kennan, ambassador to Yugoslavia, wrote that limiting the president's ability "to handle intelligently and effectively a delicate problem of international affairs" would only increase Soviet influence over Yugoslavia. Morris Rubin, editor of *The Progressive*, chastised Proxmire for an oversimplified view of foreign relations that failed to recognize the relative independence of Yugoslavia compared to other communist nations and the importance of maintaining good relations.[73]

Why was a senator going to such lengths to oppose a president from his own party? "What has happened to Bill Proxmire?" wrote one baffled reader to the *Capital Times*.

I see by the *Milwaukee Journal* that he and that reactionary, [Frank] Lausche of Ohio, have tied for the most times voting against the Kennedy administration. Wisconsin likes mavericks. I was in the

Progressive movement for 10 years before becoming a Democrat. But we have always loved mavericks, like Old Bob La Follette, who were to the left of the center, not those who, like Proxmire, are to the right.

A *Congressional Quarterly* survey of key administration measures that passed by fewer than five votes showed that Proxmire voted against the president every time—the same record as Republican senator Strom Thurmond. Willard Edward of the *Chicago Tribune* wrote that Proxmire had in four years shifted from a liberal to a moderate conservative, much to the irritation of some of his colleagues. When the Milwaukee County Democratic chair chastised him for not being more supportive of the president, Proxmire snapped back, "I was elected by the people of Wisconsin, not appointed by the president."[74]

University of Wisconsin political scientist and former staffer Ralph Huitt had a different take on Proxmire's role in the Senate. Proxmire, according to Huitt, rejected the traditional path to power, exemplified by Hubert Humphrey, of becoming an "insider" by diligently carrying out mundane tasks, currying favor with those in power, and gaining seniority. Proxmire would have none of it and instead of exhibiting deference to leaders like majority leader Johnson or President Kennedy was willing to take an independent role. He made few friends and suffered the displeasure of those who dispensed patronage, but being an outsider gave him the opportunity to bring up unpopular issues that other senators might shun for fear of breaking Senate collegiality. An energetic outsider could be more useful than a dedicated organization man, Huitt argued, and the Senate needed both. Proxmire himself embraced this role. "I think I'm a more effective Senator adopting my independent attitude than I would be if I were bucking for membership in the 'inner club,'" he wrote Huitt early in 1961. "I am able to speak out vigorously and emphatically for the positions I support whether they happen to correspond with leadership and administration position or not." He predicted that his fight against Navy secretary Connally would "keep him in line."[75]

One of the best examples of Proxmire's "outsider" status was his impromptu investigation of Fort Lewis, Washington, in the winter of 1961–1962. In October 1961, in response to the escalating tensions over Berlin, when the Soviet-backed East German government began constructing the Berlin Wall, the Thirty-Second Infantry Division of the Wisconsin National Guard was called to active duty and reported for training to Fort Lewis, just south of Tacoma. Within a few weeks, soldiers stationed there and their families in Wisconsin began complaining about lack of food, equipment, and clothing and about inadequate facilities. Congressmen Melvin Laird and Alvin O'Konski asked the Pentagon about the situation at Fort Lewis, and O'Konski began a battle of words with Division Commander Major General Hubert Smith, demanding a congressional investigation of the "criminal negligence" of the army's preparation of Fort Lewis to receive the Thirty-Second Division. In an attempt to reassure them, the secretary of the army invited the entire Wisconsin congressional delegation on a tour of the base in December. Refusing to be placated, O'Konski announced he would travel by train on November 21 to see the base for himself. After the trip, O'Konski refused to back down and continued to berate the army.[76]

In the midst of the controversy and political posturing, Proxmire decided to travel to Fort Lewis to see for himself. Arriving after dark and unannounced ("the only way we can have an effective inspection is not to let the brass know that you are coming," he said), Proxmire introduced himself to a startled soldier in the first orderly room he found and asked to sleep in his bunk since the man was on duty for the night. The next two nights he bunked with enlisted men in randomly chosen barracks and ate with them in seven different mess halls. Refusing to be accompanied by any commissioned officers, he toured the base without a schedule, wearing fatigues and riding in an open jeep through pouring rain and slogging through mud to talk to the troops. At a press conference at the Seattle-Tacoma airport at the conclusion of his impromptu inspection, he reported that he had talked to more than a thousand men and found only a few deficiencies in supplies and housing. O'Konski's charge that the Thirty-Second was a "lost division," Proxmire insisted, was an exaggeration. He provided Secretary of the Army Elvis Stahr with seven specific recommendations for improving camp conditions, but most important was the need for better communication with the enlisted men. Overall morale was good, though most men did not understand why they had been mobilized; this lack of explanation was the army's principal failing, and he recommended the army make a greater effort to explain to troops the situation that required them to be called away from their homes and families. By the end of January, Stahr reported that he had acted on Proxmire's recommendations and that camp conditions and supplies had improved.[77]

By early 1963, it was clear that Proxmire preferred to be an independent senator rather than a party man. In some ways, that threatened his political future since the party leadership was reluctant to assign him to important committees if they could not depend on his vote. He requested appointment to the Senate Finance Committee, with appropriations being his second choice, but the party steering committee, dominated by conservative southerners, denied him a seat. Paul Douglas, Joseph Clark, and other northern liberals saw this as punishment for his independence and for his votes on limiting debate, part of the ongoing battle over civil rights. Not until Estes Kefauver died in August did Proxmire finally get a seat on the Senate Appropriations Committee, though he had to give up his seat on the Agriculture Committee to do so.[78]

The Kennedy Administration was not pleased to see Proxmire on such a powerful committee since he had continuously balked at the president's tax program and the administration's spending priorities. Faced with persistent unemployment of 12 percent among young and unskilled workers, President Kennedy proposed tax cuts to spur economic growth. Proxmire doubted the tax cuts would work as an economic stimulus and fretted over the effect they would have on balancing the federal budget. In March he told University of Wisconsin economics professors the president's proposal was a "gimmick" that would "shove the burden on future generations of taxpayers" by increasing the national debt.[79] Proxmire also attempted to block administration budget proposals. He fought vigorously against $5 million for the Glen Eider reclamation project in Kansas ("the most conspicuously wasteful of all government throw-aways"), pointing out that the value of the project was measured in increased agricultural production at a time of general agricultural surplus. The Senate approved it anyway.[80] He opposed a bill to increase Senate salaries from $22,500 to $33,000, attempted to cut $25 million from a program that provided federal aid to airports, and worked to defund Kennedy's National Service Corps after two years. Proxmire also attempted to cut $95 million from the Departments of Labor and Health, Education, and Welfare, but the Senate rejected that amendment as well. His single biggest target was NASA, and in November, he moved to eliminate $90 million from its $5.19 billion appropriation, and the Senate adopted his amendment by one vote, much to the irritation of the White House.[81]

Part of Proxmire's growing independence was caused by Gaylord Nelson, who defeated longtime incumbent Alexander Wiley in 1962. Despite their friendship and good working relationship in the Wisconsin Democratic Party, Proxmire was wary of having a colleague from the same side of the aisle. Both Democrats would try to position themselves on the same issues and appeal to the same constituencies, a problem he rarely had with the conservative Wiley. Moreover, the two had very different personalities: Proxmire was a disciplined hard worker, a loner who seldom socialized with his colleagues, who found him stiff and difficult to relate to; Nelson was approachable and affable, and enjoyed sharing a drink with reporters and staffers. Dinner parties at the Nelsons' became regular events full of freewheeling and good-natured discussion. Proxmire must certainly have been reminded of his own brother as he watched the popular Nelson, and the two at times became just as competitive. When Nelson cosponsored a $500 million transportation bill, Proxmire criticized it as wasteful spending. Proxmire prided himself on physical fitness and to his chagrin found himself outdone by Nelson, who impressed the Senate gym with his ability to do one-armed pushups.[82] Proxmire was also discomfited by the inevitable comparisons of the two. Analyzing the 1963 congressional session, the ADA awarded Nelson a perfect score for voting the liberal position every time. Proxmire received only a 71 percent rating. And while the two agreed on many of Kennedy's proposals, they disagreed on a mass transit program and increased funds for employment training (Nelson favored and Proxmire opposed) and cutting funds for the development loan fund and imposing 2 percent interest on foreign aid loans (Proxmire favored and Nelson opposed). With Nelson in the Senate, Proxmire now looked even less liberal.[83]

In Wisconsin, voters puzzled over Proxmire's positions. As Proxmire bucked the Democratic Kennedy almost as much as he had the Republican Eisenhower and aligned with conservatives on issues of taxation and appropriations, some thought he had taken a decided turn to the right. He described himself as an "eclectic middle-of-the-roader," but some wondered if he was attempting to strike a more conservative position with an eye toward his own reelection in 1964. A visit by Vice President Johnson to Milwaukee seemed to underscore some kind of transformation in Proxmire, who introduced his old nemesis at a $100-a-plate fund-raising dinner in May. "We have differed," he told the audience, "but we have agreed in far more areas than we have disagreed." Unsatisfied with Proxmire's outline of Johnson's liberal accomplishments as majority leader and as vice president, the *Capital Times* editorialized that Proxmire had not only forgotten his insurgency against Johnson, but he had "mutilated his finest hour."[84]

The Johnson introduction occurred at about the same time that Proxmire received some of the most damning criticism of his career over the hiring and eventual firing of Frank J. Campenni. Proxmire hired Campenni full-time even though he was also a full-time graduate student at the University of Wisconsin and began paying him an annual salary of $14,596 in August 1962 before he even moved to Washington. In March 1963, the *Milwaukee Journal* reported that Campenni was on Proxmire's staff while still a university student, and other newspapers picked up the story and started to pester the senator for details. Campenni insisted he was in fact doing full-time work for Proxmire's office, describing his meetings with manufacturers and university officials about getting more defense contracts for Wisconsin and sending in weekly reports. Working full-time while enrolled as a full-time student was a violation of Graduate School policy, and the *Wisconsin State Journal* quickly lambasted Proxmire's "Aid to Education" program, and even the *Capital Times* reported on the apparent contradiction between Proxmire's public stance on economy while paying a full-time student far more than most Wisconsin taxpayers earned. Proxmire defended his employee and insisted his office was getting its money's worth from Campenni. Republicans delighted in depicting the famously stingy Proxmire as a sudden spendthrift. Melvin Laird and other congressmen claimed their offices were being flooded by letters protesting such a salary, and Laird himself claimed that his staff was suddenly disgruntled with *their* salaries.[85]

Finally, on April 22, Proxmire tried to end the controversy by repaying Campenni's salary to the US Treasury and wrote a personal check for $9,007.85, writing the secretary of the treasury "I have decided that Mr. Campenni's salary can only be justified when he joins my staff as Administrative Assistant in mid-June." Moreover, he announced that he would personally pay the next three months of Campenni's salary while he was in Madison, another $3,000. The total he ended up paying was nearly half his own salary as a US senator. "I made a mistake," he told reporters. "I am paying $12,000 for that mistake and it hurts. It hurts to admit the mistake publicly as much as to pay out this money, but it's the right thing to do." Newspapers continued to report on the issue, and Republicans vowed to make Campenni a campaign issue in 1964. Faced with this publicity, Campenni resigned from Proxmire's staff in mid-June before he moved to Washington.[86] The incident upset Ellen. Not only had it cost the family financially, it was profoundly unfair: "He had done nothing unethical or immoral, he had not absconded with public money, but in the light of the recent Congressional disclosures of conflict of interest and even outright bribery, the people seemed in the mood to lump all legislators together— on the lowest shelf of human behavior."[87]

His campaign for reelection did indeed loom large in Proxmire's mind. The 1962 elections in Wisconsin had brought mixed results for Democrats. Governor Gaylord Nelson had won election to the United States Senate, and John Reynolds had taken the governorship. Yet Republicans had retained the offices of secretary of state and state treasurer and reclaimed the office of attorney general, and Republicans controlled both houses of the legislature. Proxmire's reelection was by no means certain, and the Campenni incident had brought him a great deal of negative press. In late 1963, Republican candidates began lining up, with Lieutenant Governor Warren Knowles planning to run for governor, and Sun Prairie farmer and former University of Wisconsin Board of Regents president Wilbur Renk the leading candidate to challenge Proxmire. Proxmire hosted fundraising dinners throughout the spring and summer and began arranging television advertising with Dayton, Johnson & Hacker. He braved the snowy winter with a series of thirty-eight meetings in the rural western and northern part of state in December and January 1964.[88]

In mid-January 1964, Wilbur Renk formally announced his candidacy. Unlike Proxmire's opponent in 1958, Roland Steinle, Renk presented a much more significant challenge. He was a liberal Republican, vocally opposed to the John Birch Society, and frequently at odds with the state party, supporting Eisenhower over Taft in 1952 and Nelson Rockefeller over Goldwater in 1964 and challenging the party-endorsed candidate

Philip Kuehn in the Republican gubernatorial primary in 1962. In his announcement, he characterized himself as a thoughtful moderate and criticized Proxmire as a better campaigner than senator with an inconsistent voting record who had taken "a firm position on both sides of the issue[s]." The same independent voters who had been critical of Proxmire's success in 1957 and 1958 might now turn against the incumbent after the repeated criticism Proxmire had received in state newspapers over the Campenni affair. Proxmire immediately issued a press release praising Renk as a businessman and for his service on the Board of Regents. "He will make the most formidable candidate for Senator the Republican party of Wisconsin could put into the field," Proxmire stated. "He has an excellent chance to win."[89]

Insiders at first gave Renk little chance of victory, based largely on Proxmire's reputation as a tireless campaigner who was already well-known. Columnist Art Buchwald wrote humorously about Proxmire's ability to shake hands with thousands of voters in a variety of situations. Anecdotes began circulating about his frequent campaign appearances. Aldric Revell described an encounter at the Ladish factory in Milwaukee, when one worker encountered Proxmire shaking hands at the gate: "Bill, you shook my hand Sunday at the Packer game. . . . What are you doing? Following me around?" Adding to Proxmire's stature was the publication of his first book, *Can Small Business Survive?*, based on his experience chairing the small business subcommittee. It was a well-reviewed handbook full of practical advice for small business owners and a thoughtful critique of government policy. Behind it all lay the argument that future economic health depended on the success of small businesses. Voters seemed to appreciate Proxmire's honesty and hard work. A detailed survey conducted by Oliver Quayle and Company in July found that Proxmire had a 62 percent favorable rating among voters and led Renk 59 percent to 41 percent.[90]

The survey cautioned against too much early optimism, especially since there was a potential backlash among small-town and suburban voters against Proxmire's support of civil rights. While in the Senate, Proxmire had supported limiting the rule allowing southern senators to filibuster civil rights legislation and participated in the March on Washington led by Martin Luther King Jr. in August 1963. He had also cosponsored a civil rights bill that included banning discrimination in public accommodations; he stated his belief that the majority of people in Wisconsin favored civil rights but worried that he might nonetheless lose votes because of his position. Alabama governor George Wallace's segregationist presidential campaign posed a special problem for Proxmire since Wallace counted on a strong showing in a northern state. Wallace's candidacy in the presidential primary election horrified the senator, who called it "a terrible insult to the state" and vowed that "we want to do everything we can to defeat him." Proxmire refused an invitation to debate Wallace in person. Civil rights was only just beginning to become an issue in Wisconsin, but in a close election, any backlash against a pro–civil rights senator could tip the balance. Wallace got 24 percent of the vote, suggesting that a sizable number of voters in Wisconsin were hostile toward civil rights and might take out their frustration on Proxmire.[91]

Proxmire faced another handicap when the Senate remained in session for most of the summer, giving Renk plenty of time to get a head start campaigning. Renk hoped to stir up dissatisfaction with Proxmire's term as senator. He called Proxmire "the most fantastic political switch-hitter Wisconsin has ever seen" and accused him of changing his position on tax cuts and on a pay raise for members of Congress, both times publicly arguing against them but then voting for them. Renk also adopted some traditional Democratic positions, calling for a 5 percent increase in social security payments and criticizing Proxmire for voting against funds for cancer research. Proxmire was a demagogue rather than an effective senator, Renk told voters, citing the fact that only 6 out of 101 bills introduced by Proxmire had been passed by the Senate. Tied up in the sweltering Washington summer as the Senate remained in session, Proxmire was the unusual underdog in getting his message to voters. Not until late June did his campaign office start sending out questionnaires to local supporters to plan campaign stops at shopping centers and factories. Proxmire easily won his primary fight against two other Democrats, but the results looked ominous. Renk polled 300,258 votes compared to Proxmire's 295,676, making Proxmire one of the few incumbent Democrats who ran behind his likely opponent in a primary. The total Democratic vote was only 333,031, and one candidate, Kenneth Klinkert, garnered about 6 percent of the Democratic vote and was running as an independent in November. Proxmire would have a serious fight on his hands then.[92]

Faced with a candidate whose views were closer to his own, Proxmire strove to appear senatorial. The advertising campaign he developed with Robert Vail of Dayton, Johnson and Hacker emphasized his position on the Senate Appropriations Committee and his efforts to combat spending. He was particularly proud of an article from *Life* that called his ten-hour speech against the Glen Eider dam in Kansas his "most glorious defeat."[93] Paul Douglas spoke eloquently on the floor of the Senate, praising Proxmire for making every one of 618 roll-call votes in the session while spending forty-five weekends in Wisconsin. Yet this diligence now threatened his effort to keep his seat. Congress remained in session into October, when Proxmire desperately wanted to be in Wisconsin campaigning, especially since Renk had been on the campaign trail nearly every day since January. Senate business—Proxmire was leading the fight against a measure introduced by Everett Dirksen to circumvent the Supreme Court ruling requiring equal representation in state legislatures—thwarted negotiations between his campaign manager and Renk's since Proxmire refused to commit to a debate date if he might get called back to Washington. Renk charged Proxmire with trying to avoid talking about his record, though Renk himself was reluctant to face questioning by the press, which Proxmire insisted was vital. Short of funds and prevented from running the kind of campaign that he was best at, Proxmire fretted about his chances of reelection.[94]

Disaster struck on October 15 when the new issue of *Pageant* magazine published the results of a survey of senators and congressmen. The article claimed to be based on two polls, one of members of Congress, and the other on Washington reporters. The Washington Press Corps poll ranked Proxmire the fourth-least-effective senator. The story was written by freelancer William B. Levy, who had pitched the idea to the magazine a year earlier. It was hardly the rigorous survey it purported to be and its results were highly suspect. No senator admitted to responding to the survey, and the president of the National Press Club found that none of its thousand members had taken part. The publisher of *Pageant*, Gerald Bartell, was a Madison Democrat and friend of both Proxmire and *Capital Times* executive Miles McMillin. He had initially been skeptical of the poll but published it anyway after consulting with McMillin; now both believed it to be a hoax. When Bartell tried to access the surveys themselves, the author claimed he had destroyed them to protect the anonymity of those who had responded. Later, when called to testify at a Senate committee, Levy claimed that he had sent survey forms to every member of congress and to 220 Washington reporters and that 25 percent had responded. Editors altered the version of the story to make it appear that the survey had received a far greater response rate and that the article had accurately captured the sentiment of the press corps. Wisconsin newspapers pounced on the story, and the *Wisconsin State Journal* trumpeted on the front page: "Proxmire Fourth Worst Senator, Poll Shows." Proxmire was furious. "Although you refuse to repudiate this poll now," he warned Bartell, "I will continue to press, so long as I live, for the fullest possible investigation of this poll and will seek disclosure publicly of the fraud it is. I will do so whether I win this election or not." Republican Party workers shadowed Proxmire's factory-gate appearances and distributed fliers about the poll. Reporting on the poll as if it were a valid assessment of Proxmire's Senate career boosted Renk's campaign and forced Proxmire to completely retool his message, putting him on the defensive for the first time.[95]

His colleagues leaped to his defense. Nelson issued a press release calling Proxmire the hardest-working man in the Senate and an effective spokesman for Wisconsin on the three great issues that faced Congress: civil rights, nuclear testing, and reapportionment. McMillin—regretting his initial encouragement of Bartell's publication of the *Pageant* article—launched an investigation in the *Capital Times* trying to find any journalist had who responded to the poll. Newspaper ads quoted journalists Lawrence Spivak, Drew Pearson, Jack Anderson, and others calling Proxmire one of the best and most effective senators. Proxmire went on two television stations in Madison to challenge the *Wisconsin State Journal* to produce one reporter who answered the survey and to defend his record in the Senate. On Halloween, President Johnson appeared in Milwaukee and urged voters to reelect Proxmire as a crucial independent voice in Congress: "When we agree I know I'm right, and when we disagree I always take another look."[96]

Despite the hostility toward him by the press, the Campenni scandal, and the *Pageant* story, Proxmire won by 112,000 votes on Election Day with 53 percent of the vote, down sharply from his 1958 victory, and carrying only thirty-one of seventy-two counties, some by only a few hundred votes.

He ran well behind the president, who carried the state by 400,000 votes. Ironically, riding in on Johnson's coattails helped propel him to victory even though he had begun his term highly critical of the former Senate majority leader. His six-year term had been a transformative experience. Proxmire continued to show his mastery at campaigning, soliciting votes almost nonstop while serving in the Senate, but he also began to earn a reputation as a hardworking and thoughtful senator, a reputation that would grow in his next term as he moved up in seniority. Subsequent re-election campaigns would be easier, but he never forgot the importance of staying connected to his constituents.[97]

6

BUILDING A GREAT SOCIETY

William Proxmire returned to Washington in January 1965 after a brief vacation in the Caribbean, but his lingering resentment over the *Pageant* poll and the close election it caused made him rethink his approach to being a United States senator. Perhaps, he thought, being an insurgent had made him ineffective after all, or at the very least threatened to cement in the public mind his reputation as a gadfly, bouncing from one issue to another for the sake of publicity. Proxmire's core political philosophy remained unchanged, but in his new term he made sure his staff kept the press supplied with stories of his accomplishments so that his constituents would never doubt his effectiveness. He also resolved to develop a better reputation among his fellow senators, to be "a more pragmatic senator." "You do learn more about the job—the mechanics," he told a reporter for the *Wisconsin State Journal*. "You learn how to be more effective and efficient, how to get things done."[1] Within months, it appeared that Proxmire had become a team player. A *Congressional Quarterly* review of his votes showed he cast party-line votes 62 percent of the time in 1963 and 1964, but between January and November 1965, he voted with his party 87 percent of the time, sharply higher than the average northern Democrat and surpassed only by Walter Mondale and Daniel Inouye. One Washington insider reported that Proxmire "is not as free-wheeling as he used to be. He is now working through the committees more and he's finding that it pays off." It did indeed, and he accomplished much more in his second full term than he had in his first seven years. More importantly, he established a clear identity for himself as a Midwestern liberal, supporting most aspects of Lyndon Johnson's Great Society programs but promoting efforts to cut government spending, especially on the military. Most important of all, he demonstrated what an effective senator he could be.[2]

President Kennedy's assassination in 1963 brought Vice President Lyndon Johnson, Proxmire's old nemesis, to the White House. Lyndon Johnson's legislative accomplishments and electoral landslide in 1964 guaranteed new Great Society initiatives (including Medicare, Medicaid, federal aid to education, and federal funding for the arts, and the greatest expansion of the welfare state since the 1930s), but it was unclear at first if Proxmire would join other congressional liberals in supporting the president. Indeed, his 1964 voting record showed great reluctance to increasing government spending. Although he did vote for the Economic Opportunity Act in July 1964, he voted against the Revenue Act that cut income taxes by $10 billion in February 1964. Despite Johnson's effort to appease the "economy bloc" in the Senate by capping government expenditures at $100 billion—$2 billion less than the ceiling proposed by President Kennedy just a few months earlier—Proxmire thought the cuts insufficient.[3] "You and I enjoyed the biggest tax cut in history this year," he wrote constituents in June. "Now the other side of the tax-cut coin. Congress must keep spending down or any benefits from the tax cut will go up in the smoke of inflation." In July, he again reminded Wisconsin voters that he voted against the tax cut and highlighted his efforts to trim spending as a more fiscally responsible approach to balancing the budget.[4]

This strategy of helping shape national policy while defending Wisconsin's interests was one of several ways in which Proxmire was able to demonstrate his determination to be an effective senator. As the new session of Congress began in 1965, he suddenly emerged as one of the president's most enthusiastic supporters. Proxmire's January newsletter trumpeted Johnson's "great job" on the economy—no president had ever "jammed the economy screws as tight as LBJ did this time." He also predicted that new education legislation would reduce unemployment and long-term poverty, an idea at the very heart of the Great Society. Throughout the spring and summer, he continued to support the president's initiatives, voting for the Elementary and Secondary Education Act (Wisconsin's share amounted to $21 million), the Higher Education Act, the creation of Medicare and Medicaid, Highway Beautification, and other Great Society legislation.[5] Proxmire himself, despite his reputation for pinching pennies, valued education highly and willingly paid for his five children's education in private schools and college. And while he agreed with the president's emphasis on education, it was possible to spend unwisely. The one Great Society bill he could not bring himself to support was the Appalachian Redevelopment Act, which he saw as simply a $1 billion public works program that would benefit only a small section of the country. Proxmire defended his break with Johnson, and with fellow Wisconsin senator Gaylord Nelson, who supported it, by criticizing the bill for its regional approach to a national problem. He cited Johnson's own statement that poverty was a national problem, and efforts to end it should not be focused on one region. Proxmire would vote for money for education and health care, but this was simply another pork-barrel road construction project.[6] He also supported the administration's civil rights measures, as he had done in 1957 and 1964, cosponsoring the Voting Rights Act of 1965, though he favored an amendment that would have included a ban on poll taxes, offered by Edward Kennedy and rejected by a 49–45 vote. When southern senators attempted to filibuster, he gleefully joined northern liberals in voting to end debate. Proxmire thus acquired a perfect record on civil rights, which stretched back to his first few days in the Senate when he had witnessed Strom Thurmond's filibuster and voted for the Civil Rights Act of 1957.[7]

Proxmire had challenged Johnson's leadership as Senate majority leader, and now Proxmire's support for civil rights pushed him into open conflict with another of the most powerful figures in Washington: Senate minority leader Everett Dirksen of Illinois. Two US Supreme Court rulings, *Baker v. Carr* (1962) and *Reynolds v. Sims* (1964), required that both houses of a state legislature be apportioned among districts of equal population. Chief Justice Earl Warren's decision that established the "one man, one vote" principle alarmed Dirksen, who saw it as an unprecedented intrusion of the federal government on a state's constitutional makeup. Combined with the court's ruling against mandatory school prayer in *Engle v. Vitale*, the court seemed to Dirksen to be actively attacking the values of rural America. Politically, Dirksen hoped reapportionment would give congressional Republicans a cause to rally voters around and push back against the liberalism of the Great Society. Proxmire's assessment was much more straightforward: voters should be represented equally in their government, and the fight against reapportionment was simply a means for Republicans to maintain legislative majorities against the will of the people. Dirksen's first effort occurred in late summer and early fall of 1964, when he attempted to amend a foreign aid bill with a rider that allowed states to delay reapportionment until January 1, 1966. Only a few senators recognized the tactic—the delay would allow congressional elections under existing apportionment, thereby increasing the likelihood of Congress approving a constitutional amendment to overturn the court decisions of 1965. Proxmire, Douglas, and Clark quickly organized an effort to block the rider long enough to draw attention to its effects and turn public opinion against it, a sort of educational filibuster. Proxmire held the floor, yielding occasionally to allow other business to be completed, for two weeks. Proxmire's staff, led by Thomas van der Voort, supplied the senator with reams of material, including earlier court decisions and even debates from the Constitutional Convention. Proxmire's efforts finally succeeded on September 24, when the Senate approved a watered-down version introduced by majority leader Mike Mansfield that merely "urged" delay. The liberals had not only defeated Dirksen's effort to overturn the Supreme Court's decision, they had made it a major public issue, largely due to Proxmire's inexhaustible efforts on the floor.[8]

Now at the beginning of a new congressional session, Dirksen was ready to try again. To circumvent the court's rulings, Dirksen introduced a constitutional amendment, S.J. 2, which would allow one house of a state legislature to be apportioned based on criteria other than population. The Supreme Court, Dirksen argued, should have no authority to dictate to sovereign states the makeup of their legislative bodies. The issue was an irritating one for Democrats, since before the court ruling, many state legislatures skewed heavily toward rural—and therefore often conservative—interests. Moreover, Dirksen seemed to have the votes necessary for Congress to approve the amendment and propose it to the states for ratification. By late May, he claimed seventy certain votes in the Senate, and his staff estimated 294 votes in the House, four more than needed to get the required two-thirds majority. President Johnson, having no constitutional role in proposing amendments, could not veto the measure. The best option to defeat the measure was for Proxmire, Douglas, and Clark to stall it in the Senate Judiciary Subcommittee on constitutional amendments, chaired by Indiana senator Birch Bayh. They were able to persuade Bayh to keep hearings going for nearly three months before the subcommittee finally approved the amendment in late May.[9]

Nonetheless, the delay did allow the liberals to talk publicly about the issue, and Proxmire led the discussion. He debated Idaho representative George Hansen before the District of Columbia Bar Association, and Dirksen himself on television in Pennsylvania. "Regardless of how you slice it," Proxmire told his television audience, "the fact is that the Dirksen amendment is going to result in citizens in one part of the state having less influence in selecting their legislature than citizens living in another part of the state." Urban areas and suburban areas would be underrepresented, even though those regions had much larger populations.[10] The amendment initially failed in the Senate Judiciary Committee, but Johnson intervened when Dirksen threatened to filibuster the president's immigration reform bill. Johnson persuaded Connecticut senator Thomas Dodd to switch his vote when the committee reconsidered the measure, allowing Dirksen's amendment to pass 9–7. Yet by the time the proposed amendment came to the floor of the Senate, liberals had largely won the popular debate. The Senate voted 59–40 in favor of the Dirksen amendment, seven votes short of the necessary two-thirds majority. A subsequent effort by some state legislatures to call a constitutional convention failed in October. A gleeful Proxmire reported this victory as one of his greatest achievements of the session.[11]

In January 1966, Dirksen announced a second attempt to amend the constitution, this time establishing the Committee for Government of the People, an organization to promote the idea. As before, Douglas, Proxmire, and Joseph Tydings of Maryland promised to lead the fight against it. Dirksen's group hired the California-based firm Whitaker and Baxter to generate publicity and sway votes in Congress, an effort Proxmire initially dismissed as a "synthetic public revolt." He grew more cautious, however, when the group opened an office in Washington to lobby for the proposed amendment but refused to disclose the amount of money being spent or who their donors were. Proxmire had been deeply suspicious of lobbying groups since his single term in the state assembly fifteen years earlier and feared that "the slickest, most effective, high-pressure political public relations outfit in the country" would subvert genuine democracy through a carefully orchestrated campaign of misinformation.[12] When

the proposed amendment came to the senate floor on April 13, Proxmire depicted the issue in its simplest terms: whether or not every citizen
should have an equal vote. Dirksen's retort—that "the people should have
something to say about the composition of at least one branch of their
state legislature"—revealed two conflicting interpretations of democratic
government. Did a state's sovereignty preclude the federal government's
dictating the rights of its citizens, as Dirksen argued? Or did the federal
government have an obligation to individual citizens to ensure that they
have equal representation in state government, as Proxmire insisted?
Proxmire's interpretation—shared by most northern liberals—was the
foundation of the civil rights legislation and clearly held sway. Once again,
the Senate fell seven votes short of passing the amendment.[13] Dirksen
vowed to keep up the fight, but Proxmire could not resist crowing a bit in
triumph. This third effort was "the end of the road, the third-strike-and-
out for malapportionment . . . The real winners are the people, not the
special interest who stood to gain by malapportioned, one-man, 10-vote
legislatures."[14]

Having failed to get congressional approval twice, Dirksen turned to
the alternative route of amending the Constitution. If thirty-four states
passed resolutions calling for a constitutional convention, that convention
could propose amendments to the states independently of Congress. If
three-fourths of the states approved, the amendment would be adopted.
By late March 1967, that was a genuine possibility when Colorado, Illinois,
Indiana, and North Dakota applied to Congress for a convention, bring-
ing the total to thirty-two states. Proxmire objected to such action for
two reasons. First, he argued that twenty-six of those thirty-two petitions
were invalid because they had been passed by legislatures that had not yet
complied with the Supreme Court decision. "For Congress to accept such
petitions," he insisted, "would be like permitting all Democrats to have two
votes in a referendum to determine whether or not Democrats should have
two votes."[15] Second, he objected to Congress calling a constitutional convention without setting guidelines. If state delegations voted as a block, the
twenty-six smallest states, representing only 16 percent of the population,
could control the convention. Ratification of any amendment required
approval only from the thirty-eight smallest states, which could be as little
as 40 percent of the population. Proxmire instead proposed that if a con-

stitutional convention were held, each state should be entitled to the same number of delegates as it had in Congress, and each delegate would have one vote. This would be far more democratic and prevent a small minority from altering the constitution against the will of the majority. By the fall of 1967, however, it was largely a moot point. No additional states petitioned for a convention, and Dirksen's death in 1969 removed the prime mover in the battle against fairly apportioned legislatures. Proxmire could legitimately claim a major accomplishment in defending the principle of one person, one vote.[16]

Abstract principles were one thing, but Wisconsin voters expected their senators to protect their interests, which Proxmire focused on in his second term. In January, he proposed a $50,000 appropriation to study the development of a deicing system for the Great Lakes to allow year-round shipping. When his measure was approved by the Senate Public Works Committee in February, Proxmire trumpeted the potential benefit of keeping Great Lakes ports open, predicting millions of dollars of added revenue for the port cities of Superior, Green Bay, Milwaukee, Racine, and Kenosha.[17] Throughout the next few years, Proxmire eagerly joined with other senators from Great Lakes states to protect their states' ports. Their actions ensured that the Defense Department included these ports in competitive bidding for military cargo, prevented tolls from being raised on the St. Lawrence Seaway, and limited subsidies for American ships too large to use the seaway.[18]

Even more vital to Wisconsin was dairy farming, and Proxmire never missed an opportunity to protect the state's major agricultural product. In September 1965, the Senate approved Proxmire's amendment to the farm bill that made major changes to the federal dairy subsidies, moving from a one-price system to a system with separate prices for fluid milk and milk for manufacturing. Offering farmers two levels of subsidies allowed dairy farmers to increase their incomes—as much as several thousand dollars a year—while decreasing the production of lower-priced manufacturing milk. Under the existing system, dairy farmers could increase their income only by producing more milk, which tended to glut markets and drive prices lower. The proposal had been a long time in development. First suggested by William Knox, editor of *Hoard's Dairyman*, in 1961, the measure was approved by the Senate in 1963, but the House of Representatives rejected it. Now, two years later, the House included Proxmire's proposal in its version of the farm bill, but the Senate Agricultural Committee rejected it by a 13–2 vote. Taking his amendment directly to the floor, Proxmire fiercely debated the chief opponent, George Aiken of Vermont, ultimately gaining passage of the amendment by a vote of 57–27. Proxmire called the passage of his amendment, known as the Class I Base Plan, a "break-through," the first substantive change to dairy subsidies since 1937. He predicted that the changes would benefit dairy farmers who could re-duce production and still earn higher prices for their fluid milk. Farmers whose milk was used for manufacturing would also benefit, since lower production would naturally raise the prices they received. Finally, taxpay-ers would benefit since the system would ease overproduction of milk, requiring less federal subsidy money. This was one of the most important pieces of farm legislation in decades.[19]

Proxmire continued to promote Wisconsin dairy interests over the years. In January 1966, he picked a new fight over a $3 million cut to the federal school milk program. He wasted no time in rising on the floor to denounce the cuts, which he predicted would prevent poor schools from participating in the program and would require the federal government to pay to purchase the surplus milk, dehydrate it, and store it. In an un-usual display of self-righteous indignation, he promised to "rise on the floor day after day to hammer into the heads of this government" the foolishness of the cut.[20] He did more than talk. In March, he introduced a bill—cosponsored by sixty-two other senators—to make the milk program permanent and fund it with $110 million for the next fiscal year. On this point, he broke sharply with the Johnson administration, which proposed classifying the school milk program as a welfare program and imposing a needs test, a change that Proxmire predicted would cut the program by 80 percent. Testifying before the Senate Appropriations Committee in April, Proxmire called the cuts "phony economy" because the excess milk would end up in government warehouses rather than in schools. Prox-mire's arguments—as well as the testimony of school officials—proved persuasive, and the Senate rejected the cuts that October, after more than 150 daily speeches.[21] Proxmire clashed with the administration's budget-cutting again the following year, when he and Gaylord Nelson wrote Sec-retary of Defense Robert McNamara, urging him to reinstitute the use of butter on military bases, using a similar argument: using cheaper oil-based margarine was a false economy if the federal government was already spending millions storing dairy products.[22]

The larger problem was, of course, overproduction, which had plagued dairy farmers for decades. The trick was to somehow raise the prices farmers received for milk without increasing consumer cost. One approach to this problem led Proxmire to take up the fight against dairy imports. The National Milk Producers Federation calculated that imported dairy products averaged 884 million pounds between 1961 and 1965; they amounted to about 2.5 billion pounds in 1966 and were predicted to increase even more. That year, Proxmire introduced a bill to permanently limit imports to the 1961–1965 average to improve what he saw as "scandalously" low farm income. The benefit to milk producers and cheese makers was obvious, but Proxmire also defended the import ban as a benefit to consumers: "If you buy and eat cheese, you also pay taxes. You may think that the imported cheese drives your prices down. But, as a taxpayer, in the long run you turn right around and pay—in your federal taxes—the cost of taking an equivalent amount of milk out of production under our price support laws and putting it in storage. Whatever you save in cheese prices, you pay right back in higher taxes."[23] After the import ban failed in 1966, Proxmire introduced it again in 1967. This time, however, dairy farmers were much more vocal in their demand that Congress protect their economic interests. In March, for example, the National Farmers Organization sponsored a "holding action" to protest low milk prices by withholding milk from manufacturers. Proxmire was quick to lend his support, calling farmers "the victim[s] of one of the worst cost-price squeezes in years." Support for the dairy ban grew in the Senate, and Proxmire's bill eventually gained fifty-six cosponsors. The House of Representatives, however, blocked the bill, and limiting dairy imports was left to the discretion of the president. In June, President Johnson signed a proclamation limiting dairy imports, telephoning Proxmire personally from his Texas ranch with the news. Johnson imposed quotas again in 1968, much to the relief of dairy state senators and representatives, but Proxmire continued to urge legislation establishing permanent limits on dairy imports.[24]

The fact that the dairy industry was so important to Wisconsin opened Proxmire up to criticism that in protecting it he was simply engaging in the same kind of pork-barrel legislation he so frequently decried. He was always careful, however, to emphasize the economy of his proposals, which usually made federal milk policy less expensive. Yet beyond the economy there was a genuine concern for the plight of farmers. When challenged by staffer Martin Lobel to defend the government subsidies, Proxmire thought back to his first run for office in 1950. He had traveled to every dairy farm in the district and saw firsthand how hard they worked and how little money they earned—without federal aid, they would be forced out of business. Senators, too, noted the apparent contradiction. Alan Simpson once asked Proxmire how much money his support of dairy farmers had cost. "I have no idea," Proxmire responded. "But it's a critical thing. . . . These are little communities of four hundred or six hundred or eight hundred people." Although he sometimes voted for legislation that reduced the cost of dairy price supports, he had no choice but to support them in principle.[25]

Although he had some success protecting Wisconsin's dairy interests, Proxmire was less successful in securing federal spending in the state in other areas, perhaps because of his problematic relationship with Johnson. One of the most pressing issues was an atomic accelerator for the Midwest University Research Association. Proxmire's interest in the accelerator dated to late 1963, when he met with President Johnson in the White House to plead for funding. Aware of the irony of an avowed budget cutter demanding new spending, Proxmire followed up his meeting with a letter that revealed his conflicted feelings. Noting that his request was "the one and only time I have gone to the White House to ask a President of the United States for anything," he urged Johnson to include an appropriation for the project in the 1965 budget. "I recognize that this will cost some $170 million over the next six or seven years," he wrote, "but I am convinced that this is an excellent investment in the nation's scientific knowledge and its educational excellence."[26]

Once the project was funded, Proxmire was determined to get the accelerator located in Wisconsin, and he lobbied the Atomic Energy Commission (AEC) hard to pick a site like the Badger Ordnance Works near Baraboo. Wisconsin's chief competitors were sites in Texas, California (near the University of California at Berkeley), Washington State, Appalachia, Colorado, and Minnesota. Proxmire's former staffer Ralph Huitt, a professor of political science at the University of Wisconsin, confidentially assured Proxmire that a Wisconsin site was among the best options but that the decision would be essentially political. After the AEC completed its initial study, it named a site near Stoughton as one of six finalists for the $375 million project, much to the delight of Proxmire and University of Wisconsin officials. "It is great news that Stoughton is still in the running," he announced. "It is most essential that the accelerator be located in the Midwest in view of the tragic brain-drain from our area." To secure the Wisconsin site, the state's congressional delegation went to the White House to appeal personally to the president. Proxmire sat next to Johnson and walked him through all the arguments in favor of the Stoughton location. When he finished, Johnson responded, "Bill, now you know how much I'd like to help ya." "That was the trouble," Robert Kastenmeier later recalled. "We did know how much Johnson wanted to help Prox, which was not at all." Personal appeals to the president proved useless, and the AEC ultimately selected Weston, Illinois, for the site, though Proxmire remained hopeful that other federal research projects would be located in Wisconsin.[27]

Proxmire tried again to secure federal research dollars in 1967 when the Food and Drug Administration (FDA) announced plans for a new $16.5 million laboratory. Representative Melvin Laird of Marshfield quickly introduced an amendment to the appropriation stipulating that the laboratory could not be built within fifty miles of Washington, DC. Denied a site on existing federal property in Maryland, FDA officials made clear that the next-best option was a site in Madison. The Senate Appropriations Committee, however, deleted Laird's provision, despite Proxmire's successful efforts to maintain full funding for the site. Outraged that his efforts had been stymied, Laird blamed Proxmire for failing to protect the state's interests. Proxmire defended his actions by noting that his amendment made clear that it would be considerably less expensive to build the laboratory in Madison than in Maryland, and he believed—perhaps naively—that the economy would be sufficient to ensure a Madison location. A House-Senate conference committee restored the Laird language, and the FDA ultimately decided to locate the lab in Madison.[28]

Even more mundane federal appointments caused problems that threatened to divide Wisconsin Democrats and tested Proxmire's ability

to obtain federal patronage. After the death of federal judge Patrick Stone
in January 1963, President Kennedy had appointed David Rabinovitz of
Sheboygan to fill the vacancy in the western district of Wisconsin. Despite Proxmire's enthusiastic support for Rabinovitz, opposition developed because he resided outside of the district and because of his widely
publicized representation of labor unions. As a result, Senators Sam Ervin,
James Eastland, and John McClellan blocked the nomination in the Senate Judiciary Committee, despite Proxmire's strenuous efforts to push
it through before Congress adjourned in October 1964.[29] Following the
1964 elections, Proxmire urged Johnson to appoint John Reynolds, who
had just lost his bid for reelection as governor, bluntly telling the president
that he owed Reynolds the appointment because of Reynolds's loyalty to
the administration and his support for the president's civil rights agenda
against a Wisconsin backlash inspired by George Wallace, implying that
Reynolds's loyalty to the president had cost him his own reelection. Yet
Johnson delayed. A Justice Department spokesman explained the president was waiting to appoint a judge "in the hope Wisconsin's two senators
can resolve their disagreement over who should be selected." The disagreement stemmed from the fact that Nelson recommended either Reynolds
or James Doyle, and Proxmire recommended only Reynolds. Nelson's staff
hotly denied any split between the two senators, but rumors continued to
swirl that Proxmire refused to support Doyle, and that Nelson's support
for Reynolds was only pro forma. Nelson himself wrote Attorney General Nicholas Katzenbach, forwarding a copy to Proxmire, insisting that
both Reynolds and Doyle were qualified and had his support. Nonetheless,
newspapers continued to speculate about the delay and describe a rift between Nelson and Proxmire factions in the state party. Johnson eventually
solved the issue by appointing Doyle to the western district in April and
Reynolds to the eastern district when an anticipated vacancy opened a
few months later. This "peace maneuver" settled the dispute, but it left
lingering distrust between Nelson and Proxmire.[30]

Perhaps Proxmire's most overtly populist effort to effectively represent
the people of Wisconsin was his attempt to preserve major-league baseball
in the state. In October 1964, the new owners of the Milwaukee Braves
announced plans to relocate the team to Atlanta, which had just con-
structed a new stadium in the hope of luring away a professional baseball

or football team. The announcement shocked Wisconsin residents, and Proxmire saw this as the ideal situation in which he could demonstrate his effectiveness as a senator in the 1965 session. In February, he introduced an amendment to a bill placing the major leagues under federal antitrust laws that would require teams to pool all radio and television revenue and divide it equally. Conventional wisdom held that the owners of the Braves hoped to cash in on the lucrative Atlanta television market, and Proxmire's proposal would remove that incentive since each team would receive similar revenue regardless of the size of its media market. He struck a populist note testifying before the antitrust and monopoly subcommittee, stating that the owners had "abdicated their responsibilities to the community which provided an outstanding facility for their team and to the millions of fans who supported the team in Milwaukee." The pooling of revenue would end the practice of "opportunistic" teams relocating to larger media markets.[31] His stand struck a chord with baseball fans as well as voters who still remembered the antimonopoly rhetoric of the progressive movement. Unable to amend the bill in committee, he offered an amendment on the floor of the Senate that summer, even though the Braves had already signed a contract with Atlanta and there was no real hope of retaining them in Milwaukee. The principle of standing with fans against big money was still important: without the pooling of revenue, he told the Senate, the antitrust exemption "would hand a few teams located in rich TV markets an immense advantage. This TV advantage will build a financial imbalance into baseball permitting domination by one or two teams." The purity of baseball fell to wealth as the Senate rejected Proxmire's amendment 62–26.[32]

Proxmire moved easily from populist efforts to global issues, and during the 1960s his views on Vietnam evolved in response to growing evidence that the war was costly and ineffective. It was not surprising that a northern Democrat like Proxmire would support Johnson's Great Society programs and civil rights legislation; what was surprising was his early and enthusiastic support for Johnson's war in Vietnam throughout the mid-sixties. Proxmire had voted for the Gulf of Tonkin Resolution in 1964—only Ernest Gruening of Alaska and Robert Morse of Oregon had opposed it—and he continued to support Johnson's escalation of the war in early 1965. An Associated Press poll of senators released in early

January revealed that he was not alone. Proxmire and thirty other senators favored increased support for the government of South Vietnam and opposed immediate negotiations with North Vietnam. They would favor negotiations only once South Vietnam improved its military position, which at the moment seemed unlikely. "It's a mistake to negotiate when losing," Proxmire told the reporter.[33] In fact, Proxmire stood by his support for the president's retaliatory strikes after a Viet Cong attack on an air base in Pleiku that killed eight Americans: "I support the Administration whole-heartedly. This was a deliberate attack on Americans. We had to reply with force and we did so. The Administration position is the right one." He called Johnson's handling of the war "very proper." Two weeks later he again praised Johnson on the floor of the senate chamber: his policies "offer the best chance, in this enormously complex situation, for an enduring peace." Any negotiations, he argued, would simply reward communist aggression. Moreover, he described the material assistance the United States had provided to the people of South Vietnam: food aid (he reckoned in the millions of tons), medical care and supplies, education, and highway construction. Too much attention paid to American military aid obscured this vital effort in combating communism, as he wrote to his constituents in March: "We have helped make South Viet Nam a healthy, well-fed, prosperous and shining contrast to the pitifully depressed North Viet Nam brand of Communism. The contrast is as sharp as West Berlin and East Berlin. This the communists can't stand." Proxmire continued to emphasize American aid to South Vietnam over the next few months, citing, for example, the educational and economic advances made there in a May speech to the Yale Alumni club in Baltimore.[34] On March 2, after two months of discussion with his advisors, Johnson ordered the beginning of Operation Rolling Thunder, the sustained bombing campaign against North Vietnamese targets. Six days later, 3,500 marines landed at Da Nang. Proxmire continued to defend the president's escalation of the war and even began appearing publicly with Morse to debate it. Their first appearance together was in Portland, Oregon, drawing a crowd of over three thousand. Arguing with the irascible Morse in his own home state was, columnist Alfred Maund joked, "heroism beyond the call of duty."[35]

Wisconsin reporters delighted in the spectacle of one of Joseph

McCarthy's most vocal critics now flying with the hawks. Proxmire's support for the war put him out of step with Wisconsin's other congressional Democrats, particularly Gaylord Nelson and Robert Kastenmeier, and the war quickly turned into a divisive issue among the Wisconsin Democratic Party. The breaking point between the two Wisconsin senators came in May, when Congress debated Johnson's $700 million request to fund the war, a request that Johnson made clear was more about gaining Congress's approval of his policies than about obtaining money. Proxmire voted for the appropriation, defending Johnson's escalation as the best chance to end the war, but Nelson gave an impassioned speech refusing to support its expansion. He, Morse, and Gruening were the only three senators to vote against the administration's request. Even as Johnson increased the number of US troops in South Vietnam to seventy-five thousand that summer, Proxmire continued to support the escalation.[36]

Why did Proxmire so enthusiastically support the war? Wisconsin voters were growing skeptical of his position, as demonstrated when he was confronted by a woman at the State Fair in August who demanded to know how he could claim to be for peace in Vietnam while supporting continued military involvement. The growing antiwar movement in Wisconsin forced him to again defend his position, and he continued to insist that only a strong military presence would compel North Vietnam to negotiate. Proxmire saw only two alternatives: either the United States would convince the leaders of North Vietnam that it was willing to defend South Vietnam and use its air force to destroy military installations in the north, or the United States would hesitate and allow North Vietnam to believe that "the United States doesn't mean to keep its commitment to South Vietnam if it gets much rougher; that America would—if North Vietnam keeps fighting—pull out, give in to Communist aggression because resistance is too costly, too unpopular, too painful."[37] As a veteran of World War II, Proxmire had witnessed the mistakes of appeasement and fully embraced the policy of containment, as advocated by George Kennan and Harry Truman. Many politicians, both liberals and conservatives, failed to view the conflict as a civil war and shared the view that the United States could not afford to defer a vigorous effort to contain aggression. As he contemplated the prospect of more teach-ins against the war, he worried that public debate would serve to encourage North Vietnam. Academics, he warned, "should be fully aware of the remarkable efforts President Johnson has made to secure negotiations."[38]

The spring of 1965 witnessed the beginning of those widespread antiwar teach-ins on university campuses, first at the University of Michigan and then spreading to the University of Wisconsin, Stanford, Harvard, and others. An antiwar protest in Washington drew a crowd of twenty thousand in April. Yet even as the student protests resumed—and increased—in the fall, Proxmire refused to join others—including Johnson—in denouncing the public dissent. Senate majority leader Mike Mansfield, who privately shared his reservations to the president but never challenged him publicly, expressed shock at those burning their draft cards in October and accused them of furnishing propaganda for the North Vietnamese government. While other senators called for new laws to use against antiwar protestors who disrupted military deployment, Proxmire took a much more measured tone. The right of petition, he insisted, must be maintained, but added that if the protesters really wanted peace, they should talk to Hanoi instead. Protests—here he agreed with Johnson—served only to lengthen the war. Nonetheless, he recognized the danger of the administration working too strenuously to silence the opposition.[39]

During 1966, however, Proxmire's views on the war started to change. After the State of the Union message in January, in which Johnson vowed to continue the war while maintaining Great Society programs, Proxmire initially claimed that the president's renewed commitment "will do more to persuade North Vietnam to come to the bargaining table than any action this country has taken in a long time." Nelson was more skeptical, calling for further congressional debate over the scope of the war and declaring escalation a "tragic mistake" a few days later. Proxmire countered Nelson's criticism of escalation with a reiteration of the need to negotiate from a position of strength. It was "obvious we were losing badly before we increased our forces. We aren't winning now but we have stopped losing. If we had tried to negotiate before stepping up our forces it would have been pretty much [a] surrender."[40]

Yet Proxmire didn't want to be seen as a war hawk. He still insisted that the military buildup was necessary to force North Vietnam to the negotiating table, but he did join Nelson and thirteen other senators in urging Johnson to continue the suspension of bombing that had begun in December. Proxmire tempered his call, however, by reserving the right to support the president if he ordered a resumption of bombing. When the president did just that in January, Nelson, as well as congressmen Kastenmeier and Henry Reuss, were quick to criticize the move. Proxmire's response to reporters seeking his views was an unusually terse "no comment."[41] In February, he continued to defend the president's handling of the war, specifically stating that the United States had met almost all of the demands made by the Committee for a Sane Nuclear Policy, which had sponsored a twenty-thousand-person march on Washington the previous November. On the floor of the Senate and in his February newsletter, Proxmire insisted that the Johnson administration and SANE had exactly the same objectives. Peace activists, he insisted, should save their criticism for the North Vietnamese government. SANE's political action director, Sanford Gottlieb, responded incredulously, noting that calling for a cease-fire while increasing the number of troops and resuming bombing was hardly a move toward peace. Yet even then Proxmire continued his defense of the Johnson administration by calling for increased nonmilitary aid for South Vietnam, especially funds for land redistribution, to prevent Vietnamese peasants from supporting the Viet Cong. Johnson had promoted a vast program of economic development (dubbed the "TVA on the Mekong") a few months earlier, but little progress had been made. Proxmire even praised dissenting senators at a Jefferson–Jackson Day dinner in Colorado as a vital part of democratic government in keeping with the Senate's long tradition of advising the president on foreign policy. As Johnson's habit of prevaricating threatened public understanding of the war, such a commitment to full disclosure was a significant break from the president.[42]

Indeed, free and open discussion remained important to Proxmire, and he again teamed up with Wayne Morse to debate the war publicly, this time at Carthage College in Kenosha in March. Echoing Johnson's private political worries, Morse predicted disaster for Democrats in the 1966 elections, and he said he would support Robert Kennedy in the 1968 primary if Johnson did not move to withdraw American troops. Proxmire dismissed a potential primary challenge to the president as ridiculous. "You get 10,000 coffins back and he'll be in serious trouble," Morse retorted. Proxmire insisted that Americans needed to be patient with the

war, and that American involvement would make negotiations with North
Vietnam more likely. He was aware, however, that the audience responded
more warmly to Morse—interrupting him with applause six times—than
to himself.[43] Proxmire acknowledged that the war critics, including Morse
and Nelson, had influenced the administration's actions, a theme he am-
plified in his April newsletter. "I have supported the Administration's
position in Vietnam," he wrote. "I still do." However, he declared that
there had never been a war in which criticism had been incorporated into
national policy, citing the bombing pause, two cease-fires, cooperation
with the United Nations, and efforts to reconvene the Geneva Convention. The difference between Johnson and his critics was "no more than a
hair's breadth." Neither would withdraw from South Vietnam or invade
North Vietnam, and both wanted a negotiated peace as soon as possible.
Proxmire insisted that there was a basic consensus on Vietnam that was
far more significant than the differences between the administration and
the growing peace movement. Accordingly, Proxmire voted in favor of two
supplemental appropriation bills for the war totaling nearly $18 billion
and against Morse's amendment to repeal the Gulf of Tonkin Resolution.[44]

Proxmire became more openly critical of the Johnson administration
in late 1966 and early 1967. When McNamara suggested a program of uni-
versal service to replace the draft, Proxmire quickly attacked the idea, preferring the current system that called up only what the military needed.
After the US bombed Hanoi and Haiphong, Wisconsin congressmen Reuss
and Kastenmeier denounced the decision, and Proxmire offered only a
faint defense, stating that he hoped "the president will confine our bombing to strictly military targets" and avoid civilian casualties. In July, North
Vietnam threatened to execute captured American pilots, and Proxmire
found himself joining war critics Morse, Gruening, Nelson, McGovern,
and others in a statement warning of military reprisals if the pilots were
not treated as prisoners of war. In August, he joined McGovern and Nelson
in calling for a sharp cut to the defense budget.[45] By 1967, the antiwar protests in Wisconsin and across the nation had increased, and Proxmire again
seemed to waffle on his support of the war. He remarked on a television
news program in January that the president's policy was basically right,
but then stated that the United States needed to focus on more than just
the military situation in Vietnam. Winning required serious efforts in land

reform and improvements to sanitation and education, he said, and noted that the United States had only one thousand people working in those areas and four hundred thousand in military service. He also continued to defend the rights of protestors, and joined Nelson in challenging the National Democratic Committee's expulsion of the University of Wisconsin College Democrats for its antiwar position.[46]

The biggest issue eroding Proxmire's support for the war, however, was the sheer cost, which the Johnson administration acknowledged for fiscal year 1967 would be about $22 billion, twice the estimate it had given Congress in January 1966. As the new session of Congress began in January 1967, Proxmire called that underestimation "the blunder of the year" and promised that the Joint Economic Committee would hold hearings to investigate why the administration had misjudged the costs, and whether it deliberately misled Congress. Within a week, Proxmire was publicly questioning the continued bombing of North Vietnam. Reversing his earlier position, he stated that the attacks "have strengthened, not weakened the will of the North Vietnamese people." Stopping the bombing and the search-and-destroy operations, he thought, might lead to a greater opportunity for peace negotiations. In March, he outlined the ways in which the war was hurting the US economy, particularly through the diversion of money from education and antipoverty programs. The blunt fact was that this was the first major war to depress the economy.[47] Despite his shock at the escalating costs of the war, he still stopped short of calling for a withdrawal. In another debate with Wayne Morse in February 1967 in Milwaukee, Proxmire conceded that the United States should halt the bombing of North Vietnam, but insisted that it had to honor its obligations to South Vietnam. He referred to the Southeast Asia Treaty Organization (SEATO) repeatedly to demonstrate the need for the United States to remain committed to containing communism.[48]

While Proxmire fretted over the cost of the war, he was also influenced by his staffers' antiwar arguments. Despite being—as Thomas van der Voort recalled—"dead set against anything that would support any Communist effort," Proxmire was willing to entertain differing views on Vietnam. Student protests had little effect on him, but he did value the opinions of those who worked for him. "It took him a long time to sort through his thoughts on [the war]," Martin Lobel recalled, "because he'd

call us in and we'd sit around in his office and discuss." Proxmire challenged staffers' opinions, and different members loaned him books to
read. Gradually, Proxmire began to see the war as a civil war and wondered
whether any amount of US support could succeed in propping up a series
of unstable and unpopular governments in Saigon.[49] Proxmire grew so
concerned with the costs of war, the economic impact, and the potential
tax increases for Americans that by the summer of 1968, he offered an
amendment to a $9 billion spending bill to cut $268 million earmarked
for bombing sorties in South Vietnam. After a detailed criticism of the
bombing strategy, he remarked, "If we don't set a limit, there's not going
to be anything left of South Vietnam." He also called for a halt to bombing
of North Vietnam. By the time Richard Nixon took office in January 1969,
Proxmire had become an avowed dove and regretted his earlier support
for escalation. After Nixon ordered troops into Laos, he commented on his
vote for the Gulf of Tonkin Resolution to John Finerty: "I made a serious
mistake when I voted for that."[50]

Supporting Johnson's domestic agenda while becoming increasingly
critical of his foreign policy showed Proxmire's eagerness to assert his
independence rather than simply toe the party line. Proxmire wanted to
find one issue that he could embrace as his own to define himself as a national leader. That issue ultimately became unchecked military spending.
Proxmire's concern for federal spending was not new—he had emphasized
the need to limit it in his previous term, and it now became a major part
of his senatorial career. At first it was small things, like a federal subsidy
for helicopter airlines, which amounted to a mere $5 million in fiscal
year1965. Proxmire called the subsidy "the most conspicuous example of
a frill that we have in the entire Federal spending program," and argued
against "a general tax on the 999 people in a thousand who do not use them
so that one person, being among the most affluent in this society, can use
them."[51] This populist rhetoric carried over into criticism of other federal
expenditures. A headline in his August newsletter, for instance, declared,
"The Old Pork Barrel Rolls On." Proxmire's amendment to cut $850 mil-
lion from government projects had just been defeated, but he promised
to continue: "I intend to carry on as long as I remain in the Senate. Right
now it looks mighty discouraging. Nothing is more appealing than the
I'll-vote-for-your-dam-you-vote-for-mine psychology on which Congress

operates." In September, he lamented a $150 million canal in Florida that he was unable to stop since it was backed by the president and both appropriation committees. "I know I'll lose a lot more of these than I'll win," he acknowledged. "But this kind of fight is the only way this waste can be dramatized so that eventually Congressmen will recognize they can't expect to be re-elected by promising to do more for their constituents—no matter how wasteful the project."[52]

When Johnson introduced his budget in January 1966, Proxmire responded that Congress would still need to reduce expenditures: "Congress can and should cut this budget sharply," he said. "The president asks for a $100 million increase in pork barrel public works. In both World War II and the Korean War, these were cut. With a Viet Nam [sic] war, it is time to reduce this spending again." He again targeted what he saw as extravagance to draw attention to spending. In August, he attempted to reduce NASA's budget by 10 percent, but the Senate rejected it by a 65–18 vote. Proxmire then proposed to cut spending on the supersonic transport project (a "jet-set thrill") from $280 million to $80 million; it failed 55–31. He did succeed, however, in eliminating $18 million earmarked for new buildings for the FBI and United States Tax Court in the District of Columbia.[53] Proxmire targeted his most vigorous attack on efforts to enlarge the west front of the Capitol that began when minor structural repairs quietly escalated into a major renovation project. That summer, a special commission that included Dirksen and Speaker John McCormack approved a $34 million extension to provide nearly five acres of additional space for restaurants, offices, and restrooms. Proxmire called it "an insult to the intelligence of Congress." The Capitol already had two restaurants ("notorious money-losers") and tourists could use restrooms in the National Visitors' Center, just three blocks away. Additional office space would simply provide more perks for congressional leaders to use to reward loyalty and were totally unnecessary following the recent extension of the East Front (1958–1962) that had created ninety additional (mostly unused) rooms. Marshalling public indignation at the expense and threat to the historical integrity of the Capitol itself, Proxmire convinced the Senate to reject the extension in favor of a much more restrained restoration study.[54]

Particularly irritating to Proxmire was the continued existence of the Subversive Activities Control Board (SACB), established in 1950 to register communist activity in the United States. By the late 1960s, the board had ceased to have any real function but continued to exist as a source of patronage. This was obvious in 1967 when Johnson appointed Simon F. McHugh, the husband of his former personal secretary, Victoria McCammon, to head the board. The Senate, ignorant of the relationship, quickly approved the nomination with no discussion, but within a few days, Delaware Republican John Williams moved for reconsideration when the *Wall Street Journal* published a story depicting McHugh as the lucky recipient of a government sinecure. Proxmire outdid Williams by introducing a bill to abolish it altogether. The position, Proxmire argued, paid $26,000 for almost no work on a board that had not met in six months. Funding its budget of nearly $300,000 was "a ridiculous extravagance" in the era of rising war costs.[55] In response to this criticism, Everett Dirksen introduced a bill to assign the SACB the duty of conducting hearings and issuing findings when any organization was denounced as subversive. Dirksen was determined to preserve the board because he had engineered two of the current appointments and used it to provide patronage jobs. Proxmire vowed to fight the bill and told reporters he was prepared to speak at length and carry on the debate for days; as a result, Senate leaders withdrew the Dirksen bill.[56] Joined by Robert Kennedy of New York and Edward Kennedy of Massachusetts, Proxmire successfully blocked Dirksen's first effort to attach his proposal to an appropriations bill. Still irritated by the Proxmire-led defeat of his reapportionment effort, Dirksen was determined to preserve the board and introduced the bill again a few days later. Abolishing the board held special significance for Proxmire, who had first been elected to the Senate following the death of Joseph McCarthy, whose scare tactics and wild assertions held sway when Congress created the SACB in the first place, and he urged senators to remember the red scare's threat to free speech: "We know of the black list and the willingness and even the zeal of some to equate dissent with disloyalty and to punish error as though it were high treason." Enraged, Dirksen poked his finger in Proxmire's chest and shouted that he and his fellow liberals would lose. Proxmire continued to hold the floor and speak against the bill, effectively blocking its passage. Majority leader Mike Mansfield managed to negotiate a compromise between Proxmire and Dirksen, and the Senate extended the SACB until June 30, 1969. If the SACB did not hear at least two cases of communist subversion by the end of 1968, the board would automatically die. Proxmire agreed to the compromise, assuming that the Democratic attorney general would let the board die by refusing to refer cases to it by a June 30, 1968, deadline.[57]

Contrary to Proxmire's expectations, however, Attorney General Ramsey Clark reversed his position just days before the deadline, requesting the investigation of seven state communist party officials, thereby extending the SACB indefinitely. The announcement shocked Proxmire as it conjured up the possibility of another red scare, even though "there is nothing that the board can possibly do with these names that contribute one iota to this nation's security." Political insiders quickly connected the dots and concluded that Johnson had persuaded Clark to send the board some cases in order to gain Dirksen's support for the president's nomination of his longtime political ally Abe Fortas to the Supreme Court. When the board met in September to hold the hearings, Proxmire called them "an affront to our wisdom and common sense" and "the first honest day's work put in by the SACB in more than two and a half years."[58] He vowed to strip the board of its funding in the next budget, but the SACB continued until the Senate finally eliminated its funding in 1972, ending a long, bitter fight.[59]

By far the biggest target for Proxmire's cuts was the military budget, which had ballooned by 1967. The surprising defeat of his close friend Paul Douglas, running for his fourth term as senator from Illinois, boosted Proxmire's prominence, since he became chair of the Joint Economic Committee, a "bully pulpit" from which he could preach the virtues of frugality. He immediately began plans for hearings into the $10 billion increase in war spending. Proxmire told White House budget director Charles Schultz that the underestimation was "devastating" and had ruined Congress's chances of pursuing sound economic policy. Had Congress been informed of the increased war costs, he insisted, it could have cut spending on other projects or considered a tax increase to pay for the war. Instead, Johnson requested an increase to the debt ceiling, much to the fury of war critics. As a result of Proxmire's efforts, and those of Thomas B. Curtis of Missouri, the ranking minority member of the Joint Economic Committee, the Defense Department began publishing monthly reports on spending in Vietnam.[60] The immediate impact, however, was negligible. In September, Congress passed a $70 billion defense bill, the largest single appropriation in American history. Within weeks, the Senate also approved $4.6 billion for NASA, rejecting Proxmire's amendment to cut $100 million from its budget, and passed a $4.77 billion public works bill, which Proxmire and only two other senators voted against. Proxmire could preach, but his fellow senators proved hard to convert.[61]

As he watched defense spending increase, Proxmire began to see that the war was a threat to the entire economy, and this brought him into open conflict with the Pentagon. In May 1967, the Joint Economic Committee again held hearings investigating Pentagon spending. The committee learned from comptroller general Elmer Staats that the Defense Supply Agency (DSA) had failed to abide by the Truth in Negotiations Act, a 1962 law prohibiting excessive profits for defense contractors, and frequently awarded contracts without competitive bidding. He also reported widespread misuse of government-owned equipment in contractor-owned facilities, usually contractors using government-owned equipment for nongovernmental purposes. Proxmire characterized the DSA's performance as "incredibly sloppy" and—perhaps mindful of his military witnesses—"a clear dereliction of duty." Summing up the findings of the four days of hearings, Proxmire later wrote in the *Capital Times* that the Pentagon's failure to postaudit contracts led to cost overruns in the billions of dollars.[62]

Proxmire continued his crusade against military spending in 1968 and inevitably earned the enmity of Pentagon officials and defense contractors. In a January press conference in Madison he revealed the names of twenty-three contractors who were wasting "hundreds of millions of dollars a year" through the misuse of federal property. He cited a GAO report, requested by his own committee, that disclosed how the Defense Department failed to enforce its own regulations and allowed contractors to use government equipment for commercial purposes without permission and without paying rent. His list included some major corporations, including Boeing, Sikorsky, Raytheon, the FMC Corporation, and the Universities of Maryland and Chicago. Pentagon officials disputed the charges, and contractors rushed to insist they had done nothing wrong, but Proxmire won the public relations war: according to a *New York Times* article, "The names are being made public to dramatize the needless waste of the taxpayers' money as a result of poor management by the Pentagon, to illustrate in concrete terms how it is being wasted, and to encourage swift improvement in the Pentagon management procedures." It was a dramatic affirmation of former president Eisenhower's famous warning against the "military industrial complex" and lent greater momentum to those who opposed the war. As a result of these findings, Proxmire introduced a bill to place greater restrictions on the private use of government-owned property.[63]

Round two occurred in April, when a subcommittee of the Joint Economic Committee charged the Defense Department with "loose and flagrantly negligent management practices" in awarding defense contracts. The report claimed that over 86 percent of contracts by value were awarded based on negotiation, usually a cost-plus agreement, rather than competitive bidding, resulting in what Proxmire characterized as massive overcharges. It also labeled increasing private use of government-owned equipment a "multibillion-dollar backdoor subsidy." Pentagon officials again disputed the findings and insisted that most contracts were actually competitive, even if the department received only one bid. Proxmire scoffed at the semantic difference between a "competitive negotiated contract" and a "true competitive contract" and challenged defense officials to defend their management at a public hearing. In June, the Defense Department adopted new regulations on contractor use of government equipment, largely based on his committee's recommendations, placing Proxmire in the highly unusual position of praising the Pentagon.[64]

Proxmire's concern for spending moved him ever closer to the antiwar faction in the Senate. In late June, he called for a $268 million cut to a supplemental defense spending bill to fund B-52 bombing missions in South Vietnam. Reiterating a point he had made a year earlier, he remarked that if Congress did not limit the bombing of targets in the south, there would be nothing left of the country to save from communism. He urged the Senate to send a message to the Pentagon "that the blank check days are over."[65] Throughout the autumn of 1968, Proxmire escalated his war of words with the Pentagon over its spending. When the Renegotiation Board, charged with reviewing military contracts to prevent excessive profits, expired in August, Proxmire called for it to be renewed and strengthened, citing $45 billion in defense spending and the fact that the board saved the United States nearly $1 billion between 1953 and 1967, roughly $10 for every $1 in its appropriation. During hearings before his Subcommittee on Government Economy, Proxmire called on the

Government Accounting Office—the "Watchdog of Congress"—to study defense contractors' profits. Such an investigation, he reasoned, was necessary because of the decline of competitive bidding. By 1968, only 11.5 percent of military contracts were awarded through competitive bidding, leaving plenty of room for companies to take advantage of the increased need for equipment. At the same time, contracts awarded on a cost-plus basis increased the profit awarded to contractors, from 7.7 percent to 9.4 percent between 1963 and 1967, figures Proxmire gained from an internal Pentagon report that it had refused to make public.[66]

What Proxmire needed in his fight against excessive defense spending was a single example of extraordinary overspending to capture the attention of the public, and he found that example in the C-5A Galaxy cargo plane developed by Lockheed. The Galaxy was the largest airplane in the world: 242 feet long with a wingspan of 222 feet and a tail six stories tall, it could carry fourteen fighter jets or 345 troops and fly at six hundred miles per hour. It was also expensive and a prime example of extravagant and unchecked spending. Joint Economic Committee staff member Richard Kaufman learned about cost overruns associated with the project and contacted A. E. Fitzgerald, a deputy for management systems in the office of the assistant air force secretary for financial management, who confirmed them. Proxmire then invited Fitzgerald to testify at the Subcommittee on Economy in Government hearings that November, but the Defense Department ordered him not to and refused to allow him to provide a written statement. At the hearing, however, Proxmire saw him sitting behind the official air force witnesses and invited him to the microphone. His testimony proved explosive. Fitzgerald explained that the Defense Department awarded Lockheed an initial $1.4 billion contract to build 58 of the panes for an estimated $127.8 million profit, to be followed by a contract for 57 more. Cost overruns, according to Fitzgerald, made it likely that the Pentagon would end up paying twice that amount; original estimates put the cost of 115 planes at $2.5 billion, but it seemed likely that the total cost would be nearer $6 billion. How, Proxmire demanded, could Lockheed run up costs double those of its initial estimate? Fitzgerald attributed it to a combination of faulty cost estimates; bad planning; and a corporate strategy that encouraged low bids that lost money, which could be recouped on subsequent contracts. In short, Fitzgerald charged, Lockheed chose to lose money in the short term in order to make more money in the long term. When Proxmire asked why the Defense Department would go along with that, Fitzgerald said, "Because we want the aircraft badly enough." He then hinted at another factor: the factory assembling the plane was located in Marietta, Georgia, and Richard Russell of Georgia chaired the Senate Armed Services Committee.[67] The air force denied that the cost overruns would reach the level estimated by Fitzgerald and insisted that cost increases would be only $1.2 billion, caused by rising labor costs and technical difficulties. Proxmire nonetheless demanded an investigation by the Government Accounting Office and requested that Defense Secretary Clark Clifford postpone the additional order of C-5As pending his own internal investigation of cost overruns. Clifford initially assured Proxmire that there would be no new orders until the Pentagon reviewed the contracts.[68]

Despite Clifford's assurances, the controversy over the C5-A was far from over. In November, the air force stripped Fitzgerald of his civil service protection, which it had awarded him just two months earlier. Defense Department officials quickly explained that it had erred in granting civil service protection and was simply fixing a personnel mistake, but Proxmire drew the obvious conclusion:

> The recent action taken against Mr. A. E. Fitzgerald seems to lend weight to charges that the Defense Department stifles criticism from within and severely penalizes those who speak out about waste and mismanagement in military procurement. If this action constitutes a reprisal against a government employee for testifying to Congress, it is a very grave matter and one that the Congress cannot tolerate.[69]

Air force secretary Harold Brown told Proxmire that he was "shocked" that the senator had "misinterpreted my explanation of the facts concerning Mr. Fitzgerald" and instead blamed the mistaken classification on a computer error. The Defense Department assured Proxmire that there were no plans to punish Fitzgerald, a promise repeated by assistant secretary Robert Charles at a hearing before the Joint Economic Committee on January 16. After receiving Charles's assurances, Proxmire suddenly produced a memo written by Charles's administrative assistant dated January 6 outlining three potential ways to fire Fitzgerald. Proxmire did extract a public promise that the Pentagon would not retaliate against the whistle-blower, thus protecting his job. Fitzgerald later testified about other defense contract costs before Proxmire's subcommittee, despite efforts by the Defense Department to prevent his testimony, providing Proxmire with abundant examples of wasteful military spending. Fitzgerald was fired in 1970 but petitioned the Civil Service Commission successfully for reinstatement.[70]

The C5-A continued to fly, but the Joint Economic Committee hearings did produce an internal review, ordered by new secretary of defense Melvin Laird. Proxmire asked the Justice Department and the Securities and Exchange Commission to launch investigations into whether air force officials covered up the cost overruns in order to prevent a decline in Lockheed's stock prices. In late July, the senator attempted to eliminate funding for an order of 62 planes, but the Senate rejected his proposed cuts 64–23 in September. The Defense Department, however, reduced its order to only 23 additional planes, to bring the total to 81 rather than the original 120. Proxmire was pleased with the reduction but noted that the 81 C5-As would still cost $500 million more than the original 120 ordered. Ironically, the C5-A proved to be one of the most useful airplanes in service. Ultimately, Proxmire had a lasting influence on government spending oversight, using his role as chair of the Joint Economic Committee to scrutinize wasteful defense spending.[71]

In addition to his efforts to fight wasteful spending, Proxmire showed that he could do more than just oppose by championing a much-needed piece of consumer legislation to protect Americans from predatory lending practices. One of Proxmire's most significant accomplishments in his third term was the passage of a truth-in-lending bill. It was not an original idea, and in fact had been championed by his close friend Paul Douglas, who had fought unsuccessfully for the measure for six years. Douglas wanted to make loans easier for consumers to understand, especially since banks could hide the true cost of a loan, and different banks used different formulas for calculating and applying interest. Former senator Walter Mondale, serving his first term, recalled that "many lending institutions would obscure credit costs. It was impossible for a person who was going to borrow to be told the simple rate that was being applied so that you could compare and make good choices. It was deliberate. The financial institutions didn't want you to know, and it was deceptive." Without uniform disclosure laws, consumers faced considerable difficulty in understanding the financial costs of loans.[72] Though generally popular, the bill repeatedly died in the Senate Banking Committee, chaired by conservative Democrat Willis Robertson of Virginia, who opposed the bill. After Douglas lost his bid for reelection in November 1966, Proxmire announced in December that he would introduce a truth-in-lending bill during the next session of Congress and continue the battle.[73]

Proxmire introduced the Consumer Credit Protection Act on January 11, 1967. Like the Douglas bill, Proxmire's measure required lenders to inform consumers of the total cost of a loan both in dollars and as an annual percentage rate. Ironically, Douglas's defeat greatly improved the bill's chances of passage, since Proxmire was willing to compromise with its opponents to a degree that Douglas never was. Douglas insisted that his truth-in-lending bill cover all consumer loans and that lenders disclose the precise APR. Proxmire agreed to modify the proposal to allow approximate rates (within 1%) in response to lenders who complained about the difficulty in accurately calculating interest rates. He also agreed to exempt first-mortgage loans, loans with $10 or less in annual interest, and revolving-credit loans that required a minimum monthly payment. In addition, the makeup of the Senate Banking Committee changed, and new members Edward Brooke of Massachusetts and Charles Percy of Illinois seemed willing to support it. Their backing would mean approval by an 8–6 margin. With these changes, the Proxmire bill easily made it through committee and passed the Senate 92–0 in July. The House passed its version of the bill, introduced by Robert Kastenmeier, in May 1968, and President Johnson signed the bill in a large ceremony in the East Room of the White House, with Douglas in attendance. Proxmire's staff had been invited, too, but the senator refused to attend the signing for fear of missing a roll-call vote. He remained on the floor of the Senate to vote on an amendment to an agriculture appropriations bill that increased federal food aid programs; the amendment passed by one vote. Ken McLean, the Proxmire legislative aide largely responsible for working on truth-in-lending, also assumed that Proxmire did not want to play second fiddle to Johnson.[74]

Proxmire felt strongly about truth-in-lending in part because of his own thriftiness and his growing suspicion of consumer credit. By the end of 1967, short-term consumer debt had increased to $96 billion and cost borrowers $13 billion annually in interest payments. Proxmire wanted consumers to be able to shop around for credit and understand the cost of borrowing accurately. Committee hearings uncovered examples of interest rates of nearly 300 percent for automobiles and over 200 percent for television sets. Consumers baffled by financing agreements fell for these plans without realizing the true cost of the loan. "The central aim of the bill," Proxmire told a meeting of the American Management Association in New York in December, "is to permit consumers to shop as carefully for credit as they shop for merchandise." To drive home this point, he often used specific examples to illustrate the misleading nature of financing offers: in one instance, a new refrigerator was at $300 and available for no down payment and only $22.50 a month for eighteen months. His bill required the seller to reveal the total cost of financing this refrigerator to be $105, or over 40 percent. A bank loan of $300 could be obtained for 12 percent, saving the customer $75.[75]

As with Johnson's foreign policy, Proxmire was generally supportive of the president's economic policies through 1965 and the early months of 1966, just as inflation was starting to become a real threat for the first time in years. Americans, in fact, ranked inflation as the third-most-pressing problem facing the country, behind the Vietnam War and racial violence. The root cause of the inflation of the late 1960s was the war. In July 1965, the rate of inflation was only 1.6 percent, with an unemployment rate of 4.5 percent. That same month, however, Johnson announced the use of ground troops in Vietnam, marking a dramatic increase in military spending and a de facto economic stimulus, much to the delight of Keynesian economists who relished the possibility of full employment for the first time in history. With increased—and consistently underestimated—defense spending, the economy began to overheat as increased demand outpaced increased productivity, and some economists began to worry about inflation. In the fall of 1965, the Council of Economic Advisors urged Johnson to persuade employers and labor unions to adhere to its guideposts on wages and prices. These guideposts, established under the Kennedy administration, were supposed to control inflation by keeping wage increases in line with productivity increases. As long as wages and productivity kept pace, prices should have remained stable. Yet by the beginning of 1966, the economy was expanding at a rate of 7 percent, well beyond increased production capacity, driving up inflation and causing Johnson's advisors to call for a tax increase to slow down economic growth and curb inflation. Desperate to avoid calling for a tax increase and reveal the true cost estimates of the war, Johnson instead sent Congress a $112.8 billion budget based on the assumption that the war would end by July 1967 and require no further spending after that date. Johnson assured Congress that the United States could have both guns and butter, but the unstated consequence was the end of a decade of price stability. The consumer price index, the standard measure of the costs of goods and services, increased between 4 and 6 percent for each of the next four years.[76]

Proxmire initially supported Johnson's efforts to use the guideposts to curb inflation. Speaking at length on the Senate floor in March 1966, he told his fellow senators that "the Johnson administration has repeatedly and skillfully used the guideposts . . . to persuade labor and management to reach wage agreements that would not put pressures on prices." Johnson's heavy-handed intervention in the steel industry, he continued, was evidence that he could persuade both union and management to keep wage and price increases within the guidelines. Proxmire acknowledged that inflation was possible, but urged adjustments to the guidelines rather than the adoption of a large tax increase, as some economists recommended. Concern over inflation continued, however, and a few weeks later Proxmire complained that this worry was caused by "newspaper nervous nellies" and tried to downplay the evidence of rising prices, pointing to lower housing starts and declining inventories as signs that prices would soon level off. A tax increase to curb inflation, he insisted, was unnecessary, and he confidently asserted that the president had no plans to propose one. An unexpected increase in unemployment to 4 percent in May 1966 seemed to confirm Proxmire's assertion that an anti-inflation tax increase was unnecessary.[77] It was only a temporary lull. By the summer of 1966, Johnson's economic advisors recognized that inflation would reach at least 4 percent within a year and urged a tax increase to level off prices. At the same time, Federal Reserve chairman William McChesney Martin, influenced by the monetarist theory of Milton Freeman, sharply reduced the money supply to commercial banks, which had been increasing at a rate of 6 percent a year. The resulting credit crunch drove up interest rates and slowed down lending, threatening to launch a recession. The Fed's tight money policy slowed inflation, but the potential cost was higher unemployment.[78]

Proxmire opposed both a tax increase and tighter monetary policy. In August, he delivered a speech in the Senate and argued that using tax increases to fight inflation was like using a meat cleaver instead of a scalpel and would increase unemployment by two million. He also urged a loosening of the Fed's tight money policy, telling constituents that such a policy would make it easier to borrow money and thereby lower interest rates. Most importantly, Proxmire insisted, was the need to reduce federal spending as a way to combat inflation. Specifically, he proposed cutting $500 million from the space program ("highly inflationary frills"), $40 million from the FAA toward developing a supersonic aircraft (a "jet-set giveaway"), $300 million from subsidies to mass transportation, and $31.5 million from new buildings in the District of Columbia. Each one of these proposals, he told his constituents, "was zeroed in to cut back government spending in the most inflationary part of the economy. . . . American business has sharply increased its spending for plan and equipment, breaking all records. Competitive government spending in this area where manpower and materials are especially in short supply is sure to drive prices up."[79] By the end of the year, Proxmire had grown quite critical of the president. He opposed Johnson's major anti-inflationary weapon of ending the 7 percent deduction for business investment in new equipment, arguing that it would have no effect for at least a year and might actually make long-term inflation worse by preventing production capacity from increasing to meet consumer demand. Instead, he again called for major spending cuts amounting to more than $6 billion, more than double the amount suggested by the president.[80]

By January 1967, the battle lines were drawn: Proxmire would fight any tax increase. Even before the new session convened, Proxmire warned that a tax increase, added to the higher interest rates and declining prices for stocks and municipal bonds, would produce a recession. Cutting federal spending remained his favored way of reducing inflation, and he suggested withdrawing four divisions from Europe to save $1 billion, cutting the space program by $1 billion, and reducing public works expenditures by $7 billion.[81] In his State of the Union message, Johnson called for a 6 percent surtax on corporate and individual income taxes for two years to help pay for the war. Proxmire announced his opposition to any tax increase and repeated his earlier assertions that cutting spending would have a greater effect on inflation. Treasury secretary Henry Fowler disputed Proxmire's claims. Testifying before Proxmire's Joint Economic Committee in February, Fowler defended the need for a tax increase because he had no confidence Congress would actually cut spending by $4 to $6 billion, and dismissed Proxmire and others as critics who "had nothing to recommend . . . except the time tested cliché of cutting Federal spending." Fowler insisted that the economy was strengthening and the real danger was inflation, not recession. Much to Proxmire's shock, Federal Reserve secretary Martin also backed the tax increase when he testified before Proxmire's committee a few days later, forecasting a "new surge of inflationary pressure" as the economy improved. Proxmire thought the administration was over-optimistic about the economic forecast, a position shared by two former chairs of the Council of Economic Advisors, Arthur Burns and Walter Heller, both of whom appeared before his committee. Both warned that the economic outlook was uncertain and that hasty action could cause an economic slowdown. Burns particularly agreed with Proxmire's assessment of federal spending, which he predicted would weaken the economy as the federal government continued to grow beyond tax receipts.[82] Proxmire's efforts to use spending cuts rather than a tax increase to halt inflation, however, met with little success. Yet as he warned, "Spending cuts are hard to get through Congress. The painful alternative: a tax increase. YOUR taxes will depend on which choice Congress makes."[83]

More than any other figure in Congress, Proxmire had the ability to steer the debate over a potential inflation-fighting tax increase, and in late June his Joint Economic Committee held hearings on the economy, which he frequently characterized as "sluggish." Announcing the hearings, Proxmire warned of a return to the high interest rates and tight money that plagued the country in 1966. The situation was possible, he reasoned, as military spending drove the federal budget deficit higher and the administration failed to persuade employers to follow its wage and price guidelines. Essentially, Proxmire was using the committee to back the

Johnson administration into a corner. Throughout 1966, the administration underestimated—or deliberately misled Congress about—the cost of war in Vietnam, for which Proxmire's committee had taken administration officials to task. Updated cost estimates were due the following month, but Proxmire's hearings would establish the context under which Congress would consider the costs of the war and the president's request for a tax increase.[84] In some respects, the strategy worked. Gardner Ackley, chair of the Council of Economic Advisors, testified that "there is no escape" from a tax increase to prevent a bout of inflation. Ackley acknowledged that there was no immediate need for a tax increase but refused to say when the tax increase should go into effect or whether the administration would stick to the 6 percent figure Johnson suggested in his State of the Union message. His evasiveness irritated members of the committee, already wary of unanticipated increases in cost estimates for the war.[85] For Proxmire, the June hearings provided conclusive proof that a tax increase was a bad idea. Economic growth was flat and a tax increase would worsen conditions, and since production averaged about 87 percent, there was enough room to increase production as demand increased before inflation became a problem. A tax increase would be warranted only if defense spending rose sharply and could not be offset by other spending cuts, cuts that Proxmire argued would be as effective as a tax increase in easing inflationary pressure.[86]

Throughout the late summer and fall, Proxmire emerged as one of the most vocal critics of a surtax. In a Senate speech on July 17, for example, he warned that industrial production had declined to its lowest point in fourteen months, unemployment was at its highest in eighteen months, and employment remained flat. "It is the most elementary economic fact," he concluded, "that a tax increase at a time when unemployment is increasing and when consumers are not significantly increasing their buying would worsen economic conditions."[87] Johnson finally sent his long-anticipated and already controversial tax proposal to Congress on August 3, and it demonstrated how badly the war was affecting the economy. Johnson's proposal included a 10 percent surtax on individual and corporate income taxes, necessary to fund an additional forty-five thousand to fifty thousand new troops for South Vietnam. Proxmire immediately called it a "serious economic mistake" and warned that it would badly weaken the economy. Moreover, he asserted, it would not actually do anything to control inflation—costs for food and medical expenses would continue to rise anyway.[88] He was not afraid to be openly critical of Johnson, either, and demanded in another Senate speech that the president reduce budget requests by $9 billion rather than increasing taxes, which he could "easily" do.

This challenge to the president earned Proxmire a summons from the White House, and he met with Johnson in the Oval Office on August 31. It was not a pleasant meeting as the two argued for half an hour over the tax bill. Neither was willing to budge.[89] By mid-November, Proxmire was trying to rally support behind a combination of spending cuts and a revival of wage-price guidelines as a means of preventing inflation. "Since the President asked for this 10 per cent surtax last summer," he insisted, "the economic case for it has collapsed completely." The excessive demand that the administration alleged was causing inflation simply did not exist, and industrial production continued to decline. A tax increase "could throw another million out of work." He went so far as to hint he might filibuster any tax increase and suggested that Johnson continued to press for the surtax to avoid running a $29 billion deficit heading into his 1968 bid for reelection.[90]

Proxmire ultimately won the argument when Congress failed to enact Johnson's surtax proposal in December. Looking ahead to 1968, Proxmire called for a three-part program to combat inflation based on reducing federal spending on public works, reviving the wage-price guidelines that had worked earlier, and slowing down the Fed's injection of money into the economy. Unchastened by the congressional rebuff of its surtax proposal, the Johnson administration continued to support a tax increase. At Joint Economic Committee hearings in February, Council of Economic Advisors chair Gardner Ackley made clear that he opposed restoring wage and price guidelines even if Congress refused to pass a tax increase and those same wages and prices rose significantly. When Ackley asserted that the economy would remain strong even with a tax increase, Proxmire responded that higher income taxes would simply reduce savings rates and have little impact on spending or inflation. In fact, Proxmire publicly predicted an economic slowdown in the second half of 1968, based on consumer pessimism and declining production. Inflation was caused by increased costs, not excessive demand, and tax increases would only weaken the economy further.[91]

Proxmire may have read public opinion accurately, but by March, two things occurred that began to make Congress more amenable to a tax increase: escalation of the Vietnam War and new worries about the budget deficit. After reviewing Johnson's economic report, the Joint Economic Committee issued its own assessment calling for spending cuts, tax reform, and tighter monetary policy. Absent was any recommendation for or against a tax increase. Despite Proxmire's resistance, some members of the committee announced their support for a surtax. Democrat Henry Reuss of Wisconsin favored a surtax if certain tax loopholes were closed, and Democrat William Moorhead of Pennsylvania agreed, provided there was no escalation in the war. Another Democrat, Richard Bolling of Missouri, supported a surtax without any qualifications. Republicans were even more supportive, with Senator Wallace Bennett of Utah calling it "inevitable" in the light of growing budget deficits.

Concerns over the deficit rather than fear of inflation ultimately drove the tax increase through Congress. In April, the Senate passed a 10 percent tax surcharge coupled with $6 billion in spending cuts. Proxmire introduced an amendment to eliminate the tax increase and leave the spending cuts in place, but it was easily defeated as Republicans remained solidly behind the tax increase. Proxmire commented bitterly that it "was a vote for unemployment, for a slowdown in the nation's economy, and it could produce a world-wide recession." After much bitter negotiation the House passed its version of the bill in June, and Johnson reluctantly agreed to the spending cuts as the price for the tax increase. Proxmire promised to fight any efforts to extend it beyond its expiration date of June 30, 1969, and to fight for additional spending cuts as a more effective check on inflation.[92]

By the end of 1968, Proxmire had become a major figure in Congress, although his positions had evolved. In January 1965, he was an enthusiastic supporter of President Johnson's domestic and foreign policies, but by 1968 he had become one of the president's most persistent critics. Proxmire could also claim significant legislative accomplishments in getting the truth-in-lending bill passed and revealing excessive military spending through his masterful chairmanship of the Joint Economic Committee. The *Pageant* poll had completely faded from public memory, and no one could doubt that Proxmire had become a truly effective senator.

A young Bill Proxmire, August 1938. WHI IMAGE ID 39241

Women, often the wives of candidates, played a vital role in the Democratic Party of the 1950s. In October 1952, several women hosted a Dane County Democratic club luncheon in honor of presidential candidate Adlai E. Stevenson. Left to right, Mrs. Eleanor (Thomas E.) Fairchild, Mrs. Marion (Horace) Wilkie, Mrs. Elsie (William) Proxmire (Elsie Rockefeller, his first wife), Mrs. Marian (Carl) Thompson, Mrs. Ruth Doyle, Mrs. Helen (Ervin) Bruner, and Mrs. Dolores (Walter) Linderud. WHI IMAGE 34530

William and Ellen's blended family. From left, Ted Proxmire, Jan Cathy Sawall, Elsie (Cici) Proxmire, and Mary Ellen Sawall. *MILWAUKEE JOURNAL SENTINEL* © JOURNAL SENTINEL INC., REPRODUCED WITH PERMISSION

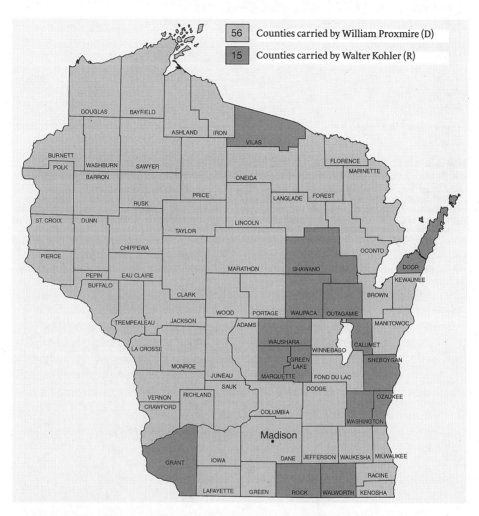

Jubilant Proxmire supporters celebrate in Milwaukee after his election to the US Senate on August 28, 1957. WHI IMAGE 30197

Proxmire and Ellen board a plane for Washington, August 1957, the day after his upset election as US Senator. WHI IMAGE 79823

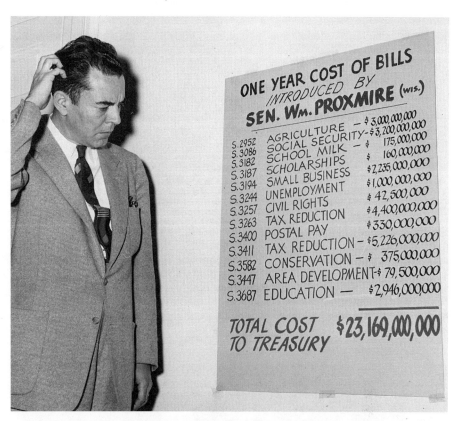

Proxmire's support for spending on social programs during his first term earned him the derogatory nickname "Billion Dollar Bill." John Byrnes, Republican representative from Wisconsin, puzzles over a list of bills introduced by Proxmire in 1958. WHI IMAGE 104913

Proxmire shocked the political establishment when he openly criticized Democratic Majority Leader Lyndon Johnson's perceived dictatorial hold over the Senate in 1959. JIM BERRYMAN, *WASHINGTON STAR*

David's Not Apt to Win This One

'This One-Man Rule Stuff Is a Myth!'

Proxmire jogs on the mall in front of the US Capitol, July 11, 1967. WHI IMAGE 30090

Proxmire meets with President Lyndon Johnson in the Oval Office, September 1, 1967. WHI IMAGE 30136

Proxmire hands his cards to constituents outside a Milwaukee grocery store, 1969. Traveling back to Wisconsin nearly every weekend, he became a familiar sight in small towns around the state. WHI IMAGE 30083

Proxmire greets three women seated on a bench at the Capitol Square, July 1969.
WHI IMAGE 30085

Proxmire giving a speech, ca. 1970. WHI IMAGE 58409

An informal moment with Senator Gaylord Nelson (right) and Congressman Robert Kastenmeier during a photography session in Nelson's office, September 1972.
WHI IMAGE 45447

Proxmire walked thousands of miles in Wisconsin to meet constituents. Here he is shaking hands with a woman outside the post office in De Soto, December 22, 1972.
WHI IMAGE 30129

Proxmire was known for making as many personal connections as he could with Wisconsin voters.
WHI IMAGE 39242

Proxmire tackles a mountain of correspondence, November 19, 1975. WHI IMAGE 39243

The senator on the set of the CBS news program *Face the Nation*, ca. 1980. WHI IMAGE 30141

OFFICE OF

SENATOR WILLIAM PROXMIRE

WISCONSIN

FOR RELEASE AFTER 6:30 A.M. FRIDAY, JULY 10, 1981 FOR PM PAPERS

Sen. William Proxmire (D-Wis.) announced Friday that, "I am giving my Golden Fleece of the Month Award for July to the United States Army, which spent $6,000 to prepare a 17-page document that tells the federal government how to buy a bottle of Worcestershire sauce.

"That's right: 17-eye-glazing pages of single-spaced type on how to buy a 15-ounce bottle of Worcestershire sauce that retails for about $1.50. What's more, in order for our hapless buyer or seller to use those 17 pages of federal specifications, he must refer to another 2,270 pages of government and commercial regulations and references.

"I can see having complex federal specifications if the military is buying a weapons system. But Worcestershire sauce? That 17-page specification and the 2,270-page backup is nothing more than a recipe for stuffed paperwork souffle that left the taxpayer with an indigestible $6,000 check. Even a dollar spent on writing and using this document is a dollar too much."

Proxmire, who is ranking minority member of the Senate Appropriations Committee, gives his Golden Fleece Award each month to the biggest, most ridiculous or most ironic example of wasteful federal spending.

"The 'Federal Specification: Worcestershire Sauce', which the Department of Defense estimates cost $6,000 in 1981 dollars to draft, was prepared for all agencies by the Army's Natick Research and Development Laboratories in Natick, Massachusetts.* It should have been entitled 'Everything You Wanted to Know About Worcestershire Sauce; But Would Never Bother To Ask.'

"Chemical analyses in the specifications are spelled out for every last molecule in the Worcestershire sauce -- from the pH for the tamarind to the salt content of the anchovy paste.

"Only the federal government could devote a 7-line paragraph to show someone how to check if the bottle cap to the Worcestershire sauce is screwed on tightly.

"The federal specifications also are written in a jargonese that would make a bureaucrat's mouth water.

"For example, I can't imagine a supermarket shopper wanting to check whether the label is stuck tightly onto the Worcestershire sauce bottle. But if he did, he'd probably just pick at the label to make sure it didn't come off.

(OVER)

Proxmire is widely known for the Golden Fleece Awards, a monthly press release dedicated to exposing wasteful government spending. Pictured here is the infamous Worcestershire bulletin from July 1981. WIS MSS 738, BOX 158, FOLDER 2

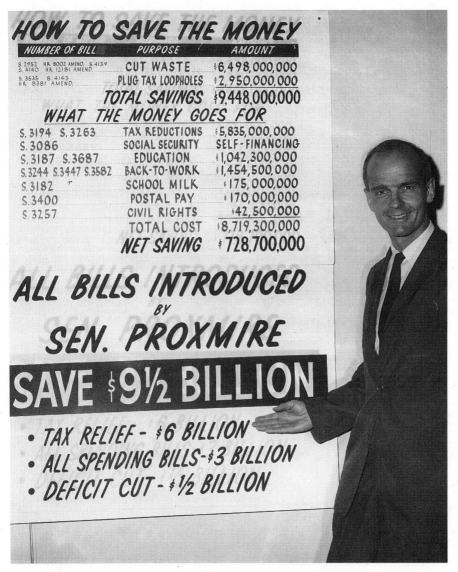

Throughout his tenure in the Senate, Proxmire demanded fiscal accountability from government agencies and worked to close tax loopholes. WHI IMAGE 39239

Proxmire and Nelson: Wisconsin's two Democratic senators. Although they were never close friends, they respected each other's expertise. WHI IMAGE 30135

Proxmire, perhaps more than any other senator, made sure to keep in touch with the people of Wisconsin, and encouraged visitors to the capital to drop by his office and say hello. AUTHOR'S PERSONAL COLLECTION

UNITED STATES SENATOR
BILL PROXMIRE

YOUR HIRED MAN IN WASHINGTON

7

HIGH-COST POLITICS

By 1969, Proxmire had established a clear identity. No longer the gadfly of the Senate, he focused on a few issues that brought him national acclaim and resulted in actual legislation, like the truth-in-lending law. As chair of the Joint Economic Committee, Proxmire demonstrated his command of the military budget and his willingness to challenge the Pentagon in wartime. The publication of his *Report from the Wasteland* in 1970 further cemented his reputation as the leading congressional critic of wasteful military spending. Despite his early support for the war in Vietnam, Proxmire had also established himself as an old-fashioned liberal by leading the fight to preserve the Supreme Court's ruling on legislative apportionment and against the anticommunist Subversive Activities Control Board. Proxmire had accomplished exactly what he intended to after the bruising 1964 campaign: he had shown that he was a senator of substance. Even more importantly, he had accomplished much in Washington without losing touch with his constituents in Wisconsin. He traveled home nearly every weekend and established legendary rapport with voters. A *New York Times* sportswriter researching a story on the Green Bay Packers noted his surprise when he was approached outside Lambeau Field before the NFL championship game by a friendly man who said, "I'm Bill Proxmire, your senator. I hope you enjoy the game." Senators in larger cities, the reporter noted, "do not do that very often."[1] Yet in Wisconsin, Proxmire had become a fixture at sporting events, factory gates, street corners, and fairs. This success in Washington and in Wisconsin, however, began to take a toll on the Proxmire family.

Proxmire's wife, Ellen, one of the most perceptive observers of social life in Washington, had collected her newspaper columns in *One Foot in Washington: The Perilous Life of a Senator's Wife* in 1963 to much critical acclaim. By that point, she had developed a realistic view of the effects a political career had on family life:

> I must confess that my life might seem more glamorous than many others, for Bill's position has enabled me to meet and come to know some of the most fascinating and important people of my time. But for every hour I have spent in the White House I have spent thousands typing or stuffing envelopes in the office. Even though I am invited to diplomatic receptions, I am, most of the time, just a working wife who doesn't even get a paycheck.[2]

This disillusionment grew after the 1964 campaign that required her to uproot her family for several months and devote almost all of her time to saving her husband's career. Writing about potential campaign finance reforms for *The Progressive* in December 1966, she described the endless fund-raising dinners and receptions over several years that were needed to generate enough money to run a statewide campaign, calling it "a long time, a lot of money, and a terrible burden for a family."[3] The Senate's often long hours and Proxmire's determination never to miss a roll-call vote made family time unpredictable. Most days, Ellen managed dinner for her family by feeding their youngest at five o'clock, the four teenaged children at six, and her husband whenever he got home. Even when the Senate was not in session, on weekends and during recesses, family life was complicated because Proxmire traveled to Wisconsin and his children might not see him at all.[4]

The five children also coped with both the opportunities and the frustrating realities of being a political family. Helping out at Proxmire's office gave the children the chance to sit in the Senate galleries to watch debates and meet other senators. Hubert Humphrey—an admirer of Ellen—always addressed Mary Ellen as "Beautiful Junior." At the occasional dinner parties hosted by the Proxmires, Jan and Mary Ellen had the job of taking guests' coats, including a glamorous mink coat belonging to Jackie Kennedy, which they could not resist trying on.[5] Theodore and Cici spent most of the year with their mother, which meant they saw their father less than their stepsisters did, but Proxmire made a point of always being available to them, and they typically spent summers in Washington. When they were in Wisconsin, Theodore once explained, "I could get my father any time I wanted to on the phone. He was always available whenever I would call him. And if he was voting or if he was tied up or anything, he would give me a call back within thirty minutes. He would always try to be very responsive." Likewise, when Cici was in college, Proxmire made a point of calling her weekly at the same time, an appointment that he looked forward to.

Maintaining family connections remained important to him after the older children moved away, though his political commitments often limited more immediate events. Theodore played sports all summer at the Wisconsin Avenue branch of the Washington Boys' Club, but long days in the Senate meant Proxmire missed his games. Very few fathers were able to make daytime games, however, so Ted never thought it unusual. Politics did, however, offer different opportunities for Ted to spend time with his father. Once Ted was old enough to drive, he occasionally ferried his father around the state on summer visits, dropping him off in small towns to shake hands while he found the nearest tavern to cool off with a soft drink, since Proxmire refused to spend money on a car with air-conditioning. The unavoidable criticism that comes with being a public figure irritated Ted, so he had to learn from an early age not to get upset by political differences or snide comments about "crooked politicians."[6]

Criticism of politicians could indeed affect their children, as Theodore and Mary Ellen found out in the summer of 1965. As part of his Youth Opportunity Program, President Johnson instructed federal agencies to fill as many summer job openings as possible with "needy" young people. The intent was noble: to steer jobs to teenagers from impoverished families. In practice, however, the presidential order created job opportunities for well-connected youngsters. The US Post Office, for example, hired 8,600 young workers for summer jobs; 3,380 of them had been recommended by senators and representatives, and many of those were in fact children of legislators. One of these "needy youths" was seventeen-year-old Ted Proxmire, who had asked the Postmaster General, John Gronouski from Wisconsin, for a job and was hired as a student assistant at the Post Office Department for $1.91 per hour for seven weeks. Mary Ellen, nineteen and a student at the University of Wisconsin, worked that summer at Yellowstone National Park as a maid and in a gift shop, earning $179. The summer before, she had worked in the Navy Department in a civil service position and had earned just over $600. When the story of congressional children receiving federal jobs broke, Proxmire moved quickly to forestall any criticism, even though both Mary Ellen and Ted had procured jobs on their own, and even though Mary Ellen's salary was paid by a private contractor rather than the National Park Service. He issued a press release announcing that he had written a check to the US Treasury for $1,806.80 to cover the salaries, Mary Ellen's room and board at Yellowstone, and 4 percent interest. Proxmire insisted that they had earned their pay, but noted that "the fact that they are related to a US Senator and worked for the federal government in summer jobs might, through no fault of theirs, make their jobs subject to misunderstanding or misinterpretation.[7] Proxmire had set such a precedent by returning the salary his office paid to Frank Campenni and by converting almost all of the stocks he had inherited from his father, worth about $175,000, to US securities in 1963. He estimated his loss at about $6,000 a year from the divestment, but it allowed him to avoid any appearance of a conflict of interest. It was a high standard that he expected his family to follow as well.[8]

The fact that the Proxmire household was also a blended family added another layer of complexity. Ellen had full custody of her children, and Proxmire developed a close relationship with them as well. When he was home, dinner included conversations about politics and current events, and he was eager to hear their opinions. He bestowed nicknames on the children: Jan he called "Jazz Bones," "Jake," or "Jacob Jasper Stall," and Mary Ellen became "Melom." Shortly after his election in 1957, he casually mentioned that he thought they should start calling him "senator" at home. The children laughed—"You're out of your mind if you think that's going to happen!" The girls did eventually settle on a nickname for him: "The Bear," because he would growl at them if they came home late. Indeed, Proxmire showed a particular vigilance in enforcing curfew for his stepdaughters, setting his alarm to wake up at eleven p.m. to wait for the tardy teenagers on the couch. Once when Jan was on a date and came home five minutes late, she was met at the door by her stepfather, who was wearing fuchsia pajamas. When she turned to say goodnight to her date, he was already in the car racing away at the sight of a growly senator up past his bedtime. Having boyfriends over while babysitting was another infraction, but it too had its humorous side. When her parents inadvertently discovered Mary Ellen with her boyfriend while babysitting, Proxmire couldn't help laughing at the situation; as Mary Ellen remembers, "I got grounded, but he was laughing. He thought it was hysterical because I always got caught." Not surprisingly, the most explosive disciplinary issues with the health-conscious Proxmire were smoking and drinking, which most of the children experimented with in high school. Again, Mary Ellen would get caught if she hadn't hidden her cigarettes. Proxmire "would walk in and he would pick up my cigarettes and tear them . . . 'God dammit, Melom! You can't smoke! It's terrible for you!'" In desperation, Proxmire offered each of them $1,000 if they did not smoke and $1,000 if they did not drink until they were twenty-one. Only two earned any reward. He gave Cici $1,000 for not smoking, and gave Douglas $2,000 despite his son's admission that he had actually consumed alcohol. "Well, you know," Proxmire told his youngest son, "the rate of inflation since the time your siblings got it, and I don't think you drink very much, so I'm going to give you two thousand dollars now."[9]

Despite his well-earned reputation as a cheapskate, the one expense Proxmire never complained about was education, and he paid willingly to enroll all five children in private school. As their parents had, both Cici and Ted attended boarding schools, Cici in the Master's School in Dobbs Ferry, New York, and Ted at the Salisbury School in Salisbury, Connecticut. Mary Ellen and Jan initially attended public school after they moved to Washington. John Eaton Elementary and Alice Deal Junior High were near the house on Ordway Avenue and affiliated with Woodrow Wilson Senior High School, their mother's alma mater. They, too, shifted from public to private school. When Mary Ellen had finished ninth grade and Jan Cathy had finished sixth, they were admitted to Sidwell Friends School, much to the dismay of Mary Ellen, a popular student who was looking forward to being a cheerleader at Woodrow Wilson. Children from many prominent political families attended Sidwell, including Julie Nixon. Jan loved her time at Sidwell, though Mary Ellen, having lost most of her friends in the transition, had a less happy time.[10]

All of the children did well in school, although Ted had inherited his

grandmother's love of socializing rather than his father's diligence. Proxmire had hoped Ted would follow in his footsteps and attend The Hill,
but Ted struggled with reading and writing. As a final effort to get him
accepted, Proxmire enrolled him in Wolfeboro in 1962, a summer camp
run by The Hill to provide remedial work. He also hired a tutor from the
University of Wisconsin to work with Ted and sent him to a remedial education center in Washington during the summer. After much research,
Proxmire settled on Salisbury as an acceptable alternative for his son.[11] Ted
proved to be something of a rebel at Salisbury, and had a difficult time staying focused on his schoolwork. In 1966, he was expelled from Salisbury for
drinking and finished his senior year of high school in Washington in 1966,
graduating in 1967 and enrolling at the University of Wisconsin. Cici also
struggled to keep her grades up but worked hard and worried about letting
her father down. Cici earned a degree at Northwestern University and then
moved back to Washington to enroll in a physician's assistant program at
Georgetown.[12] Mary Ellen enrolled at the University of Wisconsin in the
fall of 1964, during the difficult campaign. Jan started at Beloit College
in 1967. In July 1970, Mary Ellen confided in her stepfather that she was
considering law school, but had not signed up for the LSAT exam and had
missed the application deadline for Marquette Law School. Proxmire's
response was "no problem," and had his staff arrange for her to take the
exam and for Marquette to accept her late application. Education provided
the lone exception to his refusal to use his position to obtain special consideration for his children. Moreover, he paid for her tuition and gave her
$150 a month to help with her expenses. Altogether, Ellen calculated that
they paid for eighty years of private and higher education for their five
children—and didn't resent it at all.[13]

Douglas's position as the youngest child meant that he saw far more of
his parents than any of his half-siblings. Like his brother, Douglas occasionally accompanied his father on his trips to Wisconsin in the summer.
Douglas would sit and listen to his father make a speech, or watch him
shake hands with people, and they carried on conversations about school
or sports in the car between stops. When meeting voters at factory gates
or in restaurants, Proxmire would jocularly introduce his son as "the future Senator from Wisconsin" or "the real boss of the family." This was
certainly not ideal father-son quality time, but if Douglas expressed irri-

tation with politics interrupting his time with his father, Proxmire took it in stride: "You know this is what I do," he would gently remind his son, "and I love doing this. It doesn't mean that I . . . love you any less. It's just something I do."[14] Unlike Cici and Ted, Douglas remained in day school in Washington until he left for college, beginning with the National Child Research Center for preschool and continuing with the progressive Beauvoir School at the National Cathedral, both of which were near their house, and Landon, a prep school in Bethesda. This gave father and son considerably more time to spend together, especially since Proxmire seldom went out during the week, giving them time together most mornings and evenings. They played golf together regularly, which generated a sometimes intense father-son competition. When Douglas went to summer camp, Proxmire wrote his son every day. Proxmire's entire life revolved around his family and the Senate, and his children recognized his dedication: Douglas later recalled that "I never felt like—as important as his career was—never felt like that meant that he was going to exclude his family from any part of it. He always found a way to make them both work."[15]

Among his children's most lasting memories was the disciplined exercise routine Proxmire developed in the 1960s and continued until the end of his life. Proxmire was a competitive athlete at heart and relished sustained physical activity. His devotion to exercise stemmed from his two other idiosyncrasies: his impatience and his frugality. Throughout his first full term, Proxmire rode the bus to the New Senate Office Building (renamed the Dirksen Senate Office Building in 1972). The nearly hour-long ride through Washington traffic gave him time to read the morning newspaper and other material, which at first proved to be an efficient use of his time. By 1965, however, he had grown impatient waiting for the bus every morning and irritated at the slow pace of morning rush hour. At age forty-nine, he decided that he could get to his office more quickly if he ran the nearly five miles and read the morning papers in his office before his staff arrived. The decision quickly turned into an obsession with exercise and diet and transformed the lanky former college athlete into a fitness zealot, much to the consternation of his family and the amusement of his colleagues.[16]

Proxmire quickly settled into a morning routine that rarely varied. He got out of bed by five forty-five a.m. to have time for breakfast and thirty minutes of calisthenics before beginning his run. It was an old habit that he now increased to include 250 push-ups in sets of 60 or 70 interspersed with other exercises. By six thirty a.m., regardless of the weather, he was out the door and running down Ordway Avenue toward the Capitol at a steady eight-mile-per-hour pace. His run took him down Connecticut Avenue past the National Zoo and across the Taft Bridge over Rock Creek Gorge. By seven o'clock he reached the Washington Hilton, where he swam thirty-six laps in the pool (a total of 900 yards) before continuing on his run. At Dupont Circle ("where the long-haired kids hang out"), he turned on Massachusetts Avenue and headed toward Lower Senate Park, reaching his office around seven thirty. For the first few years of his routine, he washed up in his office bathroom before his staff arrived; later he kept a locker in the Senate gym and showered there before he went to his office.[17]

Until the summer of 1968, Proxmire ran home again in the evening, but recurring tendonitis forced him to walk instead, which he found to be "a marvelously well-spent hour." He became a familiar sight striding along Massachusetts and Connecticut Avenues. Residents sometimes tried to stop him to talk about their problems or about politics, and he always offered to listen provided they walked along with him. He also waved a friendly hello at the homeless people camped out near Seventh Street. In addition to his walk home, Proxmire took great pride in walking while at work, and since he never missed a roll-call vote, he frequently had to leave his office and walk to the Capitol. In good weather, he took two flights of stairs down to the exit and walked along Constitution Avenue to the Capitol, about one-third of a mile; in wet weather, he walked through the tunnel that connected the Senate Office Buildings to the Capitol and up three flights of stairs to the Senate floor. He never rode the elevator or the tram line normally used by senators and could make the trip in about six minutes, only slightly longer than those who waited for the tram. On days with frequent roll-call votes, he might easily get in two or three miles of walking. Washington offered him other, more tranquil, routes as well. He particularly liked walking the old towpath along the Potomac River and the Glover Archibald Nature Walk in Rock Creek Park, free from whizzing bicyclists and car exhaust fumes. All told, Proxmire typically walked or ran about ten to twelve miles each day. He took some smug satisfaction at being one of the most physically fit members of the Senate and suffered acute embarrassment when outdone. After boasting to Gaylord Nelson that he could do two hundred pushups, Nelson beat Proxmire at his own game by dropping to the floor to demonstrate one-armed pushups, which Proxmire couldn't do at all.[18]

Although his newfound routine was enjoyable and rewarding, Proxmire did admit that he looked a bit goofy, decked out in white running shoes and a sweatshirt, shorts in the summer and a stocking cap in the winter, jogging in place while waiting for lights to change. Once a construction worker hollered at him, "Hey, you skinny old man, put some clothes on!" Home from college, his stepdaughter Jan was on a bus slowly working its way through thick Washington traffic. A fellow rider laughed at a runner jogging in place at stoplights and repeatedly passing the bus as it sat in traffic; she sunk down in her seat, embarrassed by Proxmire's antics and fearful he would catch sight of her on the bus and wave. Early on, Capitol police routinely stopped traffic so that he could cross busy streets without waiting for the light to change. Proxmire had them stop when four unimpressed employees of the *Washington Daily News* received tickets for disobeying a traffic officer trying to hold traffic for the senator one June morning. Yet as he became a regular fixture on his route, other commuters applauded his efforts. Bus drivers and mail truck drivers waved at him. One woman who passed by him on a bus sent his office a dozen roses with a note: "Keep it up, Senator. You look great!" Only occasionally did the senator have to interrupt his run to talk to a constituent, as when a police officer stopped him to ask if he supported a 17 percent pay increase for District of Columbia police. "You fellows do a great job," Proxmire assured him. "I'd like to do all we can to help. Let me look into it."[19]

Proxmire's commitment to exercise both worried and amused his staff. Part of Massachusetts Avenue ran through what the senator called a "semi–skid row area," worrying because of the dangerous reputation many Washington neighborhoods had acquired. He was mugged twice. As Proxmire was walking home from a talk at the Cathedral School at nine thirty p.m., two men with a gun demanded his money. Proxmire shouted at them that he had terminal cancer and would be dead in two weeks anyway, so they should just shoot him. The shocked muggers ran off. The incident left Proxmire shaken but undeterred from his routine.[20] Another time, in the fall of 1973, he was mugged by two teenagers, whom he fought off rather than giving them his money. "I had a funny reaction," he recalled. "I got mad. I was mad that kids tried to hold me up. They weren't really that imposing." The two were quickly apprehended, and he marveled to his staff about how responsive the police were to his ordeal: "I had a captain, two lieutenants, four sergeants, and I don't know how many policemen in my house taking [notes]." Legislative assistant Martin Lobel quickly asked him, "Do you think your being a Senator had anything to do with it?" Proxmire met their families at their court hearing and hired the two to work off their sentences in his office helping with the mail a few hours each afternoon, though he did not publicize this.[21]

When Proxmire began his exercise regimen, he changed his diet as well. He made his own breakfast in his office after his run, which typically consisted of ten ounces of orange juice, three ounces of lean protein (tuna, herring, beef, or chicken breast), two slices of toasted sprouted-wheat bread, and eight ounces of skim milk mixed with one ounce of wheat germ. Everything was carefully measured and accounted for, and Proxmire kept track of every calorie he consumed by consulting a calorie-counting booklet he kept in his pocket. Lunch in the Senate dining room consisted of a plate of fruit and four ounces of cottage cheese or occasionally soup, if his weight hadn't crept up. More often, he ate fruit and cottage cheese at his desk. An apple at three thirty tided him over until dinner, which was usually about 350 calories of protein (usually fish, veal, or chicken breast), vegetables, and V-8 juice. When traveling to Wisconsin on the weekends, he survived on canned tuna or sardines in his hotel room, with sunflower seeds and fruit from the local grocery store. Only occasionally would he eat a large steak dinner in a restaurant, and even rarer was an evening indulgence of ice cream or peanut butter on crackers. Proxmire had a notorious sweet tooth, so giving up pie, ice cream, and cookies was a particularly heroic act of self-denial. He ended his day by going to bed early—typically nine thirty or ten o'clock—and he kept his family's telephone number unlisted so his private life would be uninterrupted.[22]

Where did this sudden obsession with diet and exercise come from? Certainly this regimented lifestyle fit Proxmire's personality, and he had been physically active all his life. Yet this new health consciousness proved to be a transformative experience. Proxmire called himself "one of the worst athletes who ever put on a football uniform at Yale." He had certainly been in much better shape than most college students, but he could not run more than a mile or swim more than fifty yards without gasping for breath. At age fifty-seven, however, after eight years of running and dieting, he could easily run five miles, swim one mile, and do more pushups than he could as a young man. He was far less tired and had lost fifteen pounds. Proxmire recalled that his father had experienced a similar transformation when he was in his forties, reducing his weight from 200 to 170 pounds through careful dieting, eventually dropping to 143 pounds by his fifty-sixth birthday. Acquaintances noticed his weight loss and sometimes thought he was starting to look ill. Journalist Frank Aukofer once noted that he looked a bit peaked and asked if he was well. "Why is it," Proxmire demanded to know, "that in this country you're not considered healthy unless you have fat cheeks?" Proxmire was ahead of his time, but by the late 1960s he had found inspiration in several recent books that launched a new physical fitness craze. In 1968, physician and retired air force colonel Kenneth Cooper published *Aerobics*, which confirmed to Proxmire why his running had improved his stamina and endurance, as well as his muscle tone. Likewise, Adelle Davis's *Let's Eat Right to Keep Fit* (1954) guided his ideas on nutrition and the importance of minimally processed foods, though he avoided some of her less scientifically credible assertions.[23]

Health was really a matter of commitment and discipline, and if Proxmire could do it, so could anyone. In 1972, he published *You Can Do It! Senator Proxmire's Exercise, Diet and Relaxation Plan* in which he outlined his methods. A person's youth, he wrote, "is likely to be a period of uncertainty, frustration, and depression" despite good health. Those who followed his recommendations could have the energy and health of a twenty-year-old at age sixty or older. "With glowing good health," he promised, "maturity can truly be a happy, joyful, full, exuberant time of life." Beyond individual fulfillment, good health was a national necessity since prosperity and abundance had made Americans overweight, weak, and lazy. It was "your patriotic duty" to improve. Self-discipline, Proxmire solemnly warned readers, was the price of freedom.[24] His recommendations included vigorous, sustained exercise like walking, running, or swimming. He dismissed popular sports like baseball, football, and tennis as worthless since they did not keep the cardiovascular system continuously working hard. Americans, Proxmire advised, should avoid refined sugar and processed foods, especially commercially baked bread ("a nutritional disaster"), and eat smaller, more frequent meals based on lean protein, fruits, and vegetables.[25]

The worst offense was alcohol consumption. Proxmire called cocktail hour "the single most destructive habit in the civilized world." Here again, he was recalling his own family experience. His father had lectured him about the dangers of alcohol, and Proxmire was well aware that his mother had been a borderline alcoholic. With his own competitive nature, Proxmire knew that alcohol was a danger to him. He did everything quickly, and in a social setting would feel compelled to stay ahead of everyone else. His stepdaughter later recalled his aversion to drinking: "The first time he had a drink . . . he realized right then, because of his personality, that he wouldn't be able to stop at just one."[26] Proxmire thrived on self-denial and self-discipline, and he was convinced his personal improvements would benefit his family and the nation.

In response to the charge of ineffectiveness that threatened his re-election in 1964, Proxmire reorganized his office staff during his second full term and by 1970 was widely acknowledged to have one of the best office staffs in Congress. When he first went to Washington in 1957, Proxmire hired Robert Lewis as his administrative assistant. Lewis, who had worked for the Wisconsin Farmers' Union and edited the *Wisconsin REA News*, had tutored Proxmire extensively on farm issues, which Proxmire in turn used to court rural voters by sending press releases to small-town radio stations about his agricultural policies. Lewis's influence was obvious when Proxmire took on secretary of agriculture Ezra Taft Benson, against whom Lewis had railed for years in the pages of the *REA News*. Almost immediately, the new senator received a call from a furious Senator John F. Kennedy, angered at Lewis's very public criticism of the Massachusetts senator's support for Benson's policies. Proxmire couldn't very well repudiate the farm policies he had endorsed for years, but he also did not want to risk alienating the most popular senator. Lewis was able to smooth things over with Ted Sorenson, then Kennedy's administrative assistant, but the relationship between Lewis and Proxmire never recovered. Lewis thought Proxmire's public fight with Lyndon Johnson was little more than pandering to Wisconsin voters, and wanted him to behave more collegially rather than develop a reputation as a maverick. Proxmire, in turn, was

furious with the number of part-time staff Lewis hired to send out boiler-
plate letters to constituents under the senator's signature. By March 1959,
Proxmire's staff had ballooned to seventy-five, mostly low-pay, part-time
workers, but nonetheless the largest in the Senate by far. The public revelation damaged Proxmire's reputation for efficiency and frugality: Senate
staffs typically numbered between ten and fifteen, and even Johnson had
only twenty-eight. Proxmire told Lewis that he needed to find another
job, and he was quickly hired by Governor Gaylord Nelson to serve as the
agricultural expert on his staff.[27] After the fiasco with Lewis, Proxmire
did not hire an administrative assistant until 1969, preferring to run his
office himself. This, too, caused problems because Proxmire was a difficult
senator to work for. Many staffers found him aloof and hard to approach.
His tendency to work on his own speeches and press releases rather than
delegate those tasks—or even consult others—tended to leave them with
little to do. One press secretary had to admit to UPI that he knew nothing
about a press release that Proxmire had issued without his knowledge, and
another wanted to quit after just a few months on the job. Consequently,
Proxmire had one of the largest turnovers of any congressional office. "It
is easy to find former Proxmire aides in Washington," one former staffer
noted. "The town is full of them."[28]

By the late 1960s, Proxmire recognized his need for talented people
who could support him, and he began assembling a smaller but more effective office staff. He hired a new press secretary, Mark Shields, in reaction to
the *Pageant* poll. Shields's job was to write a monthly column for the Wisconsin AFL-CIO newspaper under the senator's name and to disseminate
stories to the press about Proxmire's accomplishments. He was also tasked
with reducing Proxmire's reputation as a loner, "to improve relations with
the Senate and help to get him on the Democratic Steering Committee."[29]
In 1964, Proxmire hired former intern Thomas van der Voort as a legislative assistant, and he worked closely with Proxmire on the reapportionment fight and on specialized agricultural issues, most importantly
dairy subsidies. Van der Voort had no connection to Wisconsin, but he had
degrees from Princeton and Harvard Law School, which reflected Proxmire's own Ivy League background.[30] In fact, few of Proxmire's staff came
from Wisconsin, but most had advanced degrees, and Proxmire delighted
in summoning one of them to his office every week to debate whatever

issue the staffer wanted. Martin Lobel, originally from Boston and with law degrees from Boston University and Harvard, joined the staff in 1967 after teaching law at the University of Oklahoma. Ann Purcell became the office receptionist in 1965, but Proxmire quickly promoted the New Yorker to the position of legislative assistant, and she, with Shields, wrote many of the senator's speeches on the Genocide Convention. The most important addition to the staff came in 1969, when Proxmire hired Howard Shuman as his first administrative assistant in nearly a decade. Shuman had worked in the same capacity for Paul Douglas, and he brought stability to the office and ended the days of high turnover. Shuman was tasked with hiring intelligent people who could quickly learn complicated subject matter and write well. Legislative assistants were each given a portfolio of subjects and reported directly to the senator. Ronald Tammen, who succeeded Shuman as administrative assistant in 1982, recalled that by 1972, "the office had become quite permanent . . . because we'd had the opportunity to hire new people who were very loyal and who were compensated fairly and who had a free hand to do what they wanted to do and liked to do and felt good about coming to the office every day."[31]

Proxmire expected his staff to work hard—constituent mail was to be answered within twenty-four hours—and he, of course, led by example. His staff was considerably smaller than it had been in the early 1960s, but he paid them fairly and was still able to return unspent money from his office budget, an accomplishment he made sure Wisconsin voters knew about. Indeed, the lack of turnover in the 1970s and 1980s demonstrates the loyalty the staff showed Proxmire and the respectful way he treated his staff. Proxmire never lost his temper or yelled at any employee, unlike some of his famously short-tempered colleagues, and he encouraged his staff to share their opinions. Ann Purcell recalled that "most of the time he kept his door closed to the office, but I think most of us felt like when we wanted to talk to him, we'd just open the door to go talk to him."

Proxmire was just as loyal to his staff as they were to him. Sometime after Purcell joined the antiwar group Congressional Employees against the War, she risked embarrassing the senator by inadvertently sending out a letter from the group from Proxmire's office. Proxmire immediately issued a press release defending the right of congressional staff to have their own opinions. In another instance, when an executive from a large Wisconsin company tried to intimidate Martin Lobel, Proxmire summoned the businessman into his office and told him, "You will never, ever talk to my staff [like that] again. If you do that one more time, you will never cross the threshold to my office." On the other hand, Proxmire had no tolerance for disloyalty or corruption. He fired one staffer who surreptitiously wrote a gossipy column for his hometown newspaper about the inner workings of the office. When his home secretary in Milwaukee, Luther Dyb, was alleged to have accepted bribes to help procure Small Business Administration loans, Proxmire hired a lawyer to investigate the matter, turned his findings over to the FBI, and demanded Dyb's resignation. Dyb was convicted of bribery in September 1969. Despite these few instances, however, throughout the 1970s and 1980s, this small, dedicated staff wrote speeches, researched issues, and responded to constituents with incredible effectiveness. "They make me look good," Proxmire beamed.[32]

As the Senate office was fast becoming a second family, Proxmire's own family underwent some significant changes. Mary Ellen, then a student at the University of Wisconsin, married Dr. Richard Katz in June 1967 in Washington. Enduring some financial difficulties, the Katzes were unable to provide the rehearsal dinner, as was customary. Ellen graciously offered to organize and host the dinner at the Proxmire home as well as plan the large wedding. Proxmire gamely joined in the work and busied himself finding chairs and setting up tables on the deck and backyard when more people than expected arrived. For Ellen, successfully planning a large, complicated event was an eye-opening experience; she recognized that there was a demand for wedding planning and that she had the ability to organize and host events. Wanting to do something other than organizing car pools for their children, Ellen and two friends, Barbara Boggs and Gretchen Poston, decided to found their own company. Each put in $150 for startup money, and Wonderful Weddings was born. In its first year, the company made each of the partners $400. Soon afterward, however, a guest asked if they could help plan a convention, and the company began organizing tours, conventions, meetings, and other events. In 1969, Harriet Schwartz and Dorothy Mickler joined as partners to handle the growing workload. In 1970, the company changed its name to Washington Whirl-Around, and Ellen and her partners were making $6,000 each and had to add full- and part-time staff. After nearly twenty years focused on family and politics, Ellen had suddenly developed a new life outside of her husband's career and children's lives.[33]

A mostly permanent staff allowed Proxmire to play a more prominent role in the Senate, and with the inauguration of Richard Nixon in January 1969, he again became an opposition senator. Yet it was abundantly clear that the independent-minded Proxmire would continue to chart his own course no matter who sat in the Oval Office. In his January newsletter, he outlined five ways to reduce the federal budget; number one was "Slash Military Spending." Throughout 1969 and 1970, Proxmire used his position as chair of the Joint Economic Committee's Subcommittee on Economy in Government to expose Pentagon waste. Moreover, after his explosive investigation into the C5-A and with a Republican president, a growing number of his congressional colleagues joined his fight against excessive defense department spending.[34]

At first, the Nixon administration, eager to distance itself from the increasingly unpopular war in Vietnam that Johnson had escalated, appeared supportive of reduced military spending. On February 18, budget director Robert P. Mayo told the Joint Economic Committee that he had hired an assistant director to critically review all military spending proposals in an effort to eliminate inefficient or unnecessary programs. Proxmire was delighted at Mayo's pledge that nothing would be "sacrosanct" and that military spending would receive the same scrutiny as domestic spending. New secretary of defense Melvin Laird, however, had markedly different views of what could be cut, and in March submitted a fiscal year 1970 budget reduction recommendation to the White House of $78.5 billion, only $500 million less than Johnson's final request; pressure from Mayo later resulted in a slightly lower $77.3 billion.[35]

Even before the White House submitted a final budget proposal to Congress, Proxmire made clear that he intended to push for far greater cuts to military spending. On March 10, he took to the floor and, with a comprehensive list of projects that cost double their estimates and underperformed in tests, declared that the "day of the blank check for military spending must end." He demanded competitive bidding to replace the current system of negotiated contracts that incentivized unrealistic low estimates and a more effective auditing of defense contracts with stiffer penalties for contractors who failed to deliver systems on time. Proxmire's new blast at the military-industrial complex in the waning years of the Vietnam War marked a turning point: from now on, the Pentagon's budget would be met with more skepticism than support on Capitol Hill.[36] The problem, as Proxmire saw it, was a revolving-door relationship between the military and a small number of defense contractors. In March, he released a study showing that 2,072 retired high-ranking officers (colonel or navy captain or higher) worked for the ninety-five leading defense contractors. A similar report produced in 1959 by Paul Douglas's office showed 721 retired officers working for eighty-eight contractors, indicating a nearly threefold increase in ten years. The list included many of the largest manufacturers of military aircraft. General Dynamics employed 113; Lockheed, 210; McDonnell Douglas, 141; and Boeing, 169. This was the military-industrial complex at work, and Proxmire argued that it was a very real threat in a system in which the Pentagon awarded 90 percent of military contracts by negotiation rather than competitive bidding. "How hard a bargain," Proxmire wondered, "will officers involved in procurement planning or specifications drive with contractors when they are one or two years away from retirement and have the example to look at of over 2,000 fellow officers doing well on the outside after retirement?"[37]

Proxmire called the Nixon administration's proposed $1.2 billion cut to the Pentagon's budget "grossly inadequate" and asserted that defense spending could be easily reduced by $10 billion without threatening national security. Many in Congress now agreed. In an interview with reporter John Finney, Senate majority leader Mike Mansfield explained the sudden change in attitude: "They've been able to get about everything they've asked for up to this time. The Senate and Congress I think has, in part, been shirking its responsibility, and it's up to us to take up the slack and achieve a balance." He credited Proxmire's criticism of military spending with helping to move the Senate in a new direction. In addition to Mansfield, Proxmire was joined by Mark Hatfield, George McGovern, John Sherman Cooper, Philip Hart, Ted Kennedy, Stuart Symington, Edmund Muskie, Albert Gore, and Gaylord Nelson, each of whom was determined to challenge Pentagon requests.[38]

Proxmire's Joint Subcommittee on Economy in Government issued a blistering report in May, calling for a $10 billion cut to the Pentagon's budget and referring to the current procurement method as "a vast subsidy to the defense industry" and the single biggest cause of inflation. Rather than backing a proposal by George McGovern to impose a surtax on defense contractors, Proxmire urged that the General Accounting Office be granted greater authority to investigate Pentagon spending as a means of controlling costs. Proxmire's subcommittee began eight days of hearings in early June that featured former White House officials admitting lax oversight of the defense budget, and John Kenneth Galbraith's stunning recommendation that any company doing more than 75 percent of its business with the Defense Department be nationalized. The hearings revealed more examples of cost overruns that suggested the C-5A debacle was not an isolated case. The Minuteman missile system was expected to cost nearly $4 billion more than originally estimated, for example, and the cost of the navy's Deep Submergible Rescue Vehicle program had increased an astounding 2,700 percent. Witnesses testified that employees who tried to rein in costs routinely suffered retaliation, including termination. Conversely, officers who blocked efforts to reduce costs were hired by contractors, a conflict of interest that was referred to attorney general John Mitchell. In August, the committee heard testimony that B. F. Goodrich had falsified test results for a braking system it was developing for the air force in order to conceal the fact that the brakes failed to perform to Pentagon specifications.[39]

The hearings eventually produced a backlash from the administration when President Nixon, in a commencement speech at the Air Force Academy, questioned the patriotism of "new isolationists" who were jeopardizing American interests abroad. This was disturbing and reminded Proxmire of the tactics of Joseph McCarthy, since the president was blatantly trying to intimidate those who questioned ever-increasing military spending as the best way to advance American interests.[40] The subcommittee's hearings also faced stonewalling from those inside the military industrial complex itself. Former defense secretary Robert McNamara declined the subcommittee's invitation to testify, stating that testifying while head of the World Bank would set a precedent that would open him up to demands from the legislatures of member states, much to the irritation of Proxmire and other senators. Likewise, the chief executives of some defense contractors refused to appear before Proxmire's subcommittee, including the presidents of Lockheed, Boeing, and General Dynamics.[41]

Proxmire's hearings marked a turning point that led to increased congressional scrutiny of military spending. The Senate approved the administration's controversial antiballistic missile system by just one vote, despite desperate lobbying by administration officials, and Congress voted to make major weapons contracts subject to audit by the General Accounting Office. This new concern over defense spending that Proxmire had initiated was more than just Democratic doves criticizing a Republican-led Defense Department. Eighteen Republicans joined twenty-nine Democrats in voting for the auditing authority amendment, introduced by Republican Richard Schweiker of Pennsylvania. An editorial in the *New York Times* commented on "the irritation with the military now prevalent on Capitol Hill" as a result of the recent revelations: "For this lack of candor and heedlessness of the public welfare, the military now finds itself paying a price. Fortunately the evidence is overwhelming that there are still billions of dollars to be trimmed from the defense budget before that price becomes a threat to the national security. All that is happening now is a desirable reassertion of civilian review responsibility on Capitol Hill."[42]

Proxmire's views were now shared by many of his fellow senators, but in the end, the new mood of congressional scrutiny had far less impact on defense spending than Proxmire had hoped. As the Senate debated a Pentagon spending bill in the fall, Proxmire vowed to cut $10 billion, including $533 million for twenty-three more C-5A planes, from the budget. Proxmire's amendment to cut funding for the planes failed by a vote of 64–23, but the Senate did pass his amendment to require public disclosure of former Pentagon officials working for defense contractors, which he had identified as one of the principal causes of cost overruns. Another Proxmire amendment placed a $468 million ceiling on Pentagon funding for "independent research" conducted by defense contractors. He and his fellow critics managed to cut only about $71 million from the $20 billion weapons appropriation bill before it was finally passed in November. Proxmire voted for the bill but promised that he would continue to fight wasteful defense spending. He nonetheless felt optimistic about the effect that he and his fellow spending critics had on reining in the Pentagon. For the first time, a major weapons system backed by the president had been openly challenged in Congress, and public concern over military spending and lax Pentagon oversight, to a large degree the result of Proxmire's work, resulted in a reduction of nearly $3 billion from former President Johnson's initial request, though almost all of that reduction occurred in committee or in the White House budget office.[43]

President Nixon responded to the Subcommittee on Economy in Government hearings by forming a panel to investigate Pentagon procurement policies and management. This sixteen-person committee, however, included nine members with connections to the largest companies with defense contracts. "Obviously," Proxmire complained in a Senate speech, "this panel is caught in the embrace of the very bureaucracy it is supposed to evaluate and constructively criticize." Clearly, Proxmire and other Pentagon critics would have no support from the administration, and another showdown on the Senate floor loomed over the fiscal year 1971 defense budget. Proxmire's subcommittee recommended a $10 billion cut to the Defense Department budget, which he estimated to be between $75 and $78 billion, arguing that the United States already had significant military superiority over the Soviet Union and did not need to continue developing new weapons programs. Although Republican members of the subcommittee accused Proxmire of pulling those figures out of thin air, the General Accounting Office subsequently confirmed his figures. Cost overruns in thirty-eight major weapons systems over the past few years had added up to $20 billion. Proxmire's demand to cut $10 billion suddenly seemed like a more than reasonable way to curb defense spending.[44]

Even when the Defense Department announced budget reductions in January 1970, Proxmire found reason to raise the alarm. Laird proposed a "rock bottom" Defense Department budget of $71.8 billion for fiscal year 1971, a reduction of $5.2 billion from the previous year. Yet the total amount of savings gained by the troop reductions, civilian job cuts, and reduced spending in Vietnam contained in the department's budget projections, Proxmire argued, should actually add up to nearly $25 billion. By adding the $5.2 billion reduction to $10 billion to account for pay raises, inflation, and other unavoidable costs, he concluded that there was still $10 billion hidden in the budget that would be used for new and unnecessary weapons systems. He announced that the Pentagon had thereby "stolen" $10 billion of the "peace dividend" heralded by the Nixon administration rather than making that money available for domestic spending.[45] Throughout the spring, Proxmire continued to make the argument against the current system of defense contracting and published a book based on his subcommittee's findings: *Report from the Wasteland: America's Military-Industrial Complex*, a clear explanation of the connections between defense contractors and the military that drove defense spending higher and a clarion call for Congress to rein in the Pentagon.

In the Senate in the summer and fall of 1970, Proxmire led a bipartisan group of senators calling for reductions in defense spending, but as in the year before, they met with little success. The main battleground was the $19.2 billion appropriation for military hardware approved by the Armed Services Committee, chaired by John Stennis of Mississippi, one of the Senate's major hawks. Its 121-page report defended the need to maintain military spending and recommended only a modest $1 billion reduction to the administration's request. The same day the Armed Services Committee released its report, a bipartisan group calling itself "Members of Congress for Peace through Law" issued a 150-page rebuttal that called for $5.4 billion in cuts.[46] There were some small victories. The Senate almost unanimously passed Proxmire's bill to require uniform cost-accounting procedures for defense contractors, and Proxmire also secured passage of a $20 million ceiling on loans from the Pentagon to private businesses. The Senate, however, rejected amendments to cut a $322 million expansion of the Safeguard antimissile system and require the Pentagon to report to Congress if it was following its new "fly-before-you-buy" policy of testing new systems before purchase. The senate also rejected 42–31 Proxmire's amendment to place a $66 billion ceiling on total Defense Department spending for fiscal year 1971, a cut of about $5.2 billion, though he took some satisfaction in seeing one-third of the Senate agree with his desire to significantly reduce military spending. In the end, the Senate approved nearly all of the Pentagon's requests, leaving Proxmire vowing to fight on.[47]

Criticism of Pentagon spending, however, did not translate into outspoken opposition to the Vietnam War. Proxmire considered himself a "lean hawk" and continued his move toward the other congressional doves with caution. At their state convention in June 1969, Wisconsin Democrats passed a resolution calling for an immediate withdrawal of all US troops from Vietnam, a position far beyond that of Proxmire, and even that of Nelson and Kastenmeier, who were the state's biggest critics of the war. Although he repeatedly defended the right of individuals to criticize the government, Proxmire did remain concerned about the potential impact the antiwar movement might have on those subject to the draft. While shaking hands at a Milwaukee shopping center, he chatted with several young men who told the senator that they planned to refuse to serve in the army if drafted. He responded that he was encouraged by the combat lull and by developments in peace negotiations, and advised them not to risk their own futures by making a "hasty" and "ill-advised" decision. He did, however, support public rallies calling for an end to the war, again based on his respect for free speech: "We have a new president who desires to end the war," he wrote in a cautious statement read at the event. "We owe him not the moratorium on criticism that Senate Republican leaders requested, but constructive work for peace which is what the Vietnam moratorium should be." He did, however, refuse to take part personally. Ever mindful of public opinion, Proxmire surveyed his constituents about their thoughts on Vietnam. More than twelve thousand responded to his questionnaire, though the results demonstrated lingering divisions among Wisconsin voters. Most respondents wanted the war to end, but the survey revealed contrasting attitudes on how to do that. Presented with three options, those completing the survey could vote "yes" or "no" to each. As a result, 64 percent favored gradual withdrawal of US troops ("Vietnamization"), but at the same time 54 percent said "yes" to taking whatever action necessary to win the war quickly, and 60 percent said "yes" to a withdrawal of all US troops within a year.[48]

When Nixon widened the war by invading Cambodia in early 1970, however, Proxmire quickly joined with other congressional critics in denouncing the move. "We should stay out of Cambodia completely and wholly," he declared on April 29. "I am unqualifiedly against intervention. If we haven't learned our lesson after 40,000 dead Americans in Vietnam and $100 billion in spending, we never will." The optimism for a peace settlement he had expressed the previous year evaporated. He warned that for the first time in American history, Congress might force the president to reverse his action and withdraw troops. Within a few days, Proxmire announced plans to offer a resolution to ban the deployment of draftees to Vietnam and Cambodia and instead rely on an all-volunteer force.[49]

As the Senate debated the war and the Pentagon budget in the summer of 1970, Proxmire's voting record became decidedly antiwar. He voted against an amendment proposed by Robert Dole to prohibit any restrictions on the president's actions in Cambodia (it failed 36–54). Likewise, he voted against an amendment offered by Robert Byrd that gave the president the authority to commit troops to Cambodia without prior congressional approval, which failed 47–52. He also voted for an amendment to restrict future military operations in Cambodia, which passed 58–37. Never before had the Senate offered such clear opposition to presidential foreign policy, but there were limits. In August, the Senate rejected a proposal to end the draft, and in September, it rejected an amendment, introduced by George McGovern and Mark Hatfield, to set a December 31, 1971, deadline for the withdrawal of all US troops. Proxmire supported both amendments. His own amendment, to exempt draftees from serving in Vietnam, was rejected 71–22.[50]

Although military spending was Proxmire's biggest concern, he also worried about nonmilitary spending and the effect that it was having on the economy, which was increasingly plagued by inflation. In addition to wanting $10 billion cut from the defense budget, Proxmire also called for reductions in federal public works, the space program, and the SST, totaling an additional $5 to $6 billion. Proxmire's goal was not simply cutting spending for the sake of cutting spending—he hoped that doing so would ease inflation and make the 10 percent surtax, scheduled to expire on June 30, 1969, unnecessary. Treasury secretary David M. Kennedy, however, told the Joint Economic Committee in late February that he was more concerned about a recession, and warned that anti-inflationary efforts would slow down the US economy. Labor secretary George Schultz likewise recommended a much more gradual approach to fighting inflation. Despite urging from Nixon administration officials, Proxmire remained adamant that ending the surtax and cutting spending were the keys to limiting inflation. When the Joint Economic Committee issued its report in April, it called for inflation reduction to be the primary objective of federal economic policy, either through a continuation of the surtax or, as Proxmire demanded, reductions in federal spending of at least $12 billion.[51]

Why did Proxmire insist on greater spending cuts to finance the repeal of the surtax? A large part of the answer likely lies in the fact that he was up for reelection in 1970, and Wisconsin voters continued to identify taxes as their major concern. Tax fairness, therefore, was a sure winner with voters as well as a familiar issue that dated back to his gubernatorial campaigns in the 1950s. Accordingly, Proxmire called for ending tax loopholes that benefited the wealthy and corporations—the oil depletion allowance was a favorite target—and reducing taxes paid by families. Throughout the summer and fall of 1969, Proxmire continued to demand cuts in federal spending and tax reductions, but fears of recession resulted in a federal budget that continued the surtax at 5 percent and maintained spending.[52]

Throughout 1970, the specter of recession haunted the Nixon administration, and the president's economic advisors continued to advocate for policies that would combat growing unemployment without fueling inflation. Proxmire's position on the Joint Economic Committee again gave him the perfect platform from which to challenge the administration. When Paul W. McCracken, chair of the Council of Economic Advisors, predicted that unemployment would reach 4.3 percent in 1970, the highest in years, Proxmire demanded to know what the administration would do if unemployment increased beyond that figure. McCracken ruled out wage and price controls, even though Congress had authorized the president to issue them, but he vacillated on what further action the administration might take. The new Federal Reserve Chair, Arthur F. Burns, depicted a positive overall economic picture but also received sharp questioning from Proxmire, who insisted that the economy was already slowing down. Treasury secretary Charles Walker also received a hostile reception at the Joint Economic Committee when he urged patience with inflation and unemployment. After Proxmire pressed him on any plans that the administration was developing for an economic slowdown, Walker exploded, "No you listen here. I quarrel with the idea that there's going to be a lot of unemployment." An exasperated Proxmire shot back, "We want to know what you're going to do about inflation and unemployment and you won't tell us!"[53] Proxmire's criticism finally produced a more specific answer from Burns, who wrote Proxmire that inflation would gradually but significantly slow in 1970 and that the Federal Reserve would become more flexible in monetary policy to counter "unexpected variations in the performance of the economy." In other words, the Nixon plan was to walk a narrow path to keep both unemployment and inflation low.[54]

Yet as the unemployment rate continued to increase throughout 1970, Proxmire kept prodding the administration to take a more active role in the economy while cutting government spending to prevent inflation. In June, Nixon called for voluntary wage and price controls, a move welcomed by Proxmire, who had criticized the oil and automobile industries for what he called inflationary price increases. Congress, however, resisted Proxmire's continued efforts to reduce spending, particularly in the space program. In August, the Senate approved a $5.2 billion public works bill, with Proxmire casting the lone vote against it. The economic outlook was dismal indeed, and economists began using the term "stagflation" to describe an economy that defied conventional remedies. Rather than falling as confidently predicted by Burns and other administration officials, inflation rates had risen to 6 percent by the fall. Unemployment increased from 3.5 percent to 5.5 percent, despite the optimistic predictions of McCracken. Moreover, interest rates remained close to record highs, further limiting economic growth. Proxmire called for the Nixon administration to develop a jobs program, making the federal government "the employer of last resort," whenever the unemployment rate exceeded 5.5 percent. He also called on the president to fund the Emergency Housing Act to stimulate the housing industry, which would have a positive ripple effect throughout the economy. Characterizing then-current inflation as cost-push inflation driven by wage increases rather than demand inflation, Proxmire urged the president to enact wage and price guidelines. Finally, Proxmire pressed Nixon to reduce military spending and redirect those funds to domestic programs. This set of sober recommendations would become the main focus of Proxmire's economic ideas as he began his third full term in 1971.[55]

While he was fighting increased military spending, Proxmire also continued to develop his reputation as an advocate for consumer credit reform, building on his success in getting Congress to pass the landmark truth-in-lending bill in 1968. That fall, Proxmire announced plans to introduce more safeguards against credit card abuse. Citing the case of a janitor who earned $55 a week and declared bankruptcy after racking up $3,000 in debt on an unsolicited credit card, Proxmire proposed ending the common practice of banks sending credit cards indiscriminately to unwary, mostly young, consumers. He also announced plans to introduce legislation allowing consumers to correct errors in credit reports and require credit bureaus to keep those reports confidential.[56] When Congress convened in January 1969, Proxmire introduced an amendment to the Truth-in-Lending Act that would require credit card issuers to check an individual's credit history before sending an unsolicited credit card and imposed a $50 limit on that individual's liability for its unauthorized use. A second bill, the Fair Credit Reporting bill, gave individuals the right to correct wrong information, know when they were denied credit due to a negative credit report, and find out when adverse information was added to it. The issue affected more people than perhaps any other measure before Congress, since credit bureaus had files on over one hundred million Americans. The bill was subsequently endorsed by Paul Rand Dixon, chair of the Federal Trade Commission, and by Virginia H. Knauer, the president's special assistant for consumer affairs, who recommended several ways to strengthen the bill during hearings in late May. Opposition to the measure came from the American Bankers Association, which insisted that credit bureaus were capable of policing themselves and that the bill unfairly depicted all of them as engaging in sloppy work. Proxmire was delighted with their stance: "That makes their record perfect," he commented. "They opposed the Federal Reserve Act, the Federal Deposit Insurance Corporation, the Truth-in-Lending Act. If the bankers had endorsed this bill, it would have been the kiss of death." In March, Proxmire introduced a third measure, which would require the Federal Reserve Board to set maximum rates for credit insurance policies that guaranteed minimum payments in the case of disability. He claimed that the public was overcharged more than $220 million in these policies, selected by credit issuers but paid for by consumers. The Senate passed the Fair Credit Reporting Act by voice vote in November.[57]

Proxmire's other bills proved more controversial. During an unusual Sunday morning hearing before the Senate Banking Subcommittee on Financial Institutions, witnesses described how mass mailings of unsolicited credit cards were regularly stolen and sold for $100 on the black market, increasing mail fraud cases by 700 percent in just a few years. Proxmire used a pair of scissors to dramatically cut in half one card he himself had received in the mail to illustrate the potential danger to unwitting consumers who found themselves liable for charges made on cards they had not requested. The Nixon administration, however, was much less willing to support this bill. A representative from the President's Committee on

Consumer Interests warned that limits on this common practice could insulate established issuers from competition, driving up interest costs for consumer credit. Republicans on the Senate Banking Committee also opposed the bill, supporting instead a proposal that would allow unsolicited cards to be issued if companies sent a letter forty-five days in advance giving individuals the right to opt out. With full Democratic support, the committee approved the bill to ban unsolicited cards and cap consumer liability at $50 by a vote of 9–6. Despite misgivings from the Nixon administration and Republican opposition on the committee, the bill passed the Senate by an astonishing vote of 79–1. Both of Proxmire's consumer credit protection bills stalled in the House of Representatives, which took no action on either measure. To get his bills passed, Proxmire introduced them as amendments to a previously passed House bill dealing with foreign bank accounts, and the president signed them into law in October 1970.[58]

As the 1970 Senate election neared, Proxmire was determined to emphasize his role as an effective legislator to finally exorcise the painful allegations made by the *Pageant* poll in 1964. Even before the 1968 election, he was worried about his own reelection, the potential effect of Nelson's reelection, and a potential challenge from Governor Knowles. Proxmire was about the only one who had any doubt about the outcome, and he wasted no time in laying the groundwork. Shortly after the 1968 elections, Richard Cudahy and John Finerty organized a reelection committee and laid out a fund-raising plan. At first, rumors swirled about a potential challenge to Proxmire in the Democratic primary, with some suggesting that attorney general Bronson La Follette or former Green Bay Packers coach Vince Lombardi might run, each depending on his famous name to unseat the incumbent. But who would Proxmire face in the general election? The obvious Republican candidate, popular governor Warren Knowles, announced his retirement from politics after completing his third term in 1971. Republican leaders then tried to recruit a big-name "glamorous" candidate, and state party chair Ody Fish worked hard to get astronaut and Milwaukee native James Lovell or former Packers quarterback Bart Starr to enter the race.[59] Starr quickly denied having any political aspirations, but Lovell entertained the idea through the spring of 1970, fueling speculation when he announced that he would retire after the Apollo 13 mission and refused to rule out a Senate run. Not until the last week in April did

Lovell conclusively rule out a challenge to Proxmire.[60] Republicans then turned to another celebrity: former University of Wisconsin basketball coach and Milwaukee Bucks general manager John Erickson, who had begun talking to Republican Party leaders about a potential candidacy in February. Once Lovell announced he would not run, Erickson quickly leaped into the race, and Republicans hoped that his name recognition would match Proxmire's, especially since other announced candidates, state senators Gerald Lorge of Bear Creek and Milo Knutson of La Crosse, former state representative Robert Johnson of Mondovi, and Outagamie district attorney James Long, were almost unknown to most Wisconsin voters. At the state convention in May, Republicans enthusiastically endorsed a well-known and athletic candidate to run against the well-known and athletic Democrat.[61]

Proxmire formally announced his reelection campaign on Friday, May 22, with a series of press conferences around the state. Beginning at the La Crosse airport, he then flew to Madison, Mosinee, Green Bay, and Milwaukee, meeting reporters at each stop. In answering reporters' questions, Proxmire reinforced his position as an independent senator by taking some liberal Democratic positions as well as some that sounded strikingly conservative. He called for an end to the Vietnam War and the complete withdrawal of US troops within one year, a dramatic shift from his position just a few years earlier when he enthusiastically backed President Johnson and debated antiwar senator Wayne Morse. Yet at the same time, he had sharp words for campus protestors who resorted to violence, stating bluntly that they should be "kicked out of school." He vowed to continue his fight against wasteful military spending and promised to work for lower interest rates and a new housing program as a means of reducing unemployment. As for Erickson, he called his likely opponent "a pleasant, decent gentleman" with "literally thousands of friends throughout the state" and predicted a close election. He criticized Erickson's inexperience that contrasted his thirteen years in the Senate and his record streak of over one thousand roll-call votes.[62]

In the weeks leading up to the September primary, Erickson began traveling around the state in a large camper with his family in an effort to mimic Proxmire's own whirlwind campaign style, but he had a hard time differentiating himself from his opponent. Both candidates favored an end to the war, but Erickson fully supported President Nixon's "Vietnami-zation" policy and the Cambodian invasion. He reminded voters that Prox-mire had been an enthusiastic supporter of Johnson's escalation of the war, but Proxmire's current demand for withdrawal of troops made it hard for Erickson to identify Proxmire with the unpopular war. He tried to depict Proxmire as a grandstanding politician who was out of touch with the lives of ordinary citizens, despite the senator's frequent weekend trips to the state.[63]

Erickson was clearly flailing, but without a primary opponent, Prox-mire saved most of his campaigning for September and October, and even then he seldom mentioned Erickson. Erickson continued trying to provoke a response from the "elusive" Proxmire by mocking him as a "security risk" or "kidnapper" of the president's appropriation bills for his criticism of defense spending, or "billion dollar Bill" for his support for housing and welfare funds. The Nixon administration tried to boost Erickson's candi-dacy by sending Vice President Spiro Agnew to a Milwaukee fund-raising dinner, and Erickson met with Nixon in the White House to discuss the campaign. Nixon himself praised Erickson during a late-October visit to Green Bay, transforming a celebratory event in honor of Bart Starr into a de facto GOP rally. Erickson also embraced Nixon's outreach to working-class whites by calling for voluntary prayer in public schools and an amendment to the Constitution to overturn the "one-man, one-vote" Supreme Court decision. Proxmire's advertisements promoted his efforts to curb military spending: "Invest in Senator Proxmire's Economy Campaign," urged one that asked for donations of $1 to $5. "The fight for economy," trumpeted another; "Proxmire wrote the book on it!" Referring to *Report from the Wasteland*, Anne Purcell and Thomas van der Voort developed a series of effective television commercials that emphasized the senator's fight against wasteful military spending, his support of the truth-in-lending act, and his frequent travels around Wisconsin. Erickson tried to depict Proxmire's economy drive as a danger to American security and accused the senator of underestimating the Soviet Union's military strength. Cutting military spending, he warned, would encourage the Soviets and could precipitate World War Three.[64] Election Day delivered astounding results. Proxmire completely overwhelmed Erickson 948,445 to 381,297, winning 70.8 percent of the total vote, the largest total in state history.

The other four candidates won less than 10,000 votes. Proxmire carried
every county in the state and ran far ahead of the gubernatorial candidate Patrick Lucey, who won 54.3 percent. In only seven counties (Door,
Grant, Green Lake, Marquette, Walworth, Waupaca, and Waushara) did
he win less than 60 percent of the vote, and he did equally well in heavily
urban counties and rural counties. Proxmire's accomplishment was unprecedented: he had become a liberal Democrat who appealed equally to
conservative Republicans.[65]

Proxmire's triumph at the polls finally put to rest the worry that had
haunted him since 1964; he viewed his landslide as popular acclamation
for his Senate work. The cost, however, was high. All those weekends back
in Wisconsin, his total commitment to being a senator, and his disincli-
nation to attend social events wore heavily on his marriage, which began
to unravel over the course of the campaign. In June 1971, Proxmire announced that he and Ellen were separating. Proxmire bought a house a few
blocks away on Ordway Street, and Douglas began spending time at both
houses. About a year later, Ellen reflected on the situation, noting how
commitment to public service interfered with family life. That, she mused,
"was often very disappointing to the young people. If Bill had to be in the
Senate . . . he couldn't go to a graduation. It's a constant conflict . . . you
can't ever plan anything."[66] His triumphant return to the Senate in 1971
and his move into the national spotlight was thus marred by the apparent
disintegration of his family life.

8

A Senator of Substance

Living apart from Ellen in the early 1970s, Proxmire seemed to be going through a minor midlife crisis and exhibited a sudden interest in his appearance. In February 1972, he showed up at a committee hearing wearing sunglasses, barely concealing two black eyes. Ignoring the substance of the hearing, reporters instead wanted to know about the glasses, only to receive a terse "no comment" in reply. The truth came out a few days later: Senator Proxmire, the champion of thrift and healthy living, had gotten a facelift, though he refused to talk about it publicly. A few weeks later, press secretary Carl Eifert arrived in the office to find a press release on his desk, already written and ready to be issued, about Proxmire's hair replacement. Eifert's first reaction was that it was inappropriate to comment on the senator's medical procedure, but when he entered Proxmire's office and saw his head swathed in bandages like a turban, he realized such an outlandish appearance needed to be addressed, since he would preside over a Joint Economic Committee hearing. Calling the issue a nonevent but wanting to quash any rumors, he noted that "I will still be a semibaldy, but a little more semi and a little less baldy. I expect humorous, critical, amused, outraged or even ridiculing reactions. But I will acknowledge none of them. This statement is it. I consider this hair transplant to have no public significance." Privately, he admitted to one of his staffers that he thought he would look better on television with more hair.[1] The fifty-three-year-old Proxmire may have been feeling his age, but the early 1970s saw Proxmire at his most influential as he embraced his roles as leading expert on government spending and passionate fitness promoter. He relished his role as a popular, if somewhat eccentric, figure, a frequent guest on television news programs and a common sight in Wisconsin towns on the weekends.

Although he was already well-known, Proxmire dominated the news leading the fight against federal funding for the supersonic transport (SST) that Boeing was developing. The SST already had a long history by 1971. The Kennedy administration had enthusiastically supported the development of an American SST, and Congress began appropriating money to fund research in 1961. On June 5, 1963, President Kennedy formally announced at the Air Force Academy that the United States would fund the construction of a prototype SST to compete with the Anglo-French Concorde. The project reflected the boundless optimism of the time. The SST would fly at nearly two thousand miles per hour, making any city in the world reachable within hours. Supporters of the project argued that American prestige was on the line and that American airlines needed to be able to compete with European airlines. Moreover, the SST might have military applications as well if the Soviet Union developed a supersonic aircraft. NASA, the Department of Defense, and the FAA all supported federal funding for the SST. Additionally, its chief backer in Congress was the influential senator from Washington, Warren Magnuson, who was keenly aware of Boeing's importance in his home state. Above all, the SST represented the future. Just as Americans should be the first to reach the moon, American passengers should fly on American-built airplanes as a symbol of American power, or, as Kennedy put it privately, "We'll beat that bastard de Gaulle." In June, Kennedy sent his program to Congress: the federal government would pay for 75 percent of the cost of developing and testing a prototype SST up to $750 million, and Congress quickly voted a $60 million appropriation, the first of many to fund the program.[2]

Proxmire was one of the few in Congress willing to question the wisdom of federal funding to support private enterprise, even if it was a national prestige project, especially when very few Americans would actually benefit from the SST. If an SST was commercially viable, he reasoned, Boeing should not need a federal subsidy to develop it, and if it was not commercially viable, the federal government had no business funding it at all. He also doubted that federal spending could be kept under the $750 million limit set by Kennedy. By September 1966, Proxmire had begun calling the SST program a "jet-set giveaway" and tried to block funding in the Senate. Striking a populist note, he mocked the typical passenger as a playboy flying his girlfriend to Paris in two and a half hours, leaving behind a trail of sonic booms and broken windows. According to Proxmire: "For the federal government to provide this kind of massive subsidy to a private industry is virtually unprecedented." The playboy imagery was an exaggeration, but he was right about the cost. In April 1967, after Boeing and General Electric won the competition to build the prototypes, President Johnson announced that he would request $198 million in funding for fiscal year 1968. Transportation secretary Alan Boyd projected a total cost of over $1.14 billion to have two planes built by 1970 and to begin commercial service by 1974. Proxmire called it a "wasteful blunder" and predicted the costs would rise to $4 billion. It was not just the cost, either. Many were concerned that the sonic booms generated by the SST were a threat to property and human health, a charge ignored by the FAA in its promotion of the SST. Proxmire tried to remove funding for the SST, but the Senate rejected his budget amendment 54–19.[3] Throughout the rest of the decade, Proxmire continued to call for the elimination of funding for the SST, to little effect. In September 1969, President Nixon, after months of uncertainty, stated bluntly that development of the SST would continue and that he would ask Congress for an additional $662 million to finish the project, with an immediate appropriation of $95.5 million for fiscal year 1970. His request easily passed the House, but the Senate Appropriations Committee reduced the amount to $80 million. Proxmire again offered an amendment to the $2.14 billion transportation funding bill to strip the $80 million, but he lost again, 58–22.[4]

The heady optimism of Camelot made it hard to argue against an American SST, but by 1970, the atmosphere in Washington had become decidedly more cynical, especially after Proxmire's Joint Economic Committee had revealed systemic cost overruns by defense contractors. In May, the Joint Economic Committee held hearings on the SST, and for the first time, an administration official acknowledged that federal commitments to the program could reach as high as $4 billion, as Proxmire had warned, if private financing could not be found to fund production. In its report, issued in August, the committee recommended an immediate halt to the program and the removal of the current $290 million appropriation in Congress. The principal issue was financial liability. If the SST did not perform as expected, or if Boeing sold fewer than the three hundred needed to break even, then taxpayers would be on the hook for up to $4 billion. Beyond simple numbers, environmental activists began demanding an end to the SST program because of potential adverse impacts. Transportation officials denied charges that supersonic flight would cause environmental problems or be noisier than standard jets that operated at a much lower altitude. Yet the environmental argument proved effective, especially when Proxmire pointed out that the Department of Transportation had not filed an environmental impact statement as required by the 1970 Environmental Protection Act, suggesting that Boeing had something to hide. Until it did so, he argued, the Senate should not vote on the appropriation request.[5]

With dire predictions of massive cost overruns and concerns over the environmental impact, the debate reached fever pitch in the fall of 1970. Advocates insisted that an American-built SST was critical to maintaining a positive balance of trade with Europe, while many economists dismissed that argument as simplistic. Neil Armstrong warned that Soviet-built SSTs might outcompete American manufacturers if the program was ended, resulting in a military, as well as economic, threat. In November, the Senate Appropriations Committee approved $290 million for the SST, setting up a showdown on the floor of the Senate. Desperate, pro-SST senators introduced two measures to placate anti-SST advocates and reassure uncommitted senators: they set strict noise limits for supersonic planes and banned supersonic flights over land. Proxmire supported both measures but remained resolute in his opposition to the program as a whole. By now, Proxmire had convinced many former SST supporters, and the next day the Senate approved Proxmire's amendment to remove SST funds 52–41. Proxmire admitted that he was surprised by the eleven-vote margin, much wider than even he had expected. After years of fighting, it looked like he had finally won.[6]

The battle against the SST, however, was not quite over. A few days after the Senate vote, the House refused to concur with the Senate's decision, sending the issue to a conference committee. Now there was a real chance that the funds could be restored, especially since the White House and Washington senators Magnuson and Henry Jackson, taken by surprise by the Senate vote, could lobby committee members vigorously for the funds.

Proxmire and Gaylord Nelson quickly promised to filibuster any attempt to restore the SST funds. On December 10, the conference committee approved a compromise appropriation of $210 million, which ironically was projected to increase long-term costs. Many of the fifty-two senators who had voted against funds for the SST now shifted sides, but Proxmire vowed he would continue to fight. "The conferees' action," Proxmire warned, "has increased the cost of the SST to the taxpayer by more than $150-million. It has provided no further assurance against environmental pollution, which was obviously a prime concern of many Senators who opposed the SST." He prepared for a filibuster, which threatened to keep the Senate in session through the holidays and until it adjourned on January 3, while Washington state residents began considering a retaliatory boycott against Wisconsin dairy and manufactured products, since both Proxmire and Nelson were prime movers behind the SST filibuster.[7]

The actual filibuster lasted two weeks and kept Congress in session over the holidays. Proxmire began on December 17 and almost immediately clashed with Magnuson over his last-ditch bills to limit SST noise, suggesting he introduced the bills only as a ploy to gain funding and knowing the House would not pass them. An infuriated Magnuson roared that he would spend the rest of the session lobbying house members if Proxmire would just allow a vote on the appropriation. Was his action undemocratic? Proxmire defended the filibuster as a way not to thwart the will of the majority but to protect the majority decision already made to eliminate funding. His floor speeches were all fact-filled arguments against the SST, delivered as pain from a back injury made it nearly impossible for him to stand. As negotiations to restore the funds and efforts to close debate failed, tempers flared. Senator Gordon Allott accused Proxmire and anti-SST senators of listening to "pseudoscientists" with "ridiculous" arguments; when Proxmire tried to respond, Allott refused to yield the floor: "No, I will not yield! I've been listening to you for three weeks!"[8] After a brief recess for Christmas, the Senate reconvened, but compromise suddenly seemed possible. Senate majority leader Mike Mansfield suggested separating the SST funds from the transportation bill, thus funding the program for three months, allowing a final vote on the SST in March 1971. Proxmire was added to the conference committee tasked with negotiating the compromise, which it approved over Proxmire's objections on

December 31. Proxmire finally gave in and announced he would not try to amend or filibuster the compromise, contenting himself with a long speech as a kind of last word on the subject before allowing the Senate to finally vote on the last piece of unfinished business before the Ninety-First Congress adjourned on January 2.[9]

Backers of the SST had snatched victory from the jaws of defeat, and the first two months of 1971 made it look increasingly likely that Proxmire would again fail to end the program. The Nixon administration would aggressively push for the SST, and job losses in the aerospace industry rallied organized labor behind it as well. Technical advances made the SST quieter, so environmental concerns faded into the background as economic stagnation became a more palpable problem. Yet when the $290 million appropriation came to a vote, the House rejected it in a surprising 215–204 vote, paving the way for a final showdown in the Senate, where the vote was expected to be much closer. New evidence suggested that the exhaust from the SSTs would harm the ozone layer, potentially raising the risk of skin cancer. When Proxmire raised this issue, SST backers accused him of using scare tactics. The Nixon administration brought intense pressure on Margaret Chase Smith and other Republicans who opposed the program, and the AFL-CIO put pressure on Hubert Humphrey, who also voted against it. On March 24, the Senate killed funding for the SST 51–46. As his office staff celebrated with champagne (Proxmire abstained), journalists gave Proxmire most of the credit for ending the program, citing the credibility he had earned exposing cost overruns in defense contracts, and his tireless efforts to argue against the SST. Proxmire effectively combined conservative arguments against federal spending with liberal arguments against potential environmental effects to end the program. It was the high point of his career, and his office was flooded with interview requests. In May, the whole SST saga had a farcical final encore when a procedural vote in the House to close out the SST contract was amended to continue funding the project by SST backers while many members were absent. All the old arguments made a final appearance before the Senate finally killed the SST by a wide margin on May 19.[10]

Proxmire's subcommittee hearings revealing cost overruns in the Defense Department and his advocacy of consumer legislation had already made him a national figure, and his final defeat of the SST suddenly made him one of Congress's most influential members. By 1971, reporters began floating his name as one of several prominent politicians likely to pursue the Democratic presidential nomination. As early as January 1970, his name appeared alongside fellow senators Nelson and Harold Hughes of Iowa as possible dark horse candidates. Other reporters thought him more likely to be the vice presidential nominee running alongside early favorite Edmund Muskie.[11] Such speculation was all but meaningless, of course, but after Proxmire's landslide reelection and the national publicity he gained by ending the SST program, an effort that united both fiscal conservatives and political liberals, a presidential campaign seemed like a real possibility. In November 1970, Richard Cudahy, William Drew, and John Finerty—all close political backers of his senatorial campaigns—organized a presidential campaign committee, ostensibly without the senator's knowledge. Proxmire told a reporter that he was flattered but insisted he was "going to work on being a good senator" and had no presidential ambitions. The formation of a committee was not significant in and of itself—ambitious politicians tested the presidential waters all the time—but Proxmire did seem to have an outside chance. A November 1970 Gallup poll showed two major figures leading: Edmund Muskie, not yet an announced candidate, at 33 percent, and Edward Kennedy, who had stated publicly he would not run, at 31 percent. Since it was not certain that Muskie would run and since Kennedy had stated bluntly that he would not, the field was actually wide open. Hubert Humphrey came in a distant third at 16 percent, but he had not yet announced a third bid for the White House. Eugene McCarthy, unlikely to run again, came in at 6 percent in the poll, and New York mayor John Lindsay received 4 percent but had not yet switched from the Republican to the Democratic party. Proxmire was favored by 2 percent of responders, alongside Mike Mansfield and eventual nominee George McGovern. On paper, he made an excellent candidate: fiscally conservative but a proven liberal, antiwar but also critical of student protests, and a Midwesterner popular among blue-collar voters. As he watched interest in "Prox for Prez" slowly grow, Proxmire remained cagey about his willingness to run, appearing on *Face the Nation* and saying he hoped for a "vigorous campaign" in the Democratic primary but would wait to see what 1972 looked like. A few weeks later, when asked about a potential presidential campaign, he told a *Wisconsin State Journal* reporter,

"If lighting strikes, I'd be delighted." Ellen was less than enthusiastic at the prospect of a national campaign for president or vice president: "I really don't like to think about that. And to be honest, I don't see it."[12]

The strategic importance of the Wisconsin presidential primary gave Proxmire's candidacy a greater air of legitimacy than that of other potential dark horse candidates like Birch Bayh of Indiana or Henry Jackson of Washington. The election would occur in April and would include a long list of names, since a recent law allowed for the removal of a candidate from the ballot only through filing an affidavit of noncandidacy. Wisconsin voters would thus be able to express their opinions on a large array of candidates before almost any other state. If Proxmire ran as a favorite-son candidate, he could potentially prevent the nomination of someone who was too liberal or too antiwar to be palatable to the national party leadership. Proxmire quickly denied any plans to run as a spoiler and promised that—if he decided to run—he would campaign everywhere and not just in Wisconsin.[13]

Throughout 1971, candidates flocked to the state to speak at party fund-raising events, and Proxmire continued to flirt with a presidential candidacy, refusing to commit one way or the other. When the enthusiasm for a Proxmire candidacy seemed to be waning by April, he offered statements that seemed to suggest he would run. After criticizing Muskie and Bayh for not opposing Nixon's record budget, he made clear that he would make reduced spending the centerpiece of his still-theoretical campaign: "There's a possibility I might run. We ought to have one candidate who's concerned with wasteful and excessive spending." He also traveled to New Hampshire to speak at a party fund-raising event and a commencement address at Nathaniel Hawthorne College and talked openly about entering the New Hampshire primary, which occurred a month before Wisconsin's. He presented himself as the most conservative Democrat in American politics by questioning the desire of other Democrats to launch new anti-pollution, welfare, health, unemployment, and housing programs ("We cannot have everything at once"), and mocked Hubert Humphrey's proposal for a $6,500 minimum income for families as "ridiculous." At the June state Democratic convention, he happily shook hands with attendees but refused to comment on the many sporting "Prox for Prez" buttons. All summer he refused to either announce or repudiate his candidacy, worrying state Democratic leaders, who feared that a Proxmire candidacy would render the Wisconsin primary meaningless. He even traveled to California in August to see what kind of support he might have on the west coast after his repeated attacks on the aerospace industry. He told reporters that if the economy continued to stagnate, there was "a possibility that I may decide to run." In September, he made his strongest statement yet, noting that he was "seriously" thinking about it since recent polls showed him leading every other Democratic candidate, as well as Nixon, in Wisconsin. If he entered the Wisconsin primary, he promised, he would make it a national campaign, too.[14]

Proxmire's presidential bid, however, stopped abruptly in November, when he held a press conference in Milwaukee to announce that he would not run. He cited two reasons for his decision. First, his repeated attacks on military spending had made him unpopular with labor unions and industrial workers, especially as unemployment exceeded 6 percent; and any Democrat would need strenuous blue-collar support to defeat Nixon. Second, despite his accomplishments as a senator, he still lacked the popularity of either Humphrey or Muskie. He remained a maverick at heart, and the vast sums of money required for a national campaign would be hard to get for a politician who had repeatedly upset banks, industries, labor unions, and the Democratic Party itself.[15]

Having slain the SST, Proxmire continued to wage war against federal spending, especially defense spending and foreign aid as détente reshaped the contours of the Cold War. Moreover, as the Vietnam War was finally winding down, members of Congress were more willing to question whether American foreign aid was still essential to counter international communism. Making the whole issue murkier still was the fact that no one was quite sure what the status of foreign aid even was: how much was being spent, and for what purpose? During Joint Economic Subcommittee hearings in January 1971, controller general Elmer Staats revealed the disquieting reality behind the multiple foreign aid programs: no one actually knew the exact amount the United States was spending on foreign military aid. More disturbing than the lack of information was the revelation that nearly $700 million in "Food for Peace" program funds was actually used to purchase military equipment and weapons between 1965 and 1970. Direct military aid was intended to help US allies defend themselves, and thereby maintain peace, but Proxmire pointed out the absurdity of this by noting that Pakistan used US military equipment in its war with India, and El Salvador and Honduras both used US weapons against each other. Just how much the United States spent on foreign military aid proved to be a baffling question. One Pentagon aide testifying at the hearing calculated the total to be somewhere around $4.896 billion spread across multiple programs. The Pentagon's fiscal year 1971 budget listed only $625 million for direct foreign military aid but acknowledged that the total amount spent was probably closer to $2.9 billion. Whatever the exact amount, Proxmire insisted it was too much, and subsequently introduced a bill requiring the president to submit an annual report to Congress detailing military and nonmilitary foreign aid spending.[16]

If foreign military aid no longer served a strategic purpose, why did it continue? Proxmire saw it as an extension of the same military-industrial complex that fleeced taxpayers for the benefit of weapons manufacturers, and he continued to target domestic military spending as well, calling for the curtailment of new weapons programs in the dawning post-Vietnam era. Nixon's fiscal year 1972 budget called for $77.6 billion in defense spending, but Proxmire quickly insisted that at least $8 to $10 billion in waste could be easily cut without jeopardizing American defense. In fact, programs that he identified as "wasteful," such as the new B-1 bomber, an early warning system for Chinese and Russian bombers, antisubmarine systems, and attack carriers, actually made the United States less safe because they diverted money to new and unreliable systems that could very well balloon in actual cost, just as the C-5A had, rather than maintaining funding for proven equipment. When Nixon derided critics of military spending as "neo-isolationists," Proxmire accused the president, secretary of defense Melvin Laird, and Senator Henry Jackson of using scare tactics to extort money from the American people.[17] With Nixon publicly committed to ending the war in Vietnam, Proxmire thought this was the best chance in years to limit defense spending and proposed a ceiling of $68 billion. Laird responded that that would require cutting 50 percent of civilian personnel and 40 percent of contractors, resulting in a potential crisis in military security, to say nothing of the negative impact on the economy. This idea that reducing military spending would result in massive job losses and an economic slowdown was a powerful new rhetorical weapon in the fight against military cuts that would frame the debate for the next twenty-five years. The Senate rejected Proxmire's amendment 63–24 in late June.[18] Despite this setback in limiting overall military spending, Proxmire continued to fight appropriations for specific new weapons systems, though he again met with little success. Calling the new F-14 jet "a lemon," he predicted that cost overruns would drive the total cost of the program to $4 billion, or $18 to $20 million for each jet, a prediction that the GAO subsequently showed was not far off the mark. During debate over the $21 billion weapons procurement bill, Proxmire argued that the American withdrawal from Vietnam should lead to a 10 percent reduction in defense costs, and he demanded the elimination of the F-14, the B-1 bomber, and the Safeguard ABM system as unnecessary programs that made the military too dependent on unreliable technology. Despite his efforts, the Senate rejected his cuts by large majorities before approving the weapons bill on October 6. The military industrial complex continued to have a significant influence in Congress, though the war was winding down.[19]

Part of Congress's reluctance to cut military spending came from Laird's warnings of the economic consequences of defense cuts at a time when the US economy was reeling from high unemployment and high inflation. When Nixon took office in January 1969, unemployment was around 3.5 percent and inflation was just under 5 percent, but conditions worsened significantly over the next eighteen months. More worried about inflation than unemployment, Nixon continued the surtax on large incomes and excise taxes on automobiles, tried to reduce federal spending, and urged the Federal Reserve Board to pursue a tight-money policy by keeping interest rates high. By 1970, the nation had entered a recession: unemployment reached 6 percent, the GNP dropped by $3.5 billion, and inflation increased to 6.1 percent. Nixon responded with voluntary measures to control inflation: the establishment of a National Commission on Productivity, a voluntary incomes policy, and "inflation alerts" to warn consumers of high prices. Congress reacted to the economic problems by passing the Economic Stabilization Act, which authorized the president to control prices, wages, and rents, despite Nixon's determination to rely solely on voluntary measures.[20]

Proxmire was highly critical of President Nixon's reluctance to take aggressive action to improve the economy. In November 1970, he called Nixon's management of the economy a failure and instead proposed that Congress grant the president much greater authority to impose wage and price controls to combat inflation. He also urged a $10 billion cut to defense spending as an additional means of holding down inflation, while at the same time calling on the president to allocate $335 million under the Emergency Mortgage Credit Act to encourage new home construction. In short, he wanted an activist federal government that would fight inflation while encouraging economic growth in nonmilitary sectors. Proxmire was, of course, well aware that the traditional inflation-fighting methods could result in higher unemployment and that standard efforts to spur economic growth could be inflationary, but he was optimistic that a solution was possible. Nixon's method of allowing businesses and unions to negotiate wages and set prices would exacerbate demand-pull inflation, and depending solely on fiscal and monetary policies alone was ineffective in combating cost-push inflation. Wage-price guidelines were no panacea, he cautioned, but would at least provide a short breathing spell and potentially break the upward inflationary spiral and moderate future upward pressures.[21]

Indeed, rising inflation and unemployment rates were particularly vexing in the new year. By February 1971, despite increased federal spending in order to produce full employment, unemployment remained at 6 percent and inflation still hovered at around 5 percent. Proxmire, now chair of the Joint Economic Committee, was the leading voice in Congress criticizing the president's lack of action and holding early hearings in January, rather than waiting for the president's economic report, as he typically did. The hearings produced a grim economic picture: declining real wages, slowing output, state and municipal budget deficits, and a $15 billion federal budget deficit. New York mayor John Lindsay predicted a $1 billion budget deficit for the city. The White House did begin to take some more aggressive measures in the face of the growing economic crisis. Nixon publicly criticized Bethlehem Steel's 12 percent price increase and threatened to allow more steel imports to lower prices and announced the implementation of new tax credits to spur business investment. Proxmire applauded these moves as steps in the right direction, but he was much more skeptical of the president's $5 billion revenue-sharing plan to help financially strapped states that he proposed in his State of the Union message. Proxmire argued that the amount was too small—most governors agreed with him—and that states should have to abide by federal guidelines for using federal money rather than the no-strings-attached grants that the president envisioned. Moreover, Nixon's budget for fiscal year 1972 projected a $30 billion deficit, which Proxmire argued would undermine other efforts to control inflation. He again suggested that the president use an advisory board to make recommendations for wage and price levels and speculated that the worsening economy may need strict controls in the near future.[22]

In early February, the White House issued its annual economic report, which struck many economists as unrealistically optimistic. Proxmire and other Democrats reacted with stunned disbelief at the report, which predicted that inflation would drop to 4 percent and ultimately remain steady at 3.5 percent. Paul McCracken, chair of the Council of Economic Advisors, could offer little substance to support the report's predictions during Joint Economic Committee hearings. He forecast that GNP would increase to $1.065 trillion—an astounding 9 percent increase—but he had no predictions for individual sectors of the economy that would produce such growth. A few days later McCracken produced more specific predictions for Proxmire, who called them "nothing short of sensational" and amounted to the economy growing nearly 10 percent and state spending increasing by nearly 12 percent with no new administration policies to explain the growth. Surprisingly, Proxmire's dismissal of the report as merely political led to his being criticized by the president and other Republicans as a "doom and gloom" naysayer who would undermine confidence and prolong economic stagnation. Proxmire thought Nixon's response to the economy was still too tepid. The president announced a wage and price freeze in construction industries in late February but ruled out controls over the whole economy. The Joint Economic Committee report, however, insisted that it was impossible to reach the administration's target GNP, slow inflation, and reduce unemployment without stronger efforts from the federal government. It called for injecting $20 billion into the economy through a combination of an immediate increase in the personal income tax exemption, reduction in personal income tax rates (both scheduled to take effect in 1972), and delayed implementation of planned social security taxes. The top priority had to be economic expansion, and wage and price controls might become necessary to prevent inflation from wiping out gains made by economic growth.[23]

The Nixon administration, however, still refused to take action, and the economy continued to worsen. In March, unemployment rose to 6.1 percent after slight declines in January and February. The White House press secretary dismissed the news as only a temporary blip—unemployment, he insisted, had bottomed out and would be improving in the months to come. There was some indication, however, that the administration was not at all confident in its prediction, since the president had ordered the Bureau of Labor Statistics to stop giving its own regular press briefings. Federal Reserve staffers, too, were skeptical of the president's management of the economy, issuing a highly critical report of Nixon's economic forecast, which was modeled on the supply-side theories of California economist Arthur Laffer and predicted unlikely economic growth. In April, however, unemployment crept up further, to 6.2 percent, and the inflation rate increased by .4 percent. Proxmire held Joint Economic Committee hearings again, and in an unusual move, invited unemployed people to testify, hoping their "tales of woe" would motivate the president to shift federal spending away from defense and back to cities in an effort to create more jobs.[24]

Unemployment hovered around 6 percent for most of the summer, but inflation continued to rise, especially in the steel industry. Steel prices rose 8 percent in July, and steelworkers' wages increased by an astounding 30 percent, driving up prices of many consumer goods and adding increased pressure on other employers to raise wages. When General Motors announced the price of 1972 models would increase by an average of $1,500, Nixon finally conceded that he would keep an open mind on the need for a wage-price review board. Proxmire and other senators continued to pressure the president to take stronger action. The senator echoed the feelings of many consumers in a speech to the Wisconsin Chamber of Commerce that called for Nixon to establish wage-price guidelines as a way of curbing inflation. Normal free-market conditions no longer existed, he insisted, and prices and wages were being driven by "powerful industries and powerful unions" at the expense of the majority of the population, much to the irritation of Wisconsin labor leaders.[25]

Nixon finally acted on Sunday, August 15, appearing on television that evening (and interrupting *Bonanza*) to announce a series of measures that would become known as Phase I of his New Economic Plan to limit inflation while spurring economic growth. Phase I consisted of a ninety-day freeze on wages, prices, and profit margins; a reduction of federal employees by 5 percent; a new investment tax credit; tax cuts totaling $6.3 billion; a reduction of federal spending by $4.7 billion; and the creation of a Cost of Living Council, chaired by Treasury Secretary Connelly. Proxmire applauded the move, calling it "long overdue," but he did offer some criticism. Nixon's tax credits would go into effect in 1973, and Proxmire wanted them to be retroactive to January 1971 for a more immediate effect. While he was always in favor of reduced federal spending, he wanted the cuts to come primarily from defense and called for increased spending on public services. He later proposed limits on corporate profits and interest rates as well, to protect consumers. Joint Economic Committee hearings also revealed the lopsided nature of Nixon's tax cuts and credits: corporations would receive about $9 billion in cuts, according to an estimate by Joseph Heller, and individuals only about $2 billion, thereby limiting the expansionary effect of increased consumer spending. And what would happen after the ninety days of Phase I? Secretary of Commerce Maurice Stans testified that some kind of controls would be needed after November 12 to prevent inflation from becoming even worse than it had been.[26]

Nixon announced plans for Phase II in October, after much disagreement within the Council of Economic Advisors. With a goal of cutting the rate of inflation in half, the president proposed creating separate boards to control wages and prices, though cooperation would be largely voluntary. Proxmire tentatively supported the idea, but only if the president's appointees to the boards had to be approved by the Senate. Indeed, Proxmire suddenly seemed to be advocating caution. He opposed a one-year extension of the Economic Stabilization Act of 1970 that gave the president authority to control wages and prices in order to give Congress a chance to evaluate the result of the new economic policy. The president's proposal was to extend his authority until April 30, 1973; Proxmire favored an April 30, 1972, end date. Until there was evidence to show that the wage and price freeze worked, he was unwilling to give such unilateral authority to the president. Even more troubling, consumers had no legal recourse to sue violators. The Justice Department could impose fines but might be reluctant to do so against a politically influential company.[27]

Congress quickly passed Nixon's proposals, but once Phase II was under way, Proxmire began to question whether wage and price controls would work. Their byzantine complexity made them all but impossible for most Americans to understand, which he feared would lead to resentment and anger, especially from employees receiving raises that did not match the rate of inflation. A Citizens' Price Commission established guidelines for prices, and a Pay Board established guidelines to prevent inflationary raises. Yet there were many exceptions, and there was essentially nothing to prevent businesses from disregarding those guidelines. Proxmire's fears seemed to be well-founded. The price board approved an 8.5 percent increase in coal prices, significantly higher than the administration's own guidelines. Proxmire told reporters he was "shocked, stunned, and surprised" that the fifteen-person board would approve such a rate increase just as winter was getting under way. Negative public reaction might discredit the entire plan. A week later, Congress voted to extend the president's economic authority another year. Proxmire criticized the measure as a "blank check" in a three-hour speech protesting the move, a last-ditch effort to change his fellow senators' minds. Had Proxmire flip-flopped? Not exactly. Even though he had advocated for some kind of voluntary wage and price controls for over a year, the hurried way in which they were being implemented worried him. The seemingly arbitrary decisions by an appointed board would alienate consumers and workers, and the guidelines themselves had become too complicated and cumbersome. The president and Congress, in other words, had veered too much in the opposite direction and could overregulate prices and wages, potentially crippling economic growth. He argued that such powerful regulation should be extended only to big industries (those with over $50 million in annual sales) and big unions (those with over 1,000 members). The purpose remained the same, but the tools did not work. The goal of the controls, he insisted, should be to "break up monopolistic concentration of power," and big corporations and big unions were at fault for driving up prices. Instead, he favored eliminating controls from small businesses and wage limits from state and local government employees. Inflation in these areas would be kept in check by consumers and by taxpayers. Proxmire was speaking in terms that Theodore Roosevelt and Robert La Follette would have understood.[28]

Inflation and unemployment continued to be a major problem for the rest of Nixon's presidency, and Proxmire used his position on the Joint Economic Committee to criticize the administration's handling of the economy, especially after the president's overly optimistic assessment in the 1972 State of the Union Address. Congressional Democrats responded to the president's message with a panel discussion and fielded questions from reporters. Proxmire took a particularly critical view of Nixon's handling of the economy, arguing that the administration's fixation on inflation was doing nothing to ease unemployment, which he thought was the more serious problem. Economic statistics seemed to support Proxmire's pessimism: unemployment was at 6 percent and would likely remain there since any economic growth would be offset by an expected increase in the labor force. Even more worrying, long-term unemployment had tripled since Nixon took office, and the unemployment rate among nonwhite men was 10 percent. At Joint Economic Committee hearings in February, Herbert Stein, chair of the Council of Economic Advisors, defended the president's plans, which featured a $38.8 billion budget deficit designed to spur economic growth. A few days later, when treasury secretary John Connally glibly predicted unemployment at 5 percent or lower by the end of the year and ruled out a tax increase to offset the budget deficit, Proxmire retorted that Nixon's deficit was "the wrong dose of the wrong medicine at the wrong time." Promoting deficit spending as means of lowering the unemployment rate was of course going to bother Proxmire, the chief congressional critic of spending (what Henry Reuss called "bastardized Keynesianism"), but Proxmire also seemed to be interested in more radical action. After hearing from administration officials, Proxmire summoned three "radical" economists to testify before the committee about the growing maldistribution of wealth and the necessity for massive government intervention to address what they saw as an unsustainable economic system.[29]

Proxmire was by no means a radical, but the testimony did indicate that he thought more action was necessary. In March, he proposed the creation of one hundred thousand jobs per month until the unemployment rate reached 5 percent. The cost, estimated at $2 billion for the first year, would be almost entirely recouped by the reduced spending in un-employment compensation and welfare payments that would result. As for inflation, Proxmire urged changes in enforcing the Phase Two wage and price controls by focusing on big businesses and large labor unions, exempting small businesses and those industries with sufficient competition to keep prices in check. Government guidelines seemed arbitrary and burdensome to most Americans, while being totally ineffective at reining in wage and price increases by corporations and labor unions. The argument that small-business owners were burdened by price controls while large businesses were allowed to raise prices gained more currency in April when Pay Board officials admitted that they allowed raises for corporate executives to double while capping hourly wage increases at 5.5 percent. Unemployment remained high, the gap between the wealthy and poor was increasing, and productivity was decreasing, all problems exacerbated by the Nixon administration's ineffective policies on inflation.[30]

As Proxmire continued to criticize the Nixon administration's handling of the economy, popular support for wage and price controls diminished. By the end of the year, unemployment remained near 6 percent, though Proxmire estimated that 8 percent was probably more accurate. Corporate profits were up, suggesting that Nixon's wage controls were significantly more effective than his price controls. To Proxmire, it appeared that the whole wage and price control system had been hijacked by big businesses as a means of increasing their own profits at the expense of workers, consumers, and the economy as a whole. A prolonged recession seemed a very real possibility.[31]

In January 1973, Nixon announced the end of Phase Two and the easing of wage and price controls on everything except food, health care, and construction. Although Proxmire did advocate for an end to controls on small business and those sectors of the economy with enough competition to keep prices low, he objected to the fact that a few large corporations and labor unions would be able to drive up prices without any real regulation from the new federal agency, the Cost of Living Council, which received after-the-fact reports from businesses on wage and price increases. Petroleum, steel, and chemical producers, he feared, would be able to raise prices that inflated their profits while fabricating justification to placate a largely toothless federal agency. Indeed, the first big test of "decontrol" was heating oil, as prices rose sharply and shortages loomed. Proxmire had long argued against the oil-depletion allowance and oil-import quota, which allowed oil companies to make record profits while prices soared. At a Senate Banking Committee hearing in early February on extending the Economic Stability Act (ESA) another year, Treasury Secretary Schultz defended the administration's ability to roll back unjustifiable price increases made by oil companies but expressed reluctance to require companies to refund overcharged customers. Proxmire pounced on a visibly irritated Schultz over the inability of the Cost of Living Council to benefit consumers: "I think that, instead of a shotgun in the closet, the Secretary has a peashooter under the pillow."[32] Congress approved a one-year extension of the ESA in March, but Democrats demanded that the president do more to address the deteriorating economic situation. Citing the second devaluation of the dollar, the first balance of trade deficit in sixty years, and a looming $19 billion budget deficit, Proxmire called for reduced military spending and new investments in housing and job training. He proposed a six-month freeze on wages, prices, and profits as an amendment to the ESA extension, which fell just two votes short of adoption in the Senate. Increased inflation (4.6 percent in March alone, and nearly 13 percent over the previous year) caused others to join Proxmire's call for tighter control over prices, and the Senate Democratic caucus unanimously called for a ninety-day freeze. Phase Three—"decontrolling"—simply wasn't working, and the average family struggled with soaring food and fuel costs.[33]

In June, President Nixon, facing growing discontent and eager to settle domestic issues before an upcoming visit from Soviet leader Leonid Brezhnev, announced changes to Phase Three that included a sixty-day freeze on prices but not on wages. The administration would then develop Phase Four to deal with the long-term problem. The new controls, which went into effect in August, included some of what Proxmire and other Democrats had wanted. Companies with less than $100 million in annual sales could raise prices immediately; larger companies had to give thirty days' notice to the Cost of Living Council. Wage increases, however, remained capped at 5.5 percent and there were no limits on corporate profits. The intent was not to stabilize prices but to prevent price "bulges" occurring all at once. With prices for food, health services, construction material, and utilities all unfrozen, consumers looked forward to a long period of inflation and

another recession in 1974.[34] Indeed, inflation remained stubbornly high in
the early months of 1974, despite Nixon's assurance that it was the number
one problem facing the country and could be dealt with by cutting federal
spending. Though Proxmire and others urged continued controls targeting
those sectors of the economy with lack of competition or excessive demand,
Nixon announced the end of controls in February, and the ESA expired
in April. The whole experience had been profoundly discouraging, and
Proxmire believed that the Nixon administration had made the situation
worse with halfhearted efforts to address the problems of rising prices and
by repeatedly trying to placate special-interest groups.[35]

Proxmire found other aspects of the Nixon administration to criticize, especially with some of his appointments. He took the "advise-and-
consent" role of the Senate quite seriously, but he also refused to join his
fellow Democrats in opposing a nomination for purely partisan reasons. In
February 1971, for example, President Nixon nominated New York tax attorney William J. Casey to chair the Securities and Exchange Commission.
It was a noncontroversial nomination, and the Senate Banking Committee
approved his nomination unanimously after only one day of hearings.
Nonetheless, Proxmire abstained. At issue was a civil suit against Casey
charging that he and his publisher, Prentice-Hall, had plagiarized pages
of a book on tax law from another author. It was not enough to derail the
nomination, but the committee did delay forwarding the nomination to
the full Senate until transcripts of the case were made available. Within
days, however, a new revelation surfaced that Casey had been involved in
another civil suit that alleged he had been involved in an illegal stock deal
in 1962. Proxmire, along with fellow Democrat Harrison A. Williams Jr.,
demanded that the committee reopen hearings, and Proxmire had his
staff begin its own investigation of other possible lawsuits in Casey's past.
In response to Proxmire's letter asking for disclosure of any other suits,
Casey admitted to a third lawsuit alleging financial misconduct, this time
involving the merger of two companies in California. Moreover, Proxmire questioned the judge who presided over the plagiarism case, who
presented a dramatically different account of the trial than Casey had at
his hearing. The judge denied that he had threatened to set aside the jury's
decision against Casey as unsupported by evidence, that he had ordered
the parties to settle, and that he had ordered the court records sealed, all

of which Casey had claimed. With this new evidence of Casey's evasiveness, the Banking Committee reopened hearings on March 9. After five hours of testimony from Casey, the committee once again approved his nomination, this time with Proxmire, Williams, and Adlai Stevenson III voting against. Behind the scenes, Proxmire's staff worked hard to find experts to testify against Casey, consulting two former chairmen, three law professors, and three former commission lawyers; two said there was too little evidence to publicly oppose Casey, and the others thought the allegations serious enough to warrant opposition but did not want to do so out of fear of retaliation when they appeared before the SEC in the future. Once again left standing alone in opposition, Proxmire cast the lone "no" vote against Casey when the Senate confirmed Casey on a voice vote in which only eight senators were present. Casey went on to a long career in the federal government, culminating in his appointment as CIA director under Ronald Reagan.[36]

In contrast to his stand on William Casey, Proxmire infuriated liberals by supporting Nixon's appointment of William Rehnquist to the Supreme Court that same year. Nixon's third choice for the seat, Rehnquist generated significant opposition from Senate liberals who questioned Rehnquist's position on civil rights. To their dismay, Proxmire announced during Senate debate on December 9 that he would vote in favor of the nomination, citing his "strong intellectual qualifications" and denying that Rehnquist's appointment was a threat to the Bill of Rights and instead sided with the Nixon administration's desire to bring conservative voices to court to provide "a better balance between the forces of law enforcement on one hand and law violation on the other." Proxmire had expressed similar "law and order" sentiments before, but this time he received blistering criticism from Wisconsin Democrats, who unanimously opposed the nomination. A *Capital Times* editorial called Proxmire's stand "disgraceful," and even his own staff opposed Rehnquist. Proxmire would not be swayed—as long as the president's nominations were qualified and not too far outside the mainstream, the Senate should confirm. This time, Proxmire joined the winning side in the debate as the Senate confirmed Rehnquist 68–26.[37]

Proxmire's support of Rehnquist signaled a growing split with his fellow Democrats on other major issues in the early 1970s. He opposed busing

as a means of integrating public schools and voted for a Senate bill prohibiting federal courts from ordering it, one of three northern Democrats
who provided the slim margin. Gaylord Nelson, who voted against the
bill, called the vote "irresponsible and politically cowardly," a thinly veiled
swipe at Proxmire and others. A *Capital Times* editorial accused Proxmire
and the others of aiding racists. Columnist Nicholas von Hoffman called
Proxmire "a slipping liberal." Proxmire defended his position—and that of
President Nixon—by arguing that busing was bad for education and race
relations because it fostered resentment among white families who might
otherwise support racial integration, and he cited a poll of Wisconsin voters that indicated overwhelming opposition to busing.[38]

On other national issues, however, Proxmire adhered to the party line.
Despite his vocal support for the war in the 1960s, by 1971 Proxmire had
firmly lined up with antiwar Democrats, a position much easier now that
a Republican was commander in chief. After years of watching debates
among his staff over the war, usually between the older, more conservative
Howard Shuman against the younger, more liberal staffers, Proxmire had
grown more skeptical of the conflict. Yet he was also mindful of the mood
of Wisconsin voters. Responding to one of his questionnaires, Wisconsin
voters favored a gradual withdrawal by a 2–1 margin, but confusingly, 54
percent supported taking whatever actions were necessary to win. The
American invasion of Cambodia was the final straw, and Proxmire finally
admitted that his earlier support for the war had been wrong and that he
had made a serious mistake by voting for the Gulf of Tonkin Resolution
in 1964.[39]

Proxmire joined other antiwar Democrats who targeted the draft, and
he enthusiastically supported efforts to end it, participating in a filibuster
against extending the draft beyond June 30, 1971, and voting to increase
military pay in an effort to increase voluntary enlistments. Both attempts
failed, but the Senate did pass an amendment calling on Nixon to withdraw all American troops within nine months despite passing a two-year
draft extension.[40] Proxmire also supported limiting the president's war-
making ability, and in April 1972, he joined a 68–16 majority that passed
a bill requiring congressional approval before a president could commit
American troops to fighting abroad. He also became one of the most vigorous critics of continued bombing in North Vietnam, calling on the Air

Force to court-martial generals who authorized bombing raids without congressional approval.[41]

Proxmire's shift from hawk to dove was partly due to a general shift in public opinion against the war, but his continued hostility toward unchecked military spending motivated him as well. As the war began to wind down in the early 1970s, Proxmire ratcheted up his criticism of Pentagon spending, and, buoyed by his success in publicizing the C-5A program, he sought out egregious examples of military programs to garner similar public awareness of the cozy relationship between military leaders and defense contractors. The Navy unwittingly provided him with a prime example when it replaced its civilian review board with a military board at a time when numerous shipbuilders had claims for overruns pending. "If the Navy intended to replace an effective claims review group with a figurehead body intended to grease the skids for gigantic claims against the government, it could have chosen no better mechanism," he complained.[42] The removal of the Navy's top civilian procurement officer, Gordon Rule, particularly angered him, since it seemed like a deliberate effort to eliminate a figure with a long record of rejecting additional payments based on contractors' claims that costs exceeded original contracts. For example, the Navy approved a $25 million payment to Louisiana-based Avondale Shipyards, in addition to the original $23.5 million contract for twenty-seven destroyer escorts in order to guarantee quick delivery of the final fourteen. Another contractor, Litton Industries, charged the government $7 million for work done on commercial ships. Proxmire again used his chairmanship of a minor subcommittee of the Joint Economic Committee, the Subcommittee on Priorities and Economy, to publicize these and similar cases. The hearings revealed a long pattern of lax oversight and cost overruns in naval procurement. A classified memo from chief of naval operations Admiral Elmo R. Zumwalt actually recommended "expedited" payments of claims and unlimited overtime in order to deplete a newly released $400 million outlay quickly and justify increased budgets for the following fiscal year. Proxmire saw this as nothing more than theft of taxpayer money facilitated by unethical military officers. For example, in 1971, the Navy purchased three hundred altimeters for naval airplanes without competitive bidding for $1,700 each. Identical altimeters purchased by the Air Force with competitive bidding cost only $565 each.[43]

Proxmire's scrutiny of naval spending quickly zeroed in on the F-14 fighter jet, manufactured by the Grumman Aerospace Corporation. The F-14 was intended as a "multi-mission" aircraft, functioning as both a fighter and an interceptor. The original cost estimate was $11.5 million each, but delays and cost overruns drove the price per aircraft close to $20 million. In contrast, the Soviet MIG-21 cost only $1 million, the French Mirage 5 cost $1.5 million, and the American F-4 Phantom, the F-14's immediate predecessor, cost only $2.5 million. And all of them were more effective than F-14 prototypes seemed to be. After the crash of a prototype in December 1970 stalled production, Grumman claimed that it had lost $65 million on the eighty-six jets already ordered. The Navy's decision not to make a $4.1 million payment on April 1, 1972, violated the terms of the contract and would allow Grumman to reopen negotiations for increased payments. In fact, the Navy was already planning an additional $40 million payment to offset those losses, essentially a "backdoor bailout" for the company.[44] A General Accounting Office report subsequently supported Proxmire's criticism of the F-14 program and revealed that the new plane was in some ways inferior to fighter jets already in use and cost four times as much. Grumman chair E. Clinton Towl responded that the increased costs were due to inflation and that fulfilling its contract as it was would force the company into bankruptcy and shut down its operation on Long Island, which employed twenty thousand workers. Completing the full order would require an additional $545 million, or $2 million more per jet. Even then, the company would have to take a $23 million loss.[45]

Yet the costs kept spiraling higher. On May 29, Proxmire issued a statement charging the Pentagon with trying to conceal the magnitude of the F-14 cost overrun: the 313 fighter jets were estimated to cost over $6.5 billion. Another test flight crashed on June 30, killing the pilot and further discrediting Grumman. In fact, the Navy had already documented forty-three major flaws in the F-14s already constructed, sixteen of which were related to safety.[46] By the end of the year, Proxmire's criticism of the F-14 program bore results. On December 11, the Pentagon announced that it would require Grumman to produce the remaining forty-eight F-14s and would not allow any increase in price. This was a distinct break with the Pentagon's past practice of shocking generosity in paying for cost overruns. Because the Pentagon deemed the F-14 essential, however, the Navy had other ways of keeping Grumman afloat. It had already directly loaned the company $36 million at 6⅞ percent, and now the company was receiving an additional $18 million. Grumman officials defended the loan as an advanced payment for the final lot of fighter jets, necessary since the company was unable to get private credit from commercial banks, to which Proxmire retorted that the Navy was acting "as Grumman's private banker" and called the loan "a shocking indictment of the navy's professed determination to make the company live up to its existing contract obligations." After further efforts to negotiate price increases in February 1973, the Navy ordered Grumman to produce the final lot of fighters for the price stipulated in the contract. Such firmness earned the Pentagon rare praise from its chief critic: "If the Navy sticks by its guns," Proxmire announced, "our losses on the program might be held in check and, more importantly, a valuable precedent could be established for handling other mismanaged weapons systems."[47]

Grumman's problematic production of the F-14 was not an isolated case, as Proxmire made abundantly clear in Joint Economic Committee hearings. Lockheed's sloppy management of the C-5A had almost bankrupted the company until the federal government guaranteed $250 million in bank loans. Lockheed claimed the loan guarantee was necessary to protect six hundred thousand jobs, though Proxmire noted that only thirty thousand worked on civilian aircraft construction and fourteen thousand of those had already been laid off. Most infuriating to Proxmire was that this loan guarantee was in addition to a $400 million overpayment by the Pentagon, most of which was due to Lockheed's own mismanagement. Compounding the issue was the Treasury Department's Emergency Loan Guarantee Board's failure to monitor Lockheed's use of the guarantee or provide access to its records to the Government Accounting Office for a routine audit. Treasury secretary John Connally refused to testify before the Senate Banking Committee, fueling more speculation that the Treasury Department was trying to hide Lockheed's true financial health. The company itself announced plans to increase pensions for its top executives from $40,000 to $65,000, suggesting that government-backed loans were being used to line the pockets of company managers. It was, simply, "socialism for big business and free enterprise for the mom and pop stores."[48]

Using Pentagon money to fund commercial work proved to be another common problem as companies upgraded their facilities for government contracts and then used that new equipment for nongovernmental work. The best example of this is the case of Litton Shipyards, which in 1970 received a contract to build thirty DD-963 class destroyers. The company subsequently requested an additional $7 million to pay for the overhaul of its production facility, which it claimed was necessary to manufacture the destroyers. The problem was that the overhauled facility would also produce ships for nongovernment sale, thereby using the Pentagon to subsidize its commercial projects. Litton then filed a claim with the Navy for an additional $450 million, allegedly to cover the costs of Pentagon-ordered changes to the contract, a claim that would be used to rescue the company from bankruptcy. Litton executives, Proxmire charged, knew that the Navy would rather pay the claim than risk delays in production. As with the Grumman contract, Proxmire's revelations forced the Navy to reject cost increases beyond the original contract.[49]

The actions of Grumman, Lockheed, and Litton revealed that the military-industrial complex was still very much alive during the waning years of the Vietnam War. Proxmire's frequent hearings on the subject clearly showed the public how companies won defense contracts under the assumption that they could successfully claim additional payments from the Pentagon for cost overruns caused by contract changes, production errors, or simple sloppy management. In the case of Lockheed, Grumman, and others, federal loan guarantees would allow them to further leverage private capital. These claims and loan guarantees would then be used to subsidize nongovernment construction projects or make the company look more profitable than it really was. Military officials in charge of the projects had no reason to object, since rejecting claims would slow down, or halt altogether, the production of needed military equipment, and those same military officials often benefited by getting high-paying jobs in those same companies when they retired from military service. Threats of factory closures spooked representatives and senators who wanted to protect their districts and states, and until Proxmire began challenging the Pentagon, no one wanted to question the Defense Department's assertion of what it needed to counter potential Soviet threats. Internal critics who questioned defense contracts or claims—like Ernest Fitzgerald in the case of the C-5A or Gordon Rule in the case of the F-14—were fired or reassigned if they testified before Proxmire's committee.[50]

Proxmire, more than any other elected official, revealed the true extent of the military-industrial complex, and his use of well-documented examples of extravagant overruns reshaped public understanding of government spending. Despite his mastery of this complicated topic, he could never resist publicizing sensational stories of military waste that were actually minor in cost but tended to stoke public outrage. For example, in November 1972, he revealed that the Air Force was spending $179,000 to pay twenty-four enlisted men to work as cooks, clerks, and waiters and in other service jobs at the Alaskan Chateau and Health Club at Elmendorf Air Force Base in Anchorage and demanded an investigation into the military's use of enlisted men as "servants." In response to Proxmire's inquiry, the GAO reported that a total of 1,722 enlisted men worked as servants to high-ranking officers—chauffeuring, cleaning, shopping, even babysitting and laundry—at a cost of about $22 million annually. Leaders from all four branches defended the use of "aides" as necessary to allow officers and their wives to devote themselves full-time to their duties and communities, an explanation Proxmire called "absurd": "Generals making over $50,000 a year in salary and equivalent benefits shouldn't be running home at 5 o'clock. At that rank and pay, they should be putting in long hours like the farmers, businessmen and construction workers of this country. Furthermore, when these other Americans go home after a hard day's work, they have to mow their own lawn and carry out their own chores." Defense Secretary Elliot Richardson ordered an investigation and eventually curtailed the use of servants.[51]

Proxmire furthered his reputation during the early 1970s as the leading critic of federal spending by targeting several high-profile projects he deemed a waste of taxpayers' money. For example, the Department of Transportation funded "Transpo 72," an international trade fair held at Dulles International Airport, which Proxmire ridiculed and called "a gross misuse of tax dollars." Congress appropriated $5 million for the event, but expenses included a $10,000 salary for a Disneyland entertainment director to stage programs, expensive dinners, and weekly first-class air fare to and from Anaheim, California. Transportation secretary John Volpe defended the event as having a positive impact on the economy by promoting the American aerospace industry. Given the cost involved, however, Proxmire dubbed it the "most inept federal undertaking since the Battle of Little Big Horn."[52] Similarly, Proxmire, a longtime skeptic of NASA, became an early critic of the space shuttle program, estimated to cost $5.5 billion over six years. Proxmire was not opposed to space exploration per se, but he recognized that the economic conditions of the early 1970s made the federal budget essentially a zero-sum game. The president would never propose a tax increase to pay for new programs, so money spent on the space shuttle would have to be cut from federal welfare programs, thereby diverting resources from the poor to the aerospace industry that Proxmire had frequently blamed for excessive Pentagon spending. With the Apollo program scheduled to end in 1974, the space shuttle was up next, but it offered no benefits, according to Proxmire, that could not be realized with a much less expensive, unmanned exploration program. In August 1972, a reshuffling of the Senate Appropriations Committee made Proxmire the chair of the subcommittee in charge of NASA's budget, and he vowed to bring witnesses to contradict the administration's support of the shuttle program. Despite his influence on the committee, Proxmire made little headway in cutting the program.[53]

It was not just federal spending that benefited the aerospace industry that Proxmire fought. He also tried to cut spending on other programs that he thought were a waste of money, which brought him into conflict with his fellow Democrats when he proposed cutting federal arts spending. In April 1973, he proposed limiting spending on the National Endowment for the Arts and the National Endowment for the Humanities by about $700 million. Proxmire was far from a philistine, but he gave three reasons for his sudden willingness to cut these popular programs. First, the amount was too large to be spent efficiently, and much of it would therefore be wasted. Second, so much spending would produce "stale, sterile, and second-rate art." Finally, federal money might lead to stifling federal censorship. Drawing on populist rhetoric, Proxmire defended his amendment by arguing that "primarily the enjoyment of a great deal of the concerts, the museums, the opera is by the upper and upper-middle classes." His reasoning met with swift response from various arts organizations that pointed out that government spending on arts programing in other countries did not result in censorship and that NEA and NEH programs reached many impoverished children. Senator Jacob Javits of New York insisted, "The poor don't live by bread alone. . . . We're talking about ennobling and enriching their lives, too." Proxmire's amendment failed, and the Senate approved the $840 million arts bill 76–14.[54]

This assault on federal spending certainly scored points with voters, but Proxmire's obsession with cutting spending often put him at odds with his own party. In 1972, the Nixon administration proposed a $250 billion limit on federal spending as part of its anti-inflationary effort. Proxmire's own committee recommended rejecting this limit, but Proxmire himself dissented and called for an even lower spending cap: $240 billion. The additional $10 billion, he insisted, could easily be cut by ending the war, reducing the defense budget by 5 percent, and eliminating foreign military aid. Even after Congress rejected such a spending ceiling, Proxmire continued to urge the president to impose spending limits through impoundment—simply by ordering executive departments not to spend money even though it was authorized.[55] In early 1973, Proxmire again advocated a bigger budget reduction than the president recommended for fiscal year 1974 (bringing total federal spending to $265 billion rather than the president's $268 billion), including not only defense and foreign military aid but also public works, health, and education. To the dismay of state officials and his congressional colleagues, Proxmire reiterated his suggestion that Nixon simply refuse to spend funds included in the budget. It was not that he was opposed to spending on these areas, but he was convinced that there was a great deal of waste in federal programs that needed to be eliminated, and these cuts would force departments to make do with less.[56]

Proxmire's budgetary zeal and his embrace of impoundment frustrated his Democratic colleagues. Proxmire fought to impose a $265 billion spending limit, but he agreed with Texas senator Lloyd Bentsen in requiring that the president cut programs in equal proportions. Other Democrats, however, objected to the very idea of giving the president that much discretion over spending congressionally appropriated funds. Minnesota senator Walter Mondale promised to tie up the Senate for months to strike impoundment authorization.[57] Yet Proxmire was not entirely on Nixon's side, either. Even as he was urging the president to reduce federal spending, he was also arguing for increased spending on housing and criticizing the housing freeze that had been announced in January. It was a matter of priorities: "President Nixon," he cracked, "has decided to spend several billion dollars a year more in bombing Asians and to spend several billion dollars less in housing needy Americans . . . the effect of this is to increase the housing shortage both in Asia and the United States."[58] Dropping by the offices of the *Capital Times* unannounced in March, Proxmire again emphasized that he was not a doctrinaire or arbitrary budget cutter. Cuts to inefficient programs that benefited only a small number were good, but he opposed cuts to programs that aided many Americans directly or indirectly. Housing programs helped not only those who lived in subsidized housing, but also those who rented or wanted to purchase a home since shortages in housing drove up costs. Farm subsidies—he was ever a fighter for dairy farmers—likewise kept food prices down. In 1974, for example, he suggested a federal budget that reduced spending from $304 to $295 billion, cutting $12 billion from defense, space exploration, public works, and foreign aid; and adding $3 billion to housing, public service jobs, consumer protection, health care, and education.[59]

Proxmire's complicated relationship with his Democratic colleagues spilled over into the presidential primary. Early in 1972, Edmund Muskie was the favorite to win the Democratic nomination, but Hubert Humphrey's decision to enter the Wisconsin primary threatened to split the state party much as it had twelve years earlier. Proxmire avoided a formal endorsement, but after he cast his absentee ballot for South Dakota senator George McGovern, an aide shared the information with the McGovern campaign. Proxmire denied that he intentionally leaked his ballot, but went on to enthusiastically praise his fellow senator: McGovern

has a marvelous, marvelous character. He's such a decent man. He has strength, stability, and such a positive outlook. He never back-bites or criticizes. Furthermore, George's record is closer to mine. I've been trying to hold down spending on the military and on space, to re-order priorities, to cut waste where it hurts. If I had run for president myself, those would have been my issues. The only candidate who's saying those things is George.

Proxmire's nonendorsement gave McGovern a decided boost in the state, and he was already doing well courting some of the groups Proxmire had always depended on: factory workers, senior citizens, and farmers. By summer, Proxmire was confidently predicting a McGovern victory.[60]

The emerging Watergate scandal, however, overshadowed all of these economic issues. Shortly after the arrest of the Watergate burglars, Proxmire played a critical early role in tracing the break-in back to the White House. Noting that the Federal Reserve Board required banks to keep records of large transactions, he requested the board to identify the bank that issued the sixty-three $100 bills found on one of those arrested. Federal Reserve Board chair Arthur Burns, a former Nixon advisor, refused, revealing to the senator privately after testifying at a Joint Economic Committee hearing that the FBI wanted to keep that information confidential. When the investigation revealed a financial connection between one of the burglars and the Nixon campaign, Proxmire requested that the Office of Federal Elections in the General Accounting Office conduct an audit of Nixon campaign funds. The GAO reported to Congress directly, so such an audit would bypass the Justice Department. When the audit began to reveal additional financial irregularities, Proxmire called for a full investigation, led by former senator John Williams and former Supreme Court Justice Arthur Goldberg, with a full report due within thirty days, well before Election Day. Proxmire's early effort to "follow the money" failed, and the president won reelection. Not until February 1973, after the burglars' conviction and the increasingly clear connection to the White House, did the Senate establish the Select Committee on Presidential Campaign Activities to investigate.[61]

Proxmire played no significant role in the Senate hearings, but the unfolding scandal revealed that he had himself been targeted by the Nixon administration. A former FBI agent had surveilled Proxmire's office, and the offices of seven other members of Congress, in early 1972.[62] Despite these revelations, Proxmire was cautious in his public comments on the scandal. Speaking at Cornell in April 1973, he told his audience that "we continue to have confidence in the President until definite evidence of his involvement is found," much to the consternation of his liberal supporters. He quickly clarified in a Senate speech that he thought the press was unfairly demonizing Nixon—he compared it to the tactics of McCarthy—and that the president deserved the same presumption of innocence as any other citizen, especially given his long record of public service. Privately, however, he was more cynical, telling *Capital Times* editor Miles McMillin that the president was "involved in Watergate up to his ears." Nonetheless, he wanted Nixon's guilt proven by evidence, not innuendo or hearsay. Proxmire's criticism of the perceived rush to judgment in the press came up the next morning in an Oval Office conversation between the president and Alexander Haig, who wanted to use Proxmire's statements to defend Nixon. The *Wall Street Journal*, the *Washington Post*, the *New York Times*, and many other newspapers bristled at Proxmire's comparison to McCarthyism and defended the investigative journalism that exposed the scandal as a vital part of protecting a democratic society.[63]

Proxmire's surprising defense of Nixon reminded voters of his iconoclastic independence and his willingness to break with his own party. When the Wisconsin Democratic Party convention voted for a resolution calling on the president to resign, Proxmire called it "completely premature." A *Capital Times* editorial called Proxmire's reaction "shortsightedly wrong" and compared his defense of Nixon to his enthusiastic support of the Vietnam war seven years earlier. When Nixon's "Enemies List" was made public, Proxmire was astounded to find his name on it. He claimed that his relations with the president "have always been warm and friendly . . . and I'm sure he doesn't regard me as an enemy. There may be other people who are calling the signals and saying let's get these people who are opposed to the President. That's just not the way President Nixon would think, I'm sure." He continued to assert that the evidence of criminal activity would never implicate the president himself and that there was no chance for impeachment. Yet it was not just blind support of Nixon, either. When the president called on the Senate to end its hearings on Watergate as a waste of money and a distraction, Proxmire insisted that they must continue to ferret out the evidence, wherever it may lead, and he called on Nixon to release all the White House tapes. After Spiro Agnew resigned as a result of his own corruption scandal, Proxmire approved of Gerald Ford's appointment as vice president, but he promised a vigorous investigation, including a comprehensive audit of his finances and tax returns, before a confirmation vote. After the Saturday Night Massacre, when Nixon ordered special prosecutor Archibald Cox fired and attorney general Elliot

Richardson and deputy attorney general William Ruckelhaus resigned in protest, Proxmire rejected outright Nixon's plan for the appointment of a new special prosecutor to replace Cox as "an insult to congress."[64]

In January 1974, Proxmire still thought impeachment unlikely, despite the growing evidence of the administration's abuse of power, but it was clear that he no longer had any trust in the president. Met by reporters at O'Hare International Airport, Proxmire refused to say whether he supported impeachment: "I'm part of the jury . . . so I can't commit myself, even in my own mind." He feared impeachment proceedings and a Senate trial would be too politically divisive, and public opinion seemed to support his position. His office conducted a poll of Wisconsin voters and found that 55 percent of respondents wanted Nixon to resign, but only 44 percent wanted him impeached. For most of the spring and summer, Proxmire simply stopped commenting on the unfolding scandal, refusing to speculate about impeachment as late as August. When Nixon did finally resign on August 9, Proxmire offered an uncharacteristically bland statement: his resignation "is a reminder that even a President who has won a landslide victory and has achieved greater power and influence throughout the world cannot illegally manipulate American institutions or cover-up criminal activities and remain in office." He was much harsher with President Ford's pardon, calling it "absolutely wrong" and "completely absurd" since there had been no conviction.[65]

Despite his vacillation on the Watergate scandal, Proxmire remained quite popular in Wisconsin, and he went to great lengths to ensure his likeability, often by engaging in unlikely stunts to show off his dedication to physical fitness. In November 1972, for example, he began a multi-stage, 1,200-mile tour of Wisconsin. Elected officials, of course, regularly toured their home states, but only Proxmire would decide to *run* the entire distance . . . in winter. He began his odyssey in Milwaukee and spent nine days running along state highways for over 260 miles to Lancaster in Grant County, sloshing through the snow and slush in a yellow slicker and galoshes, stopping at factory gates and shopping centers to introduce himself and talk to voters. He averaged about thirty miles a day at a pace of about four miles an hour. After a few days' break, he started a second leg in early December, and a third on Christmas. The intermittent runs continued through January and February before finally concluding in April.[66]

Proxmire's jogging tour of the state coincided with his emergence as a champion of physical fitness. In January 1973, the Amateur Athletic Union named Proxmire its honorary national physical fitness chairman. He celebrated the announcement by dropping to the floor and doing seventy-five pushups in less than two minutes. The appointment coincided with the completion of his book on physical fitness, *You Can Do It!*, released a few months later. In his book, he explained his own exercise and diet regimen, far more rigorous than that recommended by Weight Watchers, but absolutely necessary for a nation plagued by obesity and laziness. Proxmire's personal habits—running to work every day, or packing sardines and sunflower seeds for breakfast when he traveled—were well known, but now he wanted to promote his ideas widely. He went so far as to introduce a resolution to make the last Sunday in May "Walk a Mile for Your Health Day," which passed in December.[67] His views on health sometimes bordered on the cranky, which brought him into conflict with more traditional medical authorities. He claimed that the National Academy of Science's recommended daily allowances of vitamins and minerals "capricious, unscientific, and illogical," as well as "ridiculously low" and claimed that it was unduly influenced by the food industry. This drew a sharp response from UW professor Alfred Harper, who chaired the committee that spent five years developing the recommendations. Such unsubstantiated claims, he declared, undermined the credibility of the FDA and opened the doors to every quack and charlatan ready to profit from the sale of nutritional supplements. Proxmire persisted, citing studies that recommended much higher dosages of vitamins, and he introduced a bill to prohibit the FDA from classifying as illegal drugs supplements that exceeded 150 percent of the recommended dietary allowance (RDA). By that same logic, Proxmire argued, the FDA could regulate the sale of salt, sugar, and even water, all of which were dangerous if consumed in very large quantities. Doctors, Ralph Nader's Health Research Group, and even the AARP attacked Proxmire's attempt to curtail the regulatory power of the FDA.[68]

By 1975, Proxmire had become a highly respected senator, one who was regularly mentioned as a potential presidential or vice presidential candidate. Yet at the same time, he recognized he was unhappy without Ellen. For her part, Ellen had reconciled herself to the fact that her husband thought being a senator was the greatest job in the world and would continue to devote himself to it. She had her own very successful career that took up as much time as her husband's. Yet neither of them was happy being apart, and they announced their reconciliation in February 1975 after four years of separation. They would have their own careers, which would keep them both busy, but they decided to remain a family and purchased a new house on the same street. Proxmire recognized the strain his dedication to the Senate had put on their marriage ("I did all the taking and she did all the giving"), but he would never take her for granted again.[69]

9

BUILDING A LEGACY

G erald Ford assumed the presidency in the aftermath of the Watergate
scandal, struggling with a dramatically weakened office and a Democratic Congress. Proxmire, now chairing the Senate Banking, Housing,
and Urban Affairs Committee, and with a reputation of willingly clash-
ing with authority, had an ideal position from which he could criticize
the president on economic issues. And there was much to criticize as the
economy in the mid-1970s suffered from both recession and inflation. In
January 1975, Proxmire predicted a long, slow recovery within the year,
but with lingering unemployment until at least 1980. He made clear that
he would oppose increased federal spending or public employment that
would increase inflation, and he was skeptical of price controls or federal
lending to failing businesses, as many Democrats favored. In that sense he
seemed closer to the president's position than that of his own party, but
Ford discovered that Proxmire would be quick to criticize his actions if he
disagreed. Having served nearly twenty years in the Senate, Proxmire had
gained seniority and increasingly focused on building an enduring legacy
that was based on more than just criticism of whoever was president.[1]

Proxmire thought Ford an honest, but not brilliant, politician. When
the president proposed an economic plan built around $16 billion in in-
come tax cuts, reduction of federal spending, direct government payments
to low-income taxpayers, and an increased tax on imported oil, Proxmire
was quick to respond, stating bluntly it was a "bad program that won't
work." Congress added an additional $4 billion in tax cuts but refused to
make any cuts in spending. Ford reluctantly signed the bill in March. As a
result, inflation ate up discretionary spending, rendering the tax cuts far

too ineffective to stimulate the economy. The economy did indeed worsen in early 1975, with unemployment reaching 9.2 percent in May—the highest since 1941—before showing signs of recovery in the summer. These tax cuts did little to stimulate the economy and instead expanded the budget deficit to a record $60 billion in 1976 and led to worsening inflation, despite the administration's optimistic forecast of economic growth.[2]

Another early clash came over housing policy. As he had with presidents Kennedy, Johnson, and Nixon, Proxmire vigorously opposed presidential appointments that he considered unqualified, even as other senators deferred to executive prerogatives. Within months of becoming president, Ford faced Proxmire's opposition to his nomination of Carla Anderson Hills as secretary for Housing and Urban Development. As chair of the Banking, Housing, and Urban Affairs Committee, Proxmire was responsible for holding hearings on the nomination. His concern was that Hills was unqualified to run HUD during a time of ongoing crises in housing: "At a time when housing starts in the country have dropped below 900,000 and when the administration has frozen virtually all assisted housing starts," he remarked, "this is no time for on-the-job training of a new secretary of HUD." Nonetheless, Proxmire's committee approved the nomination with only two dissenting votes—Proxmire and Delaware senator Joe Biden. The Senate subsequently approved her nomination 94–5. Conflict over housing continued, however. In April, Congress passed a bill providing loans and subsidized mortgages to homeowners facing foreclosure. Proxmire called it a cheap way to fight economic recession by creating as many as five hundred thousand construction jobs, but Ford vetoed the bill and the House failed to override.[3]

One of the most controversial economic issues in Ford's brief administration involved the financial insolvency of New York City. The city's annual budget was about $12 billion a year, twelve times that of Chicago and Los Angeles, after years of pay raises to employees and free tuition in the city university system. In the fall of 1975, New York City was running a $120 million budget deficit, and projections placed its total debt near $900 million by 1976. Facing bankruptcy, Mayor Abraham Beame lobbied the federal government for aid to prevent the city from defaulting on its loans and failing to pay its employees. Proxmire was initially skeptical of the request, but he quickly realized that bankruptcy would likely require many years of federal grants—potentially hundreds of millions of dollars—to maintain basic city services and leave the city unable to find financing from private banks. Worse, it might drag New York State into bankruptcy as well, and raise interest rates for cities across the country. Additionally, he was impressed by state and local efforts to cut spending, which showed how seriously they took the crisis; the city fired 25 percent of its municipal employees, including five thousand police officers, two thousand firefighters, and ten thousand sanitation workers. As Banking Committee chair, Proxmire worked hard to develop a compromise bill that would provide federal loan guarantees to the city. The plan gave New York a $4 billion loan guarantee but would require federal monitoring of its finances and a balanced budget, which he ultimately thought would be less costly to taxpayers than bankruptcy.

President Ford, however, announced he would veto any legislation, leading to the famous October 30 headline in the *Daily News*: "Ford to City: Drop Dead." Proxmire was appalled at Ford's shortsightedness in not seeing the long-term economic consequences a city default would have on the national economy. The Banking Committee advanced the bailout by an 8–5 vote, but Proxmire recognized that there simply weren't enough votes to pass the measure on the floor of the Senate. By December, Ford had changed his mind, and Congress quickly passed a bailout bill, steered through the Senate by Proxmire, who impressed everyone with his mastery of the subject and detailed answers to senators' questions. For the next several years, the Senate Banking Committee held hearings on the city's financial health, with its chair asking hard questions about wages and costs. One reporter went so far as to wonder if Proxmire were the real mayor of New York City. When Mayor Ed Koch requested additional aid in the form of long-term federal loan guarantees in the spring of 1978, Proxmire made it clear that his committee thought the city could now manage on its own without additional aid, especially since it was offering pay increases to municipal employees and paying $48 million to refurbish Yankee Stadium. When municipal employee union negotiations broke down, Proxmire abruptly canceled committee hearings on additional aid for the city. But political pressure from New York politicians, the *New York Times*, and President Carter changed many of the committee members' minds. Only Proxmire, John Tower, and Jake Garn opposed a second

bailout for New York. That summer, Proxmire again offered his expertise
and shepherded the bill through the Senate in his capacity as committee
chair, though he himself voted against it, wary of confirming the federal
government's willingness to bear the financial risk of guaranteeing municipal bonds.[4]

Proxmire became chair of the Senate Banking, Housing, and Urban
Affairs committee in January 1975 when Alabama senator John Sparkman
resigned the position to become chair of the Foreign Relations committee.
The banking industry was wary of the new chair, who had been responsible
for the Truth-in-Lending Act and the Fair Credit Reporting Act, and with
good reason: Proxmire promised change. "The banking industry was too
comfortable under Sparkman," Proxmire said. He also wanted to make it
more competitive and increase Federal Reserve oversight. Proxmire further championed more federal spending to encourage home construction
that would address the housing shortage and create jobs in construction.
During his six years chairing the committee, it took a much more activist,
proconsumer role than it had under earlier leadership.[5]

At first, he made little headway. The committee approved a federal
mortgage bill that he predicted would create eight hundred thousand jobs,
but the measure was vetoed by President Ford. Proxmire proposed consoli-
dating into one regulatory agency the Federal Reserve System, the Federal
Deposit Insurance Corporation, and the Comptroller of the Currency, a
move that he argued would be far more efficient:

> Our present system of dividing authority between three agencies is
> characterized by interagency bickering, buck-passing, indecisiveness,
> inconsistencies, duplication of effort and most recently by large bank
> failures. A unified bank regulatory agency would have the strength,
> resources, and freedom of action to implement the additional re-
> forms needed to maintain the strength of our banking system.

He also introduced legislation limiting the consolidation of large banks
by restricting a bank from acquiring more than 20 percent of banking
assets in any one state. Congress rejected these changes to the industry,
which Proxmire blamed on intense lobbying by bankers. He did get the
Home Mortgage Disclosure Act passed, which required banks to disclose

the number of mortgages they issued by zip code as a way of identifying and publicly shaming those institutions that practiced redlining—banks refusing to loan money for homes in low-income, and often minority, areas. Banks hated the requirement, but it was the perfect Proxmire project: proconsumer legislation at no cost to the taxpayer.[6]

In 1977, however, with a Democrat in the White House and a new populist mood in Washington, Proxmire was able to steer two important pieces of legislation through Congress. The first was the Community Reinvestment Act (CRA), part of an omnibus housing bill. Despite the passage of the 1968 Fair Housing Act, the Banking Committee found evidence of widespread racial discrimination in mortgages, and the federal government had done almost nothing to address the issue. A related issue was the widespread practice of redlining. At a committee hearing in March, Proxmire played television commercials produced by the Savings and Loan Foundation and by the American Bankers Association that spoke in glowing terms of people's deposits being used for home loans in their own communities. The truth was far different, and many banks simply did not invest in the communities in which they operated, contributing to the economic decline of neighborhoods. Morris Crawford of Bowery Savings, for example, admitted to the committee that less than 12 percent of his bank's home mortgages were invested in New York City. To remedy this problem, Proxmire introduced the CRA, which required federal regulators to consider how much money banks invested in the immediate communities before approving new branches. The loans would, of course, have to meet the standards of sound operation, but now banks would have to make sure that some of their loans would remain local. The intent was not to force banks to make bad loans, but to apply standards fairly and force banks to pay attention to local customers. A similar measure, introduced by Henry Reuss, passed the House, and President Carter signed the bill into law in December. The CRA gave local groups some leverage over banks, so that a poor score would not automatically make regulators reject applications for branch openings, mergers, or acquisitions. A 1998 Urban Institute Study revealed that the CRA was responsible for increasing lending in low-income areas in twenty-two out of twenty-three cities and led to $388 billion in mortgages by 1997.[7]

The second piece of important legislation involved the defense industry. Proxmire's frequent scrutiny of its practices revealed that American business officials often bribed foreign governments to procure contracts. The extent of the practice was shocking: more than four hundred corporations had paid more than $300 million in bribes to foreign officials. Lockheed had been caught bribing the prime minister of Japan, precipitating the collapse of his government. Proxmire introduced the Foreign Corrupt Practices Act in January 1977 to outlaw this practice. It was quickly passed by Congress and signed by President Carter in December. The senator called the law "the most significant US contribution to world trade in 1977." A final legislative success came in 1980, when Congress passed the "Proxmire-Reuss Depository Institutions Deregulation and Monetary Control Act," which allowed customers of all banks to earn interest on their checking accounts and allowed savings banks to offer business loans, credit cards, and other financial services that had been the purview of commercial banks. It was a reform that would increase competition among financial institutions, and such competition would benefit consumers. When Republicans gained control of the Senate in 1981, however, Proxmire lost his chairmanship of the committee to Republican Jake Garn of Utah, depriving him of his bully pulpit and ending the committee's emphasis on consumer protection.[8]

Despite his proconsumer record, Proxmire irritated some traditional Democratic constituencies with his frugality. In February 1976, Ford vetoed a $6.2 billion public works bill. Proxmire voted to sustain the president's veto—the only member of the Wisconsin delegation to do so—and so earned the ire of labor unions and Milwaukee mayor Henry Maier, who claimed that Proxmire's opposition cost the state $50 million in federal funds for building projects. Proxmire defended his position on the grounds of efficiency: each new public service or public works job created would have cost $25,000, but investing that money in housing, Proxmire argued, would have created far more jobs at a lower cost and addressed the rising cost of homes, too. Proxmire also opposed Ford's revenue-sharing plan, which generated much criticism from Wisconsin mayors, several of whom vowed revenge in the upcoming election. Proxmire again defended his stance on the grounds of efficiency, insisting that federal funds should go directly to taxpayers rather than to local officials, who tended to spend funds on inflationary construction projects that did not address increased housing costs. As with New York City, he simply did not trust that local officials would be able to resist adding to the inflationary spiral of government spending.[9]

Proxmire's hostility toward federal spending often frustrated state and local officials who expected their congressional delegation to bring dollars to their districts. No project better illustrates this frustration than the case of a dam over the Kickapoo River near LaFarge. Begun in 1971, the dam had two purposes: to control flooding that threatened several small towns near the river, including Gays Mills and Soldiers Grove; and to create a 1,800-acre lake that would be the heart of a new outdoor recreation area and boost tourism to the region. In 1975, the Army Corps of Engineers halted work on the partially completed dam when an environmental impact statement, one of the first in the nation under the Environmental Protection Act, revealed that the lake would quickly become contaminated by runoff from nearby farms and be overwhelmed with algae and weeds, creating a noxious mess that would require continuous remediation. Governor Patrick Lucey and Senator Gaylord Nelson opposed the continued construction and instead favored a study to find other options for flood control, including relocating the communities prone to flooding. Proxmire surprised many by continuing to support the construction of the dam, despite its estimated $51.5 million price tag. He insisted that local residents supported the dam, though support was far from universal, although more cynical journalists noted that his support might also have come from the fact that he faced reelection in a year. When Nelson managed to halt construction while alternatives were considered, Proxmire urged that "non-controversial" parts of the project continue.[10]

That fall, after having his staff conduct its own cost-benefit analysis, Proxmire abruptly withdrew his support for the dam. Remarkably, he announced his position in LaFarge itself when he met with local officials and residents in the village hall. When challenged, he bluntly defended his position: "I changed my mind primarily because of the colossal increases in the cost of this project. It had gone from $15.6 million to $24.5 million to $38.4 million to $51.5 million over the years. And in order to justify it [the Corps of Engineers] had to more than double their claims of recreational benefits. I found those benefits hard to justify." Proxmire spent nearly two hours listening to the dismayed and increasingly angry crowd, some of whom broke down in tears trying to explain the dam's importance to the survival of the community. One of his aides described it as the roughest two hours he had facing his constituents; Proxmire himself later referred to as "one of the most painful days of my life." He was simply unable to persuade the people that the costs of the project would greatly outweigh the benefits. Proxmire's reversal drew praise from some journalists who saw it as a courageous act of putting the general good over pork-barrel spending that would benefit only a few, though the *Capital Times* criticized how long it took him to make what Nelson and Lucey saw as an obvious decision.[11]

Local residents remained furious at Proxmire's change of heart and his role in deleting funds for the project in December. In January 1976, LaFarge residents hanged Proxmire in effigy and held a mock funeral near the river on what would have been the bed of their new lake. For years, hope remained alive for the LaFarge dam project. President Ford proposed new funds as part of a large public works bill, but President Carter deleted them soon after he took office. In July 1978, severe flooding inundated Soldiers Grove and Gays Mills, forcing the evacuation of hundreds of residents and causing millions of dollars in property damage. Local residents bitterly blamed Proxmire for their losses, both real and imagined, and the sheriff made sure that Proxmire had an armed escort when he toured the area to see the damage. Amazingly, a majority of LaFarge residents voted for Proxmire's reelection in 1976. When asked about that strange fact, the mayor replied that although "we hate that son-of-a-bitch for what he did . . . we admired his guts for coming out here and talking to us in person."[12]

In 1975, Proxmire began what would become his most popular and longest-lasting attack on federal spending: the Golden Fleece Awards. His success in exposing the cost overruns of the C-5A and other Pentagon waste demonstrated the necessity of good publicity to expose government waste, so Proxmire decided to create "a monthly award for the most absurd example of waste accomplished by one federal agency or another during the preceding thirty days." After considering several names (such as Rip-Off of the Month, Spending Crime of the Month), Proxmire and his staff settled on "fleece" to suggest "a smooth, legalized theft from the taxpayers." Tom van der Voort, who had an interest in Greek mythology, suggested "Golden Fleece."[13] On March 11, Proxmire issued a press release awarding a Golden Fleece to the National Science Foundation for spending

$84,000 on a University of Minnesota study on why people fall in love. It set the tone for ridicule that would characterize the award for the next thirteen years:

> I object to this because no one—not even the National Science Foundation—can argue that falling in love is a science. Even if they spend $84 million or $84 billion, they wouldn't get an answer that anyone would believe. And I'm against it because I don't want the answer. I believe that 200 million other Americans want to leave some things in life a mystery, and right at the top of this list of things we don't want to know is why a man falls in love with a woman and vice versa.[14]

Professor Ellen Berscheid, the lead researcher, quickly defended the study as part of a larger project studying psychological dependence and interpersonal attraction begun in 1972 that would benefit psychologists and therapists and therefore have practical application. When Proxmire followed up by criticizing a similar $224,000 grant to the University of Wisconsin, Professor Elaine Walster responded that her study was part of a larger field of study that she called "equity theory," which she had been working on for the past fifteen years and was widely respected among social scientists. She accused Proxmire of not trying to understand a complex and relevant field of research and instead going after a cheap laugh and political points. The UW Faculty Senate condemned Proxmire's criticism as a threat to basic university research in a statement that concluded, "To the extent that in his personal opinion some funded basic research projects are wasteful, Senator Proxmire's criticisms must be directed at improving the Foundation's policies and review criteria. To instead make attacks on individual scientists' projects, through the mass media and on insufficient knowledge, is a threat to the freedom of scientific inquiry which the Faculty Senate can only view with deep dismay." Proxmire conceded that the UW faculty had a fair point and did indeed work with the NSF to improve its procedures for approving and reporting grants.[15]

Proxmire awarded the second Golden Fleece to the NSF, NASA, and the Office of Naval Research for spending more than $500,000 over seven years to fund a study by Dr. Roland Hutchinson of Kalamazoo State Hospital on why rats, monkeys, and humans clench their jaws. His press release for the second "fleece" was even more sarcastic than the first, mocking the "transparent worthlessness" of Hutchinson's research and declaring it was "time for the federal government to get out of this 'monkey business.'" Proxmire repeated this story in his constituent newsletter and on the Mike Douglas television show.[16] This time, Proxmire got more than an angry rebuke from Midwestern faculty: a year later, Hutchinson filed a lawsuit against Proxmire and legislative assistant Morton Schwartz, who had done most of the research, for libel, claiming that the award had "held him up to public ridicule and damaged his professional reputation," rendering him unable to obtain future grants. Ironically, Schwarz, a former economics professor himself, had indeed done his homework, contacting each of the granting institutions and obtaining documents that supported the grants. Before making the announcement, Schwarz contacted Hutchinson and read him the press release. Hutchinson insisted that the press release was not a fair evaluation of his work and that he would prepare a rebuttal, which turned out to be a $6 million lawsuit.[17]

Despite its origin in government-funded "monkey business," the Hutchinson lawsuit dragged on for nearly four years and actually involved some serious constitutional issues. Article I, Section 6 of the Constitution granted members of Congress legal immunity for statements made on the floor in order to guarantee free debate and prevent reprisal for controversial statements. But did that immunity extend to statements repeated in print or on television? Because this question was of great importance to every member of Congress, the Senate funded Proxmire's defense, though Senator Barry Goldwater pointed out the hypocrisy of Proxmire himself receiving federal funds to defend himself for attacking others for receiving federal funds. A federal court dismissed the suit based on the doctrine of congressional immunity (which covered Proxmire's statements on the floor of the Senate) and the freedom of speech clause of the First Amendment (which covered his newsletter and television appearance), but Hutchinson appealed the decision. In July 1978, the US Court of Appeals upheld the lower court ruling, stating that by accepting public funding for his work, Hutchinson had become a public figure. As a public figure, therefore, Hutchinson had to prove that Proxmire had acted with malice in his statements. Without evidence of malice, Proxmire's statements were protected free speech. Hutchinson refused to give up and appealed the verdict to the US Supreme Court, which agreed to take the case in January 1979. In June, the court ruled in an 8–1 decision that Hutchinson was not a public figure and had to prove only injury, not malice, and that the congressional immunity clause did not apply to statements made outside of Senate debate, meaning that Proxmire could be sued for libel. The court remanded the case back to a lower court, but in March 1980, Proxmire agreed to a settlement. Hutchinson accepted $10,000 plus $5,131.92 in court costs—paid out of Proxmire's own pocket—and a public clarification that Proxmire had not intended to disparage Hutchinson's research, a not-quite apology. Proxmire's defense costs were nearly $125,000, which Proxmire gradually repaid, beginning with royalties he earned from a book about the Golden Fleece Awards.[18]

The lawsuit was an expensive ordeal, but Proxmire continued to make his monthly award during the suit and for the remainder of his time in the Senate. Every month, his legislative assistants spent hours meticulously researching some instance of wasteful government spending, often tipped off by someone working for some federal agency, and the office would decide on a winner. Proxmire would revise the award's language, injecting his own humorous style to make them appealing as press releases. Administrative assistant Howard Shuman was responsible for editing and releasing them. Some government agencies were targeted more frequently, like NASA and the Armed Forces, and the amounts were sometimes tiny compared to other federal spending, but the press releases were always written to outrage the American taxpayer. Proxmire issued one of his favorite Golden Fleece Awards in July 1981 to the Department of the Army for spending $6,000 to produce a seventeen-page set of instructions for the purchase of Worcestershire sauce. The Senate itself received occasional awards, including a March 1978 award for spending $122 million on a new office building. Sometimes Proxmire issued special merit awards to those individuals or agencies that saved money, such as the Smithsonian Institution, which completed the Air and Space Museum ahead of schedule and under budget. Although the Golden Fleece Award remained quite popular with Wisconsin voters and certainly generated good press, not everyone was entirely comfortable with a prominent US Senator ridiculing research. NASA received several awards—spending $140,000 to pay an author to write a six-thousand-word history of the Viking Project, for example, or requesting $28 million for a building addition to store moon rocks. He bestowed an award on the Smithsonian Institution for producing a Tzotzil dictionary, a language spoken by a few thousand inhabitants of southern Mexico. Some journalists, though they admired the research put into them by Proxmire's staff, thought a few of the Golden Fleece Awards were little more than cheap shots. Even some of his staff were uncomfortable with them, seeing some as petty. Such criticism may have had an impact. Over the years, Proxmire and his staff tended to focus on government agencies funding sometimes embarrassingly inappropriate expenses rather than getting pulled into the merits of research, and later awards avoided naming names. Legislative director Ken Dameron, who had a law degree, took on the responsibility of reading the awards to make sure there would be no further legal issues. Even after Proxmire had been out of office for years, the Golden Fleece Awards remained probably his best-known work. "Where's William Proxmire when you need him?" wondered one columnist in a 2002 column bemoaning a $3.2 million study on identifying individuals by smell.[19]

The Golden Fleece Award was not the only way Proxmire kept himself in the public eye in the 1970s and 1980s. In an effort to stay in touch with his constituents and understand their concerns, he began working odd jobs for a day at a time on some occasions when he was in the state. He spent the Independence Day recess in 1975, for example, working on a garbage truck in Fond du Lac, in an electronics factory in Oak Creek, and at the Milwaukee HUD office. Over the years, he canned peas, washed dishes, delivered milk, insulated homes, milked cows, worked as a bank clerk, and helped out in factories. Each job helped him learn about the concerns of working-class men and women in Wisconsin. Proxmire also regularly greeted crowds at Camp Randall Stadium in Madison, outside the flower building at the State Fair, and at Lambeau Field in Green Bay. He worked in soup kitchens and nursing homes on holidays. He rarely traveled with any staff and stayed in inexpensive motel rooms, dining on food purchased from the local grocery store. Despite his almost constant presence in Wisconsin, Proxmire did not miss a single roll-call vote in the Senate between 1966 and his retirement.[20]

His big electoral victory in 1970 and his prominent role in the Senate allowed Proxmire to look confidently toward his 1976 reelection campaign. Republicans were equally sure that Proxmire would coast to reelection and struggled to find a candidate willing to take on the hopeless task of challenging the state's most popular elected official. Well-known figures like Melvin Laird and Vernon Thomson refused to enter the race, as did every Republican member of the legislature. Six months before Election Day, no one had stepped forward to seek the Republican nomination, even though three Socialist candidates had announced independent bids.[21] Finally, at its state convention in early June, the Republican Party endorsed an almost unknown figure: Stanley York, a former Assembly representative from River Falls who had served in the cabinets of governors Warren Knowles and Patrick Lucey. York agreed to run only if he had the full financial backing of the state party in order to run a creditable campaign and only if the state party would support him for a gubernatorial run two years later. Proxmire himself received some opposition from Milwaukee mayor Henry Maier, who criticized the senator's resistance to federal aid to cities, which he claimed cost the state $50 million. Beyond that, Democrats enthusiastically backed Proxmire's reelection campaign.[22]

The senatorial election in Wisconsin was all but a nonevent, greatly overshadowed by the close presidential race between Jimmy Carter and Gerald Ford, both of whom had survived heavily contested primary battles. York struggled to find a message that would resonate with voters. He criticized Proxmire for his frequent trips to the state that York characterized as tax-payer-funded campaign trips, and for trying to get federal funds to pay for his legal defense in the Hutchinson case. He accused Proxmire of switching positions for political expediency, as on the Vietnam War, and shortchanging Wisconsin in federal spending. Proxmire remained unflappable in his campaign appearances, affirming that he paid for his regular trips to the state out of his own pocket. He also announced that despite the Republican Party's plan to spend up to $250,000, he had only $597.08 in his campaign account and would not accept donations or spend any money at all. In fact, he donated $3,933 in campaign contributions to charity rather than spend it.[23] Complicating York's task was the fact that Proxmire was even more conservative on some issues than he was. At their first debate in Tomah in early October, the two candidates agreed on many issues, with Proxmire breaking from the Democratic Party to oppose both universal amnesty for draft evaders and deserters, and federal revenue sharing. The two candidates differed, however, on many other things. Proxmire favored a constitutional amendment banning abortion, a striking departure from party orthodoxy, but York took a very clear pro-choice position. York's overall strategy was to present himself as a moderate, thoughtful Republican and to depict Proxmire as a publicity-seeking opportunist who nitpicked at federal spending without making any real change: Proxmire, he said, "senses where the public is then latches on to that for the moment." He dramatically underestimated Proxmire's expertise, but staking out the middle ground was politically brilliant since it threatened to draw Democrats away from Proxmire over social issues. In attempting to turn Proxmire's reputation as a maverick against him, York indeed presented the most serious challenge of any Republican candidate. Proxmire responded by defending his record of accomplishments (truth-in-lending, exposing Pentagon waste, stopping the SST) and demonstrating his expertise on the complicated subject of defense spending. He bluntly declared that he had changed his position on Vietnam because he realized it was wrong, and he stubbornly stuck to his opposition to busing and abortion without a hint of vacillation. In other words, the campaign was between a maverick and a moderate in an increasingly polarized political environment. Indeed, at one candidate forum, Proxmire and York joined forces to defend capitalism against four socialists.[24]

Had the Proxmire-York campaign occurred in 1964, 1970, or 1982, the result might have been much closer. But 1976 was a Democratic year, with Republicans saddled with the uninspiring Ford, and Proxmire was at the height of his popularity. Even the candidates seemed bored as they rehashed the same arguments in thirteen debates around the state. Proxmire's campaign spent no money. Volunteers drove him from town to town, and there were no advertisements of any sort. The only real cost was Washington-to-Wisconsin airfare, and he paid for that himself. On Election Day, Proxmire earned a victory even more substantial than he had six years earlier, defeating York 1,396,970 to 521,902, winning 73 percent of the vote, and carrying every county, as well as running over 356,000 votes ahead of Jimmy Carter. He had become a phenomenon—a politician that the people genuinely liked.[25]

In many ways, Jimmy Carter and William Proxmire were very similar.

They both took public service seriously, had a strong sense of personal ethics, and tended to be aloof from other politicians. Proxmire praised Carter's moral integrity and efforts to make the presidency more accessible to the people. The new president even accepted Proxmire's suggestion that he walk during the inauguration parade from the Capitol to the White House, although Carter embraced it as a sign of being "the people's president" rather than as a means of promoting physical fitness, as Proxmire intended. Although the Senate quickly approved Carter's nominations, Proxmire was the only Democratic senator to question them. He opposed Patricia Harris as HUD secretary because he thought she lacked any experience with housing, and he opposed Thomas "Bert" Lance as the head of the Office of Management and Budget because he had no experience working in the federal government. Lance refused to divest his bank stocks after he took office and tried to interfere with legislation before the Banking Committee and later resigned after allegations of fraud emerged from his time as chair of Calhoun First National Bank in Georgia. Proxmire also opposed the nomination of attorney general Griffin Bell because he thought the attorney general should not be a personal friend of the president. As with Kennedy and Johnson, he was not going to give the president's nominees a free pass just because he was a Democrat.[26]

Carter took office at a time of continued economic problems: high unemployment, worrying inflation, a growing trade deficit, and increasing energy prices. The new president—much to the dismay of liberal Democrats, including his own vice president—decided to focus on inflation and promised to balance the federal budget by 1981. Proxmire should have been a key supporter of the president's budget cutting in Congress, but the two shared an aloofness and dislike for traditional political deal making. As a result, Proxmire found himself criticizing a president from his own party almost as much as he had criticized Nixon and Ford. Carter's fiscal year 1979 budget proposal increased spending a scant 2 percent as the rate of inflation neared 12 percent in March 1978. When the Senate cut the fiscal year 1979 budget by $11 billion in September 1978, Proxmire complained that it did not go far enough and instead tried to amend the reduction to eliminate an additional $17.7 billion. Economic growth slowed enough that Carter's goal of a balanced budget within four years proved overly optimistic, but he insisted in his 1979 State of the Union message that spending restraint was still critical in fighting inflation. He described his fiscal year 1980 budget as "lean and austere," because it cut domestic spending and forecast the lowest budget deficit ($29 billion) in six years. Again, Proxmire thought it did not go far enough and proposed to slash nearly $29 billion from the budget to make it balance, introducing a bill requiring the president to submit a balanced budget to Congress. The Senate rejected his budget cut proposals.[27]

Proxmire was even more hostile toward Carter's final budget, for fiscal year 1981, which raised defense spending and increased taxes in a time of looming recession. Proxmire wanted a balanced budget and would cut everything it took to get it, telling reporters, "I'd cut them all—the farm program, the education program, housing. You name it, I'd cut it. The number one problem now is inflation, and it is hurting low-income people more than anyone else. . . . I don't think you're doing any favor to them to spend more money on these so-called social programs." Even when Carter reduced his budget proposal by an additional $13 billion, Proxmire insisted it was not nearly enough for a balanced budget. He ultimately voted against the budget in May, one of only six Democrats to do so.[28]

Ironically, President Carter's reaction to the inflation of the 1970s—reducing federal spending—changed how Proxmire criticized it. It had been easy to rail against multibillion-dollar defense contracts a decade earlier, but with a federal budget now defined as "austere," there were fewer big-ticket items to oppose. He had already recognized the publicity he could gain through his absurdist Golden Fleece Awards, and so his staff began zeroing in on smaller-scale, but equally outrageous, examples of federal waste. Proxmire increasingly focused on examples of high-ranking federal employees enjoying the perks of employment, like limousine service, catered meals, and first-class airfare, all of which provided excellent fodder for the Golden Fleece Awards, even if they meant a smaller dent in the budget.[29]

One of the major pieces of financial legislation that Proxmire fought against was the Chrysler bailout. By 1979, the company was losing millions of dollars per month and heading toward bankruptcy, and its president, Lee Iacocca, turned to the federal government for help. The Carter administration rejected Chrysler's request for $1 billion in tax credits, but it did support a $1.5 billion loan guarantee. Already opposed to the bill,

Proxmire opened Banking Committee hearings in October and gave full vent to his concerns: "If we provide loan guarantees to Chrysler, we will be saying, in effect, to every business in the country: 'It doesn't matter if you make bad management decisions; it doesn't matter if you no longer make products that enough people want to buy; it doesn't even matter if the federal government has no direct stake in your continued existence.'" Small businesses went bankrupt all the time—six thousand in 1979 alone. That was simply how the free enterprise system worked, but bailing out Chrysler would mean that taxpayers would subsidize the risk of doing business while large corporations would keep the rewards. Yet many in Congress supported the move, mainly because bankruptcy could mean job losses. Nelson supported it for that very reason, citing the six Chrysler plants in Wisconsin that employed nearly a thousand workers. After three days of hearings, Proxmire saw the bailout, with all the political pressure Chrysler was placing on members of Congress, as inevitable. The Senate passed the loan guarantee by a vote of 53–44 in December, but the whole affair left Proxmire deeply troubled about the precedent it set. What was to stop other companies facing declining sales from asking for federal help? More critically, would those companies expect the American taxpayers to pay for their bad business decisions? He was convinced the free-market system was the best economic system, and he distrusted any efforts to skew that system to favor those with the most political or economic clout.[30]

During the Ford and Carter administrations, Proxmire continued his role as a leading congressional critic of military spending, but with the war over, Proxmire's critique changed as well. He still regularly attacked the defense industry, but not for negotiating contracts with the Defense Department. Instead, he grew increasingly critical of foreign arms sales, which had increased from about $1 billion in 1970 to nearly $9 billion in 1974, nearly half of it purchased by Iran and Saudi Arabia.[31] The one weapons program against which Proxmire fought especially hard was the B-1 bomber. On April 25, 1976, Proxmire announced he would deliver a series of six speeches opposing the production of 244 of the supersonic bombers, which had been in development for years. He noted that cost estimates had increased from $35 million each in 1970 to an estimated $100 million each. Moreover, they were unnecessary, since the current B-52 bomber could fulfill the exact same role. This time, the Pentagon was ready for him. In response, Air Force secretary Thomas Reed argued that most of the cost increase was due to inflation and that a B-1 bomber would require a significantly shorter runway for takeoff, allowing it to be deployed more widely than the B-52. In a second speech a week later, Proxmire argued that missile technology made a supersonic bomber unnecessary, that the aircraft's exhaust made it vulnerable to heat-seeking missiles, and that "design slippages" meant that the bomber would not perform as originally specified anyway. Proxmire subsequently raised other issues with the B-1, including that it would be obsolete too quickly. It was a striking public debate over the merits of a complex and expensive new weapon that demonstrated how much Proxmire's fight against defense spending had changed the willingness of Congress to give the Pentagon whatever it wanted. Proxmire won, too, when the Senate voted to halt production of the B-1 until the next president took office. President Carter, after adopting much of Proxmire's argument against the bomber on the campaign trail, subsequently canceled the program.[32]

Proxmire disagreed with the president, however, over the SALT II treaty in 1979. Two weeks after Carter announced that negotiations with the Soviet Union had produced a treaty that would limit nuclear missiles but allow the two nations to continue to develop conventional weapons systems, Proxmire, George McGovern, and Mark Hatfield announced their opposition, claiming that the treaty would simply redirect the arms race rather than actually limit it. Proxmire in particular predicted that the treaty would increase military spending by promoting the development of new bombers and other missile programs not already covered by it. When the Senate began consideration of the treaty in June, Proxmire called it a "weak, faltering step in the right direction," but contended that it did not go far enough. The Soviet invasion of Afghanistan, however, meant that the Senate never ratified the treaty, although both Carter and Reagan abided by its provisions.[33]

The Soviet invasion of Afghanistan even made Proxmire reconsider his long fight against decreasing military spending. In a December 1980 interview, he acknowledged that in some cases, increased military spending was necessary. "I'm reacting to a changing world situation," he ruefully admitted, citing Afghanistan and the Soviet threat against Poland. "I'm going to be opposed to those programs which I think are wasteful. . . . But even with cutting out all the waste, I am now convinced that there is no way we can have a strong enough military force without more money."[34] There were other signs that Proxmire was drifting back to his more hawkish positions of the early 1960s. He opposed Reagan's lifting of the grain embargo on the Soviet Union in April 1981, arguing that it might give the impression that the United States would not oppose aggressive action in Afghanistan, Poland, or elsewhere. In May, he voted for Reagan's record-breaking $136.5 billion defense budget for fiscal year 1982. He did, however, criticize military projects that he thought were inefficient or useless, such as a nuclear-powered aircraft carrier that he characterized as an easy target for Soviet missiles.[35]

By 1980, the nation had grown more conservative, and the presidential election brought Ronald Reagan to the White House, giving Republicans control of the Senate for the first time since 1954. In Wisconsin, Robert Kasten defeated Gaylord Nelson in his bid for a fourth term, a shocking blow for the Democratic Party. These events affected Proxmire as well, as he seemed to take a decided turn to the right in the early 1980s. There were some early signs that he would be a consistent opponent of Reagan. He charged that Reagan's inauguration had illegally used public funds, rather than private donations, for what he saw as a gaudy, excessive celebration. Although he voted for most of Reagan's Cabinet appointees, he opposed Terrell Bell as secretary of education and James Edwards as secretary of energy and was the lone vote against attorney general William Smith and commerce secretary Malcolm Baldrige. Yet when Reagan announced his plans to reduce federal income tax rates by 30 percent over three years, increase defense spending, and balance the budget, Proxmire was cautiously supportive, calling the proposed spending cuts "a good start." He said he would support the tax cut but warned that Reagan had not explained the enormity of the consequences: Reagan "failed to explain the great sacrifices that will be needed. . . . he will have to make the spending cuts very, very deep." He predicted that Reagan's spending cuts would still leave the federal government with a $100 billion budget deficit. In May, Proxmire voted with Republicans to pass a slightly modified version of Reagan's tax cut and budget reductions, although he did protest reductions to Social Security.[36]

Wisconsin Democrats howled at Proxmire's apostasy. In June, Proxmire, the party's highest-ranking elected official, did not address the state Democratic convention in La Crosse, fearing a hostile reception. A resolution urging Proxmire to "resume voting like a Democrat" was narrowly defeated after nearly a half hour of debate. Proxmire, however, defended his record, noting that he had voted against more of Reagan's appointees than any other senator, and that he opposed reductions in Social Security and the relaxation of environmental regulations. Even though he favored increased defense spending in some areas (military pay, tanks, and aircraft), he still opposed the MX missile program, B-1 bomber, and more aircraft carriers. As for domestic spending, it was not that he supported Reagan, it was that Reagan supported *him*. Proxmire reminded reporters that he had long advocated for federal budget cuts: "Now I am winning. I have a president who supports my position."[37]

Proxmire also defended his support of Reaganomics by pointing to voter sentiment that had become significantly more conservative. He cited a survey conducted by his office that showed Wisconsin residents increasingly supported a stronger military based on conventional weapons. An April 1982 survey of his constituents yielded ten thousand responses, the majority of which favored giving Reagan's economic policies more time to work, a reaction that surprised Proxmire since Wisconsin had been particularly hard-hit in the recession. Yet people questioning his liberal credentials did make him uncomfortable, especially after the Conservative Caucus, a national lobbying group, praised Proxmire's support for Reagan's budget reductions. He devoted his July newsletter to defending his voting record and consistent positions, however they were labeled by the media. Proxmire took even more heat from Democrats when he supported President Reagan's firing of striking air traffic controllers in August. Although he believed collective bargaining was "crucial" to democracy, he stated bluntly that the striking workers had left the president with no choice. Since the Port Authority Transit Corporation (PATCO) workers had taken an oath not to strike, they were breaking the law, making the issue very clear-cut to him. "I just hope he sticks to his position," he said of Reagan. "It's a tough position, but it's the right position."

If Proxmire found any fault in Reaganomics, it was that it did not go far enough in cutting spending, and he pointed in alarm at the ballooning budget deficit and the national debt, rapidly approaching $1 trillion. In a long-shot effort to warn his fellow senators, he staged a sixteen-hour overnight filibuster against the administration's proposal to increase the debt-ceiling limit to $1.079 trillion. All night, he described ways the government could cut spending in a nearly empty chamber before an audience of yawning pages and bored security guards. Although he expressed some criticism of Reagan's economic program, especially as it increased the budget deficit, his voting record for 1981 revealed that he voted with the president 52 percent of the time.[38]

Yet Proxmire's conservativism was not entirely new; he had been moving to the right on social issues for years. Beginning in the 1970s, he consistently opposed mandatory busing as a means of integrating schools, even though he had supported civil rights legislation in the 1960s. He also opposed abortion out of personal conviction and consistently voted to deny federal funding for abortion services, which generated a great deal of anger among Wisconsin Democrats. In fact, Proxmire favored an anti-abortion amendment to the Constitution or, at least, allowing individual states to outlaw abortion. Meeting with nineteen women's and religious groups at the UW Memorial Union in February 1982, he politely refused to alter his opinion. "You've made an extraordinarily strong case," he told them, but refused to budge from his view that life begins at conception. "I don't know how I can change that view, no matter how deeply I go into it or how strong my constituents feel the other way." He did, however, strongly support family planning and making contraception easily available. Despite the fact that his entire staff was pro-choice and regularly pressed the senator on the issue, he refused to change his position, out of both personal conviction and the belief that a majority of Wisconsin residents agreed.[39] Proxmire also irritated Democrats by supporting school prayer, another hot-button issue in the culture wars of the 1980s. In 1982, he supported a measure introduced by North Carolina senator Jesse Helms to prohibit the Supreme Court from overturning state laws reinstating school prayer. Again facing criticism from liberal supporters, Proxmire defended his position: "What's wrong with having it if the principal and the school board have decided they want to have one? A lot of kids otherwise never hear a prayer. . . . They are always uplifting. They appeal to the best spirit in man." In 1984 he even supported a constitutional amendment allowing organized prayer in public schools, declaring that any form of prayer was beneficial, and dismissed arguments that such an amendment would undermine the authority of the Supreme Court or would violate the establishment clause of the First Amendment. Further alienating liberals, Proxmire supported easing gun control laws that had been in place since 1968, a position advocated by the National Rifle Association. In 1982, the Moral Majority organization gave Proxmire a 71 percent rating, the third-highest of any Senate Democrat.[40]

As the United States slid into recession in 1982, and as Proxmire began preparing for his reelection campaign, he grew increasingly critical of Reagan's economic proposals, though he still remained out of step with his fellow Democrats. In January, Reagan announced plans to change $47 billion of federal spending into block grants to states to administer social programs and construction (the so-called "New Federalism"). While state Republicans embraced state control of AFDC and food stamps as a way to reduce fraud, and state Democrats suspected the proposal was simply a way to cut welfare spending, Proxmire warned that states like Wisconsin that were more generous with payments could become "welfare magnets": "You'll have a situation where some states in order to get rid of their poor and to ease their tax burden will cut AFDC and food stamps very low. The result will be that those states that are conscientious—like Wisconsin— likely will suffer because we'll get an influx of the poor and they will be more of a burden on us and relief for states that are less conscientious." In other words, the primary concern for most Democrats was reduced funding on poor families, but Proxmire's primary concern was for Wisconsin taxpayers. When Reagan presented his budget plan for fiscal year 1983 to Congress, Proxmire voted against it, since it contained $6.4 billion in cuts from social programs, a $21 billion tax increase, and a projected $103.9 billion deficit. He did, however, join with Republicans in supporting a constitutional amendment requiring a balanced budget, 69–31, a major victory for Reagan.[41] Later that summer, as the economy worsened, Proxmire opposed the Reagan administration's $13.3 billion in spending cuts, including $4.2 billion in dairy price supports, which passed the Senate by a 67–32 vote. He also opposed an administration tax bill that increased taxes $98.3 billion over three years by raising some income tax rates, the cigarette tax, and unemployment insurance withholding and eliminating many deductions. When Reagan vetoed a $14.2 billion supplementary

spending bill in September, Proxmire announced he would vote to override the president's veto, which the Senate did by a 60–30 vote, handing
Reagan his first major congressional defeat in his first term. The spending
was necessary to keep the federal government operating and was not a
"budget buster," Proxmire argued. Despite his fame as a budget cutter,
he did not like the arbitrariness of simply defunding government operations and was irritated that his major policy position had been co-opted
by conservative Republicans as a way of cutting domestic spending while
increasing military spending.[42]

The one aspect of Reagan's budget program that Proxmire refused to
support was a reduction for dairy price supports. This was not a new position, of course, and Proxmire had spent much of his first few years in
the Senate railing against the policies of agriculture secretary Ezra Taft
Benson. Beginning in the late 1970s, the situation facing farmers grew
significantly worse. High food prices drove many farmers to increase
production, which reached record levels by 1980. High interest rates and
high oil prices, however, drove up costs, and when agricultural prices fell
as a result of overproduction, many farmers found themselves deeply in
debt and coping with a declining income. The US grain embargo against
the Soviet Union made conditions even worse, and average farm income
dropped 25 percent in 1980 alone. It was a dark time for Midwestern
farmers. Shortly after taking office, secretary of agriculture John Block
and Office of Budget and Management (OBM) director David Stockman
began planning the reduction of agriculture payments from 80 percent to
75 percent of parity in order to cut costs associated with federal purchase of
agricultural surplus. Proxmire predicted that such a move would be disas-
trous, costing the average Wisconsin dairy farmer $5,850 in income and
driving many out of business. A scheduled price increase for milk was
to go into effect on April 1, and Proxmire promised to fight the Reagan
administration's effort to cancel it. High milk prices, however, had little
support outside of dairy states, and the Senate voted 88–5 to stop the increase; Proxmire was joined in opposition only by Robert Kasten, his new
colleague from Wisconsin, and by Robert Stafford and Patrick Leahy of
Vermont and Quentin Burdick of North Dakota. The lopsided vote was
Reagan's first legislative victory of his presidency.[43]

Throughout the spring and summer of 1981, Proxmire reassured Wisconsin dairy farmers that he would do everything in his power to prevent dairy price supports from falling below 70 percent and to fight Block's plan to cancel future milk price increases. Republicans were quick to point out the irony of Proxmire encouraging a spending *increase*, but he defended his position on dairy price supports in July, noting that the parity program was vital to the economic well-being of the nation's 166,000 dairy farmers. The dairy price support program "provides stability in milk prices, helps farmers make a reasonable living and also helps keep consumer prices in line." He told farmers that he hoped to educate the president about the farm program, noting that Reagan was "a fine, intelligent man, but he is not familiar with the dairy price support and parity programs." His efforts met with little success. He was able to stall emergency legislation canceling the next scheduled price (from $13.10 to $13.49 per hundredweight) increase on procedural grounds in early October, but resorted to a filibuster in an ultimately futile attempt to block the farm bill a few days later. As with his other filibuster, he knew he had no real chance of stopping the bill, but armed with stacks of books and articles, he wanted to read into the record the arguments against it in an effort to change senators' minds now or later. After holding the floor Friday and Monday, Proxmire agreed to end his filibuster when Senate Agriculture Committee members agreed to consider raising price supports the following year. The Senate then quickly approved the price rollback on a voice vote. Despite his frequent criticism of wasteful government spending, Proxmire's filibuster did not come cheap; one estimate put the cost of Proxmire's nineteen-day delay of repealing the automatic increase near $400,000. Congress passed Reagan's overhaul of the agricultural price support system in December, the first major change since December 1949.[44]

Realizing that dairy price supports would never return to previous levels (they cost the federal government over $2 billion in 1981), Proxmire began encouraging alternatives to maintain farm income. He began circulating a report he commissioned from three University of Wisconsin graduate students on alternative dairy price programs. The report recommended a national milk board that would set quotas on production, similar to the systems in use in Canada and New Zealand. In other words, Proxmire began encouraging farmers to adopt production limits as means of maintaining stable prices. Such a change gained a following among younger dairy farmers—the Associated Milk Producers Incorporated (AMPI) supported it, as did some county chapters of the Farmers Union. In this sense, Proxmire was essentially calling for the same ends as the Reagan administration, but he wanted a more gradual, planned program rather than the steep cuts in payments proposed by Block to reduce production. The AMPI endorsed a new program that would set limits on production of milk while at the same time establishing a national marketing campaign to encourage consumption. The consequences of continuing unlimited production were dire: the federal government might scrap milk price supports altogether if they got too expensive. In 1981, the federal government purchased 10 percent of all milk produced at a cost of nearly $2.2 billion, which Proxmire had to admit was simply unsustainable. In 1983, Congress amended the 1981 law to reduce dairy price supports and give farmers who cut production a "diversion" payment to balance their losses, which reduced federal spending on dairy subsides around $1 billion in its first year. The 1985 farm bill continued diversion payments and maintained price supports.[45]

Proxmire's vigorous support for dairy farmers and his on-and-off support of Reagan in part reflected the fact that he was up for reelection in 1982. He remained widely popular in the state, and few Republicans expressed any interest in running for his seat. In March 1981, Terry Kohler, president of Sheboygan-based Vollrath Company and son of Proxmire's first senatorial opponent, Herbert Kohler Jr., distributed a fund-raising letter for another Senate run (he lost to Robert Kasten in the 1980 Republican primary). Governor Lee Dreyfus was as popular as Proxmire, but he flatly denied any interest in running for the Senate, and when he announced he would not run for reelection, Kohler immediately jumped into the gubernatorial race instead. Marlene Cummings, an advisor to Governor Dreyfus, expressed interest, but she lacked any kind of name recognition and had never run for public office before. By the winter, a more viable candidate finally emerged: thirty-one-year-old second-term state senator Scott McCallum from Fond du Lac, a moderate Republican. Proxmire's supposed shift to the right also produced a primary challenger in former state representative Marcel Dandeneau of Racine, who accused Proxmire of deserting the Democratic Party.[46]

Campaigning against the maverick Proxmire would be both a physical and an ideological challenge, as the sixty-six-year-old senator had legendary stamina and traveled to the state nearly every weekend. His 1964 opponent, Wilbur Renk, called Proxmire the "hardest Democrat in Wisconsin to beat. When he got in, he was a liberal for bigger government. Now, he's a conservative for smaller government. He's a smart operator." Stanley York agreed: "You don't deal with Proxmire on facts and issues. People know him and he's built a reputation that he's against government waste. But he shifts with the political wind." *Capital Times* political columnist John Patrick Hunter traveled with Proxmire for a two-day visit to western Wisconsin. Dressed in old, somewhat shabby clothes and making his own breakfast in budget motels, Proxmire continued to appear at factory gates to greet arriving workers at dawn before heading to shopping centers to talk to voters, most of whom had met him at least once before. As he had in 1976, he made clear that he would accept no contributions and spend no money on the campaign—it would just be him traveling around the state to meet as many voters as possible, with the minimal travel expenses paid out of his own pocket.[47]

During the summer, the three other Senate candidates—McCallum, Dandeneau, and Republican Paul Brewer—struggled to keep up with Proxmire, raise money, and articulate a clear message to distinguish themselves from the longtime senator, who actually shared many of their positions. In the primary election on September 14, Proxmire and McCallum easily bested their opponents. McCallum won the Republican nomination 182,043 to 86,728, and Proxmire won the Democratic nomination by an overwhelming margin of 467,214 to 75,258, gaining nearly 60 percent of the total primary vote.[48]

During the autumn, McCallum based his campaign on three principal themes. First, he complained that Proxmire, the Senate's greatest critic of government spending, of misusing taxpayer funds for his own political campaign. All those weekend trips to the state, reimbursed by the federal government, were nothing more than nonstop campaigning, making Proxmire's well-publicized refusal to accept campaign contributions a sham. He requested the Senate to investigate Proxmire's use of travel and office expenses. Proxmire dismissed McCallum's charges as "absolute nonsense," and the argument made little headway with voters who appreciated their senator's diligence in keeping in contact with his constituents.

Second, McCallum argued that Proxmire's constant criticism of spending meant that Wisconsin received far less than its fair share of federal dollars. Citing a League of Wisconsin Municipalities study that showed Wisconsin received 71 cents in federal spending for every dollar its residents sent to Washington, McCallum argued that Proxmire had made Wisconsin "dead last" in federal spending. Proxmire responded that the figures were inaccurate since Wisconsin was less dependent on defense industries than other states and that its population was relatively well-off, rather than in need of welfare. Proxmire instead pointed to an analysis by the OBM that estimated Wisconsin actually received $1.10 for every dollar paid in federal taxes. Finally, McCallum hoped to attract disaffected liberals, frustrated with Proxmire's more conservative views on social issues. This tactic was actually the biggest threat to Proxmire's candidacy. McCallum took a softer stance on abortion than did Proxmire, and he thought that school prayer should be voluntary and silent. He also opposed Reagan's increase in defense spending, and he and Proxmire agreed on protecting Social Security and on calling for a nuclear freeze. Proxmire's more conservative stance angered many traditional Democratic groups. Pro-choice activists and the Freedom from Religion Foundation protested his positions at the candidate forum in Madison, normally friendly territory. Some labor groups thought Proxmire had done very little to earn their support, and his criticism of federal spending actually cost them construction jobs. The state's largest union, a chapter of the American Federation of State, County, and Municipal Employees, endorsed a third-party candidate instead, despite efforts by the Wisconsin AFL-CIO to rally unions behind Proxmire. Even the *Capital Times* refused to endorse Proxmire, as it had done in 1957, 1958, 1964, 1970, and 1976, citing his position on school prayer, abortion, and school busing.[49]

On Election Day, McCallum was simply unable to overcome Proxmire's popularity, and voters reelected Proxmire by a vote of 983,311 to 527,355. The strategy of discrediting Proxmire in the eyes of liberals failed because the stakes were high: control of the US Senate, which Democrats had hoped to recapture. There were, however, signs that Proxmire's appeal may have decreased in the Fox Valley and in central Wisconsin. He failed to carry three counties (Richland, Waupaca, and Waushara), and in twenty others, his margin of victory was considerably narrower than six years before. Proxmire thus became the last Democratic candidate to win broad support throughout the entire state, rather than winning by piling up overwhelming numbers in Madison, Milwaukee, and a few other cities, which would become the normal Democratic strategy in the near future. But for now, Proxmire basked in his victory.[50]

After his reelection, Proxmire became a more active critic, not only of Pentagon spending, but also of the president's more bellicose foreign policy, generally. The turning point was Reagan's March 23 televised address on defense in which he announced plans to develop the Strategic Defense Initiative (SDI), mockingly referred to as "Star Wars." Proxmire saw Reagan's new aggressive policy as a step away from the nuclear freeze movement, which had been gaining momentum. Although he acknowledged that the basic idea was attractive, it was a dangerous policy: "If a country can guarantee against nuclear attack with [a] space based laser, for example, that means it can dictate to its enemy, it can fire first and cut off any retaliation. And secondly, the president will be forcing us into an arms race in space [that would] careen on into catastrophe at a fantastic cost." Moreover, developing such a missile defense system would make European allies less safe. As chair of the subcommittee on defense appropriations, Proxmire commissioned a survey of NATO nations government officials, who overwhelmingly opposed the deployment of SDI. American pursuit of it, Proxmire argued, could result in the collapse of the treaty organization itself. Even after Reagan gained funding for the project from Congress, research only further demonstrated how difficult a working space-based defense system would be to develop, and three years and billions of dollars later, there was virtually no progress. When Reagan's obsession with developing the program helped scuttle promising arms reduction talks in Reykjavik, Proxmire quickly pounced on the shortsightedness of giving up a promising treaty in favor of a program that could take thirty years to develop and cost $100 million to operate. Proxmire backed up his assertions by releasing a Congressional Research Service report predicting the final cost of a functional SDI system at over $1 trillion, although Pentagon officials disputed that figure. Proxmire's final attempts to cut funds for the program failed only when Vice President George Bush cast the tie-breaking vote to reject the cut and keep the program alive.[51]

One of the big issues close to home was the Navy's Project ELF, which stood for "extremely low frequency." The project would construct underground antenna grids in northern Wisconsin and the Upper Peninsula of Michigan to communicate with nuclear submarines around the world. The granite bedrock of the region made it ideal for the communications system, but Proxmire—and many others—argued that the system was already obsolete and would only serve to make northern Wisconsin a target for a possible nuclear attack. Reagan's support for the project baffled Proxmire.[52] Proxmire also opposed the development of the MX (soon renamed "Peacekeeper") ICBM to replace the Minuteman missile in service for twenty years, voting in committee in May and again on the floor of the Senate in July against funding a $625 million appropriation to build twenty-one missiles. He tried to block it again two years later, calling the construction of more MX missiles "a moral disaster." The MX, Proxmire argued, was unnecessary: "It is vulnerable to attack by an enemy's missiles and may simply spur the Soviet Union to build more retaliatory weapons. It is far more likely to provoke a nuclear war than to prevent such a tragedy."[53]

Nuclear war loomed large in Proxmire's thinking at this time. During the 1980s, he worked strenuously to keep nuclear waste out of Wisconsin, and he supported a bill that would give states an absolute veto over the long-term storage of nuclear waste within their borders. In December 1982, he prepared to filibuster a bill that would allow nuclear waste to be stored in the state, effectively blocking plans to construct a nuclear storage facility in northern Wisconsin.[54] More alarming than dealing with the waste was the threat of an actual nuclear war. Proxmire thought that the odds of a nuclear war within the next twenty years were about 50 percent unless the United States and the Soviet Union instituted a nuclear freeze, and he took to the floor nearly every morning to warn about the consequences of such a conflict. In 1984, he brought Carl Sagan to testify before the Joint Economic Committee about a potential "nuclear winter," which did much to popularize that idea. After two years of speeches, Congress passed a resolution urging the United States and the Soviet Union to jointly study the effects of a nuclear winter. The resolution had little effect, but Proxmire had succeeded in raising public awareness of what a postnuclear world might look like as a way of limiting nuclear weapons.[55]

Increasingly, Proxmire began criticizing not just military development but, as did many congressional Democrats, much of the president's foreign policy, particularly in Latin America. Opposed to US aid to the Contra rebels in Nicaragua, Proxmire also challenged Reagan's efforts to counter left-wing activity in Central America, which he called "ham-handed, arrogant, militarism . . . the one way we can provoke Central America into a communist alignment." Using the strongest language since the height of the Vietnam War, he argued that Reagan's actions were worsening conditions in Central America and generating anti-American sentiment: "For many reasons we should do everything we can—without using military power—to keep communism out of Central America. Grinding poverty and cruel exploitation, either by communist bureaucrats or right wing plutocrats, is a bane of this area. We should press for human rights and land reforms in all regimes."[56] In October, when Reagan sent troops to invade Grenada to protect American medical students at risk of being held hostage by the new Communist ruler Bernard Coard (Operation "Urgent Fury"), Proxmire joined other senators in immediately invoking the War Powers Act to limit the duration and scope of military activity on the island. The invasion, despite being badly planned and executed with limited intelligence, did ultimately succeed in achieving its objective, but only after two days of surprisingly difficult fighting.[57]

By 1984, Proxmire had returned to his old position of demanding cuts to military spending, announcing in December 1983 that he planned to recommend eliminating $45 billion from the Pentagon's budget by ending the B-1 bomber program and by halting the construction of new aircraft carriers and MX missiles. Reagan, he believed, did not have the ability to withstand pressure from defense contractors and the Defense Department bureaucracy to increase military spending; members of Congress, eager for defense spending in their districts, did nothing to check the Pentagon's budget, either. It was the old military-industrial complex at work again, and it contributed to an aggressive foreign policy that had Proxmire's constituents worried. His frequent trips around the state convinced him that Wisconsin voters were more worried about foreign policy than about the economy for the first time in a decade. Reagan's military actions in Central America, Lebanon, and Grenada disturbed many who worried that another protracted, unwinnable war was just around the corner.[58]

Of growing concern was American aid to the Contra rebels in Nicaragua. At the beginning of his second term, Reagan requested $14 million from Congress to help the Contras in their struggle against the left-wing Sandinista government, telling members that "a vote against this proposal is literally a vote against peace." Proxmire would have none of it and insisted that Nicaragua posed no threat to the United States, calling the idea that any nation in the Western Hemisphere could threaten the United States "a ridiculous joke." He did not go as far as more liberal Democrats, such as Ed Garvey, Spencer Black, or Tom Loftus, all of whom argued passionately that US aid to the Contras directly hurt tens of thousands of Nicaraguan civilians. Instead he remained focused on the basic idea that American forces should be used to defend the United States against actual, not theoretical, threats. In 1986, when Reagan requested $100 million in aid (including $70 million in military aid) to the Contras, he opposed it even more vigorously. The Contras, he pointed out, had been fighting the government for five years with significant aid from the United States and were failing, a situation very much like American support for South Vietnam. More aid was just wasting money on a hopeless cause that endangered civilians. The Senate nonetheless approved Reagan's request by a vote of 53–47.[59]

The Iran-Contra scandal broke in late 1986, and it infuriated Proxmire, who refused to believe that only a few administration figures were involved in the illegal sale of arms to Iran and the funneling of profits to the Contras:

> Obviously, the administration deceived the Congress and the country in press conferences. The attorney general's explanation that only . . . Oliver North knew the full details of this blatant violation of law and this consistent deception of the Congress, and that only John Poindexter . . . even knew the outlines of the affair, shows an appalling lack of direction and control of critical American foreign policy. In my nearly 30 years in the Senate there has been no such conspicuous and costly incompetence in the foreign policy of any administration.

Reagan may be a good communicator and attractive figurehead, Proxmire argued, but he was guilty of delegating far too much authority with no oversight to corrupt officials who had no hesitation in breaking the law and no fear of being caught. Proxmire had just reason to be angry. In 1980, Congress passed the Intelligence Oversight Act, allowing the president to withhold information from Congress in matters of national security, the same law Reagan now used to excuse his administration's arms sale to Iran. The only vote against that bill in the Senate? William Proxmire.[60]

During his last six years in the Senate, Proxmire grew increasingly worried about the growing budget deficit and the national debt, particularly the effect they had on the economy. Although the economy seemed to recover after 1983 and the nation appeared prosperous, Proxmire saw signs of looming recession. Speaking to a large gathering of Madison-area service club members in October 1983, he noted the improvement in the economy over the past six months. He warned, however, that continued economic growth was jeopardized by the $200 billion budget deficit, driven mostly by Reagan's defense spending. Without significant spending cuts, the economic recovery would not last. Even as the economy continued to improve, Proxmire insisted that the growth driven primarily by consumer spending was unsustainable. In 1986, in response to an optimistic economic forecast, he wrote that "the administration's projections that our stumbling economy will enjoy exuberant growth during the next 18 months is unrealistic. The economy continues to falter. Our children may receive a legacy of growing interest payments on the national debt. . . . How long can [consumer spending] sustain economic growth? Personal debt is at an all-time high relative to income. Business spending continues to slump. The trade deficit continues to widen." A few months later, he again drew attention to debt as a threat to economic stability, citing the $2 trillion national debt, $2.6 trillion in consumer debt, and $3 trillion in corporate debt. The US economy was living on borrowed time.[61]

Proxmire was therefore highly critical of Reagan's budgets that significantly increased the national debt. He voted against the fiscal year 1984 budget, which raised taxes by $74 billion over three years, because it increased spending by 6 percent. In 1984, he favored a Democratic $200 billion deficit reduction program that made significant cuts to military spending and increased taxes, but that plan failed to pass the Senate by a one-vote margin, and he voted against a budget that increased domestic spending by $2 billion. These were frustrating times for Proxmire. He insisted that Congress had to take "unpleasant" action to prevent long-term economic problems. "The sacrifices are not going to be easy," he told voters in Wisconsin, "but we have to take a Puritan view." He called the fiscal year 1986 budget "a disgrace" and chastised his colleagues for lacking the political courage to raise taxes ("painful but necessary") and cut spending even in a nonelection year. He was only partially mollified when Congress passed a law mandating a balanced budget by 1991 and triggering across-the-board spending cuts if it failed to do so.

Running budget deficits was simply too easy for members of Congress who lacked the will to make difficult choices, and he voted against raising the national debt limit in 1983, 1984, and 1985. The one bright spot in the long fight against deficit spending and the ballooning national debt was the tax reform bill passed in 1986, which reduced income taxes on low-income earners and enacted a minimum tax for corporate income. It was a step in the right direction, but still not enough to deal with what he saw as a looming economic crisis, made even more ominous when the federal budget exceeded $1 trillion in 1987 and $1.1 trillion in 1988.[62]

In 1986, Democrats recaptured the Senate, and Proxmire once again became chair of the Banking Committee. As he had a decade earlier, he outlined an ambitious agenda for the banking industry. He was not anti-bank but he was very concerned over how banking was becoming increasingly dominated by a few large institutions, and particularly by "nonbank banks": corporations that provided many of the same services but did not have to abide by the same banking regulations as long as they did not both accept deposits and make commercial loans. These included large retailers that issued credit cards, like Sears and J. C. Penney; industries that offered financing to customers, like General Motors and General Electric; insurance companies like Prudential and Aetna; and financial organizations like Merrill Lynch and Transamerica. The rapid growth in nonbank banks blurred the distinction among financial companies and encouraged state- and federally regulated banks to grow larger in self-defense. Such concentrated financial power was not in the best interests of consumers. His banking bills, however, got significantly watered down. The first bill simply froze the status quo for one year to give Congress a chance to study the banking industry more carefully. It banned the creation of new "non-bank banks" and limited the growth of existing ones to 7 percent per year, rather than giving banks the authority to underwrite mortgage-backed securities and create and issue mutual funds, as Proxmire proposed. He attributed the failure to the simple fact that banks wanted to compete with those larger financial institutions. Sears alone employed twenty-seven lobbyists to argue its case before members of the committee.[63]

Although Proxmire thought that a restructuring of the banking industry was long overdue, he was initially opposed to an outright repeal of the Glass-Steagall Act, which separated commercial banking from securities. In September 1987, however, he announced that he favored repeal and giving commercial banks, in addition to offering mutual funds and underwriting mortgage-backed securities, the ability to underwrite long-term corporate debt and stock issues, essentially ending the Depression-era separation. All this was predicated on the assumption that banks would silo savings from investments so that a stock market collapse, such as the one that had just occurred, would not jeopardize consumer savings that required FDIC assistance. It looked like smooth sailing since ranking minority member Jake Garn cooperated with Proxmire in working out a bipartisan agreement and since the Reagan administration and Federal Reserve chair Alan Greenspan both supported it. The Senate approved the bill by an overwhelming 94–2 vote in March 1988, but the House failed to bring the bill to the floor that fall.[64]

In response to the insider-trading scandals of the late 1980s, Proxmire also worked to impose stricter regulations on Wall Street investment firms. Specifically, he called for risk arbitrageurs—those who invest in stocks in anticipation of large profits upon corporate takeover—to be specially registered with the Securities and Exchange Commission. He also introduced a bill requiring investors to make a formal declaration to the SEC if they intended to acquire 3 percent or more of another company beforehand, rather than ten days after. Eliminating that ten-day grace period would essentially eliminate insider trading. He was unable to get this final reform through the Senate.[65]

Proxmire's most significant accomplishment in his final term had been a long time coming. In 1986, the United States ratified the United Nations Convention on the Prevention and Punishment of the Crime of Genocide, created in 1948 and promoted by Raphael Lemkin, a Polish Jew who had escaped the Nazis and made his way to the United States, and coined the term "genocide." President Harry Truman had presented the treaty to the

Senate in 1949, but despite the fact that sixty-six other nations, including the Soviet Union, had ratified the treaty by 1967, the United States still had not. Proxmire decided to take up the cause himself and announced plans to push the Senate to ratify the antigenocide convention along with three other United Nations human rights conventions, on slavery, forced labor, and political rights for women. On January 11, 1967, he stood on the floor of the Senate chamber and vowed to speak every day on the convention until the Senate approved the treaty: "The Senate's failure to act has become a national shame. . . . I serve notice today that from now on I intend to speak day after day in this body to remind the Senate of our failure to act and of the necessity for prompt action."[66]

At first it appeared to be just another Proxmire publicity stunt, but it quickly became evident that he took the matter very seriously. His daily speeches began to prick at the consciences of his fellow senators, and he thought it would be only a year or two before the Senate belatedly approved the treaty. There seemed to be progress in the 1970s, when both President Nixon and President Ford endorsed it, and the Foreign Relations Committee sent it to the full Senate in 1970, 1971, 1973, and 1974. Each time, however, it was blocked by conservative Democrats and Republicans. In 1974, a motion to end debate and proceed to a vote failed 55–38, 7 votes short of the necessary two-thirds majority. James Allen of Alabama and Sam Ervin of North Carolina organized the opposition to block the vote. In 1976, the Foreign Relations committee again recommended passage on April 29, and again the measure was defeated on the floor.[67]

With the election of Jimmy Carter, who brought a new emphasis on human rights to American foreign policy, Proxmire became more hopeful that he could convince the Senate to approve the convention, especially after Carter publicly endorsed the treaty at a UN meeting in 1977. The foreign relations committee began new hearings in May and invited Proxmire to testify. He outlined the history of the convention, characterizing it as an attempt to protect "the most fundamental human principle—the right to live," and listing its supporters. The American Bar Association had lifted its objections in 1976, and the ACLU and Department of Defense endorsed it. It was, he argued, essential for American diplomacy because the failure to ratify the convention opened up the United States to the charge of hypocrisy and weakened its ability to act on human rights violations elsewhere in the world. Again, the measure was filibustered in the Senate. A 1978 miniseries on the Holocaust generated more awareness of the treaty, and Proxmire remained hopeful that recent events in Cambodia and Uganda would remind Americans of the necessity to ratify it. After strongly lobbying his colleagues, Proxmire thought he had enough votes in 1979, but Senate leadership refused to bring the issue to the floor, fearful that it might jeopardize the SALT II treaty that was up for debate, and Carter did not want to invest his own political capital fighting for it.[68]

All told, Proxmire delivered 3,211 short addresses on the need to ratify the convention over nineteen years, each of them unique. Staff members were responsible for producing a new speech daily while the Senate was in session. Mark Shields wrote many of them in the late 1960s, and they were later given to summer interns to write before being edited and filed for later use. Because every speech was different, no one dared test Proxmire's memory by slipping in one he had already delivered. They drew on old cases of genocides, highlighted important anniversaries, and referenced current events like the genocides in Nigeria, Bangladesh, Cambodia, and Uganda. Proxmire also solicited the views of legal experts and from the secretary of state.[69]

Where did the opposition come from? In the 1950s and 1960s, it stemmed largely from southern members of Congress, who were deeply sensitive to any criticism of the nation's civil rights record. Isolationists insisted that ratifying the convention would subject US citizens or leaders to the jurisdiction of foreign courts without the usual constitutional protections, a concern shared by the American Bar Association. During the late 1960s and 1970s, US involvement in southeast Asia made human rights a touchy subject. The Liberty Lobby, an extreme conservative organization, founded in 1958 by Holocaust denier Willis Carto, argued that ratifying the convention would subvert the Constitution and make US citizens subject to foreign governments. The John Birch Society opposed the convention, too, and both of these organizations were remarkably effective in marshalling their members to contact their senators. Proxmire thus aimed his speeches at what he regarded as the real enemies of ratifying the treaty: ignorance and indifference.[70]

The treaty languished in the Foreign Relations Committee, which continued to recommend its ratification, prevented from passage by filibuster threats by Strom Thurmond and Jesse Helms. President Reagan took no position on the treaty for three years before he finally endorsed its ratification in 1984. "Hooray and hallelujah!" Proxmire responded to the announcement. "With the Reagan administration support, there is every reason to expect that we can get it through."[71] There was still opposition, however, led by Jesse Helms, who insisted that the treaty could threaten American sovereignty, despite all the evidence to the contrary. Only after the Reagan administration agreed to support a set of reservations qualifying US approval demanded by Helms did the Senate finally ratify the Genocide Convention, by a vote of 83–11 on February 19, 1986.[72]

It took another two years before the United States formally implemented the Genocide Convention, a delay necessary to bring US law into accord with the treaty by making genocide a federal crime punishable by life in prison. President Reagan signed the law on November 4, saying he was "delighted to fulfill the promise made by Harry Truman to all the peoples of the world." Proxmire did not attend the signing ceremony, since he had already made plans to visit Eau Claire and Madison that day and, in keeping with his typical habit, did not want to alter his weekend plans to visit Wisconsin. The Senate version of the act was named the Proxmire Act, a fitting tribute to his two-decade-long crusade for the treaty, and a fitting tribute to his thirty-one years in the Senate.[73]

10

RETIRED BUT STILL RELEVANT

W illiam Proxmire frequently stated his belief that being a United States Senator was the greatest job in the world. It was widely assumed that he would run for reelection in 1988, since he was only seventy-two years old, in excellent health, and still very popular. Proxmire himself believed it, telling a reporter in 1985, "I certainly have no plans to retire. I feel great. I enjoy the job and I'm still working hard." State Republicans began planning for the 1988 Senate race assuming that Proxmire would run, and candidates started lining up for the right to take on what was assumed to be a hopeless task. Throughout the summer of 1987, Proxmire refused to commit one way or the other, keeping reporters and politicians working under the assumption that he would seek another term. His bombshell retirement announcement on August 27, then, completely reshaped Wisconsin politics, as Democrats and Republicans alike immediately began jockeying with each other to claim his seat while reporters devoted columns to his legacy. Proxmire had been totally devoted to his position—no hobbies, no outside interests, no other aspirations. Now, for the first time since August 1957, he was without that job, and it proved to be a difficult adjustment.[1]

As his staff slowly departed for other jobs, his office grew more and more melancholy. Proxmire stayed at his post until his successor, Herb Kohl, was sworn in. On the last day of his term, he worked at his desk as normal, good-naturedly refusing reporters' requests to pose with his feet up, holding a glass of champagne, and keeping Vermont senator Jim Jeffords from moving into the office early. Kohl's campaign paid for a full-page ad in Wisconsin newspapers on January 3, giving Proxmire the opportunity to express his gratitude to state voters who had sent him to Washington six times:

> Thanks for the memories. Those early morning plant gates. Those hot summer days at the flower building at the State Fair. Those icy evenings shivering at University of Wisconsin hockey games and basketball games. Those glorious fall days at Lambeau Field. And when we met at Northridge and Southridge. And all those meetings in shops from Abbotsford and Adams to Wyocena and Yuba. What a marvelous State! With its lake[s], its forests, the Horicon Marsh in the spring and fall, the exquisite ice-glittering trees in Bayfield County in February.
>
> But above all—the unfailingly friendly, warm, open-minded Wisconsin people. You've made the last thirty-one years a true delight.
>
> Thank you forever.[2]

Yet he did have ambitious plans. Proxmire arranged for a small office in the James Madison building of the Library of Congress, where he planned to research financial issues (particularly the effect of private debt on the economy), write columns for newspapers or a perhaps a book, and continue awarding the Golden Fleece in cooperation with the National Taxpayers Union. His morning routine would continue to start at five thirty a.m. with thirty minutes of calisthenics, twenty minutes on a rowing machine, and twenty minutes on an exercise bike. His walk to work would be a few blocks longer as he transitioned from senator to elder statesman.[3]

For a few years, it worked. United Features Syndicate distributed his columns, allowing him to comment on current events and bestow Golden Fleece Awards on wasteful government agencies. He occasionally telephoned former staffers to ask for their thoughts on good topics for columns or to provide him details on key issues. Despite his being out of office, politics continued to interest him, though Proxmire was dismayed at the high cost of election campaigns and the influence of special-interest contributions. He admired Bill Clinton and dismissed the scandals that later led to his impeachment as "damn hypocritical." The booming economy of the 1990s buoyed his hopes that Congress could finally balance the budget, a goal he had always supported. He nursed old grudges, too. Referring to South Carolina senator Strom Thurmond, then ninety-four years old, he noted, "One of my proudest accomplishments is that I voted against him every time."[4] In 1991, Robert Kastenmeier took an office near his in the library, and the two chatted frequently and complained about the Republican-controlled Congress. Proxmire admired the efforts of Russ Feingold and John McCain to limit the influence of money in campaigns, a problem that he thought had worsened since his retirement. But Proxmire was enjoying himself. "The last few years have been my happiest," he told a reporter for the *Capital Times* in 1997. "I'm happy in the years that most people are blue and sad and waiting to die."[5]

Friends, however, noticed that he was slowing down and seemed confused at times. He could carry on a conversation but had trouble recalling names and other details. Asked to speak at an annual Taxpayers for Common Sense dinner, Proxmire appeared with one sock on inside-out and his notes jotted down inside a matchbook. Once he started speaking, however, he gave a charming and insightful talk. After another speech in Milwaukee, he seemed anxious and uncomfortable talking to members of the audience while waiting to be picked up and driven to the airport. He had to abandon his plans for a new book on debt and the economy when he could no longer write clearly, but he did publish a book on health and physical fitness, *Your Joyride to Health*, in 1992. Unlike his earlier books, which were notable for his vigorous prose and command of detail, this one was filled with stilted dialogue as a family of four lectured each other on the benefits of nutrition, exercise, and happiness. Friends who read drafts were shocked at how bad it was, and Proxmire was unable to interest any publisher and so self-published it. He tried to sell copies directly to Washington bookstores, a humbling experience for the man who had brought down the SST. Within a few years, he started forgetting his grandchildren's names. At a dinner with Matt Flynn, he began reminiscing about the 1960 Democratic National Convention, mistakenly thinking that the much-too-young Flynn had been there with him. Proxmire also stopped writing. He no longer went to his carrel in the Library of Congress. Ellen canceled his eightieth birthday party because he was unwell. When asked about his health by John Finerty, Ellen responded that he really hadn't been feeling well, and that he wasn't his old self. Finerty responded that he hoped it wasn't serious, and Ellen bluntly told him, "It's going to be, and it's permanent."[6]

In early 1998, Proxmire announced that he was suffering from Alzheimer's. "My memory is all shot," he told a reporter, apologizing for no longer being able to recall details of his career, especially frustrating since he had a famously photographic memory. He coped by keeping a supply of three-by-five index cards in his pocket to assist his short-term memory, reminding himself, for example, where and what to eat. A caretaker shadowed him as he read newspapers in the reading room to make sure he did not wander off.[7] His announcement suddenly explained a great deal about his last few years in the Senate and his decision not to seek reelection. In the late 1980s, Richard Kaufman had noticed that Proxmire was starting to slow down a bit, becoming less dynamic, especially at committee hearings. He had been more dependent on his staff to prepare questions than he had ever been in the past. He commented frequently on those senators who hung on too long and fell asleep during committee hearings. Jacob Javits suffered from ALS, used a wheelchair, and was dependent on a breathing device. John Sparkman had to be physically supported by his staff and took to wandering the halls aimlessly. Proxmire did not want to end up decrepit and having to be rolled into the Senate chamber for votes—if he could not participate fully as a senator, there simply was no reason to be one. Years later, Ellen found a pamphlet on Alzheimer's tucked away in a drawer—Proxmire had started to recognize the symptoms and feared his intellect wouldn't last another term.[8]

At first, Ellen tried to take care of her husband at home, much to the surprise of doctors who expected him to require nursing home care early on. His highly routinized life eased the symptoms of the disease, but he became agitated if his routine was disrupted or if household objects were out of place. Proxmire started doing bizarre things, like hailing a taxi and asking for a ride to Lake Forest or claiming that he was moving to Florida. His doctor prescribed Zoloft and Aricept to help him cope with his declining mental faculties, but Proxmire chafed at the restrictions and caretakers and grew combative if someone tried to guide him. Eventually, he could not be left home alone, and after he broke his arm in a fall, Ellen admitted him to the newly created Alzheimer's ward at nearby Sibley Hospital. A few days after his admission, Ellen answered the doorbell to see her husband standing there announcing that he was home after working late—he had figured out the code to unlock the door and walked home. In 2001, he was admitted to the Copper Ridge Institute in Sykesville, Maryland, a residential center for dementia patients associated with Johns Hopkins University. His old political skills resurfaced and he shook hands with fellow residents and thought he was having conversations with former colleagues.[9]

For five years, Proxmire remained at Copper Ridge as his memory slowly faded away. Eventually, he did not even recognize family at times. Everyone who visited him was struck by the irony of the situation, that a person so dedicated to healthy living and physical fitness would live to be ninety but have his personality all but obliterated by dementia. Ellen continued to support her husband in his final years and championed research and public awareness of Alzheimer's, organizing galas to raise funds for research and giving awards in his name. In 2005, he underwent surgery and radiation therapy for cancer, which hastened his decline. Proxmire died on December 15, 2005. A private funeral was held in Lake Forest, where he was buried next to his father and brother. A public memorial service was held in the Wisconsin State Capitol Rotunda, where thousands of Wisconsin citizens—many of whom had shaken his hand—paid tribute to his legislative accomplishments and his dedication to his constituents. Former governors and other elected officials praised Proxmire's integrity and dedication to public service. Another memorial was held in the National Cathedral, where former vice president Walter Mondale eulogized his former senatorial colleague and Edward Kennedy called him a "profile in courage." Over the years, Proxmire had been called a carpetbagger, a gadfly, and a lightweight. The truth, however, is that with his untiring dedication to serving his constituents and his record of consumer protection, his stewardship of federal funds, and his determined effort to prevent nuclear war and genocide, he was the quintessential senator.[10]

NOTES

Introduction

1. Dennis McCann, "Proxmire Leaves Standing Up," *Milwaukee Journal*, August 28, 1987.

2. John Patrick Hunter, "Prox Bows Out," *Capital Times*, August 27, 1987; Frank Aukofer, "Decision Was Surprise for Ellen Proxmire, Too," *Milwaukee Journal*, August 28, 1987; Mary Ellen Poulos, interview with Anita Hecht, April 1, 2009, transcript, Proxmire Oral History Project, Wisconsin Historical Society Archives, 59–60.

3. Proxmire's record as senator still stands. Two senators, Alexander Wiley (1939–1963) and Herb Kohl (1989–2013), each served twenty-four years. On the state level, six state elected officials have bested Proxmire's length of service. Shirley J. Abrahamson has served on the Wisconsin Supreme Court since 1976; Chief Justice Marvin Rosenberry served from 1916 to 1950; State Senator Fred Risser has served since 1962; representative Marlin Schneider served from 1970 to 2010; senator Alan Lasee served from 1977 until 2011; and secretary of state Douglas LaFollette has been in office continuously since 1983.

4. For the midcentury Democratic Party revival, see William F. Thompson, *The History of Wisconsin, Volume VI: Continuity and Change, 1940–1965* (Madison: State Historical Society of Wisconsin, 1988), 612–657; and Richard C. Haney, "The Rise of Wisconsin's New Democrats: A Political Realignment in the Mid-Twentieth Century," *Wisconsin Magazine of History* 58, no. 2 (Winter 1974–1975), 90–106.

5. Sunny Schubert, "Fleece Bought Him Notoriety, Anger, Chuckles," *Wisconsin State Journal*, August 28, 1987, sec. 1, 5.

6. "The 'Famous Five' Now the 'Famous Nine,'" www.senate.gov/artandhistory/history/common/briefing/Famous_Five_Seven.htm.

7. Lewis L. Gould, *The Most Exclusive Club: A History of the Modern United States Senate* (New York: Basic Books, 2005), vii–ix.

8. *Capital Times*, August 27, 1987.

9. For the feud with Johnson, see Arthur Krok, "In the Nation," *New York Times*, February 26, 1959.

10. Charles Friedrich, "Proxmire Had No Taste for Pork Barrel Ideas," *Milwaukee Journal*, August 28, 1987, 4a.

11. "One of a Kind," *Wisconsin State Journal*, August 28, 1987.

Chapter 1

1. William Proxmire to Jay Sykes, August 2, 1971, box 206, folder 18, William Proxmire Papers, Archives Division, Wisconsin Historical Society.

2. Theodore Proxmire, interview with Anita Hecht, April 2, 2010, transcript, Proxmire Oral History Project, Wisconsin Historical Society Archives, 12–13, 20–22; Jay G. Sykes, *Proxmire* (New York: Henry B. Luce, 1972), 16–17. Adele was a devout Roman Catholic and raised her two sons Catholic. For unknown reasons, Theodore, despite being ambivalent about religion, insisted their daughter be raised Lutheran. As an adult, Proxmire attended Congregational churches in Madison and Washington.

3. WP to Jay Sykes, August 2, 1971, box 206, folder 18, William Proxmire Papers; Sykes, *Proxmire*, 17–18; Edward Arpee, *Lake Forest, Illinois: History and Reminiscences, 1861–1961* (Lake Forest, IL: Rotary Club of Lake Forest, 1963), 163, 167; Martha E. Sorenson and Douglas A. Martz, *View from the Tower: A History of Fort Sheridan, Illinois* (Highland, IL: Tower Enterprises, 1985), 25–26.

4. Arpee, *Lake Forest, Illinois*, 161–62, 252; WP to Jay Sykes, August 2, 1971, box 206, folder 18, William Proxmire Papers; Sykes, *Proxmire*, 17.

5. Sykes, *Proxmire*, 15–19; WP to Jay Sykes, August 2, 1971, box 206, folder 18, William Proxmire Papers.

6. Sykes, *Proxmire*, 15; Theodore Proxmire, interview with Anita Hecht, April 2, 2010, transcript, Proxmire Oral History Project, 28–30.

7. WP to Jay Sykes, August 2, 1971, box 206, folder 18, William Proxmire Papers; Theodore Proxmire, interview with Anita Hecht, April 2, 2010, transcript, Proxmire Oral History Project, 26–27.

8. Sykes, *Proxmire*, 19. The quotation is from WP to Jay Sykes, August 2, 1971, box 206, folder 18, William Proxmire Papers.

9. Sykes, *Proxmire*, 20–21; WP to Jay Sykes, August 2, 1971, box 206, folder 18, William Proxmire Papers; *The Dial*, 1934, box 206, folder 28, William Proxmire Papers. For the history of Hill School, see Paul Chancellor,

The History of the Hill School: 1851–1976 (Pottstown, PA: The Hill School, 1976).

10. WP to Jay Sykes, August 2, 1971, box 206, folder 18, William Proxmire Papers; Sykes, *Proxmire*, 20–21, 23. Sykes erroneously names Alfred "Greasy" Neale as the head coach of the Yale Bulldogs. Neale was the backs coach; the head coach was Raymond "Ducky" Pond, and Gerald Ford, then attending Yale Law School, was an assistant coach. Theodore Proxmire interview with Anita Hecht, April 2, 2010, transcript, Proxmire Oral History Project, 12–13, 20–22; Sykes, *Proxmire*, 32; Douglas Proxmire, interview with Anita Hecht, April 5, 2010, transcript, Proxmire Oral History Project, 9; Doris R. Corbett, *Outstanding Athletes of Congress* (Washington, DC: United States Capitol Historical Society, 1997), 76.

11. Theodore Proxmire, interview with Anita Hecht, April 2, 2010, transcript, Proxmire Oral History Project, 15, 19.

12. WP to Jay Sykes, August 2, 1971, box 206, folder 18, William Proxmire Papers; Sykes, *Proxmire*, 23.

13. WP to Jay Sykes, August 2, 1971, box 206, folder 18, William Proxmire Papers; Sykes, *Proxmire*, 21–22; Douglas Proxmire, interview with Anita Hecht, April 5, 2010, transcript, Proxmire Oral History Project, 11.

14. Theodore Proxmire, interview with Anita Hecht, April 2, 2010, transcript, Proxmire Oral History Project, 12–13; Douglas Proxmire, interview with Anita Hecht, April 5, 2010, transcript, Proxmire Oral History Project, 11.

15. WP to Jay Sykes, August 2, 1971, box 206, folder 18, William Proxmire Papers; Sykes, *Proxmire*, 22–23.

16. Sykes, *Proxmire*, 25.

17. WP to Jay Sykes, August 2, 1971, box 206, folder 18, William Proxmire Papers; Sykes, *Proxmire*, 26; Corbett, *Outstanding Athletes*, 77; Counter Intelligence Corps training manual and notes, box 2, folders 1 and 2, William Proxmire Papers; Theodore Proxmire, interview with Anita Hecht, April 2, 2010, transcript, Proxmire Oral History Project, 12–13; Douglas Proxmire, interview with Anita Hecht, April 5, 2010, transcript, Proxmire Oral History Project, 37–39; Certificates of Service (duplicates issued October 30, 1957), folder 32, box 206, William Proxmire Papers.

18. Sykes, *Proxmire*, 27; duplicate military service records, box 206, folder 32, William Proxmire Papers.

19. Class notes, box 1, William Proxmire papers.

20. "The Role of the Press in American Politics," August 15, 1946, box 2, folder 3, William Proxmire Papers.

21. Sykes, *Proxmire*, 27; Theodore Proxmire, interview with Anita Hecht, April 2, 2010, transcript, Proxmire Oral History Project, 12–13; Douglas Proxmire, interview with Anita Hecht, April 5, 2010, transcript, Proxmire Oral History Project, 5–11; "Elsie Rockefeller Engaged to Marry," *New York Times*, June 15, 1946; "Elsie Rockefeller Wed in Greenwich," *New York Times*, September 15, 1946.

22. "Let There Be Light: A Dialogue on the Public Policy and Administrative Problems Implicit in Increased Government Subsidy of Higher Education," box 2, folder 7, William Proxmire Papers.

23. Sykes, *Proxmire*, 28–30; "Clearance of Cabinet Officer's [sic] Public Statements," box 2, folder 5, William Proxmire Papers. Correspondence is in ibid., folder 4.

24. Notes for GOV 6B, March 21 [1947], box 2, folder 6, William Proxmire Papers.

25. "The Corporation Income Tax and Private Investment," May 15, 1948, box 3, folder 2, William Proxmire Papers.

26. Sykes, *Proxmire*, 30–31.

27. "The Role of the Daily Newspaper in American Politics," outline and research plan, box 3, folder 1, William Proxmire Papers.

28. Sykes, *Proxmire*, 31–32; undated autobiographical sketch, box 3, folder 5, William Proxmire Papers; for John Gaus, see Paul W. Glad, *The History of Wisconsin, Volume V: War, a New Era, and Depression, 1914–1940* (Madison: Wisconsin Historical Society Press, 1990), 378, 522; John E. Miller, *Governor Philip F. La Follette, the Wisconsin Progressives, and the New Deal* (Columbia: University of Missouri Press, 1982), 14, 25.

29. Ellen Proxmire, interview with Anita Hecht, November 18, 2008, transcript, Proxmire Oral History Project, 22; Theodore Proxmire, interview with Anita Hecht, April 2, 2010, transcript, Proxmire Oral History Project, 42–43.

30. The most comprehensive coverage of La Follette and his reforms is John Buenker, *The History of Wisconsin, Volume IV: The Progressive Era* (Madison: State Historical Society of Wisconsin, 1998). On the Wisconsin Progressive Party, see Miller, *Philip La Follette*. For Phil, see Jonathan Kasparek, *Fighting Son: A Biography of Philip F. La Follette* (Madison:

Wisconsin Historical Society Press, 2006). For Robert Jr., see Patrick J. Maney, *Young Bob: A Biography of Robert M. La Follette, Jr.* (Madison: Wisconsin Historical Society Press, 2003). The standard work on Robert La Follette remains Belle Case La Follette and Fola La Follette, *Robert M. La Follette: June 14, 1855–June 18, 1925* (New York: MacMillan, 1953). See also Bernard Weisberger, *The La Follettes of Wisconsin: Love and Politics in Progressive America* (Madison: University of Wisconsin Press, 1994).

31. Richard C. Haney, "The Rise of Wisconsin's New Democrats: A Political Realignment in the Mid-Twentieth Century," *Wisconsin Magazine of History* 58, no. 2 (Winter 1974–1975), 90–99.

32. Undated autobiographical sketch; memorandum dated January 23; and notes for the *Capital Times*, all in box 3, folder 5, William Proxmire Papers; Sykes, *Proxmire*, 43–45. For Evjue, see William T. Evjue, *A Fighting Editor* (Madison, WI: Wells Printing Company, 1968).

33. Undated autobiographical sketch, box 3, folder 5, William Proxmire Papers. A daughter, Elsie (nicknamed "Cici" by her brother), was born on April 13.

34. "Labor Sounds Off" transcripts in box 3, William Proxmire Papers.

35. "Labor Sounds Off" transcript, December 8, 1949, box 3, folder 6, William Proxmire Papers; Sykes, *Proxmire*, 45–46; *Capital Times*, December 9 1949.

36. *Capital Times*, December 9, 15, 1949.

37. Ibid., November 11, 1949.

38. "Labor Sounds Off" transcript, December 1, 1949, box 3, folder 6; undated autobiographical sketch, box 3, folder 5, both in William Proxmire Papers; Sykes, *Proxmire*, 46; *Capital Times*, October 22, 1949; *Wisconsin State Journal*, October 22, 1949.

39. Ellen Proxmire, interview with Anita Hecht, November 18, 2008, transcript, Proxmire Oral History Project, 12–15.

40. Undated autobiographical sketch, box 3, folder 5, in William Proxmire Papers.

Chapter 2

1. See biographies of Representatives in the *Wisconsin Blue Book*, 1937, 1940, 1942, and 1948; Sterling Sorensen, "Proxmire, In-Law Kin of Rockefellers and Sloans, May Seek Assembly Post," *Capital Times*, February 16, 1950.

2. Population figures from the 1950 census; see 1950 *Wisconsin Blue Book*, 472.

3. Sorensen, "Proxmire, In-Law Kin."

4. William Fletcher Thompson, *The History of Wisconsin, Volume VI: Continu-ity and Change, 1940–1965* (Madison: State Historical Society of Wiscon-sin, 1988), 529–530, 569–570.

5. Ibid.

6. Ibid.; Jay G. Sykes, *Proxmire* (New York: Henry B. Luce, 1972), 47–48.

7. *Wisconsin State Journal*, May 11, 1950, sec. 2, 4; *Capital Times*, February 21, 23, 1950.

8. *Wisconsin State Journal*, April 6, June 8, 1950; *Capital Times*, June 8, 1950.

9. Campaign notebook, box 4, folder 1, William Proxmire Papers; Sykes, *Proxmire*, 48–49.

10. *Wisconsin State Journal*, September 16, 1950.

11. Ibid., August 5, 1950.

12. Ibid., September 20, 1950; *Capital Times*, September 20, 21, 1950; Sykes, *Proxmire*, 49.

13. *Capital Times*, September 23, 1950.

14. *Wisconsin State Journal*, October 31, 1950.

15. *Capital Times*, October 17, 1950.

16. Ibid., October 26, 1950.

17. Ibid., November 1, 1950; Thomas C. Reeves, *The Life and Times of Joe McCarthy: A Biography* (New York: Stein and Day, 1982), 335. On McCarthy's ethics violations (tax evasion, giving special treatment to po-litical supporters, and kickbacks from federal contractors), see Thompson, *Continuity and Change*, 579.

18. Alonzo L. Hamby, *Beyond the New Deal: Harry S. Truman and Ameri-can Liberalism* (New York: Columbia University Press, 1973), 421; David McCullough, *Truman* (New York: Simon & Schuster, 1992), 813.

19. *Wisconsin State Journal*, November 8, 1950; *Capital Times*, November 8, 1950; Thompson, *Continuity and Change*, 576; Dane County made up one Senate district, the 26th, and contained three Assembly districts. Popula-tion changes in the 1950s would soon increase the county's representation in both the Senate (two seats in 1953) and Assembly (five seats).

20. "Hello, Wisconsin!" *Capital Times*, November 9, 1950.

21. Ibid., November 22, 1950.

22. Ibid., November 21, 1950.

23. Ibid., January 10, 1951. See, for example, Stephen Leahy, *The Life of*

Milwaukee's Most Popular Politician, Clement J. Zablocki: Milwaukee Politics and Congressional Foreign Politics (Lewiston, NY: Edwin Mellen Press, 2002), 32–33.

24. *Capital Times*, January 11, 1951; Sykes, *Proxmire*, 50.

25. *Capital Times*, January 18, 1951. The other four Democrats were Charles Schmidt of Milwaukee, Robert Lynch of Green Bay, Herman Eisner of Cross Plains, and Harold Gade of Racine.

26. *Wisconsin State Journal*, February 14, 1951. The quotation is from the *Capital Times*, February 14 , 1951; ibid., May 16, 1951.

27. *Capital Times*, May 22, 1951. Communist governments in Europe stifled free enterprise by imposing production quotas and controlling prices, enforced by committees ostensibly representing "the people." Given the economic problems in these countries, business leaders in the United States were often wary of any efforts by state or federal government to regulate private businesses, even in the name of consumer protection.

28. Ibid., February 16, March 29, April 11, 25, July 12, 1951; *Wisconsin State Journal*, February 18, March 29, 1951. Patrick Lucey had introduced a similar measure in the 1949 legislature.

29. *Capital Times*, February 23, March 2, 3, 1951; *Wisconsin State Journal*, March 2, 9, 1951.

30. *Capital Times*, March 1, May 2, 9, 1951.

31. Ibid., March 1, 9, 15, May 2, 9, June 26, 1951.

32. G. T. Owen to WP, April 12, 1951, box 4, folder 2, William Proxmire Papers; see also Vincent J. Colletti to WP, March 12, 1951, ibid.

33. *Capital Times*, April 26, 1951; *Wisconsin State Journal*, April 26, 1951. Although both newspapers quoted the lobbyist, only the *Capital Times* quoted Proxmire's response.

34. *Capital Times*, May 9, 10, 24, 1951; *Wisconsin State Journal*, May 25, 1951.

35. Typewritten notes on lobbying, box 4, folder 2, William Proxmire Papers; see also "For use in Lobbying Hearing" and "Memorandum to the Committee on Judiciary," ibid.

36. *Capital Times*, April 11, 1951.

37. Ibid., May 24, 1951.

38. Ibid., June 22, 1951.

39. Ibid., February 2, 1951.

40. Ibid., April 11, May 11, 1951.

41. Miles McMillin, "Railroads and Banks Still Go Untaxed," *Capital Times*, May 12, 1951; "Million Dollar Subsidy," *Capital Times*, May 18, 1951; William Evjue, "Hello, Wisconsin: Taft's Foreign Policy Is Made to Get Votes," *Capital Times*, December 10, 1951.

42. *Capital Times*, February 1, 28, 1951; *Wisconsin State Journal*, February 2, 28, 1951.

43. *Capital Times*, May 9, June 7, 8, 1951.

44. Ibid., February 6, March 7, 1951. The life insurance provision was aimed at discouraging the rather morbid practice of taking out policies on other people and thereby benefiting financially from others' deaths, as opposed to taking out a policy on oneself.

45. Ibid., March 9, April 5, 1951; *Wisconsin State Journal*, March 10, April 5, 1951.

46. *Capital Times*, April 10, June 5, 6, 8, 14, 1951; *Wisconsin State Journal*, June 9, 1951.

47. *Capital Times*, March 15, June 9, 12, 13, 1951; *Wisconsin State Journal*, June 10, 1951.

48. "Will the Republicans Denounce This as a 'Fake' Issue, Too?" *Capital Times*, July 6, 1951; William Evjue, "Hello, Wisconsin: New Station Added; Huge Bank Profits Untaxed," ibid., July 9, 1951; "Are Mr. Harder and Mr. Matthews Working for the State or for the Bankers?" ibid., December 17, 1951.

49. See, for example, "The Political Show on Milwaukee TV," March 31, 1951; "GOP Throttles Talk on Tax Bills," May 1, 1951; and "Tax Legislation in 1951 Session Should Please Industrialists in GOP," June 19, 1951, all from the *Capital Times*.

50. "Mrs. J" to WP, March 17, 1951, box 4, folder 2, William Proxmire Papers.

51. *Capital Times*, April 18, 25, 1951; *Wisconsin State Journal*, February 3, 1951; David Obey, interview with Anita Hecht, June 8, 2011, transcript, Proxmire Oral History Project, 17. Legislators customarily received a pen and pencil set manufactured by the Parker Pen Company of Janesville. Proxmire objected to them as a needless expenditure, and if they were donated by the company, he objected to them as an unethical gift from private business.

52. *Capital Times*, March 7, 1951; *Wisconsin State Journal*, March 8, 1951.

53. *Capital Times*, March 8, 19, 1951; *Wisconsin State Journal*, March 13, 1951.

54. *Capital Times*, March 28, 1951.

55. Ibid., June 4, 1951.

56. Ibid., June 12, 1951; *Wisconsin State Journal*, June 12, 1951.

57. "Voice of the People," *Capital Times*, June 15, 1951; WP to William B. Rubin, June 19, 1951, box 4, folder 2, William Proxmire Papers. Proxmire's generalization was not far wrong; only the *Milwaukee Journal* and the *Capital Times* consistently opposed McCarthy.

58. *Capital Times*, June 21, 23, 1951; *Wisconsin State Journal*, June 23, 1951.

59. Sanford Goltz, "McCarthy Is Democrats' No. 1 National Target," *Wisconsin State Journal*, July 2, 1951; Thompson, *Continuity and Change*, 584–585.

60. *Capital Times*, June 28, 1951.

61. *Capital Times*, July 6, 10, 1951; "Kohler and McCarthyism—a Test for the Governor," *Capital Times*, July 7, 1951.

62. Ibid., July 13,14, 18, 1951; *Wisconsin State Journal*, July 15, 1951.

63. *Wisconsin State Journal*, July 20, 1951.

64. Ibid., July 28, 1951; "Little Showoffs," letter to the editor from Gertrude Blackburn, *Wisconsin State Journal*, August 11, 1951. An identical letter appeared in the *Capital Times*, August 13, 1951. Charles Werner penned a response that appeared in the *Capital Times* on August 23, 1951.

65. *Capital Times*, July 14, 17, 1951; Sykes, *Proxmire*, 16, 18; Theodore Proxmire, interview with Anita Hecht, April 2, 2010, transcript, Proxmire Oral History Project, 13, 20–21; Ellen Proxmire, interview with Anita Hecht, November 18, 2008, transcript, Proxmire Oral History Project, 20–21.

66. *Capital Times*, August 23, 1951; *Wisconsin State Journal*, August 31, September 5, 1951.

67. Miles McMillin, "The Ladies Wield Great Power in Politics," *Capital Times*, July 23, 1951; Goltz, "Fox Retirement Forces New Decisions," *Wisconsin State Journal*, September 12, 1951; Goltz, "Wisconsin Politics Young Man's Game," *Wisconsin State Journal*, October 3, 1951.

68. *Capital Times*, August 17, October 11, 1951; Goltz, "[19]52 Congressional Races Drew Little Enthusiasm," *Wisconsin State Journal*, November 19, 1951.

Chapter 3

1. *Capital Times*, March 8, 1952; *Wisconsin State Journal*; March 9, 1952; *Milwaukee Journal*, March 8, 1952; Jay Sykes, *Proxmire* (New York: Robert B. Luce, 1972), 54; Thomas C. Reeves, *Distinguished Service: The Life of*

Wisconsin Governor Walter J. Kohler, Jr. (Milwaukee: Marquette University Press, 2006), 260. The 1938 Democratic candidate was Henry Bolens, who ran third behind Republican Julius Heil (56%) and Progressive Philip La Follette (36%). Carl Thompson ran in 1950, gaining 46% of the vote.

2. "Not His Candidate, *Wisconsin State Journal*, March 17, 1952; Reeves, *Distinguished Service*, 286.

3. "Wagon Loaded, Proxmire Hitches Up," *Wisconsin State Journal*, March 18, 1952; Sykes, *Proxmire*, 54; Leonard Zubrensky, interview with Anita Hecht, December 4, 2008, transcript, Proxmire Oral History Project, Wisconsin Historical Society Archives, 21–22.

4. *Capital Times*, October 22, 1951, February 18, 1952.

5. Robert Booth Fowler, *Wisconsin Votes: An Electoral History* (Madison: University of Wisconsin Press, 2008), 171; Richard Carlton Haney, *A History of the Democratic Party of Wisconsin, 1949–1989* (Madison: Democratic Party of Wisconsin, 1989), 8; William F. Thompson, *The History of Wisconsin, Volume VI: Continuity and Change, 1940–1965* (Madison: State Historical Society of Wisconsin, 1988), 588–589; Sykes, *Proxmire*, 55; Theodore Proxmire, interview with Anita Hecht, April 2, 2010, transcript, Proxmire Oral History Project, 43; Ellen Proxmire, interview with Anita Hecht, November 18, 2008, transcript, Proxmire Oral History Project, 16; Patrick Lucey, interview with Anita Hecht, January 13, 2009, transcript, Proxmire Oral History Project, 36–37.

6. James J. Dillman to WP, March 10, 1952; Lester Johnson to WP, March 10, 1952; Leonard S. Zubrensky to WP, March 18, 1952, all in box 4, folder 1, William Proxmire Papers, Archives Division, Wisconsin Historical Society.

7. Undated letters from Thompson to WP and Elsie Proxmire, box 4, folders 4 and 7, William Proxmire papers.

8. Press release, March 21, 1952, box 4, folder 8, William Proxmire Papers; *Capital Times*, March 22, 1952; *Wisconsin State Journal*, March 22, 1952.

9. Campaign literature in box 4, folder 9, William Proxmire Papers.

10. "Fourth spot" radio advertisement, box 4, folder 9; press release for July 8, box 4, folder 8, both in the William Proxmire Papers; *Capital Times*, August 1, 8, 14, 20, October 2, 18, 28, 1952; *Wisconsin State Journal*, September 5, 28, October 29, 31, 1952. Proxmire's statements on taxes were sometimes hyperbolic. Partly to avoid being seen as a proponent of raising taxes, Proxmire emphasized the need to combat tax evasion. To maintain

an adequate revenue stream, federal and state governments would theo-
retically have to collect more money from honest taxpayers to offset those
lost to tax evaders. Such a situation deeply offended Proxmire's sense of
fairness

11. See examples in box 4, folder 4, William Proxmire Papers; Eleanor Roosevelt to Elsie Proxmire, April 14, 1952, ibid.; Sykes, *Proxmire*, 55; *Capital
Times*, May 6, 1952.

12. Press release, March 28, 1952, box 4, folder 8, William Proxmire Papers;
Capital Times, March 29, 1952.

13. *Capital Times* and *Wisconsin State Journal*, April 9, 1952.

14. Press releases, noon April 16 and 8:00 p.m. April 16, 1952, box 4, folder 8,
William Proxmire Papers; *Capital Times*, April 16, 17, 1952.

15. Press release, April 24, 1952, box 4, folder 8, William Proxmire Papers;
Capital Times, April 25, 1952; *Wisconsin State Journal*, April 25, 1952.

16. Miles McMillin, "A Tale of Two Candidates," *Capital Times*, April 26, 1952;
Sykes, *Proxmire*, 56–57; WP to "Dear Sir," May 30, 1952, box 4, folder 4,
William Proxmire Papers. See also "Itinerary," box 4, folder 8, William
Proxmire Papers.

17. Campaign literature in box 4, folder 9; press release, May 16, 1952, box 4,
folder 8, both in the William Proxmire Papers; *Capital Times*, May 17,
1952.

18. "Proxmire Replies to Marinette Paper," *Capital Times*, June 12, 1952.

19. *Capital Times*, June 27, September 25, 1952; *Wisconsin State Journal*,
August 24, September 20, 25, 1952.

20. Howard Carpenter to WP, May 24, 1952, and "Speech by Daniel W. Hoan,"
June 28, 1952, both in box 4, folder 4, William Proxmire Papers. Proxmire
did better among farmers than most Democrats and significantly better
than expected. A poll conducted by the *Wisconsin Agriculturalist* predicted
he would receive 20% of the farm vote, but its analysis of the election gave
him 29%. See *Capital Times*, December 4, 1952.

21. Press releases, October 2 and 3, 1952, and second radio advertisement,
both in box 4, folder 8, William Proxmire papers; *Wisconsin State Journal*,
September 28, 1952; *Capital Times*, October 2, 1952.

22. *Wisconsin State Journal*, May 9, 1952; *Capital Times*, July 18, October 10,
1952; Earl H. Huth to WP, May 15, 1952, box 4, folder 4; press release,
August 13, 1952, box 4, folder 8, both in the William Proxmire Papers.

23. *Capital Times*, June 25, October 29, 1952; *Wisconsin State Journal*, June 25, 1952.

24. Minority Report on the Texas Delegation, box 5, folder 1; John Hoving to WP, August 15, 1952; Hubert Humphrey to WP, August 27, 1952, box 4, folder 5, all in the William Proxmire Papers; *Capital Times*, July 23, 24, 25, 1952; *Wisconsin State Journal*, July 24, 1952; Sykes, *Proxmire*, 57–60.

25. Press release, July 16, 1952, box 4, folder 8; Estes Kefauver to WP, July 31, 1952; Adlai Stevenson to WP, August 2, 1952; both in box 4, folder 5, William Proxmire Papers; *Capital Times*, July 17, 25; October 8, 9, 1952; *Wisconsin State Journal*, July 27, 1952.

26. Press release, June 19, 1952, box 4, folder 8, William Proxmire Papers; *Capital Times*, June 20, 1952.

27. Press release, June 20, 1952, box 4, folder 8, William Proxmire Papers; *Capital Times*, June 21, 1952; *Milwaukee Journal*, June 28, July 12, 1952.

28. *Capital Times*, August 7, 12, 21; September 2, 4, 1952; *Milwaukee Journal*, August 7, 1952; press release, August 21, 1952, box 4, folder 8, William Proxmire Papers; Reeves, *Distinguished Service*, 275.

29. Reeves, *Distinguished Service*, 263–274. On Republican disunity in the 1940s and 1950s, see Thompson, *Continuity and Change*, 535–559.

30. *Capital Times*, May 5, June 26, July 1, 1952.

31. Press releases, July 15, 16, 1952, box 4, folder 8; Walter Kohler Jr. to WP, box 4, folder 7, all in the William Proxmire Papers; *Capital Times*, July 11, 15, 1952; *Wisconsin State Journal*, July 16, 1952; Reeves, *Distinguished Service*, 275.

32. *Capital Times*, August 15, 18, 19, 26, 29, 1952; *Milwaukee Journal*, August 19, 1952; *Wisconsin State Journal*, August 30, 1952; press release, August 29, 1952, box 4, folder 8, William Proxmire Papers. The scripts for the radio spots with Elsie are in box 4, folder 8, William Proxmire Papers.

33. Election results for the 1950 election are in the 1952 *Wisconsin Blue Book*, 669. Election results for the 1952 election are in the 1954 *Wisconsin Blue Book*, 654–655; *Capital Times*, September 10, 11, 1952; *Wisconsin State Journal*, September 11, 1952.

34. "Wisconsin Rapids Speech" and press release, October 2, 1952, both in box 4, folder 8, William Proxmire Papers. Police in Oshkosh disrupted a typical appearance as a violation of noise ordinances, leading to further charges of suppression. See *Capital Times*, September 18, 19, 20, 1952.

35. *Capital Times*, September 20, 1952; press releases, October 1, 4, 1952, box 4, folder 8, William Proxmire Papers.

36. *Wisconsin State Journal*, October 19, 20, 1952; *Capital Times*, October 21, 23, 1952; *Milwaukee Journal*, October 16, 28, 1952.

37. *Capital Times*, October 31, 1952; *Wisconsin State Journal*, November 1, 2, 1952.

38. *Capital Times*, October 29, 31, November 3, 1952; *Milwaukee Journal*, November 3, 1952; Sykes, *Proxmire*, 62; Reeves, *Distinguished Service*, 287.

39. 1954 *Wisconsin Blue Book*, 752, 756–757; *Wisconsin State Journal*, November 5, 1952; *Capital Times*, November 5, 1952; Leonard Zubrensky, interview with Anita Hecht, December 4, 2008, transcript, Proxmire Oral History Project, 31.

40. WP to Robert Quinn, November 10, 1952; WP to Carl Thompson, November 15, 1952; both in box 4, folder 6, William Proxmire Papers.

41. WP to Clement Zablocki, November 13, 1952; Clement Zablocki to WP, November 28, 1952; WP to Carl Thompson, November 15, 1952; Carl Thompson to WP, November 14, 1952; WP to Thomas Fairchild, November 15, 1952; WP to Adlai Stevenson, November 15, 1952; WP to Horace Wilkie, November 15, 1952; WP to Ruth Doyle, November 13, 1952; WP to Patrick Lucey, November 17, 1952; and WP to James Doyle, November 13, 1952; all in box 4, folder 6, William Proxmire Papers.

42. Stanford Goltz, "Bice May Move to Senate," *Wisconsin State Journal*, February 16, 1953.

43. *Wisconsin State Journal*, February 19, 27, 1952.

44. Sykes, *Proxmire*, 66.

45. Paul A. Walker to WP, March 4, 1953; T. J. Slowie to WP, April 8, 1953, with enclosed memorandum from WTMJ dated March 27, 1953; all in box 5, folder 2, William Proxmire Papers.

46. John H. Rhodes to WP, April 10, 1953, box 5, folder 2, William Proxmire Papers.

47. Goltz, "Proxmire Angling for Newspaper or Radio Outlet," *Wisconsin State Journal*, March 20, 1953; *Wisconsin State Journal*, April 10, December 24, 1953; Fort Broadcasting files, box 206, folder 27, William Proxmire Papers. The corporation quickly became a headache, since it did no business but still had to file state tax returns. It dissolved in 1960.

48. *Wisconsin State Journal*, April 13, 17, 20, 27, May 4, 11, 18, 25, June 1, 8, 15, 22, 1953.

49. Press release, September 2, 1953, box 5, folder 1, William Proxmire Papers; *Wisconsin State Journal*, September, 3, 1953.

50. Haney, *History of the Democratic Party of Wisconsin*, 9; Thompson, *Continuity and Change*, 596–597.

51. Press release, February 9, 1954, box 5, folder 13, William Proxmire Papers; Edward L. Schapsmeier and Frederick H. Schapsmeier, *Ezra Taft Benson and the Politics of Agriculture: The Eisenhower Years, 1953–1961* (Danville, IL: Interstate, 1975), 17, 82–93.

52. Press release, October 1, 1953, box 5, folder 2, William Proxmire Papers; Sanford Goltz, "Coming Clash Hints Shadows for Proxmire," *Wisconsin State Journal*, October 19, 1953; *Wisconsin State Journal*, October 24, 1953.

53. *Wisconsin State Journal*, March 25, April 10, 1954.

54. Reeves, *Distinguished Service*, 299–309; *Milwaukee Journal*, May 5, 7, 1954.

55. WP to Robert K. Vail, July 17, 22, 28, 30, 31, 1954; Robert Vail to WP, August 2, 1954; WP to Len Zubrensky, July 28, 1954, all in box 5, folder 10; invoices from Dayton, Johnson & Hacker, June 10, July 21, 27, 1954, all in box 5, folder 12, William Proxmire Papers. Proxmire seems to have frequently complained to Vail about the cost of producing television spots since Vail explains the prices in some detail. Proxmire also tried to steer as much printing business as possible to Artcraft Press and only reluctantly had it sent to other printers.

56. Memorandum, July 2, 1954, box 5, folder 10; Roland Day to William Evjue, July 28, 1954, box 5, folder 4, William Proxmire Papers; *Milwaukee Sentinel*, July 11, 1954.

57. Press releases, August 13, 19, 1954, box 5, folder 13, William Proxmire Papers; Thompson, *Continuity and Change*, 597–599.

58. Radio scripts enclosed with WP to Russell J. Brown, July 28, 1954, box 5, folder 12; Robert Vail to WP, August 6, 1954, box 5, folder 10; WP to Robert Vail, August 5, 1954, box 5, folder 10, all in the William Proxmire Papers.

59. WP to Peg Brandt, August 14, 1954, box 5, folder 3; WP to William Evjue, box 5, folder 4, August 16, 1954, both in the William Proxmire Papers.

60. Vote totals from the 1956 *Wisconsin Blue Book*, 675–716; Patrick Lucey,

interview with Anita Hecht, January 13, 2009, transcript, Proxmire Oral History Project, 38–40; Dick Cudahy, interview with Anita Hecht, December 30, 2008, Proxmire Oral History Project, 21.

61. Press release, September 20, 1954, box 5, folder 13; WP to Edna Bowen, September 21, 1954, box 5, folder 3; WP to John Reynolds Jr., September 21, 1954, box 5, folder 8; William Riker to WP, October 1, 1954, box 5, folder 8; Irving Cherdron to WP, October 2, 1954, box 5, folder 4; all in the William Proxmire Papers.

62. WP to Walter J. Kohler, September 23, 1954, box 5, folder 6, William Proxmire Papers; Reeves, *Distinguished Service*, 317–318; *Milwaukee Sentinel*, August 23, September 12, 1954; Sykes, *Proxmire*, 67.

63. Press release, October 2, 1954, box 5, folder 13; "Memorandum on the 1954 Gubernatorial Race," enclosed in WP to Art Bystrom, October 21, 1954, box 5, folder 11; and WP to Edward P. Morgan, October 21, 1954, box 5, folder 7, all in the William Proxmire Papers; *Milwaukee Sentinel*, October 31, 1954.

64. Sykes, *Proxmire*, 68–70; Reeves, *Distinguished Service*, 319; *Milwaukee Sentinel*, October 26, 1954; WP to Walter J. Kohler, October 22,1954, box 5, folder 6, William Proxmire Papers.

65. Election results from 1956 *Wisconsin Blue Book*, 717–754; Sykes, *Proxmire*, 72; Reeves, *Distinguished Service*, 320.

66. *Milwaukee Sentinel*, November 6, 1954; WP to Hal Roche, November 5, 1954, box 5, folder 8; WP to Harry T. Larson, November 5, 1954, box 5, folder 6; WP to "Aunt Beebee," November 10, 1954, box 5, folder 4; Carl Thompson to WP, November 10, 1954, box 5, folder 9; WP to John Hoving, November 15, 1954, box 5, folder 5; WP to Carl Thompson, November 20, 1954, box 5, folder 9, all in the William Proxmire Papers.

67. William Benton to WP, November 10, 1954, box 5, folder 3, William Proxmire Papers.

68. *Milwaukee Journal*, January 12, 1955; *Milwaukee Sentinel*, February 11, 1955; Sykes, *Proxmire*, 75–76.

69. Elsie Proxmire to WP, no date [February 1955?]; Adlai Stevenson to Elsie Proxmire, February 15, 1955 (enclosed in Carol Evans to WP, February 21, 1955); WP to Adlai Stevenson, February 23, 1955, all in box 5, folder 14, William Proxmire Papers; Theodore Proxmire, interview with Anita Hecht, April 2, 2010, transcript, Proxmire Oral History Project, 50–51;

Ellen Proxmire, interview with Anita Hecht, November 18, 2008, transcript, Proxmire Oral History Project, 23–24.

70. "Did the Farm Vote Back Benson?" *National Farmers Union's Washington Newsletter*, November 26, 1954, in box 5, folder 6; letters from Warren Magnuson, Everett Dirksen, Paul Douglas, Harris McDowell, and others in box 5, folder 14, William Proxmire Papers; Sykes, *Proxmire*, 72–73; Thompson, *Continuity and Change*, 606.

71. WP to Walter Kohler, March 3, 1955; Walter Kohler to WP, March 4, 1955, with enclosure to Freeman; WP to Orville Freeman, March 5, 1955; press release, March 4, 1955, all in box 5, folder 14, William Proxmire Papers.

72. Press release, August 8, 1955; Joseph Schantz to WP, August 31, 1955, and other letters on endorsement, all in box 5, folder 14, William Proxmire Papers; *Milwaukee Journal*, August 29, October 8, 17, 1955.

73. Press releases, May, 7 December 14, 1955, box 5, folder 14, William Proxmire Papers.

74. John W. Reynolds Jr. to WP, June 13, 1955, box 5, folder 14, William Proxmire Papers; Robert Booth Fowler, *Wisconsin Votes*, 173–174.

75. Copy of Statement of Organization, box 6, folder 2; press releases, February 10, 18, 1956, box 6, folder 6; Bill Foster to Dan Hoan, February 8, 1956, box 5, folder 16; John Reynolds to Bill Foster, February 9, 1956, box 5, folder 16; Bill Foster to Robert K. Vail, February 15, 1956, box 5, folder 16, all in the William Proxmire Papers.

76. Reeves, *Distinguished Service*, 346; Sykes, *Proxmire*, 82.

77. Press releases, February 22, 24, April 10, 13, May 21, August 5, 1956, box 6, folder 6, William Proxmire Papers.

78. Press release, March 15, 1956, box 6, folder 6; Bill Foster to Ted Kurtz, April 23, 1956, box 5, folder 16; William Foster to "Miss Edmondson," August 18, 1956, box 5, folder 16; Election Financial Statement, box 6, folder 2; Milt Schneider and William Foster to "Mr. Frye," October 17, 1956, box 6, folder 1, all in the William Proxmire Papers.

79. Press release, July 7, 1956, box 6, folder 6, William Proxmire Papers; Sykes, *Proxmire*, 78.

80. *Wisconsin State Journal*, August 3, 8, 12, 16, 1956; press releases, August 7, 11, 1956, box 6, folder 6, William Proxmire Papers; Sykes, *Proxmire*, 78–79.

81. Press releases, August 21, September 5, 6, 1956, box 6, folder 6, William Proxmire Papers; *Wisconsin State Journal*, August 29, September 6, 1956.

82. Election results from the 1958 *Wisconsin Blue Book*, 663–664; *Wisconsin State Journal*, September 12, 1956.

83. *Wisconsin State Journal*, September 20, 21, 22, 23, 25, 26, 1956; Sykes, *Proxmire*, 80–82.

84. *Wisconsin State Journal*, October 3, 5, 7, 13, 14, 26, 1956; "Tax Figures on the Loose," *Wisconsin State Journal*, October 24, 1956.

85. Election results from the 1958 *Wisconsin Blue Book*, 766; Sykes, *Proxmire*, 82–83; John S. Denigan to WP, November 17, 1956, box 6, folder 1, William Proxmire Papers; *Wisconsin State Journal*, November 7, 1956.

Chapter 4

1. Ellen Proxmire, *One Foot in Washington: The Perilous Life of a Senator's Wife* (Washington, DC: Robert B. Luce, 1963), 2–3; Jay Sykes, *Proxmire* (New York: Robert B. Luce, 1972), 79–80, 85–86; *Milwaukee Sentinel*, August 4, 1957; John Reynolds to WP, November 14, 1956, box 6, folder 1, William Proxmire Papers, Archives Division, Wisconsin Historical Society; Ellen Proxmire, interview with Anita Hecht, November 18; 2008, Proxmire Oral History Project, Wisconsin Historical Society Archives, 7–19.

2. Ellen Proxmire, *One Foot in Washington*, 3; Sykes, *Proxmire*, 86; *Wisconsin State Journal*, November 10, 1956; Ellen Proxmire, interview with Anita Hecht, November 18, 2008, transcript, Proxmire Oral History Project, 17–25; Mary Ellen Poulos, interview with Anita Hecht, April 1, 2009, transcript, Proxmire Oral History Project, 14–17.

3. *Milwaukee Journal*, November 29, 1956; *Wisconsin State Journal*, November 30, 1956; Leon Jones to WP, December 1, 1956; John Moses to WP, December 3, 1956; incorporation papers for "Wisconsin Committee to Beat the Income Tax," all in box 6, folder 1, William Proxmire Papers.

4. *Milwaukee Journal*, March 28, 1957; *Milwaukee Sentinel*, May 8, 1957; William F. Thompson, *The History of Wisconsin, Volume VI: Continuity and Change, 1940–1965* (Madison: State Historical Society of Wisconsin, 1988), 671–672.

5. Press releases, March 18, 27, 1957, box 7 folder 2, William Proxmire Papers; *Milwaukee Sentinel*, March 25, 1957; Sykes, *Proxmire*, 86.

6. Ellen Proxmire, *One Foot in Washington*, 3; Sykes, *Proxmire*, 87; Patrick Lucey, interview with Anita Hecht, January 13, 2009, transcript, Proxmire Oral History Project, 43–44.

7. *Milwaukee Journal*, May 3, 6, 7, 8, 10, 13, 1957.

8. Press release, May 13, 1957, box 7, folder 2, William Proxmire Papers; Sykes, *Proxmire*, 87–88; Thompson, *Continuity and Change*, 606–607; Stephen M. Leahy, *The Life of Milwaukee's Most Popular Politician, Clement J. Zablocki: Milwaukee Politics and Congressional Foreign Policy* (Lewiston, NY: Edwin Mellen Press, 2002), 56; *Milwaukee Journal*, May 8, 10, 14, 1957.

9. *Milwaukee Journal*, May 13, 14, 20, June 4, 5, 1957; Thomas C. Reeves, *Distinguished Service: The Life of Wisconsin Governor Walter J. Kohler, Jr.* (Milwaukee: Marquette University Press, 2006), 379; Leahy, *Clement J. Zablocki*, 57.

10. Sykes, *Proxmire*, 89; *Milwaukee Journal*, June 7, 1957.

11. Press release, June 7, 1957, box 7, folder 2, William Proxmire Papers.

12. Press releases, May 25, June 11, 1957, box 7, folder 2, William Proxmire Papers; *Milwaukee Journal*, June 4, 9, 12, 1957; Leahy, *Clement J. Zablocki*, 56–67; Thompson, *Continuity and Change*, 606–607.

13. *Milwaukee Journal*, June 9, 1957.

14. Press release, June 19, 20, 28, July 9, 1957, box 7, folder 2, William Proxmire Papers; *Milwaukee Journal*, June 14, 17, July 10, 11, 12, 25, 1957.

15. Press release, June 13, July 11, 1957, box 7, folder 2, William Proxmire Papers; *Milwaukee Journal*, June 14, 22, July 29, 1957; Reeves, *Distinguished Service*, 385.

16. Leahy, *Clement J. Zablocki*, 58–59; Reeves, *Distinguished Service*, 382–384.

17. *Milwaukee Journal*, July 28, 1957. State law limited what a candidate could spend in a primary election, but other organizations could spend more freely.

18. Voting results from the 1958 *Wisconsin Blue Book*, 666–667; Reeves, *Distinguished Service*, 387–388; Sykes, *Proxmire*, 89; *Wisconsin State Journal*, August 1, 1957. Kohler carried Barron, Calumet, Chippewa, Dunn, Eau Claire, Fond du Lac, Jackson, Kenosha, Milwaukee, Ozaukee, Pepin, Racine, Sheboygan, Trempealeau, Walworth, Washington, and Winnebago. Of these, Chippewa, Eau Claire, Jackson, Kenosha, Milwaukee, Racine, and Trempealeau went Democratic in 1956.

19. Joe Boyd, "Campaign Cooks at Proxmire Farm," *Milwaukee Sentinel*, August 4, 1957; Ellen Proxmire, *One Foot in Washington*, 5; Sykes, *Proxmire*, 90; *Milwaukee Journal*, August 8, 1957; list of campaign contributors

and expenses, and Election Financial Statement, both in box 206, folder 34, William Proxmire Papers; Patrick Lucey, interview with Anita Hecht, January 13, 2009, transcript, Proxmire Oral History Project, 46.

20. Press release, August 16, 1957, box 7, folder 2, William Proxmire Papers; *Milwaukee Journal*, August 21 and 23, 1957.

21. Press release, August 6, 1957; *Milwaukee Journal*, August 7, 1957; Sykes, Proxmire, 90; Theodore Proxmire, interview with Anita Hecht, April 2, 2010, Proxmire Oral History Project, 45. Proxmire was a bigger "loser" than either Lincoln or La Follette. Lincoln lost one election to the Illinois Assembly in 1832 and failed in his bid to be US Senator in 1858, when voters elected a Democratic legislature that chose Stephen Douglas. Technically, La Follette lost only two elections, his bid for a fourth term in Congress in 1890 and his long-shot race for the presidency in 1924, although he did fail to capture the gubernatorial nomination in the Republican convention in 1896 and 1898.

22. Reeves, *Distinguished Service*, 389–390.

23. Ellen Proxmire, *One Foot in Washington*, 6.

24. Press releases, August 8, 12, 16, 17, 18, 19, 20, 1957; *Milwaukee Journal*, August 10, 12, 15, 17, 19, 1957; Edward L. Schapsmeier and Frederick H. Schapsmeier, *Ezra Taft Benson and the Politics of Agriculture: The Eisenhower Years, 1953–1961* (Danville, IL: Interstate Printers and Publishers, 1975), 192–193.

25. *Milwaukee Journal*, August 22, 1957.

26. Ellen Proxmire, *One Foot in Washington*, 6–7; election results from the 1958 *Wisconsin Blue Book*, 773.

27. Leon Epstein, *Politics in Wisconsin* (Madison: University of Wisconsin Press, 1958), 74; "Dairy Farmers' Revolt against Benson Spearheads Proxmire Election in Wisconsin," *National Farmers Union's Washington Newsletter* 4, no. 35 (August 30, 1957); "Why Republicans Lost Wisconsin," *US News & World Report* (September 6, 1957), 23–29.

28. *Milwaukee Journal*, August 28, 1957; Thompson, *Continuity and Change*, 610; "Why Republicans Lost Wisconsin," 25–26.

29. *Milwaukee Journal*, August 28, 29, 1957; Thompson, *Continuity and Change*, 611; Reeves, *Distinguished Service*, 395–398; "Why Republicans Lost Wisconsin," 24.

30. Sykes, *Proxmire*, 91–93; Ellen Proxmire, *One Foot in Washington*, 8–9;

Theodore Proxmire, interview with Anita Hecht, April 2, 2010, Proxmire Oral History Project, 45; John Pomfret, "Winner Thanks Plants' Workers," *Milwaukee Journal*, August 28, 1957.

31. Robert A. Caro, *The Years of Lyndon Johnson: Master of the Senate* (New York: Alfred A. Knopf, 2002), 955, 1000; Sykes, *Proxmire*, 92. Ellen Proxmire disputes the birthday reference in the conversation between Johnson and Proxmire; they did not know it was his birthday until later. On the tenth anniversary of Proxmire's election, President Johnson sent him a telegram referring to him as his "best birthday present ever." See Ellen Proxmire, interview with Anita Hecht, November 18, 2008, transcript, Proxmire Oral History Project, 29–30.

32. Caro, *Master of the Senate*, 1001; Ellen Proxmire, *One Foot in Washington*, 10–15; Sykes, *Proxmire*, 93–94; *Milwaukee Journal*, August 29, 1957; *New York Times*, August 30; 1957; Ellen Proxmire, interview with Anita Hecht, November 18, 2008, transcript, Proxmire Oral History Project, 29–30.

33. *Milwaukee Journal*, August 30, 31, September 3, 1957; Caro, *Master of the Senate*, 1001; Ellen Proxmire, *One Foot in Washington*, 12–15; Sykes, *Proxmire*, 94.

34. *Milwaukee Journal*, September 3, 13, 21, 1957; *New York Times*, September 26, 1957.

35. *New York Times*, October 12, 1957.

36. *New York Times*, December 19, 1957, March 9, 13, 1958, April 22, 1958; Schapsmeier and Schapsmeier, *Ezra Taft Benson*, 193–194.

37. *Milwaukee Journal*, September 27, 1957; Sykes, *Proxmire*, 95.

38. *Milwaukee Sentinel*, October 14, 1957; *New York Times*, October 13, 1957; Haney, *History of the Democratic Party*, 11; Patrick Lucey, interview with Anita Hecht, January 13, 2009, transcript, Proxmire Oral History Project, 46; Ellen Proxmire, interview with Anita Hecht, November 18, 2008, transcript, Proxmire Oral History Project, 32.

39. "Free Ride for Senator Proxmire," *Wisconsin State Journal*, September 4, 1957; *Milwaukee Journal*, November 14, 25, 1957; Sykes, *Proxmire*, 96–97; *New York Times*, December 2, 1957. In fact, Proxmire's father loaned him money for his trip. Proxmire was not unique in his paying his own way. See "180 Congressmen Traveled in 1957," *New York Times*, January 2, 1958. Letters from WP to EP, dated "Saturday Nov. 16," "Monday night," and "Tuesday Night," box 206, folder 20, William Proxmire Papers.

40. Ellen Proxmire, *One Foot in Washington*, 16–17; *Milwaukee Journal*, December 11, 1957.

41. Ellen Proxmire, *One Foot in Washington*, 16–17; Sykes, *Proxmire*, 101.

42. *Milwaukee Journal*, January 8, 1958; *Milwaukee Sentinel*, July 3, 1958; *New York Times*, July 5, 1958; Ellen Proxmire, *One Foot in Washington*, 17; Sykes, *Proxmire*, 101–102; Ellen Proxmire, interview with Anita Hecht, November 18, 2008, transcript, Proxmire Oral History Project, 33–35.

43. Sykes, *Proxmire*, 97–98; *New York Times*, January 29, February 28, 1958; Ralph K. Huitt, "The Outsider in the Senate," *The American Political Science Review* 55, No. 3 (September 1961), pp. 8–12, box 206, folder 17, William Proxmire Papers.

44. *New York Times*, May 27, June 3, 6, 1958; Sykes, *Proxmire*, 98–99; Huitt, "Outsider in the Senate," 12; Congress, Senate, 85th Cong., 2nd Sess., *Congressional Record* (June 5, 1958), vol. 104, pt. 8, 10266–10269.

45. *New York Times*, July 10, 1958.

46. *New York Times*, June 4, August 12, 1958; *Milwaukee Sentinel*, June 19, 1958; Sykes, *Proxmire*, 101; Huitt, "Outsider in the Senate," 13.

47. Congress, Senate, "Total Proxmire Program Saves $9½ Billion; Reduces Deficit $700 million," 85th Cong., 2nd Sess., *Congressional Record* 104, pt. 13 (August 7, 1958), 16508–16513.

48. Sykes, *Proxmire*, 99–100; Huitt, "Outsider in the Senate," 13; *New York Times*, August 24, 25, 1958; Congress, Senate, 85th Cong., 2nd Sess., *Congressional Record* 104, pt. 15 (August 23, 1958), 19554–19555.

49. *New York Times*, May 25, September 11, 1958; *Milwaukee Sentinel*, August 12, September 19, 1958; Sykes, *Proxmire*, 102–103; primary election results from the 1960 *Wisconsin Blue Book*, 653. For Steinle, see *Portraits of Justice: The Wisconsin Supreme Court's First 150 Years*, 2nd ed., edited by Trina E. Gray, Karen Leone de Nie, Jennifer Miller, and Amanda K. Todd (Madison: Wisconsin Historical Society Press, 2003), 61.

50. *Milwaukee Sentinel*, March 11, August 22, 1958; *Milwaukee Journal*, March 11, 1958; Sykes, *Proxmire*, 103; Ellen Proxmire, *One Foot in Washington*, 18–20; see also campaign finance statements and correspondence, box 206, folder 33, William Proxmire Papers.

51. *Milwaukee Sentinel*, May 8, June 18, 1958; *Milwaukee Journal*, October 29, 1958; Sykes, *Proxmire*, 100, 103–104.

52. *Milwaukee Sentinel*, September 19, October 14, 15, 24, 1958.

53. *Milwaukee Journal*, October 15, 1958; *Milwaukee Sentinel*, October 16, 1958; Sykes, *Proxmire*, 104–105.

Chapter 5

1. Ellen Proxmire, *One Foot in Washington: The Perilous Life of a Senator's Wife* (Washington, DC: Robert B. Luce, 1963), 23–24 ; Ellen Proxmire, interview with Anita Hecht, November 18, 2008, Proxmire Oral History Project, 36.

2. WP to Ezra Taft Benson, January 14, 1959; Benson to WP, February 5, 1959; WP to Benson, February 4, 1959; press release, February 4, 1959, all in box 16, folder 1, William Proxmire Papers, Archives Division, Wisconsin Historical Society; *New York Times*, February 7, 1959.

3. "Statement by Secretary of Agriculture Ezra Taft Benson before the House Committee on Agriculture," February 10, 1959; "Remarks of E. T. Benson at Sen. Ag. Committee Hearing," February 16, 1959; WP to Ezra Taft Benson, March 12, 1959; Marvin L. McLain to WP, April 2, 1959; press release, April 13, 1959, all in box 16, folder 1, William Proxmire Papers.

4. Marvin L. McLain to WP, April 2, 1959; press release, April 13, 1959, both in box 16, folder 1, William Proxmire Papers.

5. Lewis L. Gould, *The Most Exclusive Club: A History of the Modern United States Senate* (New York: Basic Books, 2005), 213–216, 220–222, 228; Robert A. Caro, *The Years of Lyndon Johnson: Master of the Senate* (New York: Alfred A. Knopf, 2002), 557–596.

6. Jay G. Sykes, *Proxmire* (New York: Robert B. Luce, 1972), 110.

7. *New York Times*, February 3, 1959; Caro, *Master of the Senate*, 1015–1016; Sykes, *Proxmire*, 112.

8. Sykes, *Proxmire*, 112; *Milwaukee Journal*, February 16, 1959; *Chicago Tribune*, February 21, 1959.

9. Congress, Senate, 86th Cong., 1st sess., *Congressional Record* 105, pt. 2 (February 23, 1959), 2814.

10. Ibid., 2814–2816.

11. Ibid., 2817–2820; *New York Times*, February, 24, March 1, 1959; *Milwaukee Journal*, February 23, 1959; Sykes, *Proxmire*, 113–116 (the quotation is on p. 113); Proxmire, *One Foot in Washington*, 24–25; Caro, *Master of the Senate*, 1016–1017.

12. *New York Times*, February 25, 26, 1959; Sykes, *Proxmire*, 117.

13. Arthur Krok, "In the Nation," *New York Times*, February 26, 1959; "A Look at the World's Week," *Life*, March 9, 1959. Krok commented further on Proxmire's violation of Senate decorum and the subsequent lack of support in the *New York Times*, March 1, 1959; Ellen Proxmire, interview with Anita Hecht, November 18, 2008, Proxmire Oral History Project, 38.

14. *New York Times*, March 2, 4, 1959.

15. Congress, Senate, 86th Cong., 1st sess., *Congressional Record* 105, pt. 3 (March 9, 1959), 3559–3566, 3582; *New York Times*, March 10, 1959; Sykes, *Proxmire*, 118–119. The best example of southern Democrats' resistance to racial integration is the 1955 "Southern Manifesto" that condemned the US Supreme Court order to integrate public schools. Ninety-nine out of 102 southern Democrats in Congress signed it. See Taylor Branch, *Parting the Waters: America in the King Years, 1954–63* (New York: Simon and Schuster, 1988), 183.

16. Proxmire, *One Foot in Washington*, 25–26; Sykes, *Proxmire*, 117–118; Leslie Bechtel to WP, February 23, 1959, box 9, folder 31; B. Smith to WP, postmarked March 4, 1959, box 9, folder 20, both in the William Proxmire Papers; correspondence about the Johnson controversy fill 14 folders in box 9. The majority of them support Proxmire's position.

17. Sykes, *Proxmire*, 119; *New York Times*, March 13, April 20, 1959; *Washington Star*, April 21, 1959.

18. *New York Times*, March 20, April 4, 9, 1959; see also Russell Baker, "Critics of Johnson Keep up the Barrage," *New York Times*, April 12, 1959; *New York Times*, April 6, 1959.

19. Congress, Senate, 86th Cong., 1st sess., *Congressional Record* 105, pt. 7 (May 28, 1959), 9256–9260; *New York Times*, May 29, 30, June 1, 1959; Sykes, *Proxmire*, 119–120; Caro, *Master of the Senate*, 1016–1018. The Russell quotation is from Caro, 1018.

20. *New York Times*, October 18, November 3, 1959.

21. Arthur Krok, "The 'Bloody Shirt' and Its Modern Substitute," *New York Times*, November 3, 1959; *New York Times*, November 10, 1959.

22. *New York Times*, December 8, 1959.

23. *New York Times*, January 8, 10, 13, February 7, 1960; *Wisconsin State Journal*, January 8, 13, 1960; *Capital Times*, January 8, 12, February 2, 1960.

24. WP to *Milwaukee Journal*, March 17, 1959; Elizabeth G. Weller to WP,

March 17, 1959; WP to Robert Brenkworth, March 16, 1959; Robert Brenk-worth to WP, March 17, 1959; form-letter responses dated April to May, all in box 10, folder 39, William Proxmire Papers; Ellen Proxmire, interview with Anita Hecht, November 18, 2008, Proxmire Oral History Project, 42–43.

25. Ellen Proxmire, *One Foot in Washington*, 25.

26. Ibid., 25–28.

27. Ibid., 38.

28. Ibid., 38–39.

29. *New York Times*, May 22, June 16, 26, 1959; *Wisconsin State Journal*, June 26, 1960.

30. Congress, Senate, 86th Cong., 1st sess., *Congressional Record* 105, pt. 14 (September 1, 1959), 17498–17539; *New York Times*, August 8, September 1, 2, 3, 1959.

31. *New York Times*, June 17, August 15, 1959; Ellen Proxmire, *One Foot in Washington*, 35, 112–113.

32. Ellen Proxmire, *One Foot in Washington*, 40–41; Ellen Proxmire, interview with Anita Hecht, November 18, 2008, Proxmire Oral History Project, 49–50.

33. *New York Times*, June 14, 1959; Bill Christofferson, *The Man from Clear Lake: Earth Day Founder Senator Gaylord Nelson* (Madison: University of Wisconsin Press, 2004), 123–125; William F. Thompson, *The History of Wisconsin, Volume VI: Continuity and Change, 1940–1965* (Madison: Wisconsin Historical Society, 1988), 683.

34. *New York Times*, April 10, 1959. Humphrey formally announced his candidacy on July 14—the first Democrat to do so. See *Wisconsin State Journal*, July 15, 1959.

35. *New York Times*, June 14, July 19, 21, August 6, 15, November 15, 16, 1959; *Wisconsin State Journal*, 26 June 1959; Christofferson, *Man from Clear Lake*, 124; "The Image of Senator William Proxmire," report by Louis Harris and Associates, box 204, folder 28, William Proxmire Papers.

36. *Wisconsin State Journal*, January 3, 19, 22, 1960; *Capital Times*, January 7, 14, 1960.

37. *Wisconsin State Journal*, January 29, February 14, 1960; *Capital Times*, January 29, 1960.

38. *New York Times*, March 23, 24, 27, 1960; *Capital Times*, March 21, 22, 29, 1960; Mary Ellen Poulos, interview with Anita Hecht, April 1, 2009, Proxmire Oral History Project, 29.

39. William Proxmire, "Appeal for the Vanishing Primary," *New York Times Magazine*, March 27, 1960; *Capital Times*, March 28, 29, 1960; *Wisconsin State Journal*, March 29, 1960.

40. *New York Times*, April 7, 1960; *Capital Times*, April 6, 1960; Thompson, *Continuity and Change*, 687–692. Kennedy won six congressional districts, delivering fifteen votes, and his statewide victory earned him another five. The state national committeeman and national committeewoman cast one vote between them, but they supported different candidates, giving each a half vote.

41. *New York Times*, December 17, 1959; WP to John E. Baker, December 30, 1959, box 207, folder 10; WP to George Maurer, March 9, 1961, box 207, folder 10; WP to George Maurer, January 22, 29, 1960, box 207, folder 11, all in the William Proxmire Papers; Ellen Proxmire, personal communication with the author, April 26, 2012; Mary Ellen Poulos, interview with Anita Hecht, April 1, 2009, Proxmire Oral History Project, 17–19; Theodore Proxmire, interview with Anita Hecht, April 2, 2010, Proxmire Oral History Project, 57–59.

42. *Capital Times*, January 6, 11, 12, 22, 25, 1960; *Wisconsin State Journal*, January 7, 12, 16, 24, 26, 1960; Congress, Senate, Committee on the Judiciary, *Nomination of James R. Durfee: Hearings before a Subcommittee of the Committee on the Judiciary*, 86th Cong., 2nd Sess., January 25, 26, 1960, 26. The subcommittee consisted of James Eastland of Mississippi, Olin Johnston of South Carolina, and Alexander Wiley of Wisconsin.

43. *New York Times*, January 26, 27, March 8, April 21, 1960; *Wisconsin State Journal*, January 26, 27, April 21, 1960; *Capital Times*, January 26, February 29, March 8, April 20, 21, 1960; *Nomination of James R. Durfee*, 41–43.

44. *New York Times*, March 19, 1960; *Capital Times*, March 18, 1960.

45. *New York Times*, June 14, 16, 18, 1960; *Capital Times*, June 13, 14, 16, 1960; *Wisconsin State Journal*, June 14, 18, 1960.

46. *New York Times*, June 21, 1960; *Capital Times*, June 20, 1960; *Wisconsin State Journal*, June 21, 1960.

47. *New York Times*, June 21, 26, 1960; *Capital Times*, June 24, August 10, 1960; *Wisconsin State Journal*, June 11, August 25, 1960.

48. *New York Times*, January 21, February 3, March 10, 1960; *Capital Times*, March 1, 1960.

49. *Capital Times*, May 12, 20, 27, September 17, 1960; *Wisconsin State Journal*, May 27, June 16, 1960.

50. WP to "Aunt Bebe," June 16, 1960, box 206, folder 32, William Proxmire Papers; *Capital Times*, June 24, 25, July 11, 13, 1960; *Wisconsin State Journal*, July 12, 1960.

51. *Capital Times*, July 15, 1960; *Wisconsin State Journal*, July 16, 1960. For liberal skepticism of Johnson, see Arthur M. Schlesinger Jr., *A Thousand Days: John F. Kennedy in the White House* (Boston: Houghton Mifflin, 1965), 50–59.

52. *Capital Times*, September 19, 20, 26, October 10, 17, 22, 24, 25, 1960; *New York Times*, November 6, 1960.

53. Vote totals from the 1962 *Wisconsin Blue Book*, 860.

54. Congress, Senate, 87th Cong., 1st sess., *Congressional Record* 107, pt. 1 (January 23, 1961), 1125–1137; Sykes, *Proxmire*, 121–122; *New York Times*, January 22, 24, 1961; *Wisconsin State Journal*, January 22, 1961; *Capital Times*, January 26, 1961. Drew Pearson reported Robert Kennedy's actions on behalf of Connally in his "Washington Merry-Go-Round" column—see *Capital Times*, February 2, 1960.

55. Sykes, *Proxmire*, 121–122; *Capital Times*, March 29, 31, April 27, 1961; *New York Times*, April 1, 27, 1961.

56. Congress, Senate, 87th Cong., 1st sess., *Congressional Record* 107, pt. 11 (August 8–10, 1961), 14863–14915, 15100–15207, 15237–15239; Sykes, *Proxmire*, 122–123; *New York Times*, July 27, August 1, 7, 9, 10, 1961; *Capital Times*, July 26, August 7, 8, 9, 1961; *Wisconsin State Journal*, August 8, 9, 10, 1961.

57. Sykes, *Proxmire*, 123; *New York Times*, September 9, 1961; *Capital Times*, September 9, 1961.

58. *Capital Times*, March 16, 17, May 26, 1961; Richard Reston, "Wisconsin and JFK's Program," *Capital Times*, October 2, 1961; Schlesinger, *A Thousand Days*, 620–629; Irving Bernstein, *Promises Kept: John F. Kennedy's New Frontier* (New York: Oxford University Press, 1991), 118–128.

59. *Capital Times*, January 10, 1961; *New York Times*, April 11, May 3, 1961.

60. *Capital Times*, May 30, 1961; *New York Times*, May 21, June 4, 1961.

61. *Capital Times*, July 24, 1961.

62. *New York Times*, July 30, August 2, 3, 4, 1961; *Capital Times*, August 2, 4, 1961; *Wisconsin State Journal*, August 2, 4, 1961.

63. In April 1962, Proxmire attempted to remove $15 million from an appropriations bill to fund a US exhibit at the New York World's Fair, but the Senate rejected his amendment 60–13 (*New York Times*, April 17, 1962; *Capital Times*, April 17, 1962).

64. *Capital Times*, October 7, 31, November 2, 1961; *Wisconsin State Journal*, October 9, 30, November 4, 1961; *New York Times*, October 13, 29, 1961. The $22 million extension to the east front of the Capitol particularly irritated him. Much of the space would be used for new private offices for congressional officials, or "hideaways," as he called them. Large new office suites were not only unnecessary—his own spartan life was already well-known—they were downright undemocratic since they further insulated elected officials from their constituents.

65. *Capital Times*, January 1, April 9, 30, 1962; *Wisconsin State Journal*, April 8, June 14, 24, 1962; *New York Times*, June 14, 24, 1962.

66. *Capital Times*, July 27, 1962; *New York Times*, August 4, September 1, 1962.

67. *New York Times*, May 29, 1962; *Capital Times*, May 29, 1962.

68. *New York Times*, June 9, July 2, August 9, 22, 26, 1962; *Capital Times*, September 7, 1962.

69. *Capital Times*, January 31, February 6, March 10, 27, 1962; *Wisconsin State Journal*, February 6, March 31, April 1, 1962; *New York Times*, March 28, 29, April 1 1962.

70. *Capital Times*, February 6, 20, 1962; *Wisconsin State Journal*, February 6, 20, May 1, 1962. The quotation is from Sykes, *Proxmire*, 124.

71. *Capital Times*, May 10, 26, 1962; *Wisconsin State Journal*, May 12, 1962; *New York Times*, May 26, 1962.

72. *New York Times*, June 7, 9, 1962; Sykes, *Proxmire*, 125–126; *Wisconsin State Journal*, June 7, 8, 1962.

73. *New York Times*, July 2, 1962; *Capital Times*, July 5, 1962.

74. *Capital Times*, August 7, 1962; Willard Edward, "Record Shows Proxmire to the Right of Wiley," *Capital Times*, September 18, 1962; Sykes, *Proxmire*, 131–132.

75. Ralph K. Huitt to WP, May 10, 1959, January 11, 1961; WP to Ralph K. Huitt, May 13, 1959, January 26, 1961; all in box 206, folder 17, William

Proxmire Papers; Ivan Kaye, "What Makes Bill Proxmire Tick?" *Capital Times*, August 4, 1962.

76. *Milwaukee Sentinel*, November 21, 1961; *New York Times*, November 29, 1961; *Wisconsin State Journal*, November 30, 1961; memorandum to Senator Proxmire from "PR," November 24, 1961, and attachments, box 204, folder 16, William Proxmire Papers.

77. *New York Times*, December 1, 7, 1961; *Capital Times*, November 29, 30, December 1, 6, 1961, January 29, 1962; *Wisconsin State Journal*, November 30, December 1 and 6, 1961, January 30, 1962; undated statement [November 27 or 28, 1961]; WP to Elvis Stahr, December 2, 1961 (copied in press release dated December 5, 1961); press release dated January 29, 1962; all in box 204, folder 16, William Proxmire Papers.

78. *Wisconsin State Journal*, January 11, February 14, 27, August 22, 1963; *Capital Times*, February 25, August 22, 1963; *New York Times*, August 23, 1963; Ivan Kaye, "The Senate Establishment," *Capital Times*, March 4, 1963; Ivan Kaye, "Appropriations Unit Post Turning Point for Proxmire?" *Capital Times*, August 27, 1963.

79. *New York Times*, January 31, February 21, March 13, 1963; *Capital Times*, February 22, 26, 28, 1963; *Wisconsin State Journal*, March 3, 18, 1963.

80. *Capital Times*, June 22, December 10, 1963; *Wisconsin State Journal*, June 22, 1963.

81. *Capital Times*, August 26, 27, 1963; *New York Times*, August 8, 15, 26, 27, November 21, 29 1963.

82. Bill Christofferson, *The Man from Clear Lake: Earth Day Founder Senator Gaylord Nelson* (Madison: University of Wisconsin Press, 2004), 167–168, 193–196; Ellen Proxmire, interview with Anita Hecht, November 18, 2008, Proxmire Oral History Project, Wisconsin Historical Society Archives, 46–47; Ellen Proxmire, interview with Anita Hecht, October 21, 2010, Proxmire Oral History Project, Wisconsin Historical Society Archives, 42–44; *Capital Times*, April 4, May 30, 1963.

83. *Capital Times*, February 10, 1964.

84. *Capital Times*, May 1, 6, 1963; *Wisconsin State Journal*, May 2, 1963.

85. *Wisconsin State Journal*, March 25, 26, 30, April 2, 4, 5, 7, 1963; *Capital Times*, March 25, 1963; Sykes, *Proxmire*, 147–149. A full professor at the university made on average less than $13,000, and the state treasurer and secretary of state each made $12,000 a year.

86. Sykes, *Proxmire*, 150–153; *Wisconsin State Journal*, April 24, 25, June 13, 1963; *Capital Times*, June 12, 1963; *New York Times*, April 24, 1963.

87. Ellen Proxmire, *One Foot in Washington*, 41.

88. Bob Vail to WP, July 16, 1963; press release, December 27, 1963, and notes planning "Operation Town Hall," all in box 207, folder 4, William Proxmire Papers; *New York Times*, October 6, 1963; *Wisconsin State Journal*, May 4, June 2, September 8, October 13, December 7, 27, 1963; *Capital Times*, June 6, July 29, September 16, October 9, 1963.

89. *Capital Times*, January 14, 18, 1964; press release, January 14, 1964, box 194, folder 5; "Proxmire Summary," no date [January 1964], box 194, folder 13, both in the William Proxmire Papers.

90. Art Buchwald, "Proxmire's Advice on Master Art of Handshaking," *Capital Times*, February 15, 1964; Aldric Revell, "Why Proxmire Is So Hard to Beat," *Capital Times*, October 26, 1964; "A Survey of the Political Climate in Wisconsin," July 1964, box 194, folder 19, William Proxmire Papers; William Proxmire, *Can Small Business Survive?* (Chicago: Henry Regnery, 1964). August Derleth, the influential Wisconsin author and critic, gave it a glowing review in the *Capital Times*, June 18, 1964.

91. *Capital Times*, August 13, 28, 1963, March 14, 27, 1964. Election results from the 1966 *Wisconsin Blue Book*, 726.

92. *Capital Times*, June 25, July 7, 30, August 6, 28, September 3, 9, 1964; campaign correspondence in box 207, folder 3; "Strictly Confidential Memorandum on Proxmire Campaign," box 194, folder 13, both in the William Proxmire papers. Election results from the 1966 *Wisconsin Blue Book*, p. 733.

93. WP to Robert Vail, August 22, 1963.

94. Press release, August 14, 1964, box 194, folder 13; Roland B. Day to Daniel H. Neviaser, September 25, October 1, October 6, 1964; press release, October 10, 1964, all in box 207, folder 2; "Strictly Confidential Memorandum," box 194, folder 13; and Day to WP, August 24, 1964, box 194, folder 5, all in the William Proxmire Papers.

95. "Our Congressmen—Who Is Best? Who Is Worst?" *Pageant*, November 1964, 6–14; Gerald A. Bartell to WP, October 20, 1964, WP to Gerald A. Bartell, October 23, 1964, all in box 194, folder 14, William Proxmire Papers; Sykes, *Proxmire*, 159–161; *Capital Times*, October 15, 28, 1964;

Ellen Proxmire, interview with Anita Hecht, November 18, 2008, Prox-mire Oral History Project, Wisconsin Historical Society Archives, 59–61.

96. Press release, October 29, 1964, box 194, folder 13; *Capital Times*, October 28, 29, 30, 31, 1964.

97. *Capital Times*, November 4, 1964; Sykes, *Proxmire*, 162–163. Election re-sults are from the 1966 *Wisconsin Blue Book*, 751.

Chapter 6

1. Jay G. Sykes, *Proxmire* (New York: Robert B. Luce, 1972), 162–163; *Wis-consin State Journal*, February 14, November 29, 1965; Ellen Proxmire, interview with Anita Hecht, November 18, 2008, Proxmire Oral History Project, Wisconsin Historical Society Archives, 60; Richard Cudahy, in-terview with Anita Hecht, December 30, 2008, Proxmire Oral History Project, Wisconsin Historical Society Archives, 28; Mark Shields, inter-view with Anita Hecht, October 21, 2009, Proxmire Oral History Project, Wisconsin Historical Society Archives, 19.

2. *Wisconsin State Journal*, October 17, November 29, 1965.

3. *New York Times*, February 8, July 24, 1964; Allen J. Matusow, *The Unrav-eling of America: A History of Liberalism in the 1960s* (New York: Harper & Row, 1984), 56–59; Robert A. Caro, *The Years of Lyndon Johnson: The Pas-sage of Power* (New York: Alfred A. Knopf, 2012), 552–557.

4. *U.S. Senator William Proxmire Reports to You from Washington* (hereinafter *Proxmire Reports*), June and July 1964.

5. *Proxmire Reports*, January 1965; *Capital Times*, April 10, July 10, November 15, 1965; *Wisconsin State Journal*, April 10, 1965.

6. *Capital Times*, February 2, 4, November 15, 1965; press release, February 3, 1965, folder 32, box 130, William Proxmire Papers, Archives Division, Wisconsin Historical Society.

7. *New York Times*, March 12, 1965; *Capital Times*, May 11, 26, 1965; *Wiscon-sin State Journal*, May 26, 27, 1965.

8. Sykes, *Proxmire*, 169–171; Edward L. Schapsmeier and Frederick H. Schapsmeier, *Dirksen of Illinois: Senatorial Statesman* (Chicago: University of Illinois Press, 1985), 177–178; Byron C. Hulsey, *Everett Dirksen and His Presidents: How a Senate Giant Shaped American Politics* (Lawrence: Univer-sity of Kansas Press, 2000), 202–203; Thomas van der Voort, interview

with Anita Hecht, March 19, 2009, Proxmire Oral History Project, Wisconsin Historical Society Archives, 35–40.

9. *Wisconsin State Journal*, March 5, 1965; *New York Times*, May 23, 1965; *Capital Times*, May 24, 1965; Schapsmeier and Schapsmeier, *Dirksen of Illinois*, 177–178; Hulsey, *Everett Dirksen*, 202–203; Sykes, *Proxmire*, 172. Bayh chaired the subcommittee on constitutional amendments and thereby authored two amendments: the 25th, which established rules for presidential disability and the appointment of a vice president, and the 26th, which gave eighteen-year-olds the right to vote.

10. *Capital Times*, July 26, 1965; *Wisconsin State Journal*, July 27, 1965.

11. *Capital Times*, August 17, 1965; *New York Times*, October 26, 1965; Schapsmeier and Schapsmeier, *Dirksen of Illinois*, 178–180; *Proxmire Reports*, November 1965; Sykes, *Proxmire*, 172–173.

12. *New York Times*, January 22, 1966; *Capital Times*, January 31, March 8, April 19, 1966; Schapsmeier and Schapsmeier, *Dirksen of Illinois*, 180.

13. *New York Times*, April 14, 21, 1966; *Wisconsin State Journal*, April 14, 1966.

14. *Wisconsin State Journal*, April 21, 1966.

15. *New York Times*, March 22, 23, 26, 1967; *Capital Times*, March 23, 1967.

16. *New York Times*, October 31, 1967; Sykes, *Proxmire*, 173–174.

17. *New York Times*, January 7, February 11, 1965.

18. *New York Times*, July 7, September 21, 26, 1966, January 5, 11, July 22, August 5, 1967; *Capital Times*, November 3, 1967.

19. *New York Times*, September 14, 1965; *Capital Times*, September 14, 27, 1965; *Wisconsin State Journal*, September 15, 1965; *Proxmire Reports*, October 1965; Thomas van der Voort, interview with Anita Hecht, March 19, 2009, Proxmire Oral History Project, Wisconsin Historical Society Archives, 57.

20. *Capital Times*, January 24, 1966.

21. *Capital Times*, March 5, 7, 13, April 8, July 9, 1966; *New York Times*, June 8, 1966; *Proxmire Reports*, February and November 1966. Proxmire's proposal funded the milk program at $110 million for fiscal year 1967, $113 million for fiscal year 1968, and $120 million for fiscal year 1969.

22. *Capital Times*, January 18, 1967; *Wisconsin State Journal*, January 18, 1967.

23. *Wisconsin State Journal*, April 26, 1966; *New York Times*, November 25, 1966; *Proxmire Reports*, June 1966.

24. *Capital Times*, January 25, March 24, May 16, June 30, 1967, July 24, Sep-

tember 25, 1968; *Wisconsin State Journal*, July 2, 1967; *New York Times*, May 17, 1967.

25. Martin Lobel, interview with Anita Hecht, November 19, 2008, Proxmire Oral History Project, Wisconsin Historical Society Archives, 59–60; Alan Kooi, interview with Anita Hecht, June 2, 2009, Proxmire Oral History Project, Wisconsin Historical Society Archives, 34–35; Ron Tammen, interview with Anita Hecht, June 5, 2009, Proxmire Oral History Project, Wisconsin Historical Society Archives, 57.

26. William Proxmire to Lyndon Johnson, December 27, 1963, box 131, folder 10, William Proxmire Papers.

27. William Proxmire to Ralph K. Huitt, March 15, 1965; William Proxmire to August E. Moulton, April 6, 1965; William Proxmire to Melvin W. Powell, May 20, 1965; Ralph K. Huitt to William Proxmire, July 9, 1965, all in box 131, folder 10, William Proxmire Papers; *Capital Times*, March 22, December 16, 1966; *Wisconsin State Journal*, March 23, December 17, 1966. Kastenmeier related the White House story to Wisconsin congressman Dave Obey; see David Ross Obey, interview with Anita Hecht, June 8, 2011, Proxmire Oral History Project, Wisconsin Historical Society Archives, 16.

28. *Wisconsin State Journal*, May 22, August 2, 11, 1967; *Capital Times*, August 1, 7, 14, October 4, 1967.

29. *New York Times*, March 21, 1965; David Rabinovitz to William Proxmire, September 11, 1964; William Proxmire to David Rabinovitz, September 14, 1964; William Proxmire to Harvey Kitzman, no date [c. October 1964]; George McDormit Schlotthauer to William Proxmire, November 13, 1964, all in box 130, folder 33, William Proxmire Papers.

30. William Proxmire to Jack Valenti, December 21, 1964; William Proxmire to Lyndon Johnson, December 21, 1964; Gaylord Nelson to Nicholas Katzenbach, March 15, 1965, all in box 130, folder 33, William Proxmire Papers; Alfred Maund, "Why the Delay in Naming U.S. Judge?" *Capital Times*, February 1, 1965; Alfred Maund, "Is Prox Blackballing Doyle?" *Capital Times*, March 29, April 30, 1965; *Wisconsin State Journal*, October 14, 1965; *New York Times*, March 21, 1965.

31. *Capital Times*, February 18, 24, 25, 1965; *Wisconsin State Journal*, February 18, 25, 1965; *New York Times*, February 19, 1965; press release, February 24, 1965, box 131, folder 16, William Proxmire Papers.

32. Press releases, July 10, 1965 [incorrectly dated 1964] and August 31, 1965;

memo, "Re: Baseball to All Senators," July 19, 1965; William Proxmire to Arthur C. Allyn Jr., July 28, 1965; "Statement by Senator William Prox-mire on the Floor of the Senate in Support of Proxmire Amendment to Hart Antitrust Sports Bill," August 31, 1965, all in box 131, folder 16, Wil-liam Proxmire Papers; *Proxmire Reports*, August 1965; *Wisconsin State Jour-nal*, September 1, 1965; *Capital Times*, September 1, 1965.

33. *New York Times*, January 7, 10, 1965; Robert Mann, *A Grand Delusion: America's Descent into Vietnam* (New York: Basic Books, 2001), 399.

34. *Wisconsin State Journal*, February 11, 27, 1965; *Capital Times*, March 1, May 10, 1965; *New York Times*, March 2, 1965; *Proxmire Reports*, March 1965.

35. Alfred Maund, "Window on Washington," *Capital Times*, May 3, 1965. Three days later the newspaper published a letter from a reader urging Proxmire to enlist. A week later, the same writer demanded to know why Proxmire was so afraid of communism but was willing to support dicta-torships in Spain and Saudi Arabia. See Alfred Maund, "Window on Wash-ington," *Capital Times*, May 6, 15, 1965; Mann, *Grand Delusion*, 392–408; Lloyd C. Gardner, *Pay Any Price: Lyndon Johnson and the Wars for Vietnam* (Chicago: Ivan R. Dee, 1995), 151–176.

36. *Capital Times*, February 27, May 7, 1965; Bill Christofferson, *The Man from Clear Lake: Earth Day Founder Senator Gaylord Nelson* (Madison: University of Wisconsin Press, 2004), 289–291; Mann, *Grand Delusion*, 433–437.

37. *Proxmire Reports*, September 1965; Alfred Maund, "Window on Washing-ton," *Capital Times*, September 20, 1965; Christofferson, *Man from Clear Lake*, 287–289.

38. *Wisconsin State Journal*, September 12, 1965; Mann, *Grand Delusion*, 413.

39. *Wisconsin State Journal*, October 19, 1965; Alfred Maund, "Window on Washington," *Capital Times*, October 25, 1965; Paul S. Boyer, *Promises to Keep: The United States Since World War II* (Lexington, MA: DC Heath, 1995), 321.

40. *Capital Times*, January 13, 1966; *Wisconsin State Journal*, January 17, 18, 22, 1966; Christofferson, *Man from Clear Lake*, 292.

41. *Wisconsin State Journal*, January 28, 1966; *Capital Times*, January 28, 31, 1966; John Wyngaard, "State Democrats Split on Viet Nam Policy," *Wis-*

consin State Journal, February 1, 1966; Alfred Maund, "Surprise from Prox-mire," *Capital Times*, February 7, 1966; Mann, *Grand Delusion*, 482–483.

42. *Proxmire Reports*, February 1966; *Capital Times*, February 8, 11, 14, 1966; *Wisconsin State Journal*, February 25, March 21, 1965; Gardner, *Pay Any Price*, 194–195.

43. *Wisconsin State Journal*, March 24, 1966; *Capital Times*, March 29, 30, 1966.

44. "Proxmire Reports," April 1966; Mann, *Grand Delusion*, 503–505. Gaylord Nelson and Proxmire voted in unison on these issues; see Christofferson, *Man from Clear Lake*, 292–293.

45. *Wisconsin State Journal*, May 23, August 17, 1966; Alfred Maund, "Cool to McNamara Idea," *Capital Times*, May 30, 1966; *Capital Times*, June 30, 1966; *New York Times*, July 16 ,1966.

46. Alfred Maund, "Proxmire Switches Stand," *Capital Times*, January 9, 1967; *Capital Times*, January 12, 1967.

47. Alfred Maund, "Prox Plans Investigation," *Capital Times*, January 16, 1967; Alfred Maund, "Proxmire's War Views," *Capital Times*, January 23, 1967; *Capital Times*, March 30, 1967; Mann, *Grand Delusion*, 478–479, 511–513.

48. *Capital Times*, February 22, 1967; see, for example, William Proxmire to Werner J. Severin, March 8, 1967, William Proxmire Papers.

49. Martin Lobel, interview with Anita Hecht, November 19, 2008, Proxmire Oral History Project, Wisconsin Historical Society Archives, 39; Thomas van der Voort, interview with Anita Hecht, March 19, 2009, Proxmire Oral History Project, 32–33; John Finerty, interview with Anita Hecht, April 23, 2009, Proxmire Oral History Project, 31–32, 36.

50. *Wisconsin State Journal*, June 27, August 19, 1968; *Capital Times*, June 27; 1968; Erwin Knoll, "Report from Washington," *Capital Times*, 1968; Ken McLean, interview with Anita Hecht, September 11, 2009, Proxmire Oral History Project, Wisconsin Historical Society Archives, 46–47; John Fin-erty, interview with Anita Hecht, April 23, 2009, Proxmire Oral History Project, Wisconsin Historical Society Archives, 32.

51. *New York Times*, March 12, 1965.

52. *Proxmire Reports*, August and September 1965.

53. *Wisconsin State Journal*, January 25, 1966; *Capital Times*, August 10, 1966; *New York Times*, August 10, 11, 1966.

54. Sykes, *Proxmire*, 163–164; *Capital Times*, June 18, 1966; *Wisconsin State Journal*, June 19, 1966; *New York Times*, June 19, 1966; Alfred Maund, "Bad Ideas Turn to Marble," *Capital Times*, July 11, 1966; *Proxmire Reports*, July 1966.

55. *Capital Times*, July 21, 1967; *Wisconsin State Journal*, July 22, 1967; *New York Times*, July 22, 1967; *Proxmire Reports*, August 1967; Sykes, *Proxmire*, 174–175; Hulsey, *Dirksen and His Presidents*, 238–239; Mark Shields, interview with Anita Hecht, October 21, 2009, Proxmire Oral History Project, Wisconsin Historical Society Archives, 21–22. Technically, the board was tasked with identifying organizations that had to register as subversive, but several Supreme Court rulings, beginning in 1956, made it impossible for the Justice Department to prosecute any organization that failed to register.

56. *Wisconsin State Journal*, August 16, September 1, 1967; *New York Times*, August 16, 30, 1967; Sykes, *Proxmire*, 175–176; Mark Shields, interview with Anita Hecht, October 21, 2009, Proxmire Oral History Project, Wisconsin Historical Society Archives, 21–22.

57. *New York Times*, October 12, 18, 21, 1967; *Capital Times*, October 17, 18, 21, 1967; *Wisconsin State Journal*, October 18, 24, 1967; Sykes, *Proxmire*, 176; Schapsmeier and Schapsmeier, *Dirksen of Illinois*, 240, 247, 260–261.

58. *Wisconsin State Journal*, July 2, 1968; *New York Times*, July 7, 1968; *Capital Times*, July 8, 10, 1968.

59. *Capital Times*, September 17, 1968; Erwin Knoll, "Proxmire Hits 'Wasteful' Board," *Capital Times*, September 30, 1968; Sykes, *Proxmire*, 176–177; John W. Finney, "Senate Bars Aid to Anti-Red Unit," *New York Times*, June 16, 1972; Sam J. Ervin and William Proxmire, "An 'Alien' Creature," *New York Times*, June 23, 1972; *Proxmire Reports*, July 1972.

60. *Capital Times*, January 8, February 3, 1967; *New York Times*, February 4, 1967; *Wisconsin State Journal*, February 5, 1967; *Proxmire Reports*, February 1967.

61. *New York Times*, September 14, October 7, 1967; *Wisconsin State Journal*, October 7, 1967. The other two senators opposing the public works bill were Republicans Strom Thurmond of South Carolina and John J. Williams of Delaware.

62. *Capital Times*, May 9, 1967; William Proxmire, "Senator Proxmire Tells of Waste in the Defense Department," *Capital Times*, July 31, 1967.

63. *New York Times*, January 6, 1968; *Capital Times*, January 5, 6, March 7, 1968; *Wisconsin State Journal*, January 6, 1968.

64. *New York Times*, April 29, May 6, 1968; *Wisconsin State Journal*, May 6, June 27, 1968.

65. *Capital Times*, June 26, 1968.

66. *Capital Times*, August 7, 1968; Erwin Knoll, "Report from Washington," *Capital Times*, August 12, November 12, 13, 1968; *New York Times*, November 12, 1968.

67. *New York Times*, November 14, 1968; *Capital Times*, November 14, 1968; Sykes, *Proxmire*, 201–202; Richard Kaufman, interview with Anita Hecht, July 7, 2009, Proxmire Oral History Project, Wisconsin Historical Society Archives, 37–43.

68. *Capital Times*, November 26, 1968; *Wisconsin State Journal*, December 16, 1968; *New York Times*, December 1, 16, 1968; Sykes, *Proxmire*, 202–203.

69. *Capital Times*, January 2, 1969.

70. *Capital Times*, January 10, 17, November 17, 1969; *New York Times*, November 13, 18, 1969; *Wisconsin State Journal*, November 18, 1969.

71. *New York Times*, January 17, May 3, 6, July 30, September 10, November 15, 1969; *Capital Times*, May 1, 6, July 30, 1969.

72. Walter Mondale, interview with Anita Hecht, May 13 2009, Proxmire Oral History Project, Wisconsin Historical Society Archives, 19.

73. *Capital Times*, December 1, 1966, January 13, 1967; *Proxmire Reports*, December 1966; *New York Times*, January 12, 1967.

74. *Wisconsin State Journal*, January 31, March 5, July 12, 1967; *Capital Times*, February 17, 1967; *New York Times*, July 12, 1967, May 30, 1968; Marjorie Hunter, "Dear Friends: Truth-in-Lending Gains," *New York Times*, April 23, 1967; *Proxmire Reports*, July 1967 and June 1968; Ken McLean, interview with Anita Hecht, September 11, 2009, Proxmire Oral History Project, Wisconsin Historical Society Archives, 32–35.

75. Elizabeth M. Fowler, "'Truth in Lending' Bill May Simplify Interest Rates That Puzzle Borrower," *New York Times*, December 18, 1967; *Wisconsin State Journal*, July 12, 1967; *Proxmire Reports*, May 1967.

76. Allen J. Matusow, *The Unraveling of America: A History of Liberalism in the 1960s* (New York: Harper & Row, 1984), 155–162; Anthony S. Campagna, *The Economic Consequences of the Vietnam War* (New York: Praeger, 1991), 21, 32–35, 52–56; Robert J. Samuelson, *The Great Inflation and Its*

Aftermath: The Past and Future of American Affluence (New York: Random House, 2008), 61–67, 93–96.

77. *Capital Times*, March 14, 27, 1966; Thomas E. Mullaney, "Investor Confidence Grows Brighter, But the Reasons Are Not Discernible," *New York Times*, March 27, 1966; *Wall Street Journal*, June 9, 1966; *New York Times*, June 12, 1966; Maustow, *Unraveling of America*, 158; Campagna, *Economic Consequences*, 21–22; Samuelson, *Great Inflation*, 94–96.

78. Maustow, *Unraveling of America*, 166–169; G. Calvin Mackenzie and Robert Weisbrot, *The Liberal Hour: Washington and the Politics of Change in the 1960s* (New York: Penguin, 2008), 318–319; Campagna, *Economic Consequences*, 39–40.

79. *Wisconsin State Journal*, August 25, 1966; *Proxmire Reports*, August and September 1966.

80. Alfred Maund, "An About Face Ires Senators," *Capital Times*, September 19, 1966; *Capital Times*, October 6, 1966; *Proxmire Reports*, October 1966.

81. *Capital Times*, November 26, 1966; *New York Times*, December 7, 1966; *Proxmire Reports*, January 1967.

82. *New York Times*, February 6, 7, 10, 16, 1967. Proxmire's agreement with Burns, a Republican appointed by Eisenhower, underscored his opposition to the administration's major economic proposal and brought him into an unlikely alliance with congressional Republicans. In the House, the views of Melvin Laird of Wisconsin's seventh congressional district most closely matched those of the Democratic senator. Both were critical of the administration's underestimation of war costs and failure to enforce wage/price guidelines, and both favored spending cuts on public works and the space program for the duration of the war. See *Wisconsin State Journal*, February 12, 1967.

83. *New York Times*, March 17, 1967; *Proxmire Reports*, May, July, and August 1967; Campagna, *Economic Consequences*, 40–42.

84. John H. Allan, "But Private Sector Shows 'High-Level Sluggishness,'" *New York Times*, June 25, 1967; Alfred Maund, "Proxmire's Economy Hearing," *Capital Times*, June 26, 1967.

85. *New York Times*, June 28, 1967.

86. *Capital Times*, July 5, 1967; *New York Times*, July 6, 1967; *Wisconsin State Journal*, July 6, 1967.

87. *Wisconsin State Journal*, July 18, 31, 1967; *New York Times*, July 23, 1967.

88. *Capital Times*, August 4, 12, 1967; *Proxmire Reports*, August 1967.

89. *Capital Times*, August 28, 1967; *Wisconsin State Journal*, August 29, September 4, 1967; *Proxmire Reports*, September 1967.

90. *New York Times*, November 18, 25, 1967; *Wisconsin State Journal*, November 18, 19, 26, 1967; *Capital Times*, November 25, 1967 (quotation).

91. *Capital Times*, December 30, 1967, February 13, 1968; *Proxmire Reports*, January 1968; *New York Times*, February 6, 18, 1968; *Wisconsin State Journal*, February 14, 1968.

92. *Capital Times*, March 18, November 21, 1968; *New York Times*, March 19, 27, November 19, 1968; *Wisconsin State Journal*, April 3, June 22, 1968; *Proxmire Reports*, April 1968; William Proxmire, "Tax Hike Will Only Aggravate Poverty," *Capital Times*, July 17, 1968; Campagna, *Economic Consequences*, 40–42.

Chapter 7

1. "Green Bay: The Littlest Big-League City," *New York Times*, January 2, 1966. The incident was also mentioned in an editorial appearing in the *Wisconsin State Journal*, January 6, 1966.

2. Ellen Proxmire, *One Foot in Washington: The Perilous Life of a Senator's Wife* (Washington, DC: Robert B. Luce, 1963), 170.

3. Ellen Proxmire, "The Fantastic Cost of Campaigns," *Capital Times*, January 30, 1967 (reprint from *The Progressive*, February 1967, 20–22). See also John Wyngard, "Ellen Tells 'Agony,'" *Wisconsin State Journal*, February 8, 1967.

4. Ellen Proxmire interview with Anita Hecht, November 18, 2008, transcript, Proxmire Oral History Project, 41, 49.

5. Mary Ellen Poulos interview with Anita Hecht, April 1, 2009, transcript, Proxmire Oral History Project, 28–29.

6. Theodore Proxmire interview with Anita Hecht, April 2, 2010, transcript, Proxmire Oral History Project, 47–48, 51–52 (quotation), 55–56. On Cici, see Douglas Proxmire interview with Anita Hecht, April 5, 2010, Proxmire Oral History Project, 37–38. On custody of the children, see Walter M. Bjork to John Sinai, May 26, 1959, folder 9, box 207, William Proxmire Papers.

7. Jay G. Sykes, *Proxmire* (New York: Robert B. Luce, 1972), 155–56; *New York Times*, September 8, 1965; *Capital Times*, September 8, 9, 10, 1965;

Wisconsin State Journal, September 9, 1965; William Proxmire to Henry H. Fowler, September 7, 1965; press release, September 8, 1965, both in folder 23, box 206, William Proxmire Papers.

8. Sykes, *Proxmire*, 154–55; *Wisconsin State Journal*, February 1, 1965. Proxmire reported that he still owned 11 shares of Milwaukee Braves stock and 10 shares of American Motors Corporation stock, all held in trust for Theodore.

9. Mary Ellen Poulos interview with Anita Hecht, April 1, 2009, transcript, 24–25, 32–33, 65–66; Jan Cathy Sawall Licht interview with Anita Hecht, November 11, 2010, transcript, 27–28, 47–48; Douglas Proxmire interview with Anita Hecht, April 5, 2010, transcript, 61–62, all in Proxmire Oral History Project.

10. Mary Ellen Poulos interview with Anita Hecht, April 1, 2009, transcript, Proxmire Oral History Project, 26–27; Jan Cathy Sawall Licht interview with Anita Hecht, November 11, 2010, transcript, Proxmire Oral History Project, 29–31.

11. William Proxmire to Ralph C. Johnson, March 3, 1961; William Proxmire to Ted Proxmire, March 3, 1961; William Proxmire to Edward Hall, March 3, 1961; Edward C. Welles to William Proxmire, April 3, 1961; William Proxmire to Edward C. Welles, April 10, 1961; William Proxmire to Elsie McMillin, June 24, 1961; William Proxmire to Ralph Johnson, July 11, 1961, all in folder 22, box 206, William Proxmire Papers.

12. Theodore Proxmire interview with Anita Hecht, April 2, 2010, transcript, Proxmire Oral History Project, 59–61; Gordon Reid to William Proxmire, June 30, 1965; Cici to William Proxmire, June 5, 1965, both in folder 23, box 206, William Proxmire Papers.

13. Mary Ellen Poulos interview with Anita Hecht, April 1, 2009, transcript, Proxmire Oral History Project, 46–48.

14. Douglas Proxmire interview with Anita Hecht, April 5, 2010, transcript, Proxmire Oral History Project, 29–30.

15. Ibid., 36–38, 45–46.

16. Sykes, *Proxmire*, 143–144; *Capital Times*, July 27, August 11, 1967; *Wisconsin State Journal*, July 28, 1967, January 19, 1969.

17. William Proxmire, *You Can Do It! Senator Proxmire's Exercise, Diet and Relaxation Plan* (New York: Simon and Schuster, 1973), 71, 88–89, 102,

113; Sykes, *Proxmire*, 143–145; Ellen Proxmire interview with Anita Hecht, November 18, 2008, transcript, Proxmire Oral History Project, Wisconsin Historical Society Archives, 55; Doris R. Corbett, *Outstanding Athletes of Congress* (Washington, DC: United States Capitol Historical Society, 1977), 80; Hal Higdon, "Jogging Is an In Sport," *New York Times*, April 14, 1968.

18. Proxmire, *You Can Do It!*, 60–73; Bill Christofferson, *The Man from Clear Lake: Earth Day Founder Senator Gaylord Nelson* (Madison: University of Wisconsin Press, 2004), 171; *Capital Times*, December 16, 1968; John Herbers, "What Makes Proxmire Run?" *New York Times*, April 4, 1971.

19. Sykes, *Proxmire*, 143–145; Proxmire, *You Can Do It!*, 90; Jan Cathy Sawall Licht interview with Anita Hecht, November 11, 2010, transcript, Proxmire Oral History Project, Wisconsin Historical Society Archives, 33; Myra MacPherson, "Train (Pant, Pant) Don't Strain (Pant, Pant)," *New York Times*, February 13, 1968; "Proxmire, Ranking Fitness Buff, Jogs Right through Red Light," *Wisconsin State Journal*, June 2, 1969; "Proxmire Won't Hold Up Traffic with A.M. Jogs," *Capital Times*, June 2, 1969.

20. Erwin Knoll, "'Go Ahead, Shoot,' Proxmire Tells Robbers, 'I'm Dying,'" *Capital Times*, May 5, 1972; *Wisconsin State Journal*, May 6, 1972; *New York Times*, May 6, 1972.

21. Proxmire, *You Can Do It!*, 71; Marc Marotta, interview with Anita Hecht, January 15, 2009, transcript, Proxmire Oral History Project, Wisconsin Historical Society Archives, 38; "Howard E. Shuman, Legislative and Administrative Assistant to Senators Paul Douglas and William Proxmire, 1955–1982," Oral History Interviews, Senate Historical Office, Washington, DC, 468–470; *New York Times*, October 2, 1973; *Wisconsin State Journal*, October 2, 1973; Mike Miller, "Foiled Again: Proxmire Stops Another Holdup Attempt," *Capital Times*, October 2, 1973; "Proxmire Aids Teens Who Tried to Rob Him," *Wisconsin State Journal*, August 15, 1975; "Proxmire Hired Teens Who Tried to Rob Him," *Capital Times*, August 19, 1975; Martin Lobel interview with Anita Hecht, November 19, 2008, transcript, Proxmire Oral History Project, Wisconsin Historical Society Archives, 41–42. Lobel had no hesitation in teasing Proxmire about his obsession with exercise. When rooming with the senator in a Green Bay hotel, the hungover Lobel was awakened by a grunting noise and rolled over to see Proxmire doing his pushups on the floor. After watching for a few seconds,

Lobel said, "Hey, you can stop now. She's left," causing the senator to lose count and start over. "That was the last time we shared a room," Lobel later noted; ibid., 95.

22. Proxmire, *You Can Do It!*, 140–143; Ellen Proxmire interview with Anita Hecht, November 18, 2008, transcript, Proxmire Oral History Project, Wisconsin Historical Society Archives, 57; Douglas Proxmire interview with Anita Hecht, April 5, 2010, transcript, Proxmire Oral History Project, Wisconsin Historical Society Archives, 63; "Howard E. Shuman, Legislative and Administrative Assistant to Senators Paul Douglas and William Proxmire, 1955–1982," Oral History Interviews, Senate Historical Office, Washington, DC, 467–468.

23. Proxmire, *You Can Do It!*, 18, 28, 80, 127; Frank A. Aukofer, *Never a Slow Day: Adventures of a 20th Century Newspaper Reporter* (Milwaukee, WI: Marquette University Press, 2009), 134.

24. Proxmire, *You Can Do It!*, 11–23.

25. Proxmire, *You Can Do It!*, 126–133.

26. Proxmire, *You Can Do It!*, 133; Jan Cathy Sawall Licht interview with Anita Hecht, November 11, 2010, transcript, Proxmire Oral History Project, Wisconsin Historical Society Archives, 46–47.

27. Robert Lewis interview with Anita Hecht, November 18, 2010, transcript, Proxmire Oral History Project, Wisconsin Historical Society Archives, 37–39, 45–55; *Wisconsin State Journal*, March 8, 11, 1959; William C. Robbins, "William the Pretender on Taxes," *Wisconsin State Journal*, April 15, 1963.

28. Sykes, *Proxmire*, 166; John Herbers, "What Makes Proxmire Run?" *New York Times*, April 4, 1971.

29. Mark Shields interview with Anita Hecht, October 21, 2009, transcript, Proxmire Oral History Project, Wisconsin Historical Society Archives, 18–20.

30. Thomas van der Voort interview with Anita Hecht, March 19, 2009, transcript, Proxmire Oral History Project, Wisconsin Historical Society Archives, 25–60.

31. Sykes, *Proxmire*, 167; Martin Lobel interview with Anita Hecht, November 19, 2008, transcript, Proxmire Oral History Project, Wisconsin Historical Society Archives, pages 13–22; Ann Purcell interview with Anita Hecht, October 22, 2010, transcript, Proxmire Oral History Project, Wisconsin

Historical Society Archives, 15–21; Ronald Tammen interview with Anita Hecht, June 5, 2009, transcript, Proxmire Oral History Project, Wisconsin Historical Society Archives, 38; "Howard E. Shuman, Legislative and Administrative Assistant to Senators Paul Douglas and William Proxmire, 1955–1982," Oral History Interviews, Senate Historical Office, Washington, DC, 433–434, 447, 472.

32. Sykes, *Proxmire*, 167; Ann Purcell interview with Anita Hecht, October 22, 2010, transcript, Proxmire Oral History Project, Wisconsin Historical Society Archives, 16, 25; Ronald Tammen interview with Anita Hecht, June 5, 2009, transcript, Proxmire Oral History Project, Wisconsin Historical Society Archives, 38, 43; Martin Lobel interview with Anita Hecht, November 19, 2008, transcript, Proxmire Oral History Project, Wisconsin Historical Society Archives, 29–30; see also Kenneth Dameron interview with Anita Hecht, December 15, 2009, transcript, Proxmire Oral History Project, Wisconsin Historical Society Archives, 54–55, and William Drew interview with Anita Hecht, November 23, 2009, transcript, Proxmire Oral History Project, Wisconsin Historical Society Archives, 41–49, and Carl Eifert interview with Anita Hecht, July 6, 2009, transcript, Proxmire Oral History Project, Wisconsin Historical Society Archives, 32–35. For Luke Dyb, see *Capital Times*, June 10, October 18, 19, 1968, September 12, 1969; and *Wisconsin State Journal*, June 11, October 18, 1968.

33. *Capital Times*, June 19, 1967; *Wisconsin State Journal*, June 26, 1967; Mary Ellen Poulos interview with Anita Hecht, April 1, 2009, transcript, Proxmire Oral History Project, Wisconsin Historical Society Archives, 39–42; *New York Times*, October 10, 1971; Barbara Gamarekian, "Selling the Capital's Social Scene—With Connections," *New York Times*, June 28, 1981.

34. "How and Where to Cut the Federal Budget in 1969," *US Senator William Proxmire Reports to You from Washington*, January 1969.

35. *New York Times*, February 19, 1969; Richard A. Hunt, *Melvin Laird and the Foundation of the Post-Vietnam Military, 1969–1973* (Washington, DC: Historical Office of the Office of the Secretary of Defense, 2015), 69–75.

36. *Capital Times*, March 10, 1969; *New York Times*, March 17, 1969; *Proxmire Reports*, July 1969.

37. *New York Times*, March 23, 1969; *Capital Times*, March 22, 1969; *Wisconsin State Journal*, March 23, 1969.

38. *Capital Times*, April 21, 1969; *New York Times*, April 27, 1969; Neil

Sheehan, "Drive Grows in Congress for Arms Spending Cut," *New York Times*, May 18, 1969.

39. *Wisconsin State Journal*, May 28, June 8, 12, 25, 1969; *Capital Times*, June 2, 7, 23, 24, August 4, 1969; *New York Times*, June 4, 12, 14, 27, August 4, 5, 6, 11, 14, 1969.

40. *Capital Times*, June 5, 1969; *Wisconsin State Journal*, June 6, 1969; Max Frankel, "Nixon and Critics: He Flings Down a Challenge on Foreign and Defense Policies," *New York Times*, June 8, 1969.

41. *Wisconsin State Journal*, June 14, 1969; Richard Kaufman, "We Must Guard against Unwarranted Influence," *New York Times*, June 22, July 6, 1969.

42. *New York Times*, August 12, 1969.

43. *New York Times*, August 31, September 3, 4, 17, 1969; *Capital Times*, September 1, 3, 10, November 7, 1969; William Proxmire, "Historic Fight to Control Military Spending," *Capital Times*, September 29, 1969; *Proxmire Reports*, July 1969. Nine senators voted against the appropriation: Democrats Gaylord Nelson, J. William Fulbright, Philip Hart, Eugene McCarthy, George McGovern, and Stephen Young, and Republicans Mark Hatfield, Jacob Javits, and Robert Packwood.

44. *Capital Times*, October 28, December 29, 1969, January 8, 1970; *Proxmire Reports*, November 1969; *Wisconsin State Journal*, December 28, 1969; *New York Times*, December 28, 1969, January 9, 17, 1970.

45. *Capital Times*, February 10, 1970; *New York Times*, February 11, 25, 1970; *Wisconsin State Journal*, February 11, 1970.

46. *Capital Times*, July 16, 1970; *New York Times*, July 16, 1970.

47. *Wisconsin State Journal*, July 21, August 29, 1970; Erwin Knoll, "Report from Washington," *Capital Times*, August 10, 13, 20, 28, 1970; *New York Times*, August 13, 18, 20, 24, 26, 28, 29, 1970; William Proxmire, *The Pentagon vs Free Enterprise* (New York: Sidney Hillman Foundation, 1970).

48. *Capital Times*, June 16, July 15, October 14, November 15, 1969; *Proxmire Reports*, August and September 1969; "Howard E. Shuman, Legislative and Administrative Assistant to Senators Paul Douglas and William Proxmire, 1955–1982," Oral History Interviews, Senate Historical Office, Washington, DC, 428.

49. *Capital Times*, April 30, May 1, 1970; *Wisconsin State Journal*, May 1, 4, 6, 1970; Erwin Knoll, "Report from Washington," *Capital Times*, May 4, 1970.

50. *New York Times*, June 4, 11, 30, September 2, 1970; *Wisconsin State Journal*, June 4, 12, July 1, September 2, 1970; *Capital Times*, August 26, September 1, 1970; *Proxmire Reports*, May 1970.

51. Erwin Knoll, "Report from Washington," *Capital Times*, January 13, 1969; *Wisconsin State Journal*, February 9, 18, 20, March 9, 1969; *New York Times*, February 21, April 2, 1969; John Wyngaard, "Wisconsin Report," *Wisconsin State Journal*, March 30, 1969.

52. *Proxmire Reports*, March and September 1969; William Proxmire, "The Tax Loophole Scandal," *Wisconsin State Journal*, April 7, 1969; *New York Times*, October 24, November 30, 1969; *Wisconsin State Journal*, November 26, 1969.

53. *New York Times*, February 17, 19, March 13, 1970; *Capital Times*, February 18, 1970.

54. *New York Times*, March 22, 23, 1970; *Wisconsin State Journal*, March 22, 1970; Albert L. Kraus, "An Ambiguous Role: Nixon Administration Wants Benefits of a Recession without Paying Price," *New York Times*, March 25, 1970.

55. *Wisconsin State Journal*, June 18, 1970; Edwin L. Dale Jr., "Economy: Nixon and Critics Disagree on Remedies," *New York Times*, June 21, 1970; *Capital Times*, August 24, 1970; William Proxmire, "Under Nixon: Jobless Up, Inflation, Stagnation," *New York Times*, October 18, 1970; Paul S. Boyer, *Promises to Keep: The United States Since 1945* (Lexington, MA: D.C. Heath, 1995), 363–364; William Proxmire, "The Need for Wage-Price Guidelines," *The Bond Buyer*, December 1970, 33–35, 93.

56. *New York Times*, November 3, December 11, 1968; *Wisconsin State Journal*, December 12, 1968.

57. *Capital Times*, January 28, March 31, 1969; *Wisconsin State Journal*, February 1, 1969; *New York Times*, March 29, May 20, 1969; Erwin Knoll, "Report from Washington," *Capital Times*, March 31, June 2, 1969; Robert J. Cole, "Personal Finance: Correcting Wrong Credit Files," *New York Times*, May 26, 1969; *Capital Times*, November 7, 1969.

58. *New York Times*, December 8, 9, 1969, February 27, April 16, 1970; *Wisconsin State Journal*, December 8, 9, 1969, February 27, 1970; *Capital Times*, December 8, 1969. The lone vote against the bill was Albert Gore of Tennessee, for unknown reasons; "Consumer Legislation in the 91st Congress," PL 91–508; *Proxmire Reports*, November 1970.

59. *Capital Times*, May 17, 1967; December 10, 11, 1968, January 21, September 9, 11, November 29, December 12, 1969; *Wisconsin State Journal*, November 27, 31, 1969, January 22, 1970; *New York Times*, January 9, 1970; memorandum from Rod Matthews, "A Political Analysis of the Effect of the 1968 Elections on the 1970 Wisconsin Senatorial Election," no date (late 1967 or early 1968), folder 25, box 131, William Proxmire Papers. Matthews suggested that a Nelson loss would make Proxmire's reelection more likely since Wisconsin voters might prefer senators from two different parties. Moreover, a Knowles Senate victory in 1968 would eliminate Proxmire's most popular opponent.

60. *Capital Times*, February 5, April 27, 1970; *Wisconsin State Journal*, February 6, April 27, 1970; *New York Times*, April 27, 28, May 1, 1970.

61. *Capital Times*, February 3, 1970; *Wisconsin State Journal*, February 6, 28, April 28, 29, May 17, 1970; *New York Times*, May 17, 1970.

62. *Wisconsin State Journal*, May 22, 23, 1970; *Capital Times*, May 22, 23, 1970.

63. *Capital Times*, June 25, July 1, 8, 17, 22, 30, August 6, 20, 1970; *Wisconsin State Journal*, June 28, July 1, 8, 23, 28, 29, 1970.

64. *Capital Times*, September 17, October 1, 17, 19, 1970; *Wisconsin State Journal*, September 20, 26, October 7, 10, 14, 1970; *New York Times*, October 21, 1970. In addition to Proxmire and Erickson, four other candidates appeared on the ballot: Edmond Hou-Seye (American Party), Martha Quinn (Socialist Workers' Party), Adolf Wiggert (Progressive Labor Socialist), and Quaker antiwar activist Betty Boardman (Independent); Anne Purcell, interview with Anita Hecht, October 22, 2010, transcript, Proxmire Oral History Project, Wisconsin Historical Society Archives, 41–48; advertising and expenses for the election are in folders 26 and 27, box 131, William Proxmire Papers.

65. *Capital Times*, November 4, 1970; *Wisconsin State Journal*, November 4, 1970; John Wyngaard, "Proxmire Win Provides Key to His Invincibility," *Wisconsin State Journal*, November 9, 1970; election results from the 1971 *Wisconsin Blue Book*, 311.

66. *New York Times*, June 12, 1971; *Capital Times*, June 11, 12, 1971; *Wisconsin State Journal*, June 12, 1971; Louise Cook, "Marriage and Politics May Not Mix," *Wisconsin State Journal*, June 28, 1972.

Chapter 8

1. *New York Times*, February 8, 24, 1972; *Capital Times*, February 12, 23, 1972; *Wisconsin State Journal*, February 12, 24, 1972; Carl Eifert, interview with Anita Hecht, July 6, 2009, transcript, Proxmire Oral History Project, Wisconsin Historical Society Archives, 49–50; Mary Frances de la Pava interview with Anita Hecht, October 20, 2009, transcript, Proxmire Oral History Project, Wisconsin Historical Society Archives, 40–41. The extent of ridicule was apparent in the *Wisconsin State Journal* cartoon on February 25, 1972, depicting Proxmire, dressed in a suit and running shoes, fertilizing his head. Months later, Proxmire eagerly talked about how successful the procedure had been, but it did have an embarrassing coda. In March 1973, Proxmire became the first senator to release his tax returns, which revealed he had deducted the $2,758 cost of the procedure as a medical expense. He quickly corrected the error, which added $1,000 to his federal and state tax bills; see *Capital Times*, March 22, 23, 1973; *New York Times*, March 23, 24, 1973; and *Wisconsin State Journal*, March 24, 1973. The mistake was the accountant's, who used all medical receipts without conferring with Proxmire. See Lawrence Knutson interview with Anita Hecht, December 16, 2009, transcript, Proxmire Oral History Project, Wisconsin Historical Society Archives, 30.

2. For general background on the early development of the SST, see Mel Horwitch, *Clipped Wings: The American SST Conflict* (Cambridge, MA: MIT Press, 1982), 22–55; Don Bedwell, "Supersonic Gamble: Should the Cancellation of America's SST Program Be Remembered as a Mercy Killing?" *Aviation History* (May 2012), 14–15; Richard Wegman interview with Anita Hecht, March 18, 2009, transcript, Proxmire Oral History Project, Wisconsin Historical Society Archives, 26–27; William Proxmire, *Uncle Sam: The Last of the Bigtime Spenders* (New York: Simon and Schuster, 1972), 224.

3. *Proxmire Reports*, September 1966, May 1967; *Wisconsin State Journal*, April 30, June 1, 1967; *Capital Times*, May 31, August 22, 1967; *New York Times*, September 28, October 6, 1967; Evert Clark, "Green Light for the Supersonic," *New York Times*, August 14, 1966; Evert Clark, "Supersonic Liner Gets Surprise Aid from Transport Agency's Measure," *New York Times*, November 13, 1966; Robert A. Wright, "Turbulence Is Still Ahead

for SST," *New York Times*, October 8, 1967; Horwitch, *Clipped Wings*, 177–181, 216–221; Richard Wegman interview with Anita Hecht, March 18, 2009, transcript, Proxmire Oral History Project, Wisconsin Historical Society Archives, 28–29.

4. *New York Times*, December 4, 1968, October 17, December 18, 1969; *Capital Times*, September 24, 1969; Christopher Lydon, "Nixon Backs SST; Battle for Funds Looms in Congress," *New York Times*, September 24, 1969; Horwitch, *Clipped Wings*, 271–274. A conference committee subsequently agreed on an $85 million appropriation; *Proxmire Reports*, May and October 1969.

5. Christopher Lydon, "US SST Commitment May Increase by $3-Billion," *New York Times*, May 12, 1970; E. W. Kenworthy, "Senate SST Opponents Acquire New Allies and Ammunition," *New York Times*, June 8, 1970; Christopher Lydon, "2 Panels to Study Effect of SST on Environment," *New York Times*, July 21, 1970; E. W. Kenworthy, "Noise and Ecology Standards for SST Are Sought," *New York Times*, August 2, 1970; *Capital Times*, May 25, 1970; Christopher Lydon, "Shelving of SST Is Urged by Panel," *New York Times*, August 20, 1970; *Wisconsin State Journal*, May 26, 1970; *Capital Times*, August 19, 1970; Richard Wegman interview with Anita Hecht, March 18, 2009, transcript, Proxmire Oral History Project, Wisconsin Historical Society Archives, 29–30.

6. *New York Times*, September 16, November 25, December 4, 1970; Christopher Lydon, "SST Backers Told Soviet Jet Is a Threat," *New York Times*, November 11, 1970; *Capital Times*, November 25, December 3, 4, 1970; Christopher Lydon, "Senate Approves Two Curbs on SST," *New York Times*, December 3, 1970; *Wisconsin State Journal*, December 4, 1970; Richard Wegman interview with Anita Hecht, March 18, 2009, transcript, Proxmire Oral History Project, Wisconsin Historical Society Archives, 30–36; Proxmire, *Uncle Sam*, 224–226.

7. Christopher Lydon, "House Declines to Back Senate in SST Fund Curb," *New York Times*, December 9, 1970; Christopher Lydon, "Senate SST Filibuster Pledged; Conferees Will Convene Today," *New York Times*, December 10, 1970; *Capital Times*, December 9, 16, 22, 1970; Christopher Lydon, "SST Compromise Greeted by Relief and Uncertainty," *New York Times*, December 12, 1970; *Wisconsin State Journal*, December 12, 1970.

8. *Capital Times*, December 17, 1970; Christopher Lydon, "Scott Fighting SST

Filibuster," *New York Times*, December 18, 1970; Christopher Lydon, "Senate Defeats Motion to Close Debate Over SST," *New York Times*, December 20, 22, 1970; *Wisconsin State Journal*, December 23, 1970; Frank Aukofer interview with Anita Hecht, November 21, 2008, transcript, Proxmire Oral History Project, Wisconsin Historical Society Archives, 38–40; Richard Wegman interview with Anita Hecht, March 18, 2009, transcript, Proxmire Oral History Project, Wisconsin Historical Society Archives, 38–40.

9. Christopher Lydon, "Senate Delays SST Plan, Returning It to Conferees," *New York Times*, December 30, 1970; *Capital Times*, December 30, 31, 1970; *Wisconsin State Journal*, December 30, 1970; Christopher Lydon, "Proxmire Accepts Extension of SST," *New York Times*, January 1, 1971; John W. Finney, "Congress Closes as Senate Votes SST Compromise," *New York Times*, January 3, 1971; *Proxmire Reports*, January 1971.

10. Christopher Lydon, "Supporters of Supersonic Airliner Making Comeback as Issue Shifts from Environment to Economics," *New York Times*, March 1, 1971; Richard Witkin, "New Ingredients in the SST Debate," *New York Times*, March 18, 1971; Christopher Lydon, "House Votes to End Fund for Development of SST: Backers See Senate Aid," *New York Times*, March 19, 1971; *Capital Times*, March 20, 1971; John W. Finney, "Miscalculations by White House and Labor Helped Defeat the Supersonic Transport," *New York Times*, March 25, 1971; Christopher Lydon, "Senate Bars Funds for SST, 51–46; Nixon Calls Vote 'Severe Blow,'" *New York Times*, March 25, 1971; John H. Averill, "SST Vote Triumph for Proxmire," *Capital Times*, March 25, 1971; *Wisconsin State Journal*, March 25, May 13, 20, 1971; Richard Witkin, "Boeing Head Sees Half-Billion Rise in Outlay for SST," *New York Times*, May 14, 1971; Richard Witkin, "Senate to Vote Wednesday on Bid to Revitalize SST," *New York Times*, May 15, 1971; Christopher Lydon, "Senate Rejects Bid to Revive SST by Vote of 58–37," *New York Times*, May 20; 1971; Proxmire, *Uncle Sam*, 226–229; Richard Wegman interview with Anita Hecht, March 18, 2009, transcript, Proxmire Oral History Project, Wisconsin Historical Society Archives, 42–50.

11. *Wisconsin State Journal*, January 12, 1970; *Capital Times*, March 13, 1970.

12. *Wisconsin State Journal*, December 13, 14, 1970, January 8, 1971; *New York Times*, November 26, 1970; *Capital Times*, December 26, 1970.

13. John Wyngaard, "State Demos Look Forward to 1972 Primary," *Wisconsin*

State Journal, February 8, 1971; John Patrick Hunter, "A Preview of the '72 Presidential Primary?" *Capital Times*, March 13, 1971; *Capital Times*, March 18, 1971; *Wisconsin State Journal*, March 19, 1971.

14. John Wyngaard, "Proxmire for President Boomlet on Wane," *Wisconsin State Journal*, March 28, 1971; *New York Times*, May 1, September 1, 1971; *Wisconsin State Journal*, April 19, 25, May 12, 22, September 13, 1971; *Capital Times*, May 24, August 28, 1971; James D. Selk, "Demo Convention: Tale of 2 Meetings," *Wisconsin State Journal*, June 20, 1971; John Wyngaard, "Proxmire Reaps Silence on Almost-Candidacy," *Wisconsin State Journal*, September 17, 1971.

15. *Wisconsin State Journal*, November 7, 1971; John Wyngaard, "Proxmire's Candidacy Killed By Home State," *Wisconsin State Journal*, November 12, 1971; *New York Times*, November 7, 1971.

16. *Capital Times*, January 5, 7, 23, 1971; *Wisconsin State Journal*, February 23, 1971; *New York Times*, January 5, 7, 1971; John Finney, "Military Aid: Some Weird Goings On in the Program," *New York Times*, January 10, 1971; Dana Adams Schmidt, "Proxmire Disputed by Pentagon on Military Aid Total for 1970," *New York Times*, January 23, 1971; Erwin Knoll, "Report from Washington," *Capital Times*, February 22, 1971; *Proxmire Reports*, February 1971.

17. Erwin Knoll, "Prox Opens New Arms Waste Fight," *Capital Times*, April 12, 1971; *New York Times*, April 13, May 12, 1971; *Wisconsin State Journal*, April 13, May 2, 1971; *Capital Times*, May 1, 5, 1971.

18. John W. Finney, "Senate Faces $7-Billion Arms Cut Fight," *New York Times*, June 27, 1971; William Beecher, "Laird Sees Peril in $7-Billion Cut," *New York Times*, June 29, 1971; John W. Finney, "Senators Reject Arms-Fund Cuts," *New York Times*, June 30, 1971; *Wisconsin State Journal*, July 1, 1971; *Capital Times*, July 1, 1971; *New York Times*, June 28, 1971.

19. *New York Times*, July 7, September 9, 23, 30, 1971; *Wisconsin State Journal*, July 7, September 30, October 7, 1971; *Capital Times*, July 8, 1971.

20. Melvin Small, *The Presidency of Richard Nixon* (Lawrence: University Press of Kanas, 1999), 203–207.

21. *New York Times*, November 29, 1970; *Wisconsin State* Journal, November 29, 1970; *Capital Times*, November 30, 1970; William Proxmire, "The Need for Wage-Price Guidelines," *The Bond Buyer*, December 1970; Erwin Knoll, "Report from Washington," *Capital Times*, December 21, 1970.

22. *Capital Times*, January 15, 1971; *New York Times*, January 17, 23, 30, 1971; *Wisconsin State Journal*, January 18, 23, February 1, 1971; Erwin Knoll, "Report from Washington," *Capital Times*, January 18, 1971; Small, *Presidency of Richard Nixon*, 207–208.

23. *New York Times*, February 5, 14, 23, March 31, 1971; *Capital Times*, February 6, 1971; *Wisconsin State Journal*, February 6, 1971; Erwin Knoll, "Report from Washington," *Capital Times*, February 15, 1971; Edwin Dale Jr., "Optimistic Economic Forecast Arouses Disbelief," *New York Times*, February 28, 1971.

24. *New York Times*, April 3, 22, June 22, July 3, August 6, 7, 1971; *Wisconsin State Journal*, April 22, 1971; *Capital Times*, April 26, June 5, 1971.

25. Edwin L. Dale Jr., "Keeping an 'Open Mind' on Wage-Price Controls," *New York Times*, August 8, 1971; *Capital Times*, August 13, 1971; *Wisconsin State Journal*, August 14, 1971; Alan Greenspan, *The Age of Turbulence: Adventures in a New World* (New York: Penguin, 2007), 60–61.

26. *New York Times*, August 16, 18, 20, 25, 1971; *Wisconsin State Journal*, August 17, 18, 28, 1971; *Capital Times*, August 17, 18, 1971; Small, *Presidency of Richard Nixon*, 209; Greenspan, *Age of Turbulence*, 61–62; Richard Reeves, *President Nixon: Alone in the White House* (New York: Simon and Schuster, 2001), 361–366.

27. *New York Times*, September 23, October 2, 8, 15, 1971; *Wisconsin State Journal*, October 2, 8, 17, 23, 1971; *Proxmire Reports*, November 1971.

28. *New York Times*, November 21, 30, December 2, 4, 1971; *Wisconsin State Journal*, November 19, 21, December 12, 19, 1971; *Capital Times*, December 2, 27, 1971; Small, *Presidency of Richard Nixon*, 210–211.

29. John W. Finney, "Democrats Score Nixon's Message in Rebuttal on TV," *New York Times*, January 22, 1972; William Proxmire, letter to the editor, *New York Times*, January 25, 1972; Edwin L. Dale Jr., "Nixon Aide Sees Jobless Cutback," *New York Times*, February 8, 1972; "Connally Backs Policies on Jobs," *New York Times*, February 17, 1972; Edwin L. Dale Jr., "Views Given to Congress By 'Radical' Economists," *New York Times*, March 1, 1972; the three were Douglas F. Dowd of Cornell University, Barry Bluestone of Boston College, and Howard Sherman of the University of California, Riverside.

30. *Wisconsin State Journal*, March 9, 1972; Philip Shabecoff, "2 Democrats in Congress Ask Reform of Economic Controls," *New York Times*, March 11,

1972; Edwin L. Dale Jr., "Democrats Ask Big Social Security Rise," *New York Times*, March 23, 1972; *Capital Times*, April 22, 1972; *Wisconsin State Journal*, April 22, 1972.

31. Philip Shabecoff, "Congress Panel Assails Controls," *New York Times*, May 22, 1972; James L. Rowe Jr., "Democrats Want Controls Relaxed from All but Largest Companies," *Capital Times*, May 22, 1972; Philip Shabecoff, "Economic Panel Asks Output Spur," *New York Times*, July 10, 1972; *Capital Times*, July 14, September 2, 30, 1972; Edwin L. Dale Jr., "As Phase III Approaches: The Virtuous Circle or . . . the Vicious Cycle," *New York Times*, August 27, 1972; Thomas E. Mullaney, "Big Debate Brewing on Issue of Price Controls," *New York Times*, October 22, 1972; "Proxmire Forecasts Check on Controls Program," *New York Times*, November 13, 1972; "Proxmire Calls Business Coddled," *New York Times*, November 15, 1972; Edward Cowan, "Business Support for Controls Appears to Decline," *New York Times*, December 21, 1972.

32. *Capital Times*, January 11, 12, 1973; *New York Times*, January 12, 30, 1973; Edward Cowan, "In Phase 3, It's Industry's Ball," *New York Times*, February 4, 1973. In March, the COLC did impose a 1% limit on oil price increases, near the end of the winter heating season, but left open the possibility for companies to request higher price increases on a case-by-case basis; Reeves, *Alone in the White House*, 556–560.

33. *Capital Times*, February 28, June 5, 1973; *New York Times*, March 1, 11, June 5, 8, 1973; *Wisconsin State Journal*, March 1, April 3, 6, 1973, Small, *Presidency of Richard Nixon*, 211–212.

34. *New York Times*, June 14, 1973; *Capital Times*, June 14, 1973; Edwin L. Dale Jr., "Rules for Phase 4 Permit Some Price Rises of 10%," *New York Times*, August 8, 1973; *Wisconsin State Journal*, August 8, 1973; Small, *Presidency of Richard Nixon*, 212.

35. *Wisconsin State Journal*, January 4, 10, 13, February 7, 20, 1974; *Capital Times*, January 9, 11, February 19, 1974; Small, *Presidency of Richard Nixon*, 212–213.

36. Eileen Shanahan, "Senate Committee Clears Casey's S.E.C. Nomination," *New York Times*, February 11, 1971; Eileen Shanahan, "Senate Likely to Reopen Hearings on S.E.C. Chief," *New York Times*, February 13, 1971; *Capital Times*, February 13, 26, March 1, 10, 26, 1971; Eileen Shanahan, "3d Suit Disclosed by S.E.C. Nominee," *New York Times*, February 26, 1971;

Wisconsin State Journal, March 1, 10, 1971; Myron S. Waldman, "Casey's Testimony at Variance with Court Case Facts," *Capital Times*, March 3, 1971; Eileen Shanahan, "Committee Backs Casey for 2nd Time," *New York Times*, March 10, 1971; Max Frankel, "The Ides of March: Nixon Aides Discover Good Omens," *New York Times*, March 16, 1971.

37. *Capital Times*, December 8, 9, 10, 11, 1971; *Wisconsin State Journal*, December 10, 11, 1971; "Rehnquist Says '52 Memo Outlined Jackson's Views," *New York Times*, December 9, 1971; *New York Times*, December 11, 1971. Proxmire also opposed Nixon's appointment of Creighton W. Abrams as army chief of staff, Richard Kleindienst as attorney general, and Roy Ash to the Office of Budget and Management; see Small, *Presidency of Richard Nixon*, 1972.

38. *Wisconsin State Journal*, February 27, 1972; *Capital Times*, February 28, March 18, 1972; Nicholas von Hoffman, "Moms, Manny's Cigar, and Buses," *Capital Times*, March 8, 1972; John Herbers, "Senate Approves Mild Busing Curb; Strong Bill Fails," *New York Times*, March 1, 1972.

39. Richard Wegman interview with Anita Hecht, March 18, 2009, transcript, Proxmire Oral History Project, Wisconsin Historical Society Archives, 20; Ann Purcell, interview with Anita Hecht, October 22, 2010, transcript, Proxmire Oral History Project, Wisconsin Historical Society Archives, 24–26; John Daniel Finerty interview with Anita Hecht, April 23, 2009, transcript, Proxmire Oral History Project, Wisconsin Historical Society Archives, 31–32; Dick Cudahy interview with Anita Hecht, December 30, 2008, transcript, Proxmire Oral History Project, Wisconsin Historical Society Archives, 28–29; *Proxmire Reports*, September 1969, May 1970.

40. *Capital Times*, May 10, 12, June 25, 1971; *Wisconsin State Journal*, May 27, June 5, 23, 25, 1971. The June 24th withdrawal amendment was subsequently removed from the final bill by a House-Senate conference committee. The Senate passed a similar resolution in October 1971.

41. *Wisconsin State Journal*, April 14, June 16, August 19, 1972; *Capital Times*, June 15, 1972.

42. *Capital Times*, February 14, 1972.

43. Richard Witkin, "Proxmire Scores Navy Claims Payment," *New York Times*, February 18, 1972; Richard Witkin, "US Auditors Question $7-Million Litton Charge," *New York Times*, March 28, 1972; Richard Witkin, "Rush by Navy to Spend Funds Charged," *New York Times*,

March 29, 1972; Richard Mintz, "Spend and Spend Some More, Top Admiral Told Navy," *Capital Times*, March 29, 1972; Richard Witkin, "Altimeter Price Called Too High," *New York Times*, March 30, 1972.

44. John W. Finney, "Proxmire Charges Navy Plans Money 'Bailout' for Grumman," *New York Times*, April 8, 1972; Proxmire, *Uncle Sam*, 80–81.

45. "New Fighter Plane of Navy Criticized in Spending Study," *New York Times*, April 17, 1972; Richard L. Madden, "Grumman Insists on Needs Fund Rise to Build 48 F-14s," *New York Times*, April 18, 1972; *Wisconsin State Journal*, April 17, 1972; Leonard Silk, "Why Overruns in the Defense Market?" *New York Times*, April 19, 1972.

46. *New York Times*, May 30, 1972; *Wisconsin State Journal*, July 1, 18, 1972.

47. David A. Andelman, "US Bars Price Increase by Grumman for F-14's," *New York Times*, December 12, 1972; Anthony Ripley, "Proxmire Criticizes Navy for Its Loans to Grumman," *New York Times*, December 22, 1972; *New York Times*, August 19, December 22, 1972, January 5, 1973; David A. Andelman, "Grumman Gets Navy Loan Despite Its Refusal on F-14," *New York Times*, January 4, 1973; *Capital Times*, January 4, 1973; Richard Witkin, "Pentagon Rebuffs Grumman, Litton over Price Rises," *New York Times*, March 2, 1973; Richard Witkin, "But Wait for the Final Out," *New York Times*, March 4, 1973; *Capital Times*, March 5, 1973.

48. Juan M. Vasquez, "Capitol Investigation Finds 'Substantial Evidence' of Mismanagement in the Lockheed C-5A Program," *New York Times*, March 27, 1972; Juan M. Vasquez, "$400-Million Lockheed Payment Scored," *New York Times*, March 28, 1972; *Wisconsin State Journal*, March 28, 29, May 1, 1972; Juan M. Vasquez, "Connally Board Said to Flout Law," *New York Times*, April 13, 1972; *Capital Times*, April 14, May 1, 1972; Juan M. Vasquez, "Proxmire Says Connally Insults Congress on the Lockheed Loan," *New York Times*, May 4, 1972; Proxmire, *Uncle Sam*, 231–23.

49. Richard Witkin, "US Auditors Question $7-Million Litton Charge," *New York Times*, March 28, 1972; Richard Witkin, "Proxmire Sees Crisis at Litton; Urges Navy to Reject Claims," *New York Times*, June 27, 1972; *Capital Times*, June 26, 1972; Richard Witkin, "S.E.C. Denounced by Proxmire on Earnings Reports by Litton," *New York Times*, July 23, 1972; *New York Times*, July 27, 1972; Richard Witkin, "US Asks to Stay Litton Payments," *New York Times*, June 20, 1973.

50. For overviews of defense contracting: Leonard Silk, "Why Overruns

in the Defense Market?" *New York Times*, April 19, 1972; Richard Witkin, "Shucks! We Need a Few More Billion," *New York Times*, April 30, 1972; Robert Sherrill, "SCRAM, SCAD, ULMS and Other Aspects of the $85.9-Billion Defense Budget," *New York Times*, July 30, 1972; Michael C. Jensen, "Musical Chairs in Business and Government," *New York Times*, November 12, 1972; Richard Witkin, "To Bail Them Out or Not," *New York Times*, January 14, 1973; "High Profits Found for Defense Jobs," *New York Times*, May 16, 1973. For retaliation against whistleblowers: "Third Proxmire Witness Fired from US Position," *Capital Times*, January 6, 1973; Anthony Ripley, "Navy Aide Asserts Military-Industrial Complex Has Invaded Administration," *New York Times*, December 20, 1972; Anthony Ripley, "Fitzgerald Says Pointless Work Filled Last Days at the Pentagon," *New York Times*, April 6, 1972.

51. *New York Times*, November 11, 23, 1972, May 4, 23, 1972; *Wisconsin State Journal*, November 11, 1972, February 16, April 23, May 24, 1973; *Capital Times*, November 22, 1972, January 24, April 18, 23, May 3 (quotation), 18, 1973. At the same time, Proxmire's populist haranguing got Congress to cut the usages of limousines by government employees from 800 to 27; see Richard L. Madden, "Senate Votes to Curb Chauffeured Cars," *New York Times*, November 17, 1973.

52. *Capital Times*, March 27, May 25, 1972; *New York Times*, April 2, May 21, 1972.

53. John Noble Wilford, "Opposition in Congress to Space Shuttle Likely," *New York Times*, January 6, 1972; *Wisconsin State Journal*, January 9, August 18, 1972, April 27, 1973; *Capital Times*, January 10, August 17, 1972; *New York Times*, August 18, 1972, June 20, 1973; *Proxmire Reports*, February 1972.

54. *New York Times*, April 16, May 20, 1973; Marjorie Hunter, "Federal Art Bill Faces Fund Fight," *New York Times*, April 28, 1973; Harold C. Schonberg, "Cash for Culture, Too," *New York Times*, April 29, 1973; Marjorie Hunter, "Senate Approves $840-Million Aid to Arts," *New York Times*, May 3, 1973; *Wisconsin State Journal*, May 4, 1973; Mel Gussow, "National Endowment Puts Government into Role of Major Patron of the Arts," *New York Times*, August 12, 1973.

55. *New York Times*, August 28, 1972; *Capital Times*, October 23, 1972; *Wisconsin State Journal*, October 24, 1972.

56. *Capital Times*, February 5, 9, 1973; *Wisconsin State Journal*, February 6, 7, 1973.

57. James M. Naughton, "Senate Slates Showdown Vote on Ceiling-Impoundment Issue," *New York Times*, 30 March 1973; *Wisconsin State Journal*, April 4, 1973.

58. Michael C. Jensen, "Romney Discloses Halt in Subsidies for New Housing," *New York Times*, January 9, 1973; *Capital Times*, January 10, 1973.

59. John Haig, "Prox Hits Nixon Fund Priority," *Capital Times*, March 10, 1973; *Capital Times*, August 27, 1973; *New York Times*, October 3, 14, 1973, January 1, 1974; Martin Tolchin, "Mayors Decry Nixon Housing Proposal," *New York Times*, October 4, 1973; *Proxmire Reports*, March 1974.

60. John Wyngaard, "Many in State Owe Much to Humphrey," *Wisconsin State Journal*, January 16, 1972; *Capital Times*, March 31, May 20, 1972; Douglas E. Kneeland, "McGovern Gets Proxmire Vote," *New York Times*, April 1, 1972; John Wyngaard, "Proxmire Endorsement Called Gesture to Left," *Wisconsin State Journal*, April 9, May 21, 1972.

61. Bob Woodward, "O'Brien Sees White House Hand in Break-In at Democratic HQ," *Capital Times*, June 21, 1972; *Capital Times*, July 27, 1972; Bob Woodward, "Order Probe of Nixon Funds," *Capital Times*, August 2, 11, 1972; *New York Times*, August 3, 1972; *Wisconsin State Journal*, August 12, 1972; Bob Woodward and Carl Bernstein, "Nixon Group Loses Bid to Slow Break-In Suit," *Capital Times*, August 12, 1972; Carl Bernstein and Bob Woodward, *All the President's Men* (New York: Simon and Schuster, 1974), 15–16, 36–44.

62. John M. Crewdson, "Spying on Capitol Offices Laid to Watergate Figure," *New York Times*, April 2, 1973. The others were senators Jacob Javits, Charles Percy, Edmund Muskie, Edward Kennedy, and Mike Gravel and representatives Shirley Chisholm and Edward Koch; *Capital Times*, April 2, 1973; *Wisconsin State Journal*, April 2, 1973; Small, *Presidency of Richard Nixon*, 283–287.

63. *Capital Times*, April 30, May 8, 9, 1973; "Proxmire's 'Bad Day'" editorial, *Capital Times*, May 2, 1973; Linda Charlton, "Proxmire Calls Press 'Unfair' to Nixon a Day after Linking Him to Watergate," *New York Times*, May 9, 1973; James Reston, "Proxmire on the Press," *New York Times*, May 9, 1973; "Reporting on Watergate," editorial, *New York Times*, May 12, 1973; "Watergate, Senator Proxmire and the Press," *Capital Times*, May 15, 1973;

Stanley Kutler, *Abuse of Power: The New Nixon Tapes* (New York: The Free Press, 1997), 420–421.

64. *Capital Times*, June 16, 18, 27, August 17, October 13, 22, 24, 27, 1973; *New York Times*, July 12, 1973; Erwin Knoll, "Prox: 'Nixon Wouldn't List Me as an Enemy,'" *Capital Times*, July 13, 1973; *Wisconsin State Journal*, August 19, October 16, 1973. Proxmire was on both the first enemies list produced by John Dean, and on the second list given to the IRS, revealed in December 1973.

65. *Wisconsin State Journal*, January 3, February 2, September 10, 1974; *Capital Times*, August 4, 9, September 9, 1974.

66. *Wisconsin State Journal*, November 13, 21, 27, 29, December 10, 1972, April 1, 1973; *Capital Times*, November 21, 29, December 26, 1972, February 17, 1973.

67. Erwin Knoll, "Prox Pushes His Luck—75 Times," *Capital Times*, January 21, 1973; Judy Klemesrud, "Senator Proxmire: Campaigning for a Healthier America," *New York Times*, August 7, 1973; *New York Times*, September 29, December 15, 1973; *Wisconsin State Journal*, September 29, 1973.

68. *Capital Times*, June 11, 13, July 8, August 3, 22, 23, 1974.

69. *Capital Times*, February 28, 1975; *Wisconsin State Journal*, March 1, 1975; "Proxmires Tell of Marriage Split, Making Up," *Capital Times*, August 11, 1975; Douglas Proxmire, interview with Anita Hecht, April 5, 2010, transcript, Proxmire Oral History Project, Wisconsin Historical Society Archives, 52–54; Ellen Proxmire, interview with Anita Hecht, October 21, 2010, transcript, Proxmire Oral History Project, Wisconsin Historical Society Archives, 17–19; Jan Licht, interview with Anita Hecht, November 11, 2010, transcript, Proxmire Oral History Project, Wisconsin Historical Society Archives, 55–59.

Chapter 9

1. W. L. Christofferson, "Proxmire Sees 'Rocky Times,'" *Wisconsin State Journal*, January 5, 1975; *Capital Times*, January 7, 8, 1975.

2. *Wisconsin State Journal*, January 16, June 3, 1975; *New York Times*, June 7, 1975; Andrew Downer Crain, *The Ford Presidency: A History* (Jefferson, NC: McFarland, 2009), 108–114.

3. *Wisconsin State Journal*, February 14, 28, March 6, June 26, September 11, 1975; *Capital Times*, February 27, April 25, November 11, 1975.

4. Crain, *The Ford Presidency*, 189–193; *Proxmire Reports*, November 1975; *Wisconsin State Journal*, October 24, 28, 30, 31, December 4, 6, 7, 1975, May 24, 31, June 30, July 28, August 2, 1978; *Capital Times*, October 30, 31, 1975, May 23, 1978; Richard L. Madden, "Anti-Spender Proxmire Helps Save N.Y.C.," *Wisconsin State Journal*, December 11, 1975; Edward Handell, "Bill Proxmire: Is He the Real Mayor of New York?" *Capital Times*, January 25, 1978; Christopher R. Conte, "Bailing Out New York City— Again," *Wisconsin State Journal*, March 15, 1978; Edward Handell, "Prox Won't Compromise on New York Problems," *Capital Times*, April 28, 1978; William Proxmire, *The Fleecing of America: The Election Issue That Hits You Where You Hurt* (Boston: Houghton Mifflin, 1980), 156–167. President Carter strongly supported the 1978 loan guarantee legislation, partly for political reasons. He noted in his diary on September 11 that Proxmire was attempting to prevent further loans to New York and that he had instructed Vice President Walter Mondale to "take charge and keep us on the side of the New York angels." See Jimmy Carter, *White House Diary* (New York: Farrar, Straus and Giroux, 2010), 464.

5. W. L. Christofferson, "Proxmire Promises Banking Changes," *Wisconsin State Journal*, January 26, 1975.

6. *Wisconsin State Journal*, May 14, June 6, 1975; Robert Pfefferkorn, "Proxmire Isn't Bankers' Pinup Boy," *Wisconsin State Journal*, August 19, December 2, 1975; *Capital Times*, December 1, 1975; Robert Kuttner, interview with Anita Hecht, June 9, 2011, transcript, Proxmire Oral History Project, Wisconsin Historical Society Archives, 20–22. The only way Proxmire was able to get the act passed was to agree to a sunset clause—it had to be renewed every five years.

7. Austin Scott, "Proxmire Study Shows Discrimination in Loans," *Capital Times*, July 26, 1975; *Capital Times*, June 1, 1976; *Wisconsin State Journal*, March 26, 1977; Paul Grogan and Tony Proscio, *Comeback Cities: A Blueprint for Urban Neighborhoods* (New York: Basic Books, 2001), 109–126; Ken McLean, interview with Anita Hecht, September 11, 2009, transcript, Proxmire Oral History Project, Wisconsin Historical Society Archives, 64–68.

8. *Wisconsin State Journal*, May 13, 1976; "Welcome Anti-Bribery Law," *Capital Times*, January 10, 1978; Sylvia Porter, "Finance Reform: Good and Bad News," *Wisconsin State Journal*, April 13, 1980; Ken McLean, interview

with Anita Hecht, September 11, 2009, transcript, Proxmire Oral History
Project, Wisconsin Historical Society Archives, 77–78; Richard Kaufman,
interview with Anita Hecht, July 7, 2009, transcript, Proxmire Oral History Project, Wisconsin Historical Society Archives, 48–49.

9. Mike Miller, "Maier, Labor Rip Proxmire on Veto," *Capital Times*, February 20, 1976; *Wisconsin State Journal*, February 20, 1976; *Capital Times*,
May 7, 8, 1976; *Wisconsin State Journal*, May 9, 1976.

10. Franklin W. Iossi, "Kickapoo Dam Delay Draws Angry Reaction in LaFarge,"
Wisconsin State Journal, April 17, 1971; "$15 Million for Two Embattled
State Projects," *Capital Times*, January 25, 1972; Whitney Gould, "Proxmire
Won't Fight La Farge Project," *Capital Times*, February 10, 1975; *Wiscon-
sin State Journal*, February 10, 13, 1975; *Capital Times*, February 11, 12,
15, 1975; Whitney Gould, "Prox Wants Some Parts of LaFarge Project to
Continue," *Capital Times*, April 10, 1975; Witney Gould, "Nelson Assured
LaFarge Work to Halt for Study," *Capital Times*, May 8, 1975.

11. *Wisconsin State Journal*, September 7, 1975; *Capital Times*, September
8, 22, 1975; Whitney Gould, "Prox Asking LaFarge Fund Cut-off," *Capital Times*, September 9, 1975; William Proxmire, *Fleecing of America*,
150–153; Ron Tammen, interview with Anita Hecht, June 5, 2009,
transcript, Proxmire Oral History Project, Wisconsin Historical Society
Archives, 48–49; *Proxmire Reports*, October 1975.

12. *Capital Times*, December 8, 15, 1975; January 9, 12, 1976, July 3, 5, 1978;
Wisconsin State Journal, January 7, 10, 1976; July 3, 5, 1978; Richard W.
Jaeger, "Debate over LaFarge Dam Heats Up in Flood's Wake," *Wisconsin
State Journal*, July 9, 1978; David Blaska, "Towns Shared a Flood, Not Ideas
for the Future," *Capital Times*, July 10, 1978; Robert H. Spiegel, "Flood Aid:
Unnatural Disaster?" *Wisconsin State Journal*, July 16, 1978l; Proxmire, *The
Fleecing of America*, 153; Ron Tammen, interview with Anita Hecht, June 5,
2009, transcript, Proxmire Oral History Project, Wisconsin Historical
Society Archives, 50.

13. Proxmire, *The Fleecing of America*, 1; Thomas van der Voort, interview with
Anita Hecht, March 29, 2009, transcript, Proxmire Oral History Project,
Wisconsin Historical Society Archives, 75; Ron Tammen, interview with
Anita Hecht, June 5, 2009, transcript, Proxmire Oral History Project, Wis-
consin Historical Society Archives, 55–56.

14. Proxmire, *The Fleecing of America*, 6–7; *Wisconsin State Journal*, March 12,

1975; "Golden Fleece Awards—1975," box 158, folder 1, William Proxmire Papers, Archives Division, State Historical Society of Wisconsin; *Proxmire Reports*, May 1975.

15. *Wisconsin State Journal*, March 13, April 10, 15, 1975; James Reston, "Proxmire Misses the Boat," *Wisconsin State Journal*, March 14, 1975; *Capital Times*, March 17, 1975; Diane Sherman, "Prof. Explains 'Intimate' Study," *Capital Times*, March 19, 21, April 3, 1975; Roger A. Gribble, "Study of Intimate Relations Defended by UW Professor," *Wisconsin State Journal*, March 19, 1975; Roger Gribble, "UW Faculty Senate Criticizes Proxmire," *Wisconsin State Journal*, April 15, 1975. Proxmire quoted the faculty senate's statement in full in *Fleecing of America*, 43–44.

16. Press release, April 18, 1975, box 158, folder 1, William Proxmire Papers; Proxmire, *Fleecing of America*, 7–8; *Capital Times*, April 18, 1975; *Wisconsin State Journal*, April 19, 1975.

17. Proxmire, *Fleecing of America*, 38–40; Irvin Kreisman, "'Fleece' Award Winner Sues Prox for Libel," *Capital Times*, April 16, 1976; Howard Cosgrove, "Jackman on Libel Suit against Prox," *Capital Times*, April 17, 1976; Anita Clark, "'Golden Fleecer' sues Proxmire for $6-Million," *Wisconsin State Journal*, April 17, 1976; Morton Schwartz, interview with Anita Hecht, September 9, 2009, transcript, Proxmire Oral History Project, Wisconsin Historical Society Archives, 42–44; Ron Tammen, interview with Anita Hecht, June 5, 2009, transcript, Proxmire Oral History Project, Wisconsin Historical Society Archives, 58–59. The lawsuit was later increased to $8 million.

18. Spencer Rich, "Proxmire Seeks Funds from Senate," *Capital Times*, May 10, 1976; "Hutchinson versus Proxmire," *American Psychologist* 35 (August 1980): 689–690; Stuart Levitan, "Prox Gets Goldwater's 'Fleece' Award," *Capital Times*, August 10, 1976; Irvin Kreisman, "Researcher Documents Suit against Proxmire," *Capital Times*, December 31, 1976; Stuart Levitan, "Judge to Dismiss $6-Million Suit against Proxmire," *Capital Times*, January 5, 1977; *Wisconsin State Journal*, January 7, 1977, July 5, 1978, January 9, 1979, March 25, 1980; Jonathan Dedmon, "Proxmire Immune to Suit?" *Capital Times*, April 13, June 26, 1979, March 24, December 24, 1980; Richard Carelli, "Proxmire's 'Fleece' Target for Libel, Court Rules," *Wisconsin State Journal*, June 27, 1979; Frederick L. Berns, "Prox Says He Isn't Fleecing Taxpayers," *Capital Times*, March 25, 1980;

Morton Schwartz, interview with Anita Hecht, September 9, 2009, transcript, Proxmire Oral History Project, Wisconsin Historical Society Archives, 45–47.

19. Carl Eifert, interview with Anita Hecht, July 6, 2009, transcript, Proxmire Oral History Project, Wisconsin Historical Society Archives, 40-42; Frank Aukofer, interview with Anita Hecht, November 21, 2008, transcript, Proxmire Oral History Project, Wisconsin Historical Society Archives, 40–41; Kenneth Dameron, interview with Anita Hecht, December 15, 2009, transcript, Proxmire Oral History Project, Wisconsin Historical Society Archives, 34–37; Howard E. Shuman, Legislative and Administrative Assistant to Senators Paul Douglas and William Proxmire, 1955–1982, Oral History interview, Senate Historical Office, Washington, DC, 456–463, 544–545; Linda Campbell, "It Doesn't Take $3.2 Million to Sniff Out Government Waste," *St. Paul Pioneer Press*, December 30, 2002.

20. *Wisconsin State Journal*, June 28, 1975, May 27, 1981, January 17, 1984; Robert Pfefferkorn, "Proxmire 'Moonlights' as Home Foam Insulator," *Wisconsin State Journal*, October 15, 1975; Edward Handell, "Prox's Style Makes Him Media Favorite," *Capital Times*, September 26, 1978; *Capital Times*, January 5, 1982; Michael V. Urban, "Is Proxmire Record Hand Shaker?" *Wisconsin State Journal*, August 11, 1975; William Christofferson, "Demand High for 23–6 Loss," *Wisconsin State Journal*, September 14, 1975; John Welter, "Prox Plans Holiday among the Helpless," *Capital Times*, December 19, 1975; Charles Fulkerson, "The Senator Came to Dinner," *Wisconsin State Journal*, December 26, 1975; *Capital Times*, January 2, December 23, 1980; *Proxmire Reports*, February 1975, August 1975, May 1978.

21. William Christofferson, "GOP Hunts Proxmire Opponent," *Wisconsin State Journal*, June 29, 1975; William Christofferson, "Challenger to Proxmire? No Consensus in GOP," *Wisconsin State Journal*, November 23, 1975; William Christofferson, "State GOP Seeking Full Candidate Slate," *Wisconsin State Journal*, April 25, 1975. William Hart (Socialist), Robert Nordlander (Socialist Labor), and Robert Schwartz (Socialist Worker) had all announced their candidacies by May 1; John Patrick Hunter, "Delegates Cheer Prox Despite Maier's Attack," *Capital Times*, June 12, 1976.

22. John Patrick Hunter, "York Seen as GOP Pick to Challenge Proxmire," *Capital Times*, June 5, 1976; William Christofferson, "State Republicans

Endorse York for Senate," *Wisconsin State Journal*, June 6, 1976; John Patrick Hunter, "State GOP Picks York with a Promise for 1978," *Capital Times*, June 7, 1976.

23. *Capital Times*, July 14, 23, 29, August 11, 30, September 2, 9, 23, 24, 1976; Stuart Levitan, "Proxmire Returns $3,933 in Campaign Donations," *Capital Times*, September 9, 1976; Howard E. Shuman, Legislative and Administrative Assistant for Paul Douglas and William Proxmire, 1955–1982, Oral History Interview, Senate Historical Office, Washington, DC, 507–509.

24. Reid Beveridge, "Proxmire Opposes Unconditional Amnesty," *Wisconsin State Journal*, October 8, 1976; *Capital Times*, October 8, 15, 1976; "York: Stalking Proxmire," *Capital Times*, October 11, 1976; Mike Dorgan, "York Says Proxmire's 'Lack of Principles' Real Issue," *Capital Times*, October 11, 1976; "Proxmire: Quest for a 4th term," *Capital Times*, October 18, 1976; Ed Bark, "It Was Proxmire and York against the 'Other Four,'" *Capital Times*, October 21, 1976; the sixth candidate was Michael MacLaurin of the US Labor Party.

25. Reid Beveridge, "Proxmire Jobs 'No Budget' Race," *Wisconsin State Journal*, October 29, 1976; *Wisconsin State Journal*, November 3, 1976; *Capital Times*, November 3, 1976.

26. Stuart Levitan, "Proxmire Speaks Mind on Carter Nominees," *Capital Times*, January 24, 1977; Stuart Levitan, "Nelson, Proxmire Vote against Griffin Bell," *Capital Times*, January 26, 1977; "Prox Claims Inaugural Walk Idea," *Capital Times*, January 24, 1977; Peter G. Bourne, *Jimmy Carter: A Comprehensive Biography from Plains to Postpresidency* (New York: Scribner, 1997), 365; Jimmy Carter, *White House Diary* (New York: Farrar, Straus and Giroux, 2010), 9; *Proxmire Reports*, June 1977.

27. *Capital Times*, February 21, 1977, January 22, April 24, 1979; *Wisconsin State Journal*, April 4, 1977, September 7, 1978, April 27, 1979; Bourne, *Jimmy Carter*, 370–374, 422–424, 435–436; *Proxmire Reports*, April 1979.

28. Frederick L. Berns, "New Carter Budget Draws Mixed Reviews from Congressmen," *Capital Times*, January 29, 1980; Patricia Simms, "State Delegation Mixed over Carter's Budget," *Wisconsin State Journal*, January 30, March 18, May 13, 1980; Bourne, *Jimmy Carter*, 458; *Proxmire Reports*, April 1980.

29. See, for example, Linda Charlton, "Big Wheels Still Get Their Low Cost

Goodies," *Wisconsin State Journal*, February 16, 1977. In addition to the monthly Golden Fleece Awards, Proxmire kept up an intermittent fight against federal largesse for the rest of his career.

30. *Wisconsin State Journal*, August 18, October 11, 22, December 20, 1979; Frederick L. Berns, "Prox Calls Chrysler Aid Inevitable," *Capital Times*, October 18, 1979; *Capital Times*, October 25, 1979; Robert H. Spiegel, "Prox: Chrysler 'Can't Lose,'" *Wisconsin State Journal*, October 23, 1979; Owen Ullmann, "$1.5 Billion Chrysler Bailout OK'd," *Capital Times*, December 21, 1979; Frederick L. Berns, "Prox Fears Bad Precedent in Chrysler Aid," *Capital Times*, December 21, 1979; Thomas W. Still, "Prox-mire Says He Opposes any Bailout by US," *Wisconsin State Journal*, December 28, 1979; William Proxmire, "'No' to More Chrysler," *Wisconsin State Journal*, January 11, 1980; Proxmire, *Fleecing of America*, 168–176; Paul Sarbanes, interview with Anita Hecht, September 10, 2009, transcript, Proxmire Oral History Project, Wisconsin Historical Society Archives, 19; *Proxmire Reports*, December 1979.

31. *Wisconsin State Journal*, May 1, 1975; *Capital Times*, August 25, 1975; February 18, March 6, 1976; *Wisconsin State Journal*, August 25, September 8, 1975, March 4, 5, 13, 1976.

32. *Wisconsin State Journal*, April 26, May 3, 13, 21, 1976; *Capital Times*, April 26, 1976; James J. Kilpatrick, "Proxmire, Goldwater Debate B-1," *Wisconsin State Journal*, May 19, 1976; Spencer Rich, "Senate Throws B-1 Off Production Plan," *Capital Times*, May 21, 1976; Dana Adams Schmidt, "B-1 vs. B-52 Debate Raises Major Issues," *Wisconsin State Journal*, January 9, 1977.

33. *Wisconsin State Journal*, March 5, 1979; *Capital Times*, March 5, June 19, 1979; Tom Wicker, "SALT II: A Matter of Trust," *Wisconsin State Journal*, March 12, 1979; *Proxmire Reports*, July 1979.

34. *Capital Times*, December 15, 1980.

35. *Capital Times*, April 25, May 30, 1981; *Wisconsin State Journal*, May 15, 31, 1981.

36. John Patrick Hunter, "Proxmire Is Undecided about Haig," *Capital Times*, December 19, 1980; *Capital Times*, February 11, May 13, 1981; *Wisconsin State Journal*, January 23, February 16, 17, May 13, 1981; Patricia Simms, "Reaction to Reagan Speech Is as Expected," *Wisconsin State Journal*, February 7, 1981; Haynes Johnson, *Sleepwalking through History: America in the*

Reagan Years (New York: W.W. Norton, 1991), 22, 28–32, 65, 110–111. On the conservative mood of the country, see Steven F. Hayward, *The Age of Reagan: The Conservative Counterrevolution, 1980–1989* (New York: Crown Forum, 2009), 59–95, 150–154, 156–166.

37. *Capital Times*, June 13, 1981; *Wisconsin State Journal*, June 14, July 30, August 1, 1981; Phil Haslanger, "Proxmire Is Confident despite Party Treatment," *Capital Times*, June 15, 1981; Patricia Simms, "Proxmire Defends His Budget Vote," *Wisconsin State Journal*, June 16, 1981; Thomas W. Still, "Slumping Dems Take Swipe at Proxmire," *Wisconsin State Journal*, June 17, 1981. The final passage of the tax cuts and budget cuts occurred in late July, reducing spending by $130 billion over three years and a 25% tax cut phased in over three years.

38. *Capital Times*, February 14, July 2, August 8, 1981, May 18, 1982; John Patrick Hunter, "'Labels Don't Count,' Proxmire Tells Constituents," *Capital Times*, July 14, 1981; *Proxmire Reports*, July, October 1981; *Wisconsin State Journal*, August 8, 9, September 30, 1981, May 18, 23, 1982; Jay Perkins, "Prox Spends Long, Lonely Night in a Fight He'll Never Win," *Capital Times*, September 29, 1981; Frederick L. Berns, "1981 in Congress: State Reps See Good and Bad," *Capital Times*, January 2, 1982; William S. Becker, "Reagan Shines on Capitol Hill," *Wisconsin State Journal*, January 11, 1982; Johnson, *Sleepwalking through History*, 153–154; Hayward, *Age of Reagan*, 169–174.

39. On busing: *Wisconsin State Journal*, September 25, 1975, November 14, 1980, December 11, 1981, February 5, 1982; *Capital Times*, August 24, 1978, May 23, 1981, January 30, 1982; on abortion: *Capital Times*, April 25, 1975, *Wisconsin State Journal*, June 30, 1977, May 22, 1981; Kaye Schultz, "Proxmire Won't Bend Anti-Abortion Stand," *Capital Times*, February 6, 1982 (quotation); Sunny Schubert, "Debate Still Continues in Madison over Abortion Issue," *Wisconsin State Journal*, January 22, 1983; Ken Dameron, interview with Anita Hecht, December 15, 2009, transcript, Proxmire Oral History Project, Wisconsin Historical Society Archives, 89–90; Ron Tammen, interview with Anita Hecht, June 5, 2009, transcript, Proxmire Oral History Project, Wisconsin Historical Society Archives, 76–78.

40. On school prayer: Bill Peterson, "Filibuster on School Prayer Lingers," *Capital Times*, September 21, 1982; *Wisconsin State Journal*, September 23, 29,

1982, March 19, 21, 1984; *Capital Times*, September 29, 1982; Jacob Stockinger, "Debate about Prayer in School Quiet in Madison," *Capital Times*, March 19, 1984; Tom Raum, "School Prayer Backers Vow to Continue Efforts," *Capital Times*, March 21, 1984. On gun control: *Wisconsin State Journal*, July 10, 1985; *Capital Times*, July 15, 1985; John Patrick Hunter, "Senate Votes to Ease Gun Controls," *Capital Times*, July 10, 1985. For Moral Majority rating: *Capital Times*, October 30, 1982. Proxmire was also hostile to the gay rights movement, arguing for a provision in a housing bill that would prioritize applicants in "stable family relationships" and telling the Senate Appropriations Committee, "We certainly don't want to say that homosexuals have equal access with families to public housing." See *Wisconsin State Journal*, June 23, 1977.

41. Hayward, *Age of Reagan*, 201–213, 232–233; Matt Pommer, "Reagan Plan Draws Quick Doubts," *Capital Times*, January 27, 1982; Frederick L. Berns, "Federal Shift Has Both Good, Bad: Lawmakers," *Capital Times*, January 27, 1982; Paul Rix, "Dreyfus Endorses Reagan's Shift to States," *Wisconsin State Journal*, January 28, 1982; *Wisconsin State Journal*, June 23, 24, August 5, 1982; *Proxmire Reports*, February 1982.

42. Hayward, *Age of Reagan*, 210–213; *Wisconsin State Journal*, August 19, 20, September 8, 11, 1982; *Capital Times*, August 19, September 10, 1982; Frederick L. Berns, "State Dems Unite against Reagan," *Capital Times*, September 11, 1982; Steven R. Weisman, "Override Vote Dents Reagan's Veto Record," *Wisconsin State Journal*, September 12, 1982.

43. Robert C. Bjorklund, "Proxmire Favors 80% of Parity," *Wisconsin State Journal*, February 8, 1981; David Blaska, "Milk Surplus Blessing, Not Curse, Prox Says," *Capital Times*, February 9, 1981; *Capital Times*, February 26, March 26, 1981; *Wisconsin State Journal*, February 26, March 26, 1981. On the farm crisis, see Neil E. Harl, *The Farm Debt Crisis of the 1980s* (Ames: Iowa State University Press, 1990); Gilbert C. Fite, "The Farm Debt Crisis of the 1980s: A Review Essay," *Annals of Iowa* 51 (1992): 288–293; Kathryn Marie Dudley, *Debt and Dispossession: Farm Loss in America's Heartland* (Chicago: University of Chicago Press, 2000).

44. *Capital Times*, April 13, July 13, October 20, 1981; David Blaska, "Block-Helms Play Parity Game," *Capital Times*, April 15, 1981; Robert C. Bjorklund, "Dreary Outlook Seen for Dairymen," *Wisconsin State Journal*, July 12, 1981; *Wisconsin State Journal*, October 6, 17, 20, December 11,

1981; Bob Fick, "Prox Filibuster Thwarts Dairy Support Rollback," *Capital Times*, October 17, 1981; Walter B. Mears, "Proxmire Fails Dairy Folks Back Home," *Capital Times*, October 21, 1981; *Proxmire Reports*, November 1981.

45. David Blaska, "Silver Lining in Dairy Cuts: Fresh Ideas Rising to the Top," *Capital Times*, January 13, 1982; Robert C. Bjorklund, "Dairy Farmers Back Self-Help Plan," *Wisconsin State Journal*, January 15, 1982; Fred Berns, "State Congressional Reps Still Back Dairy Supports," *Capital Times*, March 13, 1982; Thomas W. Still, "Reduce Milk Production, Proxmire Warns," *Wisconsin State Journal*, April 8, 1982; Robert C. Bjorklund, "AMPI Backs Plan to Cut Milk Production," *Wisconsin State Journal*, March 28, 1982; *Capital Times*, March 27, 1982, January 11, 1984; David Blaska, "Dairy Plan Doesn't Face Up to Facts," *Capital Times*, January 18, 1984.

46. *Wisconsin State Journal*, March 25, 1981; Frank Ryan, "Dreyfus Denies He Will Run against Proxmire," *Capital Times*, April 2, 1981; John Patrick Hunter, "GOP Sets Sights on Proxmire," *Capital Times*, June 6, 1981; Arthur L. Srb, "GOP Touts Marlene Cummings, Kohler for Senate," *Wisconsin State Journal*, June 6, 1981; Paul Rix, "Upbeat GOP Sets Sights on Proxmire," *Wisconsin State Journal*, June 7, 1981; John Patrick Hunter, "Cummings 'Interested' in Proxmire's Job," *Capital Times*, June 8, 1981; John Patrick Hunter, "Taking on Prox—McCallum Gets Ready for Suicide Mission," *Capital Times*, January 7, 1982; John Patrick Hunter, "Dandeneau Isn't a Token Candidate," *Capital Times*, April 15, 1982; Thomas W. Still, "Proxmire Challenger Says Issues Key to His Success," *Wisconsin State Journal*, April 18, 1982; Thomas W. Still, "Who'll Run for Governor? Lots of Possibilities," *Wisconsin State Journal*, April 27, 1982.

47. Arthur L. Srb, "Proxmire Presents a Special Problem to GOP Hopefuls," *Capital Times*, August 15, 1981; John Patrick Hunter, "After Record Senate Stay, What Will Prox Run for Now?" *Capital Times*, September 4, 1981; Thomas W. Still, "Chances of Defeating Proxmire Are Slim," *Wisconsin State Journal*, December 6, 1981; John Patrick Hunter, "Proxmire Set for Re-Election Bid," *Capital Times*, May 26, 1982.

48. Phil Haslanger, "Pols Flock Like Mosquitoes," *Capital Times*, August 11, 1982; Paul Fanlund, "Proxmire's Opponents Understand the Odds," *Wisconsin State Journal*, August 29, 1982; Nicholas D. Kristof, "If Nothing Else, 'Ed' Proxmire Still No. 1 Campaigner," *Capital Times*, August 30, 1982;

Paul Fanlund, "Proxmire, McCallum Overwhelm Opponents," *Wisconsin State Journal*, September 15, 1982; *Wisconsin Blue Book, 1983–1984*, 881.

49. John Patrick Hunter, "McCallum's Senate Drive Gets $263,000 from GOP," *Capital Times*, October 1, 1982; *Wisconsin State Journal*, October 2, 3, 11, 1982; John Patrick Hunter and Rob Fixmer, "Proxmire, McCallum Keep Debate Civil," *Capital Times*, October 13, 1982; Chuck Martin, "Proxmire Finding Labor Support Coming in Line," *Wisconsin State Journal*, October 17, 1982; *Capital Times*, October 18, 21, 1982; P. B. Seymour, "Proxmire, McCallum Mix It Up on TV debate," *Capital Times*, October 22, 1982.

50. *Wisconsin Blue Book, 1983–1984*, 903. Three other candidates received a total of 34,217 votes; Rob Fixmer, "Prox Has No Trouble," *Capital Times*, November 3, 1982; Paul Fanlund, "Proxmire Easily Beats Challenger McCallum," *Wisconsin State Journal*, November 3, 1982.

51. Dan Allegretti, "Kastenmeier, Proxmire Lash Out at Reagan Plan," *Capital Times*, March 24, 1983; *Wisconsin State Journal*, March 25, April 6, July 27, 1983, February 10, 1984, September 23, 1987; Steven F. Hayward, *The Age of Reagan: The Conservative Counterrevolution, 1980–1989* (New York: Random House, 2009), 291–299; Fred Hiatt, " 'Star Wars' Research Shows Flaws, Report Says," *Capital Times*, March 31, 1986; William J. Broad, "Rocket Problems Seen as 'Star Wars' Setback," *Wisconsin State Journal*, June 15, 1986; John Patrick Hunter, "Reagan Blew It, State Dems Say," *Capital Times*, October 13, 1986; John Patrick Hunter, "Prox: Star Wars Too Costly," *Capital Times*, August 3, 1987; Dave Zweifel, "Star Wars Won't Fly as Long as Bill Proxmire Is Around," *Capital Times*, September 16, 1987.

52. *Wisconsin State Journal*, April 13, 1981; *Capital Times*, April 13, 1981; Matt Pommer, "ELF Makes State A-Bomb Target: Prox," *Capital Times*, October 9, 1981.

53. Lou Cannon and George C. Wilson, "Senate Committee's Vote Frees MX Funds," *Capital Times*, May 13, 1983; *Wisconsin State Journal*, March 19, 20, 21, 1985; *Capital Times*, March 19, 1985.

54. *Capital Times*, April 23, October 27, 1981, December 18, 1982; David Stoeffler, "Dumping A-Waste Out Of State Is a Relief, for Now," *Wisconsin State Journal*, April 27, 1981; *Wisconsin State Journal*, August 24, 1981; Ruth Fleischer, interview with Anita Hecht, March 20, 2009, transcript, Proxmire Oral History Project, Wisconsin Historical Society Archives, 29–33.

55. *Proxmire Reports*, March 1981; *Capital Times*, July 12, 1983; Thomas W. Still, "Proxmire: Chance of Nuke War 50%," *Wisconsin State Journal*, July 12 1983; John Patrick Hunter, "Prox's lonely Fight against Armageddon," *Capital Times*, July 19, 1983; *Wisconsin State Journal*, July 12, 1984, August 20, 1985; Richard L. Strout, "One Winter that Must Never Come," *Wisconsin State Journal*, April 23, 1984; William J. Broad, "Nuclear Winter Theory May Reshape A-Weapon Thinking," *Wisconsin State Journal*, August 5, 1984; John Patrick Hunter, "Senator Urges Nuclear Winter as Summit Topic," *Capital Times*, November 11, 1985.

56. Hayward, *Age of Reagan*, 299–304; *Capital Times*, July 28, 1983; *Proxmire Reports*, August 1983.

57. W. Dale Nelson, "GOP Backs Senate War Powers Vote on Grenada," *Capital Times*, October 29, 1983; Hayward, *Age of Reagan*, 315–324; *Proxmire Reports*, November 1983; Hayward, *Age of Reagan*, 315–325; Johnson, *Sleepwalking through History*, 249–279.

58. *Wisconsin State Journal*, December 22, 1983; Andrew Pratt, "Proxmire Rips Defense Spending," *Wisconsin State Journal*, July 10, 1984; John Patrick Hunter, "Proxmire Says Foreign Policy Worries State," *Capital Times*, January 12, 1984; James McCartney, "Revolving Door Spinning Fast in Defense," *Wisconsin State Journal*, April 8, 1985.

59. *Wisconsin State Journal*, April 16, 24, 1985, March 28, April 21, 1986; Thomas W. Still, "Wisconsin's 'Sister State' Suffering at Hands of US Policy, Dems Say," *Wisconsin State Journal*, July 3, 1985; John Patrick Hunter, "Sandinistas Praised at Local Hearing," *Capital Times*, July 3, 1985; John Patrick Hunter, "Lawmakers Split over Contra Aid Proposal," *Capital Times*, March 10, 1986; Hayward, *Age of Reagan*, 299–308; Johnson, *Sleepwalking through History*, 249–279.

60. Dan Allegretti and John Patrick Hunter, "Proxmire: Prosecute Aides to Fullest Extent," *Capital Times*, November 25, 1986; John Patrick Hunter, "Iran Deal Shows Prox Was Right," *Capital Times*, November 27, 1986; *Wisconsin State Journal*, December 14, 1986; *Capital Times*, December 15, 1986; Johnson, *Sleepwalking through History*, 333–371; Hayward, *Age of Reagan*, 515–557.

61. John Patrick Hunter, "Prox Sees Recovery Tailspin without Cuts," *Capital Times*, October 13, 1983; Thomas M. Waller, "Recession Not Over, Proxmire Says," *Wisconsin State Journal*, October 13, 1983; John Patrick Hunter,

"Wisconsin's Washington," *Capital Times*, September 8, 1986; Mike Stam-
ler, "Prox Gloomy on Economy," *Capital Times*, February 10, 1987.

62. *Wisconsin State Journal*, May 20, November 17, 1983, May 9, 17,
August 24, October 17, 1984, August 3, October 11, December 12,
1985, June 7, 1988; *Capital Times*, November 17, 1983, June 25, 1987;
Thomas W. Still and Paul Fanlund, "Budget, Not Party, Keyed State Votes,"
Wisconsin State Journal, August 3, 1985; Thomas W. Still and Paul Fan-
lund, "Compromise Budget Splits State's Votes," *Wisconsin State Journal*,
August 3, 1985; John Patrick Hunter, "Prox Says Tax Bill Aids State's Poor,"
Capital Times, August 18, 1986.

63. Thomas M. Waller, "Proxmire Attacks Bank Loopholes," *Wisconsin State
Journal*, February 8, 1987; Andrew Mollison, "Proxmire: Money, Lobby-
ists Beat Banks," *Wisconsin State Journal*, March 15, 1987; "Bank Reform
Forgotten as Senators See Green," *Wisconsin State Journal*, March 18, 1987;
Wisconsin State Journal, August 5, 1987; *Capital Times*, August 28, 1987;
Ken McLean, interview with Anita Hecht, September 11, 2009, transcript,
Proxmire Oral History Project, Wisconsin Historical Society Archives,
71–74, 89–90.

64. *Capital Times*, September 24, November 13, 19, 1987, March 31, Octo-
ber 21, 1988; *Wisconsin State Journal*, September 25, November 16, 1987;
March 31, October 21, 1988; David Skidmore, "Prox Pushes Bill for Bank
Deregulation," *Capital Times*, November 4, 1987.

65. *Capital Times*, March 5, April 8, September 29, 1987; *Wisconsin State Journal*, March 5, 1987; Dave Skidmore, "Caution Urged on Takeover Intervention," *Wisconsin State Journal*, September 20, 29, 1987; Alan Fram, "Prox
May Withdraw Takeover Bill," *Capital Times*, June 22, 1988; Ken McLean,
interview with Anita Hecht, September 11, 2009, transcript, Proxmire
Oral History Project, Wisconsin Historical Society Archives, 91.

66. *Capital Times*, November 14, 1966, February 20, 1967; Jay Sykes, *Proxmire*
(New York: Robert B. Luce, 1972), 177–179; Samantha Power, *"A Problem
from Hell": America and the Age of Genocide* (New York: Basic Books, 2013),
79.

67. Power, *Problem from Hell*, 85; Spencer Rich, "Cloture Move Fails on Geno-
cide Treaty," *Washington Post*, February 7, 1974; William Proxmire to
Hubert Humphrey, April 1, 1976; William Proxmire to Richard Stone,
April 14, 1976; memorandum, May 28, 1976, signed by Hubert Humphrey,

Edward Kennedy, William Proxmire, Jacob Javits, and Hugh Scott; Lawrence L. Knutson, "Proxmire Pushing for Genocide Treaty," *Wisconsin State Journal*, April 15, 1976; *Capital Times*, February 2, 6, 1974, August 13, 1979.

68. Jacob Javits and William Proxmire to Jimmy Carter, March 2, 1977; Jimmy Carter to William Proxmire, April 5, 1977; John W. Kole, "Genocide Pact Backers See Chance for US Ratification," *Milwaukee Journal*, May 25, 1977; "Testimony by Senator William Proxmire before the Senate Foreign Relations Committee," May 24, 1977; Nicholas Daniloff, "Proxmire's One-Man Push Gaining Ground," *Wisconsin State Journal*, August 28, 1978.

69. Power, *Problem from Hell*, 81–84; William Proxmire to Cyrus Vance, September 6, 1978; Cyrus Vance to William Proxmire, October 16, 1978; William Proxmire to Louis Henkin, October 30, 1978; Bruno Bitker to William Proxmire, November 1, 1978; Thomas Franck to William Proxmire, November 2, 1978; Louis Henkin to William Proxmire, November 28, 1978; Tom J. Farer to William Proxmire, December 4, 1978; Leonard C. Meeker to William Proxmire, January 5, 1979; Mark Shields, interview with Anita Hecht, October 21, 2009, transcript, Proxmire Oral History Project, Wisconsin Historical Society Archives, 26–29; Ron Kind, interview with Anita Hecht, March 27, 2009, transcript, Proxmire Oral History Project, Wisconsin Historical Society Archives, 11–13; Ron Tammen, interview with Anita Hecht, June 5, 2009, transcript, Proxmire Oral History Project, Wisconsin Historical Society Archives, 64–66; Ruth Fleischer, interview with Anita Hecht, March 20, 2009, transcript, Proxmire Oral History Project, Wisconsin Historical Society Archives, 59–60.

70. *Capital Times*, May 29, 1967, January 20, 1969; Erwin Knoll, "Report from Washington," *Capital Times*, July 22, 1968; "Hesitancy on Genocide Pact," *Capital Times*, May 5, 1970; Powers, *Problem from Hell*, 155–156.

71. Richard Bradee, "Milwaukee Man Pushes for Genocide Treaty Approval," *Milwaukee Sentinel*, December 4, 1981; *Capital Times*, February 17, April 6, 1981, September 5, 19, 1984; Richard Whittle, "Genocide Treaty's Future Uncertain," *Wisconsin State Journal*, February 12, 1982; "Reagan Administration Backs Treaty to Condemn Genocide," *Milwaukee Sentinel*, September 6, 1984; Dale Nelson, "Prox Says Genocide Fight to End in Victory," *Capital Times*, September 7, 1984; William Proxmire, "Genocide Treaty a Moral Imperative for US," *Milwaukee Journal*, May 5, 1985; *Proxmire Reports*, June 1983.

72. *Wisconsin State Journal*, February 20, 1986; *Capital Times*, February 20, 1986; Robin Toner, "After 37 Years, Senate Endorses a Genocide Ban," *New York Times*, February 20, 1986; John Patrick Hunter, "Proxmire's Tenacity Paid Off 37 Years Later," *Capital Times*, March 4, 1986; Frank Aukofer, "Proxmire's Lonely Crusade against Genocide Wins," *Milwaukee Journal*, September 9, 1984.

73. John Patrick Hunter, "Wisconsin's Washington," *Capital Times*, February 17, 1988; *Wisconsin State Journal*, October 17, November 5, 1988; *Capital Times*, November 5, 1988; John Finerty, interview with Anita Hecht, April 23, 2009, transcript, Proxmire Oral History Project, Wisconsin Historical Society Archives, 33.

Chapter 10

1. Thomas W. Still, "Proxmire Says He'll Continue in '88," *Wisconsin State Journal*, March 1, 1985; Arthur Srb, "Proxmire's Early Declaration Seen Fending Off an Earl Bid," *Capital Times*, May 31, 1985; *Capital Times*, June 6, 1987; Doug Mell, "GOP Considers Proxmire Rivals," *Wisconsin State Journal*, June 6, 1987; *Wisconsin State Journal*, July 14, 1987; John Patrick Hunter, "Proxmire Looking Like a Candidate," *Capital Times*, August 24, 1987; John Patrick Hunter, "Prox Keeps 'em Guessing," *Capital Times*, August 26, 1987; David Stoeffler, "Proxmire Expected to Seek Re-Election," *Wisconsin State Journal*, August 27, 1987.

2. "A Message from Two Men Who Care a Lot about the People of Wisconsin," *Milwaukee Journal*, January 3, 1989.

3. Ken Dameron, interview with Anita Hecht, December 15, 2009, transcript, Proxmire Oral History Project, Wisconsin Historical Society Archives, 108–112; Ron Seely, "Proxmire Leaving Senate, but Hardly Retiring," *Wisconsin State Journal*, January 1, 1989; Joyce Hackel, "A Senator until the Very End," *Wisconsin State Journal*, January 1, 1989; *Capital Times*, November 25, 1988.

4. Jeff Mayers, "Still Pithy after All These Years," *Wisconsin State Journal*, July 7, 1997.

5. Betsy Wangensteen, "Out of the Spotlight: Kastenmeier, Proxmire Spend Their Days Reflecting on Their Congressional Service," *Capital Times*, March 18–19, 1995; Sharon Theiner, "Prox: Golden Leash Controls Congress," *Capital Times*, April 9, 1997; David Umhoefer, "Former Senate

Maverick William Proxmire Dies," *Milwaukee Journal-Sentinel*, December 15, 2005.

6. Ruth Fleischer, interview with Anita Hecht, March 20, 2009, transcript, Proxmire Oral History Project, Wisconsin Historical Society Archives, 75; William Drew, interview with Anita Hecht, November 23, 2009, transcript, Proxmire Oral History Project, Wisconsin Historical Society Archives, 71–72; Matt Flynn interview with Anita Hecht, January 5, 2009, transcript, Proxmire Oral History Project, Wisconsin Historical Society Archives, 49–50; John Finerty, interview with Anita Hecht, April 23, 2009, transcript, Proxmire Oral History Project, Wisconsin Historical Society Archives, 73–74.

7. Matt Pommer, "'I Loved Every Minute of It,'" *Capital Times*, April 18–19, 1998; Adam S. Martin, "Proxmire, Of Course, Has Regimen," *Wisconsin State Journal*, April 26, 1998.

8. Richard Kaufman, interview with Anita Hecht, July 7, 2009, transcript, Proxmire Oral History Project, Wisconsin Historical Society Archives, 60–62; Martin Lobel, interview with Anita Hecht, November 19, 2008, transcript, Proxmire Oral History Project, Wisconsin Historical Society Archives, 88.

9. "Alzheimer's Disease Strikes Ex-Senator," *New York Times*, March 16, 1998; Ellen Proxmire, interview with Anita Hecht, October 21, 2010, transcript, Proxmire Oral History Project, Wisconsin Historical Society Archives, 45–58; Theodore Proxmire, interview with Anita Hecht, April 2, 2010, transcript, Proxmire Oral History Project, Wisconsin Historical Society Archives, 90–97; David Umhoefer, "Former Senate Maverick William Proxmire Dies," *Milwaukee Journal-Sentinel*, December 15, 2005.

10. Jason Stein, "William Proxmire, 1915–2005," *Wisconsin State Journal*, December 16, 2005; Katherine M. Skiba, "To His Family, Proxmire Was a Hero, His Wife Says," *Milwaukee Journal-Sentinel*, December 15, 2005; Katherine M. Skiba, "Proxmire Called a Profile in Courage," *Milwaukee Journal-Sentinel*, April 2, 2006.

Acknowledgments

Before I began this project in 2010, I vaguely remembered Bill Proxmire as a popular senator who complained about government spending and shook a lot of hands. I was therefore a little reluctant to undertake a biography when Dave Zweifel, editor of the *Capital Times*, asked me if I was interested. Yet after talking with him, author Sandy Horwitt, and especially Ellen Proxmire, I realized what an extraordinary and important figure the senator had been, not just in Wisconsin but nationally. Beyond the quirky personality lay a uniquely dedicated and hardworking lawmaker who reshaped how the public thinks about military spending, challenged entrenched political leaders, and almost single-handedly persuaded the United States to ratify the United Nation's antigenocide convention. What a long and colorful career! Writing the first full biography of Proxmire has been both an honor and a challenge, and after eight years I am extremely grateful to my friends, family, and colleagues for their encouragement.

The University of Wisconsin–Waukesha, my academic home since 2004, provided much support over the years while I worked on this project. The campus is fortunate to have an excellent and dedicated group of librarians who aided me by rapidly obtaining whatever books I needed. My History Department colleagues—the finest group of people I've ever worked with—also supported my work, and I am particularly grateful for a sabbatical in the fall 2015 that allowed me to complete much of the archival research. The amazing staff at the Wisconsin Historical Society made researching Proxmire's long career possible. Archivists organized and catalogued the enormous collection of Proxmire papers and digitized much of the content, making it available online. At the Wisconsin Historical Society Press, I am indebted to my old friend Kate Thompson for her support for the project and to Rachel Cordasco for her thorough and thoughtful editorial work. The efforts of both improved the final work immeasurably. Anita Hecht, of Life History Services, produced an incredible oral history project, interviewing dozens of Proxmire friends and family and producing hundreds of pages of transcripts full of personal recollections and anecdotes that brought the senator to life. Without her efforts, this book would be a dull affair indeed. Ellen Proxmire read and commented on draft chapters, as did Jim Bailey and David Adamany; I appreciated their regular reassurance that I was on the right path.

In March 2011, I traveled to Washington to meet with Ellen Proxmire, who welcomed me into her home to go through several scrapbooks of newspaper clippings, as well as boxes of other material. She even made me lunch, and I still think of her every time I make myself a tuna sandwich. An extraordinarily accomplished professional in her own right, she was exceptionally gracious and kind, and I am grateful that my family and I had the opportunity to get to know her.

As I reflect on the completion of this project, I also think about how much my own life has changed and how grateful I am for my family. It has been an eventful—and often tumultuous—eight years, but I would not have missed any of it for the world. My wife, Jody, remains the love of my life twenty-five years after we first met. I take great delight in my sons, James, William, and Alden, who make me proud every day.

Jonathan Kasparek
Waukesha, Wisconsin

Index

Page numbers in *italics* refer to images.